KILLER

INVESTIGATIONS INTO 20 OF THE MOST GRUESOME MURDERS OF THE 20ᵀᴴ CENTURY

FOREWORD BY COLIN WILSON

Marshall Cavendish
Editions

Copyright © 2008 Marshall Cavendish Partworks Ltd

Chapters are excerpted from *Murder Casebook* published in 1989 by
Marshall Cavendish Partworks Ltd

This book first published in 2008 by:

Marshall Cavendish Limited
Fifth Floor
32–38 Saffron Hill
London EC1N 8FH
United Kingdom
T: +44 (0)20 7421 8120
F: +44 (0)20 7421 8121
sales@marshallcavendish.co.uk
www.marshallcavendish.co.uk

A CIP record for this book is available from the British Library

ISBN-13 978-0-462-09910-1
ISBN-10 0-462-09910-5

Images from TopFoto

Designed and typeset by Phoenix Photosetting,
Lordswood, Chatham, Kent

Printed and bound in Great Britain by
TJ International Ltd, Padstow, Cornwall

CONTENTS

Contents

FOREWORD: UNDERSTANDING MURDER

As I scanned the contents page of this volume, I found myself trying to imagine how a Victorian detective would have reacted to it – for example, Inspector Fred Abberline, who tried and failed to catch Jack the Ripper. He would, of course, have had no difficulty understanding the crimes of Peter Manuel, for the Victorian age had plenty of burglars who turned killers, or Roy Fontaine, the homosexual butler who murdered his employers, or the Kray twins, who killed to impress each other, or the muddled delinquent Donald Hume, who was simply a weak ne'er-do-well. But the 'motiveless' murders of the poisoner Graham Young, or the random shootings of David Berkowitz, the 'Son of Sam', or the trawling for victims of Dennis Nilsen, the Muswell Hill mass murderer, would have struck him as incomprehensible, while the sex crimes of Ted Bundy, or the 'Hillside Stranglers' would have suggested a dimension of evil beyond anything he had encountered. He would have felt that the world was hurtling into a dark abyss.

To some extent he would have been right. But, as hindsight enables us to understand what has happened, we can begin to see that it is not as terrifying as it first appears.

To begin with, we can see that the dawn of this new and disturbing age had already arrived in the Jack the Ripper murders of 1888. There, for the first time, we encounter a violence that suggests madness or pure wickedness. But we can also see something to which the Victorians were blind: that the key lies in the word 'sex'. The Victorians, inhibited by prudery, thought it lay in religion, and that the killer was a 'religious maniac' who wanted to rid London's East End of prostitutes. It would be another three or four decades before criminologists would recognize that the West had entered the 'age of sex crime'. In Britain, such crimes are typified by the murders of rapist Reginald Christie, in America by those of the Wisconsin necrophile Ed Gein.

It was in the mid-1970s that an American crime investigator, Robert Ressler, coined a term for the most disturbing trend so far: serial murder – 'repeat killers' like Son of Sam, although Jack the Ripper also qualifies. Ressler recognized that virtually all serial murders are motivated by sex. But his colleague Roy Hazelwood carried this an important step further when he noted that 'sex crimes are not about sex – they're about power', thereby providing a key to mass murderers from Jack the Ripper to Son of Sam.

Foreword: Understanding Murder

Without such a key, a book like this appears to be a random collection of unrelated cases. It is the word 'power' that provides the common thread. One after another we encounter murderers whose basic characteristic is a sense of weakness, of helplessness, of being a 'nobody'. The case of Crippen seems baffling because there was no need for him to kill his wife, Cora – all he had to do was to walk out on her and vanish with Ethel Le Neve. But with her open infidelities, Cora had made him feel a nonentity. Then he finds Ethel, who regards him with the kind of adoration all men feel to be their due. Now what he wants is to make a completely fresh start, and expunge years of humiliation. To poison Cora and dismember her body is the act of a man determined to assert that he is not a nonentity. This is why Cora ended up in the basement of 39 Hilldrop Crescent and Crippen ended on the gallows: he had asserted – as Buckminster Fuller expressed it – that he was a verb, not a noun.

We can recognize this underlying lack of a sense of self-esteem in most murderers in this book. Peter Sutcliffe, the Yorkshire Ripper, a quiet, shy child who grew up withdrawn and modest; Donald Neilson, the Black Panther, who changed his surname from Nappey because people laughed at it; Hillside Strangler Kenneth Bianchi, whose life was a search for self-esteem; Dennis Nilsen, who told criminologist Brian Masters 'I never felt powerful in my life'; Berkowitz, such a nonentity that neighbours refused to believe he could be Son of Sam; Gein, the quiet little necrophile who was dominated by his mother; Christie, who was nicknamed 'Reggie No-Dick' and 'Can't-do-it Christie' because of his impotence; DeSalvo, the Boston Strangler, whose father habitually raped his wife in front of the children ... Time and again we encounter men who started life as psychological cripples, and killed as a reaction to a sense of inadequacy. Even the brutal Kray twins turn out to be mother's boys who learned to box to avoid being bullied at school.

And so, again and again, psychological inadequacy and low self-esteem provide us with the key to the ultimate violence. I would like to take a bet that if ever Jack the Ripper is finally identified, he will turn out to be someone who suffered from a gnawing inferiority complex.

Colin Wilson

Chapter 1

PETER SUTCLIFFE

THE YORKSHIRE RIPPER

By the time he was caught, seven women had been savagely attacked, 13 more brutally murdered and a whole community was virtually under siege. In a reign of terror spanning nearly six years, Peter Sutcliffe managed to elude capture by the biggest police squad ever assembled to catch one man.

It was bone-chillingly cold, solid Yorkshire cold. In a northern suburb of Leeds a milkman shivered on his rounds in the icy fog of an October dawn. As he peered through the freezing mist to see his way past the bleak recreation ground just off the Harrogate Road, he saw a shapeless bundle huddled on the frosted wintry grass. It was probably only a Guy Fawkes, Bonfire Night was just a week away, but something made him go over and investigate.

The woman was sprawled face upwards on the ground, her hair matted with blood, her body exposed. Her jacket and blouse were open and her bra pulled up. Her trousers were pulled down below her knees, although her pants were still in position. Her chest and stomach were lacerated with 14 stab wounds.

Later, the pathologist's report would reveal that she had been attacked from behind, dealt two vicious blows on the back of her head with a heavy, hammer-like implement. One of the blows had shattered the back of her skull. The stab wounds were inflicted after death.

The first killing

Wilma McCann, who regularly hitch-hiked lifts home after nights on the town, had died horribly about 100 yards from her home, a council house in Scott Hall Avenue. She had always liked a good time and a drink – the post-mortem blood test showed that she had consumed 12 to 14 measures of spirits on the night of her death, 30 October 1975.

On the fatal night, Wilma wore her favourite outfit – pink blouse, white flares, dark blue bolero jacket. At 7.30, she left the house, instructing her eldest daughter, Sonje, to keep the three younger children in bed and the front door locked. Sonje followed these instructions faithfully, until five o'clock next morning when the tearful clamouring from the younger children, and her own anxiety about her mother, goaded her into action. Bleary-eyed and anxious, she took her younger brother Richard, aged seven, and went for help. They were discovered, shivering at the local bus stop, hugging each other for warmth and reassurance.

Chapeltown

The first victim was just 28. There seemed to be no sexual motive for her murder. Her purse, the clasp bearing the word 'Mummy', inscribed by Sonje, was missing. In the absence of any other motive, the police treated her killing as a callous by-product of robbery. Investigations were set up, but got nowhere.

In fact it was to be the first in a long line of vicious killings that was to strike fear into the hearts of women in the North, particularly those who lived and worked in the area of Chapeltown. This was the red-light district of Leeds. It still is, but it is a sadder place these days. Then, it had barely changed for years, supply and demand balancing each other nicely. Not all the women who worked there were professional prostitutes. Some were housewives who sold sex for a little extra money to supplement their day jobs, some were women who were bored with their home lives, some were just enthusiastic amateurs who did it primarily for fun. One such 'good time girl' was 42 year-old Emily Jackson, who lived with her husband and three children in the respectable Leeds suburb of Churwell, five miles to the west of Chapeltown.

The boyfriend?

It was early in the evening of 20 January 1976 when Emily and her husband arrived at the Gaiety public house on the Roundhay Road, an acknowledged watering hole for the Chapeltown irregulars and their would-be clientele.

Within minutes of their arrival, Emily left her husband in the main lounge and went looking for business. Less than an hour later, she was spotted climbing into a Land Rover in the car park – that was the last time she was seen alive. At closing time, Mr Jackson, still alone, drank up and took a taxi home, perhaps assuming that his wife had found a boyfriend for the night.

It was still dark next morning when a worker on early shift noticed a huddled bulky shape on the ground, covered with a coat. Underneath lay Emily Jackson's body. Like Wilma McCann, she was sprawled on her back, her breasts exposed and her pants left on; like Wilma McCann she had been dealt two massive blows to the head with a heavy hammer. Her neck, breasts and stomach had been lacerated with stab wounds. But in Emily's case, the killer had stabbed at her dead body over 50 times, gouging her back with a Phillips screwdriver.

One senior detective admitted that the sight of such a ferocious attack had left him numb with horror. Somehow more sickening was the impression of a heavy ribbed wellington boot that was stamped on her right thigh.

Double murder

The post-mortem on Emily Jackson indicated sexual activity had taken place, but before the attack and not necessarily with the murderer. Once again, there seemed to be no motive. Officially, the police admitted that the killings were linked and that they were looking for a double murderer. Privately, they admitted that they were dealing with a remarkable killer, one who so far had left only one clue: he took size seven in shoes.

Over a year went by before the murderer struck again. By now the horrific deaths of McCann and Jackson were a fading memory among the 'good time girls' of the Chapeltown area. Like Emily Jackson, Irene Richardson was a part-time amateur, who worked the street corners to make ends meet and lived a sad, precarious existence in a squalid rooming house in Chapeltown's Cowper Street. On the evening of 5 February 1977, Irene Richardson left her tawdry rooming house half an hour before midnight to go dancing.

A post-mortem

Next morning, an early morning runner was jogging across Soldier's Field, a public playing-field just a short car ride from Chapeltown. He saw a body slumped on the ground behind the sports pavilion and stopped to see what the matter was.

It was all sickeningly familiar. She lay face down. Three massive hammer blows had shattered her skull. Her skirt and tights were torn off, but her coat had been draped in pointless propriety over her buttocks. Underneath her coat, her calf-length boots had been removed from her feet and laid neatly on her thighs. In awful contrast to this decorum, her neck and torso had been savaged with knife wounds. A post-mortem indicated no sign of sexual intercourse; she had died only half an hour after leaving her lodgings on her way to the last dance of her life. She was 28 years old.

There could be no denying now that a serial murderer was on the loose.

Killer: Peter Sutcliffe

As the details of Irene Richardson's death came to light, the Yorkshire media were not slow in drawing parallels with that other woman killer who still stalks police files and the collective public imagination: Jack the Ripper, who specialized in the killing, mutilation and disembowelling of prostitutes in the foggy back streets of London's East End. The unknown murderer of Wilma McCann, Emily Jackson and Irene Richardson now had a name – the Yorkshire Ripper.

It was too much for many of the red-light girls, who moved away in droves to safer areas such as Manchester, London and Glasgow. Those who could not or would not be displaced so far from home shifted their operations to nearby Bradford, where there is a thriving red-light district in the Manningham Lane–Oak Lane–Lumb Lane triangle.

Leeds memory

Patricia (Tina) Atkinson was a Bradford girl who lived just around the corner from Oak Lane. She counted herself lucky that she did not have to ply the increasingly dangerous car trade. Her marriage to an Asian had produced three daughters in quick succession, but had not survived the culture clash. In 1976 Tina lived alone, entertaining a string of boyfriends. She was attractive, slim and dark haired and there was no shortage of admirers.

The memory of the Leeds murders simmered under the surface of most women's minds, but two months had gone by since Irene Richardson's body had been found. It was a pleasant April evening when Tina got ready to go to her local pub, the Carlisle. Dressed in her favourite black leather jacket, blue jeans and a blue shirt, she had a good drinking session with her friends, reeling out just before closing time rather the worse for wear. She was not seen all next day, and people assumed she was sleeping it off.

The boot print

The following evening, friends dropped round and found the door to her flat unlocked. When they went in, they found a lumpy bundle on her bed, shrouded in blankets. Tina had been attacked as she came into her flat, four hammer blows smashing the back of her head. Then she had been flung on to the bed, her clothes pulled off. A knife had been plunged into her stomach seven times and the left side of her body was slashed. Any doubt about the killer's identity, or fear that this was a copy-cat murder, was dispelled by one discovery – a size seven wellington boot print, found on the bottom bed sheet. It was the same as the print found on Emily Jackson's thigh.

The police rarely worry about the media nicknames for killers, but by the end of April they were concerned that the Yorkshire Ripper was thriving too much on the oxygen of publicity. They were also having to face the fact that the murderer had discovered a limitless source of potential victims whose very lifestyles put them practically beyond protection.

THROUGH THE NET

On the evening of Saturday, 25 June 1977, Peter Sutcliffe dropped his wife Sonia off at the Sherrington nursing home where she worked the occasional night shift. He then set off for a drink with his next door neighbours and regular pub crawl companions, Ronnie and Peter Barker. The trio spent the evening in three pubs in and around the Bradford area, finishing off at the Dog in the Pound, where the highlight was an ex-sailor behind the bar who dressed in drag. At closing time they went for fish and chips before heading for home. Although it was well past midnight when Peter dropped the Barker brothers at their front door, he drove on and rejoined the traffic on the main road.

At around 2.00 a.m. the following day, he spotted a lone girl wearing a gingham skirt emerging into the street lights of Chapeltown Road, Leeds. He watched her as she passed the imposing form of the Hayfield pub, turning left down Reginald Terrace, one of the many side streets running off the main road. Parking his white Ford Corsair, he got out and began to follow her.

The body of Jayne MacDonald was found lying by a wall at 9.45 a.m., when the first group of children made their way into the adventure playground in Reginald Terrace. She had been struck on the back of the head, dragged 20 yards from the pavement and hit twice more. She was then stabbed once in the back and repeatedly through the chest. The police knew at once who they were dealing with – the trademarks were unmistakeable. But there was one alarming difference.

Jayne MacDonald was only 16, had just left school and worked in the shoe department of a local supermarket. On the night of her death, she had been with friends in Leeds and the attack took place on her way back to her parents' home, just a few hundred yards from where her body was found.

The MacDonalds were typical of the other side of life in Chapeltown. They were a happy, hard-working family unit, who outnumbered the element in the suburb that survived on prostitution or worse. Jayne MacDonald was not a prostitute, not a 'good time girl'. Her only connection with the red-light world was that she lived there.

When it became clear that the Yorkshire Ripper was now killing teenage girls barely out of school, the effect on the investigation was electric. By the time Jayne's inquest got under way in September, the police had interviewed almost 700 residents in 21 streets in the immediate vicinity of Reginald Terrace, and taken 3,500 statements, many of them from prostitutes.

Pressure on the police to come up with results was mounting. Two weeks after killing Jayne MacDonald, the Ripper savagely attacked Maureen Long in some waste ground near her home in Bradford. By some miracle she survived, but the description of her assailant did little to help the inquiry – over 6 ft tall, aged 36 to 37, with collar length, fair hair.

By the time Home Secretary Merlyn Rees visited the so-called Ripper headquarters in Leeds, he was told the case involved 304 full time officers who had interviewed 175,000 people, taken 12,500 statements and checked 10,000 vehicles.

A vital clue

Had the police known the type of man they were looking for, it would have offered little encouragement. He was to be found in an immaculately kept home in a middle class suburb of Bradford. Peter and Sonia Sutcliffe had moved into 6 Garden Lane, their new home in Heaton, in August, living together on their own for the first time. At the age of 31, Peter was a polite and mild-mannered neighbour, a hard-working and trusted employee, a good son and a loyal husband. He was the sort of man who tinkered happily with his car at weekends. There was not a great deal about him to cause raised eyebrows and certainly not enough to cast him in the role of mass murderer.

On Saturday, 1 October, Jean Bernadette Jordan was climbing into Sutcliffe's new red Ford Corsair near her home in Moss Side, Manchester. She accepted £5 in advance and directed him to some land two miles away between allotments and the Southern Cemetery much favoured by prostitutes. A few yards from the car, Sutcliffe brought the full force of a hammer down on to Jean Jordan's skull. He struck her again and again, 11 times in all. After pulling her body into some bushes, he was startled by the arrival of another car and made a rapid getaway.

As he drove back to Bradford that night, he was conscious that he had left a vital clue by the body of Jean Jordan. The £5 note he had given her was brand new, taken directly from his wage packet, which he had received only two days previously.

Return to Moss Side

For eight long days Sutcliffe waited, and when the body had still not been discovered he decided to risk returning to Moss Side to find the note. Despite a frantic search, he could not find Jean Jordan's handbag and in an act of frustration he started to attack the body with a broken pane of glass. He even tried to cut off the head, thinking that this would remove his own tell-tale hammer blow signature. In the end he gave up, kicking the body several times before driving home.

One day later, an allotment owner found Jean Jordan's naked body and rang Chorlton-cum-Hardy police station. Her head was unrecognizable and there was no identifying evidence among her scattered clothing.

She was eventually identified from a fingerprint on a lemonade bottle she had handled before leaving home for the last time. Jean Jordan was 21 and had been cautioned twice for soliciting. She lived with a man she had met in Manchester on her arrival from Scotland five years earlier, and they had two sons.

When Jean Jordan failed to return to their council house that weekend, her common law husband thought little of it. As a result her name did not appear on a missing persons list file for ten days.

Air of dismay

The discovery of the £5 note near her body meant the tempo of the investigation was raised dramatically. But three months later there was an air of dismay at its complete lack of success. One of the 5,000 men they had talked to was Peter Sutcliffe. Helpful and courteous, he had failed to arouse any suspicions. After leaving Sutcliffe's spacious detached house the detectives filed a five paragraph report which left him in the clear.

Sutcliffe's was the sort of house that Helen Rytka, a striking 18 year-old girl had often dreamed of owning. By 31 January 1978, she was sharing a miserable room next to a motorway flyover in Huddersfield with her twin sister, Rita.

They tended to work as a pair, concentrating upon the limited red-light district in and around the depressed and derelict Great Northern Street area. The railway arches under the Leeds to Manchester line formed brothels, but Helen and Rita were a step above that, they believed, concentrating upon the car trade.

Because of the Yorkshire Ripper murders, they had devised a system whereby they were picked up separately outside a public lavatory, each giving their client precisely 20 minutes, and returning to the toilet at a set time. They even took the car number of each other's client before they set off.

Fatal decision

It all went terribly wrong, however, on the snowy night of Tuesday, 31 January 1978. Helen arrived back at the rendezvous five minutes early, at 9.25 p.m. The bearded man in the red Ford Corsair offered her the chance of another quick £5, possibly even before Rita returned. The sisters never saw each other again.

Helen took the stranger to nearby Garrard's timber yard, which straggles round the railway arches, a constant night-time haunt for down-and-outs as well as prostitutes.

Unusually for him, Sutcliffe had sexual intercourse with Helen, largely because the presence of two men in the yard delayed his hammer attack. He struck when the girl stepped out of the back seat to return to the front of the car, anxious no doubt to return to her twin. His first blow missed, striking the door of the car. His second attempt struck her head, then he hit her another five times. The attack was a few feet from the foreman's shed in the wood-yard, and the walls were spattered with her blood.

Helen's body was dragged to a woodpile, where it was hidden, her clothes scattered over a wide area. Her bra and black polo-neck sweater were found in the characteristic position above her breasts, and her socks were left on. Her black lace panties had been found earlier by a lorry driver on the site and pinned to a shed door. She had been horribly mutilated, with three stab wounds to the chest, and indications of repeated stabbings through the same wounds. There were also scratch marks on the chest.

Police optimism

Back at the lavatory, desperately worried as she was, Rita's fear of the police was greater and it prevented her from going to them immediately. It was three days before a police Alsatian located the hidden body. But the police were optimistic. The Ripper's latest victim had vanished in the early evening from a busy street.

More than 100 passers-by were traced, and all but three cars and one stocky, fair-haired man eliminated. George Oldfield went on the Jimmy Young radio show a week later and suggested that a wife, mother or girl-friend must have surely, by then, suspected the Ripper's identity. No one came forward because the Ripper was too careful.

A few weeks later, on 26 March 1978, a passer-by spotted an arm sticking out from under an overturned sofa on wasteland in Lumb Lane, part of Bradford's red-light district. The putrid smell from what he thought was a tailor's dummy sent him rushing to a telephone.

By any standards, 22 year-old Yvonne Pearson, was a serious professional prostitute, having worked the rich businessman trade in most of Britain's cities. Although a Leeds girl, her diary contained addresses of clients all over the country.

Return to the scene

She had been killed two months earlier – ten days before Helen Rytka – by a large blunt instrument blow to the head (Sutcliffe having progressed from ball-pein hammers to a club hammer), and her chest had been jumped upon repeatedly. Her bra and jumper were pulled above her breasts, while her black flared slacks had been tugged down. Horsehair from the sofa was stuffed in her mouth. It seemed that the killer had even returned to the scene to make her body more visible – as he was believed to have done with Jean Jordan in Manchester four months previously – by placing a copy of the *Daily Mirror*, dated four weeks after her death, under one of her arms.

Yvonne Pearson knew only too well the dangers her business held and had told a neighbour and friend of her worries about the Yorkshire Ripper. On the night of her death, she had left her two young daughters, Colette and Lorraine, with a 16 year-old neighbour, and set off for the Flying Dutchman pub.

She left there at 9.30 p.m. and within minutes was climbing into a car driven by a bearded man with black, piercing eyes. They parked on wasteland in nearby Arthington Street. He killed her with a club hammer, dragged her by the collar to the abandoned sofa and jumped on her until her ribs cracked.

Two months after Yvonne Pearson's body was found, Vera Millward – frail, ill, and looking at least 15 years older than her 41 years – died in a well-lit part of the grounds at Manchester Royal Infirmary. The Ripper had hit her three times on the head with a hammer and then slashed her across the stomach.

Spanish-born and the mother of seven children, Vera Millward had arrived in England after the war as a domestic help. She later lived with a Jamaican and soon resorted to prostitution in Manchester's Moss Side district to support her family.

On the night of Tuesday, 16 May, her boyfriend thought she was going out from their flat in Greenham Avenue, Hulme, to buy cigarettes and get pain-killing drugs from the hospital to ease her chronic stomach pains.

When a gardener discovered her body at 8.10 a.m. the following morning, on a rubbish pile in the corner of the car park, he thought at first that she was some sort of doll. Vera Millward was lying on her right side, face down, her arms folded beneath her body and legs straight. Her shoes were placed neatly on the body and rested against the fence. She was partly covered by a grey-coloured coat and a piece of paper was placed over her badly disfigured head.

The reward for information leading to the arrest of the Yorkshire Ripper was by now £15,000. No one in George Oldfield's team at this stage had any real doubts that the man they were searching for lived in West Yorkshire – and probably right under their noses in Leeds or Bradford.

By the end of 1978, in little over 12 months, detectives had been face to face with the Ripper four times. Twice they had visited him in connection with the £5 note clue. Three months after Vera Millward's death, they returned because his car registration number had cropped up during special checks in Leeds and Bradford.

On the fourth occasion, Sutcliffe was questioned about the tyres on his car. The police were checking for treads that might match tracks first identified at the scene of Irene Richardson's murder, 21 months earlier. As usual Sutcliffe was accommodating and unruffled, betraying absolutely nothing. The officers were never asked to check Sutcliffe for blood group (rare) or shoe size (unusually small for a man) – at least two of the firm facts known about the killer.

THE RIPPER'S RAMPAGE

Between June 1977 and May 1978, Peter Sutcliffe had attacked seven women, leaving five dead and two horrifically injured. But just as quickly as his killing spree had accelerated, it abruptly stopped. For the next 11 months the Yorkshire Ripper simply went out of circulation. Theories began to spread about what had happened to him. One possibility was that he had committed suicide. If he had taken his identity with him to the grave, then the eerie similarity to his Victorian counterpart would have been complete.

On the night of Wednesday, 4 April 1979, Sutcliffe drove from Bingley to Halifax. Just before midnight, he got out of his car and fell in step with 19 year-old Josephine Whitaker as she walked across Savile Park playing-fields. He spoke to her briefly, and then, as they moved away from the street lamps, smashed the back of her skull with a hammer and dragged her into the shadows.

Josephine's body was found early the next morning. Like Jayne MacDonald, she had been a respectable girl, who lived at home with her family and worked as a clerk in the headquarters of the Halifax Building Society. With her murder, the Ripper was telling women that he had not mistaken Jayne MacDonald for a prostitute: he would attack any woman who had the nerve to walk the streets after dark. Overnight, all women in the north of England lost their liberty.

Game of bluff

All this time, Peter Sutcliffe had been keeping up an astonishing game of bluff with his family and friends. He would make a point of picking up Sonia from work to 'protect' her from the Ripper, and confided to one colleague that 'whoever is doing all these murders has a lot to answer for'. On one occasion, his fellow drivers at the Clark's depot even made a bet that he was the Ripper, but Sutcliffe just laughed and said nothing.

Sutcliffe's rampage had lasted four years. Ten women were dead, and the police were no nearer to finding their sadistic killer. In fact, they were sinking further into a morass of conflicting information, conjecture and myth. Few actual details of the killer's grisly methods were publicly released, but that did not stop the wildfire spread of rumour.

It was at this point that the Sunderland hoaxer struck, tragically misdirecting the police and costing three women their lives. Three anonymous letters and a cassette tape had landed on George Oldfield's desk between March 1978 and June 1979, seemingly indicating that the Ripper was in fact a Geordie.

Disastrous summer

Peter Sutcliffe let the police clutch at this straw throughout the long hot summer of 1979. In July, he was visited by Detective-Constable Laptew about his car, which had been spotted in the Lumb Lane area of Bradford on 36 occasions. Laptew sensed something suspicious about Sutcliffe but, because all eyes were focused on the north-east, his observations went unheeded. Sutcliffe returned to Bradford a month later to claim his eleventh victim.

It was Saturday, 1 September, and Sutcliffe was cruising the streets around Little Horton – a residential area for many students. It was just after 1.00 a.m. when he saw Barbara Leach – a second year social science student – moving away from a group of friends outside the Mannville Arms on Great Horton Road.

Sutcliffe struck in Ash Grove, just 200 yards from the pub and then dragged Barbara Leach into the shadows of somebody's backyard. Here he stabbed her eight times before putting her body into a dustbin recess and slinging an old carpet over it. Barbara's body was not found until late the following afternoon.

Police impotence

Two Scotland Yard dignitaries were sent to Yorkshire as advisors. They returned to London a month later having contributed nothing to the inquiry. Men from the Manchester force returned to Bradford to review the £5 note inquiry. They narrowed their field down to 270 suspects, but got no further and returned home.

Another Christmas, another Easter came and went, and still no progress was made. As the summer of 1980 faded, the public had pushed the Ripper to the back of its collective mind. Still at Garden Lane, Peter and Sonia Sutcliffe maintained the same unobtrusive lifestyle as before, seldom entertaining and preferring to keep themselves to themselves. Peter still went out to the pub with his friends and brothers in the evening, and the combination of this and his travels at work meant that it was always going to be difficult for the police to pin down his movements on any specific night. On Thursday, 18 August, he went to Farsley, Leeds, and killed for the twelfth time.

Killer: Peter Sutcliffe

Civil servant

Marguerite Walls was a 47 year-old civil servant working at the Department of Education and Science. She had worked late to tidy up loose ends before going on a ten day holiday. She left the office at 10 p.m. to walk the mile or so home. Two days later, her body was found, buried under a mound of grass clippings in the wooded grounds of a magistrate's house. Marguerite Walls had been bludgeoned and strangled, but her body had not been mutilated. As a result police refused to include it in the Ripper sequence.

Three months later, they had no such option. Jacqueline Hill, a language student at the University of Leeds, got off the bus in Otley Road opposite the local Kentucky Fried Chicken shack. She was in sight of Lupton Flats – a hall of residence – when Peter Sutcliffe, his fingers still greasy from his Kentucky Fried supper, brutally struck her down. He dragged her body to wasteland behind the shopping parade and fell upon it in a frenzy. Death had struck Jacqueline so suddenly that one of her eyes remained open. Sutcliffe stabbed repeatedly at the sightless eye.

Public anger

After five years, women finally lost their tempers and took to the streets to voice their anger, fear and frustration. Public anger was matched by over-whelming police frustration, as more and more information flooded the system and they were unable to do anything with it.

Two days before Jacqueline Hill's murder, the Home Office – jolted at last from its complacency – had appointed a Super Squad. Six weeks after Jacqueline's death, this A-team reached the same conclusion as the West Yorkshire force – they had no idea how to crack the case.

A CRUEL HOAX

One aspect of the Ripper inquiry has all the elements of a classic tragedy. The actors were George Oldfield, Chief Constable Ronald Gregory and the anonymous hoaxer who became known as the Geordie Ripper. He perpe-trated a hideous joke on a police force so desperate to put an end to the real Ripper's appalling activities, salvage their tattered reputation and soothe the fears of an increasingly agitated public, that they were prepared to sus-pend objective judgement in the interests of nailing their man.

The hoax began modestly in March 1978. Two anonymous letters arrived in Yorkshire from north-east England. Posted in Sunderland five days apart, one was addressed to George Oldfield, the other to the editor of the Manchester *Daily Mirror*. The letters were discounted, largely because they had been written after Yvonne Pearson's disappearance but before her body was discovered, and the writer had wrongly estimated the number of victims. The letters disappeared into the obscurity of the filing cabinet.

Almost exactly a year later, a third letter arrived. It had been posted to catch the 1.45 p.m. collection in Sunderland on 23 March 1979. Handwriting experts confirmed that the same person had written all three letters. As far as police were concerned, the third letter was significant as it mentioned the fact that Vera Millward, the last victim, had stayed in hospital. They believed, wrongly and fatally, that this information could only have come from Vera herself. On this basis they made a breathtaking leap to the conclusion that the writer was the Ripper.

This third letter made it clear that the next victim might possibly be in Bradford's Manningham, but definitely not in Chapeltown – it was 'too bloody hot there' because of the efforts of 'curserred coppers'. The bizarre language, and the general caste of the letters – so close to the gleeful sadism of the original Ripper's taunting notes – rang warning bells in some police minds. Unfortunately, these bells were muffled by the urge to find a clue – any clue – to break the case open.

Two weeks after the third letter had arrived, Josephine Whitaker was murdered in Halifax. She was the second non-prostitute to meet her death at the hands of the Ripper and pressure was mounting on George Oldfield. The only credible lead he had was the three Sunderland letters.

George Oldfield called a press conference, and the Sunderland theory was aired. To back it up, traces of engineering oil had been found on one of the letters, similar to traces found on Josephine Whitaker's body. The public were asked to come forward with any information they had about anybody who might have been in Sunderland on the days the letters were posted. The response was overwhelming, as if the public too were relieved to be given something concrete to go on. But on analysis, it added up to very little.

On the morning of 18 June 1979, two months after Josephine Whitaker's death, a buff coloured envelope landed on George Oldfield's desk. It was addressed in the Sunderland writer's familiar hand and contained a cheap black cassette tape. Here was the clue that was to solidify the hypothesis in Oldfield's mind into fact. He slotted the tape into a cassette player and switched it on. From the machine came a man's broad Geordie accent. His message contained 257 words. If it was authentic, it was one of the most sensational clues in the annals of detection.

Reputations at stake

George Oldfield was convinced of the tape's authenticity, but wanted it kept under wraps for a while. Chief Constable Ronald Gregory on the other hand thought that such a distinctive voice would be easily identified if the public were allowed to hear it.

Two days later, news of the tape and its contents somehow seeped through to the press. At a hastily called press conference the world's press hounds crammed into the modest lecture hall at the police detective training school in Wakefield. The media machine was about to swamp George Oldfield. He made a last concession to objectivity, observing, just once, that it could be an elaborate hoax. After that, the idea sank without trace. George Oldfield's career and the reputation of his force was on the line. He seemed to regard the Ripper's outrages as a personal challenge to him and was desperately determined to defeat his opponent.

A huge publicity campaign was mounted. The public could dial in and listen to the 'Geordie Ripper Tape', in the hope that someone somewhere might recognize the voice. Within a few days of the press conference and publication of the tape, more than 50,000 calls flooded in.

The experts

Meanwhile, George Oldfield consulted language experts from Leeds University – Stanley Ellis, one of the country's leading dialect experts and Jack Windsor Lewis, a lecturer in the Department of Linguistics and Phonetics. They quickly verified the accent as genuine Wearside, and pinned it down to Castletown, a small tightly-knit suburb of Sunderland. West Yorkshire Police moved in – 11 detectives were installed in a Sunderland hotel and 100 officers in the town prepared to get their man. Media coverage reached saturation point.

In theory, it should have been only a matter of time before the Geordie Ripper was found. The police were moving through a very small area – only 4,000 people lived in Castletown – with a very fine tooth-comb. Men less desperate than George Oldfield began to acknowledge that the Geordie Ripper was a cruel hoaxer, who knew he would not be discovered because he had a cast-iron alibi for all the relevant times. Northumbrian police, never entirely convinced, made their doubts public.

Alarm bells were also ringing in the heads of the two dialect experts, Ellis and Lewis. They tried in vain to impress their fears on police and even suggested an alternative campaign, which did not eliminate suspects from other regions. Their advice was not taken. West Yorkshire Police persisted with their belief that non-Geordies could be eliminated from the inquiry. Oldfield and Gregory planned an even more grandiose campaign, with a million pound budget. A few days before the launch of this fateful campaign, Ellis and Lewis, increasingly unhappy about the situation, wrote separately to Oldfield and Gregory about their apprehension.

Misdirected faith

The expert opinion was not accepted. The perverse insistence that their quarry was a Geordie meant the elimination from the inquiry of all other suspects, including the bearded driver from Bradford who had featured in both the £5 note and the red-light files, and who had already been interviewed four times by police.

The infamous publicity campaign went ahead, running out of steam and credibility by 1980, having achieved nothing at all apart from clogging the already overloaded police system with a silt of useless information.

Apart from the main theme of missed clues, botched interviews and cruel misdirection, an unnoticed minor irony was being played on the theme of blood. Forensic tests showed that whoever had licked the sticky flaps of the Sunderland envelopes had blood that belonged to the rare group B – a group shared by only six per cent of the population.

At this stage, the police believed that the Ripper had been responsible for the murder of Joan Harrison in Preston, Lancashire, three weeks after Wilma McCann, his first victim, had died. Semen on Joan Harrison's body indicated that her murderer's blood belonged to group B. Peter Sutcliffe's blood was group B, but he had not been in Preston, and his accent did not fit the Sunderland hypothesis, so no suspicion fell on him.

Of course, there is no knowing, whether police would have got to Sutcliffe before the deaths of Josephine Whitaker, Barbara Leach, Marguerite Walls and Jacqueline Hill if they had not been preoccupied with the Geordie Ripper.

To this day, only one person knows who the Geordie Ripper was. Somewhere in Sunderland, there is a man who is arguably just as guilty of murdering the Ripper's last three victims as if he had wielded the hammer himself. And it was pure chance that prevented yet another victim falling foul of the Ripper hoaxer.

THE FINAL TWIST

It was the second day of the New Year, 1981, when Sergeant Robert (Bob) Ring and Police Constable Robert Hydes started their evening shift. They were cruising along Melbourne Avenue in Sheffield – a haunt of prostitutes and their customers – when they saw Olivia Reivers climbing into a Rover V8 3500. It was a toss of a coin whether they would bother to investigate alleged soliciting. They decided to stroll over.

The driver identified himself as Peter Williams and said that the car was his own – the short, bearded man wanted no trouble. He scrambled out of the car, asking immediately if he could relieve himself. Bob Ring nodded in good tempered exasperation, and the little man sidled over to the shadowy bushes lining the grubby lane. Under cover of darkness, he removed a ball-pein hammer and sharpened knife from a special pocket of his car coat, and hid them. Olivia Reivers, remonstrating with the policemen, had no idea that she was abusing the men who had saved her life.

By the time the man strolled back to his car, the police had established that the number plates on it were false and prostitute and client were taken to Hammerton Road police station for further questioning. The man's name was Peter William Sutcliffe.

At the station, Sutcliffe's main worry was that the police would tell his wife that he had been picked up with a prostitute. Otherwise, he was calm and obligingly forthcoming – after he had been to the lavatory and hidden a second knife in the cistern. He readily admitted that he had stolen the number plates from a scrap-yard in Dewsbury, West Yorkshire.

Every force in the land had been issued with instructions to inform West Yorkshire Police if they picked up a man in company with a prostitute. So Peter Sutcliffe was locked up for the night and the next morning was taken, still unprotesting, to Dewsbury police station.

Sutcliffe was a chatty, eager interviewee. He told the Dewsbury Police that he was a long distance lorry driver, travelling regularly to the north-east. Almost in passing, he told them he had been interviewed by the Ripper Squad about the £5 note and of his regular visits to the Bradford red-light district.

Within an hour of Sutcliffe's arrival, Dewsbury Police had called the Ripper Squad at Millgarth, Leeds. Detective Sergeant Des O'Boyle soon dis-covered that Sutcliffe's name had come up several times, and immediately set off to drive the eight or so miles to Dewsbury.

By six in the evening, O'Boyle was sufficiently intrigued by Sutcliffe to contact his immediate superior in Leeds, Detective Inspector John Boyle. When Boyle found out that Sutcliffe was blood group B he, too, travelled to Dewsbury, and Sutcliffe was locked in his cell for a second night.

Damning evidence

In the meantime, Bob Ring heard one of his colleagues casually mention that the Rover driver was still in the cells at Dewsbury, being interviewed by detectives from the Ripper Squad. Ring froze. He rushed back as fast as possible to Melbourne Avenue. After frantic minutes scrabbling, he found what he was looking for.

The telephone call from Sheffield to Dewsbury was music to the ears of Ripper Squad detectives. Ring had recovered a ball-pein hammer and a knife. Boyle and his sergeant stared speechlessly at each other, scarcely daring to believe it.

Sutcliffe slept soundly through a night that saw frantic police activity. Detective Sergeant Peter Smith, the oldest Ripper hand on the case, was called in. While Smith and Boyle questioned Sutcliffe, his wife, Sonia, was being questioned in a room down the corridor and his neat suburban house in Garden Lane, Heaton, was being searched by police officers.

Triumph in sight

All morning, they discussed almost everything but the Ripper murders with Sutcliffe. Then, early on Sunday afternoon, Boyle stopped talking about Bonfire Night and mentioned the hammer and knife found in Sheffield. Sutcliffe, the garrulous witness, fell silent. Boyle probed gently, 'I think you're in trouble, serious trouble.'

Sutcliffe finally spoke. 'I think you are leading up to the Yorkshire Ripper.' Boyle stayed calm, containing his mounting excitement.

'Well, what about the Yorkshire Ripper?'

'Well,' said Sutcliffe. 'That's me.'

He admitted to killing 11 women, denying that he had anything to do with Joan Harrison's death or the Geordie tape.

Boyle could hardly believe his ears. The Ripper inquiry was over. It seemed to be as much a relief for Sutcliffe as it was for his captors. 'Just thinking about them all reminds me of what a monster I am,' he confided. He did not want a solicitor present as he recalled unprompted the long list of dead, nor at this stage did he mention the voice of God conferring divine right upon him.

A terrible revenge

Over the following day and a half, Boyle and Smith took down Sutcliffe's confession. It took almost 17 hours to complete. Asked why he had done what he did, Sutcliffe said that he began killing after a Bradford prostitute cheated him out of £10 in 1969. At the time, he was feeling overcome with jealousy, and had sought the companionship of a prostitute. The encounter was a catastrophe. Sutcliffe did not have sex with the woman and was deliberately short-changed by her. 'I felt outraged and humiliated and embarrassed. I felt a hatred for the prostitute and her kind.'

At the end of the marathon dictation session, Sutcliffe signed the statement and identified the knife and hammer found in Sheffield as his. He was remanded in custody at Armley jail in Leeds. The news broke and an atmosphere of celebration filled the streets and pubs where the Yorkshire Ripper had stalked. Senior detectives could scarcely conceal their delight during the press conference given after Sutcliffe's confession.

Sixteen weeks later, Sutcliffe stood trial at the Old Bailey's No. 1 Court. That he came to trial at all was due to Mr Justice Boreham.

Even before he had been arraigned, the Crown prosecution, defence counsel and Attorney General Sir Michael Havers had agreed that the

Bradford lorry driver was mentally ill, suffering from paranoid schizophrenia. After five years of terrorizing the women in the north of England, it looked as if the Yorkshire Ripper would be quietly put away.

Mr Justice Boreham, however, was having none of this. Barely concealing his irritation with both counsels, he threw out their suggestion, ordered the court to reconvene in five days' time and made it clear that the jury would listen to the evidence and decide on behalf of the British public whether Peter Sutcliffe was a madman or a murderer.

Pleading guilty to manslaughter, Sutcliffe was calm, assured and articulate. His high-pitched Bradford voice hardly faltered as his defence counsel accompanied him through his recital of death. He even managed to laugh when he recalled that when questioned about the size seven wellington boot and the print on Emily Jackson's thigh and Tina Atkinson's bedsheet, the policeman had not noticed he was wearing the boots.

Religious hallucination

Sutcliffe's defence team had tried to dissuade him from giving evidence under oath. He refused. Departing from his police statement, Sutcliffe claimed that he had been following instructions from God. He admitted that in 1969, two years after he had first heard the voice of God, he had been planning to kill a prostitute in Bradford's Manningham Lane area. On this first attempt at 'street cleaning', he was arrested and charged with being in possession of a housebreaking implement – his hammer.

For the jury, it was a straight forward decision. Was Sutcliffe mentally ill, as the defence maintained, or a sexual sadist as the prosecution were now treating him?

Late in the afternoon of 22 May, Sutcliffe rose to his feet to hear the jury's verdict. They found him guilty of 13 murders and seven attempted murders. Justice Boreham sentenced Sutcliffe to life imprisonment, with a recommendation that he should serve at least 30 years.

Sutcliffe was incarcerated in the special top security wing at Parkhurst Prison on the Isle of Wight. During his stay he was attacked by another prisoner who slashed his face with a broken coffee jar. Three years later, in March 1984, the plan he had hatched in Armley jail came to fruition. Sutcliffe was moved to Broadmoor, to occupy a room in Ward One of Somerset House. His faking of mental illness – if faking it was – has rebounded on him. Sutcliffe's mental state has so deteriorated that he is often totally incoherent.

The passage of time has helped to cushion the horror of the five years when Sutcliffe was at large. But the question that haunted those who were close to the case still remains. How did he confound the efforts of a massive police investigation for so long?

CASE FILE: SUTCLIFFE, PETER

BACKGROUND

The eldest of John and Kathleen Sutcliffe's six children, Peter – even before he became an adult – often wondered jokingly if John Sutcliffe was his real father. After all, John was a self-proclaimed man's man, a local boy about town, as well as a famed local footballer, cricketer and actor – a man for all seasons.

Mother's boy

Unlike the other Sutcliffe children. Peter never quite managed the art of surviving daily life comfortably in the council estate world of Bingley – a somewhat dour town just six miles north of Bradford along the Aire Valley. From the start he was small and weedy, destined to be close to his mother for many years. Indeed it was Kathleen, the quiet and solid Catholic mother, who provided the round-the-clock stability, seven days a week.

Even after starting school, from which he played truant for two weeks when he was bullied, he clung to his mother's skirts at home, following her everywhere in the house and in the streets. The younger boys – particularly brother Mick, three years Peter's junior – seemed to have inherited their father's appetite for life and the opposite sex. Their capacity to spend great chunks of the day consuming large quantities of beer and spirits held no appeal for Peter.

The preener

When he left school at 15, traditionally the cross-over point into manhood, Peter still confounded his family. He continued to be methodical, meticulous and fastidious, spending hours preening himself in the bathroom – despite showing no interest in girls at the end of it all. His ability to sit in the toilet for three or four hours at a time became a family joke.

So too did one of his earliest jobs – that of a grave-digger at a cemetery in Bingley. When he allowed himself a joke, he regularly favoured a quip about having 'thousands of people below me where I work now'. His shrill and wildly uncontrollable laughter took by surprise those who heard it for the first time from such an apparently serious young man. At home, at work and even at the local pub he would sit bolt upright, knees neatly together, moving only his eyes when someone spoke to him, scarcely able to bear moving his head.

As he grew older, Sutcliffe took up body-building. He went on a course of 'bulk-builder' foods and would spend an hour or so every evening training on his Bullworker.

Too deep

Despite his body-building efforts, it was still apparent to Peter, and the friends of his brothers and sisters, that he was different. He was certainly the brightest of the family and undoubtedly regarded as good looking. Yet none of his sisters' friends were attracted to him.

Deep and introverted was how his family described his first proper girlfriend, Sonia – the first girl he had taken home to meet his mother. He met the dark, quiet 16 year-old schoolgirl with the mid-European accent in the Royal Standard, his local haunt. Her father would have been furious if he had known she was drinking under age with her girlfriends from school.

Sonia had the same introversion and hauteur as others had detected in Peter, and quickly succeeded in moving him away from his pals in 'grave-digger's corner' in their local pub.

Perfect match

On Sundays, Sonia and Peter sat on dining chairs at the back of the sitting-room, lost in their own conversation. Sonia, said the family, would speak to others only when it was absolutely unavoidable. They believed she held them in contempt, particularly father John and brother Mick, the serious drinkers for whom Saturday night and Sunday lunchtime sessions were almost sacred.

Following an often tortuous eight year courtship, Peter and Sonia married. After spending the first three years of married life with Sonia's parents, Peter became the first Sutcliffe for three generations to move out of Bingley – to a detached house in upwardly-mobile Heaton in Bradford. The Sutcliffe family claim they never felt welcome during their increasingly rare visits to Heaton. Mick and Sonia certainly made no secret of their personal distaste for each other.

Peter had always stuck up for his mother, sympathizing with the hard time he believed his domineering father gave her. Before he left the family home on the Ferncliffe Estate,

Bingley, however, his faith in her traditional Catholic purity was shattered. His father had discovered that Kathleen was having an affair with a neighbour, a local policeman.

Devastated

John Sutcliffe arranged for the children, including Peter and bride-to-be Sonia, to be present at a Bingley hotel for a grand confrontation. Kathleen arrived in the bar believing she was meeting her boyfriend, only to be forced by her husband to show the family the new nightdress she had bought for the occasion. Peter was devastated. Yet, having discovered earlier that Sonia had had a secret boyfriend, he hinted to his father that he understood.

Later that same year, 1969, Peter Sutcliffe carried out his first known attack. He hit a prostitute over the head with a stone in a sock following a row over a £10 note in Bradford.

Since his son's trial, John Sutcliffe has said that he believed the trauma of his mother's affair triggered off the Yorkshire Ripper inside Peter. 'It shook him rigid. He worshipped his mother and I think now that what I did turned his mind.'

One psychiatrist who was involved in the case agreed, explaining that Sutcliffe's mother's affair could have pre-empted him into an acute psychotic state.

PSYCHOLOGICAL PROFILE

The key question at Peter Sutcliffe's trial was his state of mind when he carried out the attacks. Was he mentally ill, suffering from the rare but clearly definable paranoid schizophrenia? Or was he a clear-thinking sadist who was fully aware of what he had done? In short, was he mad or guilty of murder?

Diagnosis?

Peter Sutcliffe's defence, represented by James Chadwin QC, maintained that he was suffering from paranoid schizophrenia. This diagnosis was based on the evidence of three eminent forensic psychiatrists – Dr Hugo Milne of Bradford, Dr Malcolm McCulloch of Liverpool and Dr Terence Kay of Leeds – each of whom had interviewed Sutcliffe.

What they believed to be crucial was Sutcliffe's claim that, since the age of 20, he had been following instructions from God. He had first heard the voice of God seemingly coming from a gravestone in Bingley Cemetery, when he worked there as a grave-digger. It told him that his mission in life was to clean the streets of prostitutes. God had even helped him by preventing the police from capturing him until now. He conceded that he had been planning to do the Lord's work on Olivia Reivers when police finally caught him.

The Crown prosecution, led by the Attorney General, Sir Michael Havers, argued that Sutcliffe's story of a divine mission was a lie and that he was 'a clever callous murderer who deliberately set out to create a cock and bull story to avoid conviction for murder.' Firstly, there was the evidence of a prison officer at Armley who had overheard Sutcliffe telling his wife that he was planning to deceive the doctors about his mental state.

He had told her that if he could convince people he was mad he might only get ten years 'in the loony bin'. This was backed up by the fact that during his original interrogation by the police, he never once mentioned a divine mission.

It had not occurred to the psychiatrists that Sutcliffe may have faked schizophrenia. His ability to do so may have been helped by the fact that he had at least one personal experience of the illness. In 1972, his wife had suffered a nervous breakdown while studying in London. She had talked of being the second Christ and had claimed pain in her hands from being nailed on the cross.

These facts made it hard to present a convincing case that Sutcliffe really was a paranoid schizophrenic with dangerous delusions. The jury's distrust was reinforced when Dr McCulloch admitted that he had taken only half an hour with Sutcliffe to reach a diagnosis. They were visibly unimpressed when he admitted that he had not even looked at Sutcliffe's own statement until a day before the trial.

The Crown prosecution was adamant that there had been evidence of sexual sadism in at least six of the attacks.

There was one point upon which the three psychiatrists were in agreement with the prosecution. They said in evidence that if they were wrong about the paranoid schizophrenia then there was only one likely alternative explanation and that was the prosecution's. Peter Sutcliffe was a sadist, a man who enjoyed killing women, a cold-blooded murderer, evil rather than mad. After the professionals had had their say the decision ultimately lay with the jury.

Chapter 2

DONALD NEILSON
THE BLACK PANTHER

In 1975, 17 year-old Lesley Whittle was abducted by a callous killer whose sinister appearance earned him the nickname of the Black Panther. For Lesley, the kidnap ended in unimaginable horror. Eleven months were to pass before the Panther was finally cornered.

On the evening of 13 January 1975, Lesley Whittle went to bed early. Lesley, a 17 year-old student, lived with her mother on the main street of the village of Highley in Shropshire. Lesley's mother returned home at 1.30 a.m. and, before going to bed, she went to check on her daughter. Lesley was asleep in her bedroom.

Soon after that, during the small hours of 14 January, a sinister figure approached the house, clad head-to-toe in black and wearing a hood with slits for eyes and mouth. Working silently and expertly, he cut the telephone wires that provided contact with the outside world, and then forced his way inside the house via the garage. Passing through the lounge, he went straight to Lesley's bedroom.

Abduction

Lesley Whittle was woken with a rough shake. A figure, of small but athletic build, was standing by her bed pointing a sawn-off shotgun between her eyes. He left her in no doubt that he would kill her if she failed to follow instructions.

Putting tape over her mouth, the black-clad figure led Lesley downstairs and outside to a green Morris. He bound her wrists and ankles and placed tape over her eyes before laying her down in the rear seat.

Retracing his steps, he went back into the lounge and left a coil of plastic

Dymo tape, which he had prepared earlier, with three ransom messages printed on it.

Returning to the car, Lesley's abductor removed his hood and put on an ordinary jacket, placing his holdall bag with his house-breaking tools in the boot. He then set off on the 65 mile route to his hiding place.

Leaving the M6 at Junction 16, he drove to Bathpool Park. After removing a manhole cover leading into the central shaft of the drainage system, he returned to the car and released Lesley's legs.

Lesley's abductor forced her underground through an inspection hole just 11in wide, and then followed her down a rusty ladder. At its base was a 5ft step over which water flowed.

They reached the main shaft after a number of obstacles, including a waterfall, and finally arrived at the lowest of three platforms, just 24in wide and 62ft below ground. On the platform lay a foam rubber mattress, along with a sleeping bag. A wire noose, 5ft long, was already attached to the ladder.

Lesley was naked when her abductor placed the wire collar, which was cushioned with sticking plaster, around her neck. He clamped it on using three metal cable clips which he tightened with a spanner.

Lesley Whittle never discovered the identity of the man who kidnapped and entombed her in the Bathpool Park drainage system. In time, the public would know him as Donald Neilson.

The day after the kidnapping, Neilson forced Lesley to make two tape-recorded messages for her family, reading from what he had written in capital letters on a writing pad. The messages were to reassure them she was safe and urge them to pay the ransom money.

He also prepared a series of Dymo tape messages, which were to be used as part of the intricate plan to guide whoever had the ransom money to the pick-up point.

On the evening of 15 January, Neilson left Bathpool Park to make the final checks on the route that the ransom carrier was to follow and to conceal the Dymo tape messages in preselected telephone boxes.

Fatal challenge

While he was looking over the final pick-up point – a Freightliner depot near Dudley in Worcestershire – he was challenged by a night supervisor. Neilson shot the supervisor six times, mostly in the back, and escaped on foot, leaving his car behind. Inside the car were Lesley's slippers and the ransom messages she had recorded earlier that day.

On the following night, a second attempt was made to hand over the ransom money. Neilson changed the pick-up point to a wall adjoining Bathpool Park. After playing a new recording of instructions in Lesley's voice down the telephone, he waited for the ransom carrier.

The plan went disastrously wrong. Ronald Whittle, who was bringing the money, got lost and drove past the wall. A courting couple had parked in the exact spot where the handover was due to take place. Neilson became convinced that a police helicopter was hovering overhead and a trap was about to be sprung on him.

Act of panic?

Neilson returned to the underground platform where Lesley Whittle was noosed. According to his account, she moved over to give him space on the platform and fell over the edge. In the opinion of most others, including the jury at his trial, Neilson had panicked and pushed his hostage over the edge of the platform, where she died of shock or strangulation.

Lesley Whittle's body was found seven weeks later, still hanging from the length of wire coil in Bathpool Park. By this time the police were sure that the man they were looking for was also wanted in connection with the murders of three sub-post office masters in the past year. They had no clues as to his identity, but his individual style and ruthless operational methods had earned him a nickname with the police and general public – the Black Panther.

THE POST OFFICE KILLINGS

Some time in 1965, Donald Neilson turned to house-breaking in order to supplement his income. Using a manual brace and bit drill, he developed a technique of making holes in window frames through which he could manipulate the catch with a piece of strong wire or a fine screwdriver.

The burglaries became very familiar to the Yorkshire police and became known as the 'brace and bit' robberies. By the time Neilson was arrested in 1975, over 400 such robberies had been committed, all of which the police felt they could close files on.

No return

The returns on these burglaries were small, however, and Neilson remained dissatisfied. He was a loner who disliked authority and was jealous of those who were wealthier than he was.

Like every other money-making venture Neilson had attempted, the burglaries did not bring in enough to change his way of life. He may have proved to be extremely proficient at getting in and out of people's homes as they slept, but he rarely seemed able to choose where much money was to be found.

Killer: Donald Neilson

In 1967 Neilson expanded his range of criminal activities when he raided a sub-post office in Nottingham. It was the first of 19 similar raids, almost exclusively in Lancashire and Yorkshire, between 1967 and 1974.

The advantages of choosing sub-post offices as a target was that the security arrangements were far less rigorous than at a main branch or local bank. In the early 1970s there were more than 23,000 sub-post offices in Britain, providing a seemingly limitless number of potential places to raid. The disadvantage was simply that the amount of money to be taken from each one was small. No one could retire from a life of crime after raiding a sub-post office.

Since his National Service in the army, Neilson had remained obsessed with military organization and planning. To carry out his night visits he had established a headquarters at his home in Grangefield Avenue. Half of the lounge was a workshop, equipped with the tools of his trade, while the other half was boarded off to serve as an office. He would sit in his office dreaming of future operations that would make him and his family wealthy.

To the outside world, the Neilson family were private to the point of being reclusive. When Donald Neilson was seen, he was working compulsively – either mending one of his vehicles or repainting the house. Mrs Neilson was hardly ever seen outside the house, and neighbours noted how poorly dressed she was when she did appear.

On 16 February 1972, Neilson broke into a sub-post office in Haywood, Lancashire. The postmaster, Leslie Richardson, was woken up and, getting out of bed, found himself confronted by a hooded man who spoke to him in what sounded like a West Indian accent. In the struggle that followed, Neilson's shotgun went off, blowing a hole in the ceiling. Mr Richardson managed to snatch off the hood and was surprised to see a white man since he used a West Indian accent.

Neilson escaped through a rear door. The police afterwards felt sure that the raid was linked with seven similar break-ins and for the first time had a witness who could put together a Photofit identification of the raider. It was to be the first of six such Photofits, none of which produced a realistic likeness.

Almost exactly two years later, Donald Neilson was in Harrogate, Yorkshire. His target was a sub-post office corner shop run by Donald and Johanna Skepper. The couple had lived and worked there for ten years and on the night of 15 February, they were asleep upstairs, with their 18 year-old son Richard in the adjoining bedroom.

Bound and gagged

Neilson drilled three holes in a rear, ground-floor casement window to gain access, and then moved silently upstairs to the son's bedroom. Richard was shaken awake to find Neilson standing in front of him pointing a shotgun at his face and wearing a black mask.

Neilson demanded to know where the safe keys were kept. After being told they were in a cupboard at the bottom of the stairs he pressed a piece of tape over the boy's mouth, bound his wrists together and taped his ankles to the bed.

Neilson could not find the keys and returned to the son's bedroom. He released him and forced him in to his parents' bedroom to find the keys. As Richard Skepper moved past the foot of the bed his mother and father woke up, instinctively reaching for the bedside light to see who was in the room.

Fatal decision

Neilson stepped quickly inside the bedroom and ordered Skepper to switch the light off again. In that split-second, Skepper made the brave but fateful decision that was to cost him his life. Jumping out of bed, he shouted to his son 'Let's get him.' Neilson, who was standing just two feet away from the sub-post master, responded by shooting him in the chest. Donald Skepper fell dying into his wife's arms.

'It was horrifying,' she said later. 'If it was someone you could have seen the face of, or someone you could have spoken to reasonably … but just to see the hood was really terrifying, so much so that I really couldn't move.'

Neilson rushed from the room, with his shotgun in one hand and a wooden-handled knife with a four-inch blade in the other. It was 5.25 a.m. when Richard Skepper raised the alarm. 'My mother woke up first and then my father sat up in bed,' he said later. 'The intruder came into the room carrying his gun in his right hand. He was not pointing it at anyone in particular, just generally around the room. My father said something like "What do you want?" to the intruder, and I said he wanted the keys. My father made as if to get out of bed, swinging his legs around to face the man. He said, "Let's get him." At that point the man who was holding the gun pointed it at my father. The next thing I saw was a flash of the gun going off and then I heard the explosion. My father fell back on to the bed.'

The police surrounded Harrogate with armed officers, but Neilson had got away. Within a few days, more than a thousand people had been interviewed and the Post Office had offered a £5,000 reward. The police had no idea that Neilson lived less than half-an-hour's drive away.

By the following September, seven months later, 30,000 people had been interviewed, but the police were no closer to identifying the Black Panther. In the early hours of 6 September, Neilson re-emerged to kill again.

It was after 4 a.m. when Mr Derek Astin woke up in his flat above the sub-post office in the village of Higher Baxendin, near Accrington, in Lancashire. He lived there with his wife Marion and their two children, 13 year-old Susan and 10 year-old Stephen. When Mrs Astin woke up she found her husband was already out of bed and grappling with a hooded figure by the wardrobe.

Mr Astin pushed Neilson on to the landing and his wife, searching desperately for a weapon, tried to hand him a vacuum cleaner. There was then a loud 'crack', and Mr Astin collapsed on the landing. At the same time, Neilson fell backwards down the narrow, steep staircase. In the midst of her terror, Mrs Astin noticed how quickly he recovered and got up again.

Mr Astin suffered a massive wound which severed both the main artery and the main vein in his arm. His daughter tried to use a bedsheet to staunch the flow of blood, before rushing out of the house to find help. Their telephone wires had been cut, and Astin died soon after arriving at the hospital.

There were already 100 policemen trying to solve the Skepper murder, and when detectives arrived in Accrington, there was no doubt that the double killer was the same person who had been unmasked by Leslie Richardson two years earlier in Lancashire.

First of all there was the tell-tale brace and bit method of entry in all three incidents. There was also the bullet taken from Astin, and a spent cartridge case, which were added to the collection of linked ballistic evidence. The police had already received further confirmation that they were dealing with a man who was ruthlessly callous. However, while the officers heading the inquiry realized they were dealing with an extremely dangerous man, the public at large remained ignorant of the fact.

Even when 55 year-old Sidney Grayland was shot and killed just nine weeks later at the sub-post office run by his wife, Margaret, at Langley in the West Midlands, the national press was still treating the shootings as isolated crimes.

Unhooded

The Graylands were stock-taking in the early evening of 11 November, when Sidney Grayland went out to the storeroom. His wife heard a shot and when she rushed to investigate, found her husband on the floor, wounded in the stomach. Neilson had entered through the back door with a bottle of ammonia strapped to the torch he was carrying. When he knocked on the door and Mr Grayland opened it, the older man was also carrying a torch. In the struggle that followed, Mr Grayland grabbed the intruder's hand and the ammonia squirted into Neilson's hooded face.

Temporarily blinded, Neilson ripped the hood from his head, lashing out with his foot at the same time. At that moment Mrs Grayland arrived and was told by her husband, 'Watch it, Peg, I have been hit.' Neilson realized that Mrs Grayland must have seen his face. He attacked her, fracturing her skull in three places. He left her in a pool of blood, covering her head and shoulders with cardboard boxes.

Before leaving, Neilson removed cash and postal orders totalling £800. It was to be more than four hours before the events at the Graylands' shop were discovered. At 10.55 p.m., two policemen noticed that the lights were still on at the shop. When they investigated they found Mr Grayland dead and his wife barely clinging to life.

The police now had more clues, including another .22 bullet, five spent cartridges and a length of blood-soaked cord that Neilson had used to bind Mrs Grayland's wrists. Mrs Grayland herself was unconscious for some time after the attack and even when she had begun to recover, could not provide a description of her attacker. At this stage, detectives were unwilling to make an official link between the Grayland murder and the previous two post office attacks.

They were also unaware that the man they were looking for was about to embark on a far more ambitious scheme. After two years of planning and physical training, Donald Neilson was ready to try kidnapping a victim for ransom.

It was only the second time such a thing had been tried in Britain. And though the first attempt had ended in failure, Donald Neilson believed that his military precision would make it pay off.

FADING HOPES

Dorothy Whittle woke on the morning of 14 January 1975, to discover that her daughter Lesley was missing. She was puzzled – in the early hours of the morning Lesley had been fast asleep in her room. After checking the house to make certain her daughter was not there, Mrs Whittle drove the length of Highley's main street to her son Ronald's house in the vain hope that Lesley had spent the night there.

Neither Ronald nor his wife, Gaynor, had seen or heard from Lesley that morning.

In deep unease, Mrs Whittle and Gaynor drove back to the Whittles' home. There they discovered the ransom demands and realized they were in the midst of a full-blown nightmare – Lesley had been kidnapped.

Ransom demands

There were three ransom messages, all on a coil of Dymo tape left on a box resting on a flower vase in the lounge. The messages read:

- No police £50,000 ransom to be ready to deliver wait for telephone call at Swan shopping centre telephone box 6 p.m. to 1 p.m. if no call return following evening when you answer call give your name only and listen you must follow instructions without argument from the time you answer you are on a time limit if police or tricks death.

Killer: Donald Neilson

- Swan shopping centre Kidderminster deliver £50,000 in a white suitcase.
- £50,000 all in old notes £25,000 in £1 notes and £25,000 in £5 there will be no exchange only after £50,000 has been cleared will victim be released.

Detective Chief Superintendent Bob Booth, head of West Mercia CID, was investigating a murder in Wellington, Shropshire, when he heard the news from Highley.

When he heard about the professionally prepared ransom tapes and the cut telephone wires, he went straight to the Whittle home.

Ronald Whittle immediately set about raising the £50,000 in used notes from his bank in Bridgnorth. At this stage, the police were not certain the kidnap was genuine, but they arranged to tap the Whittles' telephone and a telephone box at Kidderminster that Neilson had referred to in his ransom note. They also set up a tail for Ronald Whittle and informed Scotland Yard.

Like the American FBI, who had a kidnap conviction rate of 240 out of 400 in the previous four years, Superintendent Booth encouraged the family to co-operate fully with the kidnapper. He was willing for them to pay the ransom if it secured the early release of the victim on the grounds that the majority of kidnap victims do not survive more than the first 48 hours.

Booth also accepted Scotland Yard's offer of 12 experts who had been trained in techniques to deal with cases of kidnapping. Despite the acrimony that was to develop over the weeks between West Mercia CID and Scotland Yard, during the first few hours they agreed on one thing, Ronald Whittle should take the ransom money and wait in the telephone box in Kidderminster from 6 p.m. onwards for the next instructions.

But by 8 p.m., there had been a development that was to influence the entire investigation. It was crucial that the kidnapper be given no hint that the Whittle family had involved the police. Yet somehow a freelance reporter received a tip-off that a major kidnap incident was underway.

As a result, the police took the decision to withdraw Ronald Whittle from the telephone box in Kidderminster just before 9.30 p.m. When Neilson finally telephoned just before midnight, the police tapper could hear the call ringing in, but there was nobody in the box to answer it.

The following night, 15 January, police again instructed Ronald Whittle to leave the telephone box during the time that Neilson had arranged to ring. The reason this time was a hoax caller who had managed to convince them his call was genuine. As a result, Ronald wasted a night driving to a non-existent delivery destination.

On the same night, while Neilson was preparing the second part of his plan to secure the ransom money, he shot Gerald Smith, a security guard, at the Freightliner depot in Dudley.

Misleading information

Gerald Smith survived for 14 months after the attack, with the help of four operations. He provided the police with what he was convinced was a good likeness of the Black Panther. His attacker had spoken with a local accent, from the village of Tipton less than two miles from Dudley. This well-intentioned evidence proved extremely misleading.

In his hurry to escape from the depot, Neilson left his stolen car, a green Morris 1300, in a car park just 150 yards from where Gerald Smith had been shot. For eight days it remained unnoticed. As a result, the kidnapping of Lesley Whittle and the shooting in Dudley became two separate news stories.

Finally a policeman noticed that the car's registration number on the road tax did not match the number plates. Further investigation revealed that the car had been stolen from West Bromwich over three months before.

When the Morris was searched, the boot revealed some startling clues. There was a tape-recording of Lesley Whittle's voice, which was intended for the abortive ransom collection of 15 January. Also inside were tape recorders, torches, a gun and ammunition and a foam mattress. The gun provided the first positive link between the sub-post office murders and the Whittle kidnap.

On the third night of the kidnap, 16 January, the police felt sure they would get the money to the kidnapper. The Scotland Yard officers had brought sophisticated bugging and surveillance equipment. Several of them were armed. A special squad of vehicles was on stand-by and a mobile headquarters was ready to co-ordinate the investigation.

New instructions

The kidnapper called at 11.45 p.m. Leonard Rudd, the transport manager of Whittle's Coaches, answered the call. Lesley's recorded voice instructed the ransom carrier to wait by the Kidsgrove telephone box.

Ronald Whittle drove first to Bridgnorth police station where he was briefed by Detective Chief Superintendent Lovejoy of Scotland Yard, who was in charge of this part of the operation. Without Booth's knowledge, the Scotland Yard officers had also decided to record on microfilm the serial number of every bank note.

Ronald Whittle set off to deliver the ransom money at almost 1.30 a.m. His uncertainty was compounded by the fact that there was nothing but the kidnapper's word to assure him that his own life was not in danger. The Panther could shoot him and escape with the money. And there was also the chilling possibility that Lesley was already dead.

Killer: Donald Neilson

Frustrating journey

Unmarked police cars kept a discreet distance from Ronald Whittle's car. A total of 11 other surveillance vehicles were involved in the operation. Yet Whittle twice lost his way and it was 3 a.m. before he reached the first contact point. It took him a further 30 minutes to locate the hidden message.

From Kidsgrove, Ronald Whittle was instructed to go to Bathpool Park, where he was to go to a wall and wait for a flashing light signal. Once at Bathpool Park, Ronald waited with mounting frustration for the signal. It never came. Finally and reluctantly, he pulled out after lengthy consultations with the police over two radios in his car.

Whittle could not have known that Neilson had worked out in advance how long the journey should have taken. Nor did he realize that a courting couple had driven into the park at 2.30 a.m., at least an hour before he arrived, and were puzzled to see a torch flashing in their direction. The couple said later they also saw a police car inside the park, a claim fiercely denied by the police.

Wrong conclusion

Neilson had been watching all these activities through a pair of field glasses. Convinced that police were about to move in on him and that the ransom would never be paid, Neilson fell into a rage, returned to the drainage shaft and murdered Lesley Whittle. By dawn, he was on his way back to Bradford.

When daylight arrived the Scotland Yard team searched Bathpool Park as discreetly as possible. They assumed that Neilson might still be inside the park and were keen to give the impression that Ronald Whittle had gone there without their knowledge. They found none of the clues that could have led them to the underground hideout.

Local suspicions

The hunt for the identity of Lesley Whittle's kidnapper had by now centred around the family's home village of Highley. Detectives believed that anyone with a knowledge of Lesley's financial circumstances, and where she lived, was very likely to be a local. Moreover, the kidnapper seemed to have an intimate knowledge of the Whittle home. While an RAF helicopter hovered over the village looking for possible hideouts, detectives interviewed anyone who could possibly be a suspect.

Other theories circulated. One was the possibility that the kidnapper was a travelling salesman who had become familiar with Highley. Another was that he had worked at Dudley Zoo, which was situated next to the Freightliner depot where Gerald Smith was shot.

The police were prepared to clutch at such straws because they knew they were working against the clock.

Confrontation

Chief Superintendent Booth knew that the most important clues were still likely to lie within the grounds of Bathpool Park. But he was unwilling to move in until he felt certain that the chances of finding Lesley alive there were minimal. On the evening of 5 March, Booth and Ronald Whittle appeared on television and acted out a pre-arranged confrontation with each other.

Ronald Whittle pretended to reveal for the first time to Booth that he had gone to Bathpool Park and attempted to deliver the ransom money. Booth's response was to fly into a rage and terminate the interview. To the viewing public it appeared that Booth had been humiliated. For Bob Booth, however, this deception provided the opportunity to find out what was in Bathpool Park.

DARKEST FAILURE

The day after Chief Inspector Booth and Ronald Whittle had appeared together on television, the police moved into Bathpool Park, but failed to find any clues. Then two schoolboys came forward with a torch they had found in the park several weeks before. Stuck to the torch was a piece of Dymo tape with the words 'drop suitcase into hole' printed on it. It was clear proof that Ronald Whittle's visit to the park had not been intended as a dry run.

Tragic discovery

On the next day, Friday 7 March, a constable climbed down into the main shaft of the drainage system. Picked out in the light of his torch was the naked body of a young woman suspended from a wire rope near the base of the shaft. On the platform above Lesley Whittle lay a collection of objects.

For those on the investigation it was a shattering blow. 'In my wildest dreams I never dreamed he would do such a thing to the girl. It is terrible,' Booth said afterwards.

Yard in charge

Although the link between the sub-post office murders and the Whittle kidnap had already been made, different investigating teams were working on each of the murders. In order to provide the necessary co-ordination, the head of Scotland Yard's murder squad was put in overall charge of the hunt for the Panther.

A total of 800 police was drafted in to Kidsgrove, where Bathpool Park was situated and every one of the town's 22,000 population was to be interviewed. The murder squad took over Kidsgrove police station, setting up its headquarters there. A special telephone answering machine, known as Robophone, was set up for people who wished to provide information anonymously.

The squad's best hope of tracking down their man lay in the number of items left behind in Bathpool Park. There were clothes, a pair of binoculars, a pencil torch, a flash lamp and a foam mattress identical to the one found in the back of the stolen Morris. One after another, however, these seemingly promising leads turned to dead ends.

The binoculars were traced to a shop, where it was found that the purchaser had filled in a guarantee which included a name and address. Police raided the address only to find that it was not a private house but a small commercial company. The name was a false one.

As for most of the other items, their lack of distinguishing marks made it impossible to track them down to a shop, let alone a purchaser.

Many items had been left scattered around Bathpool Park and taken home by people who did not recognize their significance. One man came forward to say that he had found a food hoard near the drainage system. He was able to return saucepans, but the tinned food had been eaten.

Of more significance was a pocket memo machine, complete with its model and serial number. Nearby, was a broken cassette player and a tape, which when played back was found to have Lesley Whittle's voice on it. Police traced the owners of the memo machines bearing the serial numbers immediately preceding and following that on the one found. But they could make no more progress.

The police found out that postal orders from the post office raids were being cashed in branches throughout the north of England. A news blackout was imposed on this information so that the Panther would carry on cashing them, but because of the volume of postal orders processed by the post offices, his postal orders escaped notice until it was too late.

One of the most complex aspects of the investigation was the decision to interview every person who had been involved in the construction of the Bathpool Park drainage system.

It soon emerged that for each of the three contractors there was a series of sub-contractors who in turn did their own sub-contracting. The scale of this line of inquiry reached almost impossible dimensions. By the end, police were far from sure that they had seen everybody.

The police were also misled by four telephone calls which they mistakenly believed were made by the Panther. They were taken from recordings of incoming calls made at Ronald Whittle's home. The accent belonged to someone from the Black Country and the arrogance of the caller persuaded police it was the Panther.

Reconstruction

In an attempt to jog people's memories, a local actor was asked to drive around Kidsgrove in the stolen Morris that had been found near the Freight-liner depot. Dressed in clothes similar to the ones that Neilson was known to wear, he stood by telephone boxes and walked around Bathpool Park.

The reconstruction was shown on national television and within 24 hours more than 1,000 telephone calls had been received. Each caller had named people they thought could be the Panther. Everybody who had been named was visited, but Donald Neilson was not among them.

There was another reason why the police were particularly eager to track down the Black Panther. They believed that as long as he remained at large, certain people might be persuaded that kidnap for ransom was a viable form of crime. And in the wake of the Whittle kidnap, a number of attempted – but unsuccessful – kidnaps did in fact occur.

As 1975 came to an end, the massive and exhaustive police investigation had still not come close to identifying the Black Panther. The one remaining hope for the murder hunt team was that the Panther would come back out into the open and make a mistake.

On Thursday, 11 December, Neilson did just that. At 11 p.m., at Mansfield Woodhouse in Nottinghamshire, two policemen in a parked panda car noticed a suspicious-looking man carrying a hold-all outside the Four Ways pub. The man was Donald Neilson.

Chance encounter

The two constables – Stuart McKenzie and Tony White – called him over to the car. They asked him for his name and what he had been doing that evening.

Acting friendly, Neilson gave them a false name and said that he was on his way home from work. But when McKenzie asked him to write his name down, Neilson produced a sawn-off shotgun.

Neilson forced PC White into the back of the car and got into the passenger seat. Pressing the shotgun into McKenzie's side, Neilson instructed him to drive to Blidworth, a village six miles away.

As they drove, PC White noticed that for a split second the gun was pointing away from PC McKenzie. White took the opportunity to lunge at Neilson, forcing the muzzle of the gun upwards. As PC McKenzie slammed on the brakes, the shotgun went off into the roof of the car, slightly injuring PC White.

Killer: Donald Neilson

Tackling the Panther

The police car had come to a halt outside a fish and chip shop. As the two policemen grappled with Neilson, two customers rushed over to help them. Neilson struggled and fought with extraordinary strength, but was eventually dragged over to some railings and handcuffed there.

Neilson was driven the 70 miles to Kidsgrove. After 12 hours of questioning, his resistance gave way. He confessed to the kidnap of Lesley Whittle.

FACING JUSTICE

The trial of Donald Neilson began in the sweltering heat of Oxford Crown Court on 14 June 1976. Oxford had been chosen because it was more likely to provide an unprejudiced jury than an area where the Black Panther had operated. The locals seemed unaware that it was taking place, and in scenes untypical of a major murder trial, the streets outside the courtroom were virtually empty.

The scenes inside, however, were electric. Neilson, the ex-soldier, gave an extraordinary performance. He moved in and out of the court marching at the double, holding himself permanently erect. He stood to attention when answering questions, often replying with a snappy 'yes sir' or 'no sir' and all the time staring at a spot high on the window facing the witness box.

The basis for Neilson's defence in the Whittle case was that, while he had kidnapped the young heiress, he had not pushed her to her death from the underground ledge. He claimed she had fallen accidentally.

During the Crown's opening speech Neilson took copious notes, and only wavered once, when a tape was played of Lesley Whittle's voice giving the ransom instructions. Neilson, who had prepared for his trial by doing hundreds of press-ups each day, sobbed into a handkerchief.

Neilson claimed that he had always planned to release Lesley Whittle. The Crown countered this by suggesting that it had been Neilson's intention from the very first day to kill her. While Neilson maintained that she had never seen his face throughout her ordeal, the Crown reminded him of his own evidence, when he talked of her seeing a look of alarm on his face at one point.

'If she had seen your face,' Phillip Cox, for the prosecution said, 'she would recognize your face on a subsequent occasion and you could not have allowed her to live.'

Military precision

Neilson seemed to have an idea that if he explained everything sensibly, in a matter of fact manner, and with his favourite military precision, then the jury would understand and realize it had all been a ghastly mistake, a master plan that had gone wrong for the right reasons. He rarely looked the jury's way. If he had, he would have detected the open-mouthed revulsion among several of them as he attempted to make Lesley Whittle's journey from the safety of her home to the Bathpool Park drainage system seem ordinary.

Before leaving her in the shaft, Neilson had tethered her. He said she had made no comment when he had placed the wire noose over her head. She had not objected when he took off her dressing gown so she could dry herself with it. He even explained to the court how the police, in his opinion, would have been wise to recruit two SAS men to help track him down. He had, after all, been training for the kidnap for three years.

Tortured logic

Neilson then explained the third night in Bathpool Park, when he had flashed his torch at the wrong car when Ronald Whittle had arrived late. Looking increasingly desperate, Neilson took 34 minutes of tortured logic to explain just how and why Lesley Whittle had died. His voice rose and fell, his eyes blazed and he looked close to losing control, particularly when the Crown insisted that he had no option but to kill Lesley when his plan had gone wrong.

One of the most compromising pieces of evidence was the Dymo tape with the words 'police or tricks – death' printed on it. Neilson was adamant that it was a threat he did not intend to carry out. In the same way, he changed the emphasis of his evidence, saying the ransom money was secondary to his escape.

When Neilson was questioned about the sub-post office murders, he began to describe the extent of the planning and preparation that went into each raid.

He conceded that he was obsessed with detail when he was planning his crimes. He set off in the evenings with 'the tools of the trade' in his bag, and concentrated on sub-post offices because they contained 'Government money'. He preferred them because they would provide covering noise and ease of escape. After a raid he would escape on foot across rough ground. He would wash and disinfect his clothes in advance to reduce his body smell in case the police used tracker dogs. He would break the trail where possible by crossing streams.

When Neilson described the murder of the three sub-post masters his excuse this time was that the gun had gone off by mistake. Donald Skepper had grabbed the gun causing it to go off, claimed Neilson. He said this in spite of the fact that forensic evidence made it clear that the gun had been fired two feet away from the victim.

He said the same thing had happened in the Derek Astin shooting. This time his statement was even less believable, because Mr Astin had been shot by two different guns, the first of which had been fired from over three feet away.

Explaining a murder

He tried to explain away the murder of Sidney Grayland and the vicious assault on his wife by saying he thought he was being attacked by two men. He could not see at the time because he had had ammonia squirted into his eyes. But he failed to explain how a few minutes later, he was able to break into a safe and steal £800.

Donald Neilson was found guilty of the murders of the three sub-post masters and of Lesley Whittle. He was found guilty of causing Mrs Grayland grievous bodily harm, with intent to endanger life, during his arrest. Mr Justice Mars-Jones would not set a minimum number of years to Neilson's sentence. 'In your case life must mean life. If you are ever released from prison it should only be on account of great age or infirmity.'

CASE FILE: NEILSON, DONALD

BACKGROUND

Donald Neilson was born on 1 August 1936 in Morley, West Yorkshire, an extended suburb to the west of Leeds. He grew up in a cramped one up one down terraced house. His father was a poorly paid woollen worker and the family, like most other people in the neighbourhood, lived on the verge of poverty.

His real name was not Neilson but Nappey. This made him a natural target for bullies and teasing in his childhood. He was so affected by the experience that, when his own daughter was born, he decided to protect her from the same abuse by changing the family name to Neilson.

His mother died when he was ten years old. While his father carried on working, Neilson had to shoulder much of the responsibility of looking after his sister, who was four years younger.

By the time he was 17, he was working as an apprentice carpenter. He did not drink or smoke and his main pleasure seemed to be confined to going dancing in Bradford once a week.

It soon became clear that Neilson was a loner. None of his contemporaries can remember him having any more than one girlfriend – his future wife, Irene Tate, whom he met at a dance. Their secret wedding, to which even Irene's twin sister was not invited, took place in 1955.

Some time before that, Neilson had begun his National Service in the King's Own Yorkshire Light Infantry. He failed the initial ten week basic training course and had to be 'back-squadded' to repeat it. But his two years in the army had more of an influence on his later activities than any thing else in his early life. He positively relished the hardships that military life forced on him.

Survival skills

Neilson spent six months in Kenya where he underwent an intensive period of jungle warfare training. He was equipped with a rubber-stocked, short-barrelled .303 jungle rifle, a weapon that bears a resemblance to a sawn-off shotgun.

Then after eight uneventful months in Aden, Neilson was posted to Cyprus. It was here that he was confronted most directly with death when he had to guard terrorists awaiting execution.

On completion of his National Service, and having reached the rank of Lance Corporal, Neilson returned to West Yorkshire and his young wife. The army had instilled in him a sense of confidence and self-sufficiency. The young Neilson had played truant from school because he could not face the taunting. Now, he was beginning to feel that he was in a position to exact revenge on society.

Donald and Irene Neilson bought a terraced home in Grangefield Avenue, alongside the busy Leeds Road leading out of Bradford. Despite the close-knit nature of the neighbourhood, the couple kept themselves to themselves and seldom invited anyone to their home. Their daughter Kathryn was born in 1960.

Most of the time Neilson made a living as a jobbing carpenter. He also tried to start up a small taxi business and at one stage planned to buy Alsatian guard dogs to start up a security firm. Despite all his efforts, however, financial success eluded him.

Military bearing

People remarked that Neilson walked with a parade ground spring in his step at all times and often gave the impression of taking orders at the double. He took to wearing paratrooper's boots, battledress jackets and olive green trousers. And he bought an ex-army jeep to drive around in.

PSYCHOLOGICAL PROFILE

Donald Neilson was a cunning, devious criminal who displayed all the attributes of a psychopath. His meticulously planned and executed sub-post office raids, and the organization required to carry out the abduction of Lesley Whittle, testify to his ability to think rationally. But at the same time he was prone to panic and acts of senseless savagery.

When he failed to rendezvous with Ronald Whittle to collect the ransom money, he fell into a rage and returned to the hideout to end his victim's life.

Neilson's trail of violence showed that cold-blooded killing did not present him with a psychological or emotional problem. A clue to his behaviour lies in his relatively unloved upbringing, after which he joined the army. His poor record as a soldier demonstrates the problem the psychopath has with learning. He consistently failed to exercise reasonable judgement and was unable to profit by experience. The problem recurred in civilian life when his efforts at making a success of business failed. This is symptomatic of a failure to plan in the longer term. His future in crime was being mapped out at this time.

Paranoid

Following his arrest, Neilson was examined by several psychiatrists and psychologists. All agreed that he was of above average intelligence, psychopathic and obsessional. He was also found to be paranoid about accepting the authority of others, and deeply resentful of those who made more money than he did – which was most people.

There are many well-defined characteristics of the psychopath, but the psychology is still not clearly understood. Although Neilson exhibited many of the traits, he remains a puzzle. It may be said that no sane person kills in the way he did. Yet he was never regarded as legally insane and so was unable to plead diminished responsibility in mitigation of his actions.

Throughout the five weeks of Neilson's two trials, in the sweltering heat of Oxford Crown Court, the man who subjected Lesley Whittle to a hellish world of subterranean caverns and narrow shafts – a world in which he seemed to thrive – showed hardly a flicker of emotion. Sitting rigidly still at the geometrical centre of the airless room, only the top of his head was visible to most of the court. Just once he cracked.

Icy composure

As a recording of Lesley Whittle's tremulous voice echoed round the hushed courtroom, the Black Panther wept openly. By the time he stood to receive several life sentences, Neilson had recovered his icy composure. Turning quickly on his heel, he marched stiffly from the dock and into criminal history as one of Britain's most brutal killers.

Chapter 3

PETER MANUEL

GLASGOW'S MULTIPLE KILLER

His youth was spent mainly in approved schools and Borstals. He was a compulsive thief, burglar and attacker of women. Yet after a series of murders broke out on the outskirts of Glasgow in the mid-1950s, Manuel cunningly eluded his pursuers to terrorize his neighbourhood.

On the afternoon of Wednesday, 4 January 1956, George Gribbon was taking a stroll along a golf course in East Kilbride, a new satellite town outside Glasgow. A labourer in his late forties, he was in poor health and had been advised to get as much fresh air as possible.

At about 3 p.m. he reached Capelrig Copse, alongside the fifth fairway. As he searched for lost golf balls among the conifers, he came upon a horrifying sight. The body of a young woman lay, face down, in a hollow on the damp ground. Moving closer, he saw that her head had been savagely beaten in.

Sickened by the discovery, Gribbon ran in panic towards the road. He saw some Gas Board engineers and urgently told them what he had seen. His story came out in a babble and the gas workers thought he was joking, or had been seeing things. One of them, a young man with a dark, heavily-greased quiff and scratches on his face, was particularly unimpressed by Gribbon's appeal for help.

Despite his poor health, the labourer hurried across fields and reached Calderglen Farm, where he made a 999 call to the police. By this time, some of the gas workers, troubled by doubt, had gone into the copse and found the woman's body. They, too, called the police.

A chase

Rain had been drizzling on and off for days. One of the girl's shoes was found nearly 70 feet from her body. The other was embedded in the slope of a large ditch, which was eight feet deep and nearly twice as wide. The marks of running feet were found across fields, on barbed wire fences and in the ditch. The victim had clearly run for her life, over at least 400 yards, before the chase ended.

Detectives felt the attack had probably occurred at night, as the girl's body lay close to a gate leading on to the golf course and also to one of the tees, where golfers played their opening shots. Blood was found at the gate and fragments of the victim's skull were located on the nearby ground.

The victim had been a blonde, robust girl of 5ft 10in. After a brief examination, a pathologist concluded she had died over 36 hours before. Soon, a local man, William Marshall, came forward to say he had heard a 'squeal cry' while out walking his dogs near the golf course at 8.30 p.m. on 2 January, two days before.

Reported missing

The girl was quickly identified as Anne Knielands, a 17 year-old who had lived with her parents in converted stables on the Calderwood estate, 1½ miles from East Kilbride. She had gone out dancing during the Hogmanay holiday on 2 January and had not returned. Her parents, thinking she must have been staying at a friend's home, had waited until the morning of 4 January to report her as missing.

Forensic examination revealed that the victim's underwear had been interfered with but she had not been sexually assaulted. Semen stains were, however, found on her clothing, indicating a killer who had reached a sexual climax through violence.

The investigation was led by Detective Chief Superintendent James Hendry of the Lanarkshire CID. A large squad of detectives and constables were assembled and briefed before the huge task of door-to-door inquiries began. As some of them filed off, a desk-bound officer, Chief Inspector William Muncie, remarked, 'Don't forget Peter Manuel.' He was referring to a local burglar and sex offender whom he had arrested several times.

One of the first officers to reach Capelrig Copse, Police Constable James Marr, had asked the Gas Board foreman for a description of George Gribbon, the man who had found the body. The foreman had described the man and PC Marr was turning to leave when one of the engineers asked, 'What if this man does not want to come and starts a fight? Can we hit back?'

PC Marr turned to look at him. It was a strange question. The young man had a quiff in his greasy black hair and scratches on his face. To Marr's trained eye, they looked recent. Marr noted these details and left.

Prison record

Two days later, on Friday, 6 January, the gas workers' foreman, Richard Corrins, reported the theft of a pair of Wellington boots from the workmen's hut. PC Marr went over on Monday, 9 January.

Corrins casually mentioned that one of his workers had served a prison sentence for rape. Marr quickly ascertained that the worker had been the young man with scratches on his face. Corrins told Marr that the scratches had not been there before 2 January. Marr asked his name. 'Peter Manuel,' replied Corrins.

On 12 January, DCS Hendry interviewed Manuel at work. Hendry had had dealings with the Manuel family before and ensured that the suspect's parents, Samuel and Bridget, were questioned simultaneously at their home. They lived with their son in a council house at 32 Fourth Street, Birkenshaw, a town about five miles from Capelrig Copse.

Hendry asked Peter Manuel about his scratches. Manuel replied that he had got them during a fight on New Year's Eve. He said he had not left the house on the evening of 2 January. He became insolent towards the detective, as if toying with him. At the house, Samuel Manuel was asked the same question. His son had been at home all evening, he answered. Bridget Manuel could not remember.

Some of Peter Manuel's clothes were taken away for examination. The tests proved negative. But Chief Inspector Muncie, who had had dealings with Manuel only two months before, was able to supply a list of clothing then in Manuel's possession.

Two items on the list, a maroon jacket and a pair of grey flannel trousers, had not been found at the Manuel home. Questioned again, Manuel was openly hostile. He claimed he had given away the jacket and trousers.

Other inquiries led the police nowhere. Anne Knielands' friends, including Andrew Murnin, a member of the Parachute Regiment who had arranged to see her on the evening of 2 January, could all account for their movements. Murnin had been celebrating Hogmanay with such force that he had forgotten the date.

Some friends of the Knielands family, the Simpsons, had seen Anne Knielands early in the evening of 2 January. Anne had left their house at 6.40 p.m. to catch a bus from Capelrig Farm, near the copse where she was later found.

Manuel agreed to let a local paper publish his photograph as one of the people who had been questioned. It appeared on 14 January, but no one stepped forward to say they had seen Manuel in East Kilbride on the night Anne Knielands was murdered.

44

MASSACRE BY STEALTH

During March 1956, two months after the murder of Anne Knielands, the police received a tip-off from one of their underworld informants. There was to be a robbery at a colliery in Blantyre, a satellite town between East Kilbride and Birkenshaw, outside Glasgow. It was to take place at 11.30 p.m. on 23 March. Two burglars would be involved. One would be Peter Manuel.

Detectives knew that Manuel had changed tack by mixing regularly with other criminals, abandoning his lone-wolf tactics for burglaries. Police officers were waiting when Manuel and his accomplice attempted the burglary at the predicted time. Manuel managed to escape, but left fragments of his clothing on some barbed wire. He was arrested later at his home and appeared before the Hamilton Sheriff Court. He was granted bail and the trial was set for 2 October.

Less than three weeks before the trial, on 15 September, police were alerted to a break-in that bore Manuel's hallmarks. At a home in Bothwell, a burglar had split tins of food on the carpet and had left dirty boot marks on the bedding. The next evening, 16 September, there was a similar burglary at another small local community, High Burnside. At 18 Fennsbank Avenue, a small haul of cash and jewellery was taken. Soup tins and cigarette butts had been emptied on to the carpets, and footprints were left in the bedding.

The next morning, 17 September, police received an urgent call to go to a house a few doors away, at 5 Fennsbank Avenue. This was the home of the Watt family.

More victims

The householder, William Watt, who owned a large bakery business in Glasgow, was away on a fishing holiday in Argyll, in the west of Scotland. Left at home were his wife Marion, who had recently undergone a successful heart operation, but was still weak, Mrs Watt's sister, Margaret Brown, and the Watts' 16 year-old schoolgirl daughter, Vivienne.

On 17 September, the daily help, Helen Collison, had arrived at No. 5 at 8.45 a.m. The back door was usually left open for her. This time it had been shut. Mrs Collison had rapped on window panes and called out without reply. The curtains were drawn and a glass panel had been broken in the front door, near the handle. After alerting a neighbour, who knew the Watts well, Mrs Collison had asked the local postman, Peter Collier, to interrupt his rounds and go into the house in front of her.

Inside, they had found Mrs Watt and Mrs Brown in their beds. Both had been shot dead at point-blank range. In another bedroom, they had found Vivienne Watt. She had also been shot from close range. Though still breathing, she had died before an ambulance arrived.

The police found the same desecration as they had at No. 18, a few doors up the street. None of the victims had been sexually abused. A pathologist reported that the three women had been killed during the night.

DCS Hendry, whose file on Anne Knielands remained open, assumed command of the investigation. Less than 24 hours later, at 2 a.m. on 18 September, four detectives arrived at the Manuel house in Birkenshaw with a search warrant.

Manuel's father Samuel let the officers into the house, complaining that the police were molesting his family. He threatened to write to his Member of Parliament. A search of the house, and a close examination of Manuel's clothing, revealed no clues. Peter Manuel refused to answer any questions at all.

The investigators had, however, a second suspect on their list. This was William Watt. He had left on his fishing holiday on Sunday, 9 September 1956, with his labrador, Queenie. His wife had put his shotgun into his car for rabbit-hunting.

Watt had then driven to the Cairnbaan Hotel in Lochgilphead, on the western mainland, about 90 miles from High Burnside, past Loch Lomond. The hotel had been his base for fishing trips for many years.

At 1 a.m. on the morning of 17 September, a few hours before the murders at his house, Watt was seen at a window of the hotel by two local men who knew the sight of him well. Soon after 8 a.m. he was seen driving to look at the local fishing waters before breakfast. At 11 a.m. he was informed that his wife, daughter and sister-in-law had been murdered.

Return home

Watt openly broke down at the news. It was arranged for a local man to accompany him for about half his journey home. Then a Lanarkshire police officer, Sergeant William Mitchell, would meet him and escort Watt the rest of the way. On the first stage of the journey, Watt regained his composure. A former Police War Reservist, he seemed no longer distraught when he met Sergeant Mitchell in the town of Alexandria.

'I thought I was going to bring back a broken-hearted and bereaved man,' Sergeant Mitchell was to comment, 'and I found a man with a smirk on his face and without a tear.'

Watt was questioned several times. To some extent, suspicion of him was inevitable. Most murders are the result of domestic feuds. The local grapevine informed police that Watt had had mistresses.

Police frogmen searched the water around Cairnbaan Hotel for a .38 Webley revolver, while teams of officers with dogs searched possible hiding places. Tests were carried out to see if Watt could have pushed his car along the gravel outside the hotel without alerting the other residents.

A theory was developing that Watt had risen early on the morning of 17

September, driven 90 miles to his home, carried out the murders, and returned to Lochgilphead before breakfast. However, no one at the hotel had heard or seen his car during the night.

Another factor which undermined the theory was the length of the journey. Watt said he usually took two hours and 15 minutes. An expert police driver managed to shave 11 minutes off this time, but checks revealed that there had been a ground mist around Lochgilphead in the early hours of 17 September, which would have lengthened the journey.

Witnesses

But after a ferry master and a motorist both reported having seen a driver of Watt's description making the journey at the relevant times, and had separately picked him out at identification parades, the case against Watt seemed to have acquired substance. On 27 September, Watt was arrested and charged with three murders. He was taken to Barlinnie Prison just outside Glasgow.

On 2 October 1956, Peter Manuel was sentenced to 18 months' imprisonment at Hamilton Sheriff Court for the attempted robbery at the colliery at Blantyre. He too was confined at Barlinnie Prison, where he found that the arrest of William Watt was the main topic of conversation. Six days later, Manuel wrote to Watt's solicitor, saying he had information about 'a recently acquired client of yours.'

Manuel also hunted out Watt to say he knew the identity of the uncaught killer of the three women. When Watt's solicitor, Lawrence Dowdall, arrived on 10 October, Manuel described being told by the 'real' murderer about the shootings, which he related in exact detail. Much had not appeared in published reports of the murders.

'Look, Manuel,' snapped Dowdall, '… you were there.'

'No, I wasn't there,' Manuel insisted. But he refused to name the so-called killer and continued to ask Dowdall to work on his own appeal.

Manuel clams up

Manuel was interviewed by detectives inside Barlinnie, but refused to answer any questions. The investigators were now sensing that the wrong suspect was under arrest. This doubt was strengthened by an underworld informant's report that Manuel had illegally purchased a gun one week before the Watt family was murdered. On 22 November, there was a second search of the Manuel home, this time by a large number of officers, but nothing suspicious was found.

By now, the case against William Watt had collapsed. After 67 days inside Barlinnie, he was released on 3 December 1956. Manuel served his sentence and was freed just under a year later, on 30 November 1957.

Three days before his release, Manuel had again written to Lawrence Dowdall, Watt's solicitor. This time he referred to 'unfinished business concerning the party who was to my certain knowledge doubly unfortunate.'

Arranged meeting

When Manuel and Dowdall met, Manuel again refused to speak to the police about his knowledge of the Watt family's murderer. But he asked for a meeting with Watt himself.

Watt, determined to identify the murderer, agreed. The meeting took place on 3 December 1957. The two men talked for hours, first in a restaurant on the outskirts of Glasgow, then at a bar and finally at the home of William Watt's brother, John Watt.

Manuel on this occasion did provide the name of the alleged murderer. He accused Charles Tallis, a man he knew, who also had a criminal record. Manuel repeated his account of how the murders were described to him.

'You know far too much about the house not to have been there,' Watt remarked. Manuel flatly denied this.

Later in the conversation, Watt spoke his mind. 'If I thought you had anything to do with the murder of my family, I'd tear you to pieces with my bare hands,' he told Manuel.

Manuel sat bolt upright and replied, 'Nobody talks to Manuel like that.'

The meeting ended inconclusively and, for a while, Manuel lost interest in what he called 'the horrors' and 'the tragedy at Burnside.'

NEW YEAR RAMPAGE

At 10 a.m. on Sunday, 29 December 1957, William Cooke, a construction engineer living in the town of Mount Vernon, reported to local police that his 17 year-old daughter Isabelle was missing. Cooke explained that she had gone out to a dance the night before and had not returned. He added that the family's telephone, at 5 Carrick Drive, was temporarily unable to receive incoming calls, and perhaps Isabelle was staying with friends.

As well as making routine inquiries, police searched the nearby River Calder. One of her shoes and her handbag were recovered from a water-filled colliery shaft. Other personal effects emerged but there was no trace of the dark-haired teenager.

Murder squad

A murder team was assembled under Detective Inspector John Rae. DCS Hendry, whose file on Anne Knielands still remained open, had retired from the force on the very day that Isabelle Cooke went missing.

Chief Inspector Muncie was among the senior officers investigating the disappearance, and probable death, of Isabelle Cooke. On Monday, 6 January, Muncie was leading the search around the colliery air-shaft, where several of her possessions had been found.

He looked up to see the Chief Constable of Lanarkshire, John Wilson, standing beside him. 'There have been three people shot in a bungalow in Uddingston,' he said. Muncie thought to himself, 'Manuel territory'.

At 38 Sheepburn Road, Uddingston, police found the bodies of Peter Smart, the 45 year-old manager of a Glaswegian firm of civil engineers, his wife Doris and their 11 year-old son Michael. The family home was a well-to-do bungalow which Smart had built himself in 1954. No one realized that anything had happened to the family until Smart failed to appear for work that Monday morning.

Reconstruction

Piecing together the last week of the Smarts' lives, detectives discovered that the family planned to visit an old friend, William McManus in Dumbarton on New Year's Eve. But they had not arrived, nor even made a telephone call to wish him a Happy New Year, as Peter Smart usually did.

On 3 January, McManus had been in Uddingston, and used the journey to drop a note at the Smarts' home. The house had looked empty.

On 6 January, two colleagues of Peter Smart, Alexander McBride and William Blackwood, drove to Sheepburn Road. It was quite untypical of Smart not to let the firm know if he was unwell, or unable to go to work for any reason. They found the family cat in the garden. The neighbours could give them little information that seemed useful, but the two men sensed an unease locally about the Smarts. At 9.40 a.m. they went to Uddingston police station.

At 11 a.m., Sergeant Frank Hogg and Constable John Thomson had broken into the house. Sergeant Hogg found Peter and Doris Smart in their bedroom, and their son Michael in his room. All had been shot through the head at point-blank range.

Downstairs, there were letters postmarked from 31 December to 3 January, all unopened. The curtains in the front rooms were open while those of the bedrooms at the back were drawn. In the kitchenette, a tin of salmon had been opened and left to spoil.

There was widespread alarm across the region. The murders of the Smart family and the presumed killing of Isabelle Cooke came less than two years after the deaths of Anne Knielands and the Watt family.

Two senior detectives from the Glasgow CID, Detective Superintendent Alex Brown and Detective Inspector Tom Goodall, were seconded to the Lanarkshire inquiry. In this investigation, clues emerged very rapidly.

Peter Smart's bank confirmed that on New Year's Eve he had withdrawn

£35 in £5 notes with consecutive serial numbers. The family had died in the early hours of New Year's Day. There was no sign of the money at the bungalow, so the killer had probably stolen it.

A psychological clue to the killer emerged from neighbours' reports of the Smarts' house during the five days that the family had lain dead inside it. Curtains had been opened and closed during that time and lights had been switched on and off. The killer appeared, therefore, to have remained in the house or to have returned stealthily to it over several days.

Inspector Muncie remembered the day, over 11 years before, when he had first arrested Manuel in Sandyhills. On that occasion, Muncie had returned to a burgled house to complete an examination, and had surprised Manuel emerging from a hide-out in the basement. Muncie asked himself whether Manuel could court danger to such a degree as to return to a house where he had shot three people. He knew that Manuel lived only a ten-minute walk away.

Muncie's final doubts were removed by a series of reports from an informant named Joe Brannan, who had won Manuel's trust during a joint burglary in 1956. Brannan had been arrested while Manuel escaped, but Brannan had refused to name his accomplice to police.

In the weeks after the discovery of Isabelle Cooke's clothing in the River Calder, and the Smart murders, Brannan stayed close to Manuel. Furtively, every word of Manuel was reported back to police headquarters.

Red herring

According to Brannan, Manuel had said of the police search of the River Calder, 'What they are finding there is only a red herring.' News of the massacre of the Smart family had made Manuel laugh, Brannan added. It was clear that Manuel was prepared for another search of his house.

The detectives, however, had changed tactics and were trying to match their prime suspect's cunning. Brannan had also reported that Manuel appeared to be without cash on New Year's Eve, but had been spending freely on drink in the days after. Patient, quiet checks were made of his local pubs, and some of Manuel's banknotes were recovered and compared to those issued by the Commercial Bank to Peter Smart.

Clever charade

There was also a report from a local man in Uddingston, John McMunn, that, around 5.45 a.m. on 4 January, he and his wife had woken to see the face of a man with a deranged look at the bedroom door. 'Where's the gun?' McMunn improvised. 'Here it is,' shouted his wife. The charade worked and the intruder fled.

At 6.45 a.m. on Tuesday, 14 January, police arrived at the Manuel home in Birkenshaw. Six senior detectives and a woman police officer were among the party. Peter Manuel had been asleep on a folding chair in the living room, as the family had friends to stay. While his father Samuel protectively read the search warrant, Manuel became abusive.

Told he was being taken to Bellshill police station for questioning, Manuel replied, 'You haven't found anything yet. You can't take me.' After dressing, and drinking a cup of tea made by his mother, he left with the officers.

At 11.10 p.m. that evening, at Lanarkshire police headquarters, Manuel was charged with murdering the Smart family, and breaking into the McMunns' home. He made no reply.

PLAYING FOR LIFE

Inside his cell, Manuel was left to brood not only on his own fate, but also on that of his father. A senior detective told Manuel that his father had been arrested and was in custody at Barlinnie Prison on a charge of receiving stolen goods.

At 32 Fourth Street, police had found a pair of wool-lined gloves and a Kodak camera. One officer remembered seeing these items on a theft report. They had been stolen from a house in Mount Vernon, three days before Isabelle Cooke disappeared nearby. Samuel Manuel tried to protect his son by implausibly describing how he had bought them in a market.

Soon after his arrest, Manuel had stood in an identification parade. Several witnesses picked him out as the customer who paid for drinks with notes issued to Peter Smart by the Commercial Bank. Manuel told his interrogators he had been given the notes by a Glaswegian betting shop owner, Samuel McKay. Furious at Manuel's claim, McKay told police he had seen Manuel with a Beretta automatic in December.

A deal

At 12.30 p.m. the following day, 15 January, Manuel asked to speak to Inspector Robert McNeill, a leading member of the murder inquiry. McNeill finally entered Manuel's cell at 3 p.m., with Detective Inspector Thomas Goodall. Manuel offered a deal. If his father was released, he would help police clear up some unsolved crimes. McNeill refused.

'Bring my father and mother here,' Manuel went on. 'I will speak to them with you present, and once I have told them myself, and made a clean breast of it, you can take them away and I will take you to where the Cooke girl is buried.'

The detectives asked if Manuel wanted a lawyer. 'I want to do this myself,' he said. 'I will write something out for you.'

Killer: Peter Manuel

Manuel was led to a superintendent's office. He began writing a letter addressed to Inspector McNeill. It repeated his offer of clearing up crimes in return for his father's freedom. 'The crimes I refer to above are crimes of Homicide,' he wrote. The letter was signed 'Peter T. Manuel'. He read it through but found fault with it, and decided to write another.

The second letter to McNeill named the killings which Manuel was offering to clear up: Anne Knielands, the Watt and Smart families, and Isabelle Cooke. McNeill read the note and seemed unenthusiastic. He told Manuel that his offer would need approval from higher authorities. But by this time, Manuel could wait no longer to tell his story.

Confession

He began with the Smart murders. Manuel spoke without shame of shooting Peter and Doris, but hinted at shame in killing the 11 year-old Michael by saying, 'I thought it was a man in the bed.' Manuel spoke calmly and gave no indication of the frenzy he must have been feeling at the time. His detail was reserved for trivia. 'I then went into the living-room, and ate a handful of wee biscuits from a tray on the chiffonnier ...' he said. The gun had been thrown into the River Clyde.

Manuel's parents had been brought to Hamilton. For the first time, Manuel showed signs of remorse. Both Samuel and Bridget Manuel were devoutly religious. Manuel asked his father why he had shielded him over the gloves and camera. Finally, Manuel told them, 'There's no future for me. I have done some terrible things. I killed the girl Knielands at East Kilbride and I shot the three women in the house at Burnside.'

Manuel went on to describe each of the eight killings before his parents left. Samuel Manuel was taken back to Barlinnie Prison but the charge against him was soon dropped.

Towards midnight, Manuel led detectives to a ploughed field in Mount Vernon, and sensed the exact spot he was looking for. He told them they would find the body of Isabelle Cooke buried there. She was uncovered in the early hours of 16 January.

At 4.15 a.m. Manuel began writing out a statement, in which he confessed in detail to the eight killings. It took him until 6.15 a.m. and covered five pages of foolscap paper.

After some rest, Manuel went with police to the River Clyde. He pointed out where he had thrown the Webley .38 revolver used in the Watt murders, and the Beretta with which he had shot the Smarts. His memory was extremely accurate, and the weapons were recovered.

On 18 January, Manuel took police to a river known as Rotten Calder. He directed them to a piece of iron on the riverbed which he claimed to have used in the killing of Anne Knielands.

More vital evidence to support Manuel's confession was provided by a man called James Platt, a neighbour of the Watt family. Platt's home had been burgled shortly before the killings at the Watts' house. Later, Platt's wife found what proved to be a .38 bullet, and a wristwatch, inside a slit in their mattress.

Ballistics experts reported that the bullet was fired from the gun used to shoot the Watts. The discovery finally cleared William Watt of suspicion, because it pointed to Manuel as the owner of the fatal gun. The burgled Platt household showed Manuel's hallmarks: upset tinned food and a cigarette stub on the carpet.

Manuel's initial co-operation with the police, as they amassed evidence against him, was to turn to defiance. Few of the investigating detectives were surprised to learn that he planned to renounce his confessions. But Manuel went much further.

Under the legal aid system, he had been granted expert legal advisers. He instructed them that, in the case of the Watt and Smart family killings, a form of defence known as 'Impeachment' was to be put forward.

Impeachment had not been heard as a defence in a Scottish murder trial for nearly 100 years. It meant that, from the witness box, Manuel would accuse named individuals of perpetrating the crimes for which he would be on trial for his life.

SINGLE DEFENCE

The trial of Peter Manuel for murder opened in the Glasgow High Court on Monday, 12 May 1958, before Lord Cameron, and lasted for 16 days. The prosecution was led by M.G. Gillies QC and Manuel was represented by Harold Leslie QC. The jury consisted of nine men and six women.

Manuel was charged with several thefts and with the murders of Anne Knielands, three members of the Watt family, Isabelle Cooke and Peter, Doris and Michael Smart.

If convicted, he would be sentenced to death. The trial drew newspaper reporters from all over the world. The defendant, as usual, chose to look spruce in public, wearing a black blazer, neat grey trousers and shirt, and a blue tie. Sitting in the dock, he seemed relaxed and poised, with no trace of the savagery associated with the charges.

Manuel pleaded not guilty to all charges. There were gasped murmurs in court as the Clerk of the Court announced what Scottish law describes as Special Defences to several of the charges. One was an alibi against the charges of murdering the Smart family. Another was the Impeachment of William Watt. Manuel would accuse Watt of murdering his own family.

The prosecution spent two days outlining the eight killings to the jury. On the third day, Watt's solicitor, Lawrence Dowdall, described his meetings with Manuel.

Watt himself was called as a witness on the fourth day. Manuel's defence counsel, Mr Grieve, had a tricky task. He attempted to show that Watt might have shot his own family. Watt rebutted all such suggestions.

Broken by police

On the seventh day, Inspector McNeill took the stand. Mr Leslie, for Manuel, began the defence by holding up Manuel's successive statements after his arrest.

'I'm suggesting that the accused was broken down,' Leslie said. 'Can you account for the position any other way?'

'I'm afraid I can't account for the accused's actions at all,' McNeill replied.

There was a break in the case, during which the jury and witnesses were asked to retire, while the judge considered a defence plea that Manuel's verbal and written statements to the police should not be admissible as evidence. The defence contended that they had been produced under duress. Lord Cameron, the judge, ruled that the statements should be heard in open court.

The next day, Manuel dismissed his counsel. Supremely confident of his own powers of persuasion, and with a natural flair for the dramatic moment, Manuel effectively caused much of the evidence to be re-heard all over again. William Watt was among the first to be recalled. The impeachment was now heard again, and showed the cunning of Manuel's imagination.

'Do you remember,' Manuel asked Watt, 'that you said to me that when you shot your little girl it would have required very little to turn the gun on yourself?'

'No,' the witness answered.

'Do you remember describing to me the manner in which you killed your wife?'

'I never did,' William Watt replied.

Manuel used his experience of legal language to stunning effect in court, and was frequently able to score clever points which inexperienced counsels would have missed. Inspector McNeill was recalled to the witness box. He was questioned about the original decision to charge William Watt, not Manuel, with the Watt family murders.

'Was I eliminated at the time of the Watt murders?' Manuel asked.

'I could only express an opinion,' McNeill replied.

'What opinion?'

'... I attached grave suspicion to you, but not to the exclusion of all other persons,' McNeill answered.

'You arrested Watt?'

'Yes.'

'Held him for two months?'

'Yes ...'

Manuel concentrated on trying to cast doubt on witnesses' credibility on small points. McNeill's colleague, DI Goodall, confirmed it was dark when Isabelle Cooke's body was found.

'In which hand,' Manuel asked, 'were you holding your torch?'

'I had no torch,' Goodall replied.

'Then how could you see, if it was dark?' Manuel asked triumphantly.

The judge, Lord Cameron, gave Manuel wide scope to defend himself. Where possible, he even came to Manuel's assistance. Lord Cameron asked Manuel's mother, Bridget Manuel, to repeat some painful evidence which had been in her son's favour.

In his final speech, delivered after the closing address for the prosecution, Manuel presented a succession of complex alibis, repeated his accusation of William Watt, and alleged that Peter Smart had bought a gun off Manuel. Smart had also, according to Manuel, given him the key to his house to meet a contact in Smart's place. Manuel had let himself in and found the family shot dead. He repeated that the police had colluded to frame him.

'Which amounts to a conspiracy to have you murdered?' the judge asked.

'That is what it amounts to, my Lord,' Manuel replied.

In his summing-up, Lord Cameron commented, 'The accused has presented his own defence with a skill which is quite remarkable.' The judge said he would allow the jury to decide whether any question of weakness of mind, which fell short of insanity, should be considered. This would have allowed the jury to convict Manuel of 'culpable homicide' – which did not carry the death sentence – instead of capital murder. 'For my own part,' Lord Cameron said, 'I have had difficulty in seeing whether one scintilla of evidence can be found to warrant such a conclusion.'

The jury spent only two hours and 21 minutes considering its verdict. It found Manuel guilty of six capital murders in the Watt and Smart family shootings, and of the simple, or non-capital, murder of Isabelle Cooke. On the judge's direction, Manuel was acquitted of murdering Anne Knielands, because of the lack of evidence to corroborate his confession.

Lord Cameron sentenced Manuel to 'death by hanging: which is pronounced for doom.' The defendant watched in silence as the black triangular hat was placed for a moment on the judge's head.

The execution inside Barlinnie Prison had been set for 19 June. By appealing, Manuel automatically postponed this date, but he decided not to conduct his own defence.

Manuel's new counsel, R.H. McDonald QC, concentrated on the decision by the trial judge, Lord Cameron, to allow Manuel's confession as evidence. McDonald argued that the arrest and later release of Samuel Manuel on a receiving charge amounted to 'inducement', which would have rendered the confession inadmissible in law.

The Lord Justice-General Clyde, sitting with Lord Carmont and Lord Sorn, did not even ask the prosecuting counsel to reply to the appeal. 'The presiding judge amply justified the course which he took in allowing the confession evidence to go before the jury,' Lord Clyde said. The appeal was dismissed and the execution was set for 11 July.

Manuel took to silence inside the narrow, austere death cell at Barlinnie Prison. The prison population had little sympathy for a killer of women and children, and the prison authorities took strict measures to prevent Manuel's food being poisoned by inmates working in the kitchens.

Once, he managed to injure himself deliberately with the bed, and complained that he had been attacked by the wardens. If it was a ruse to win pity, it failed.

He spoke little, even when told that an appeal for clemency had failed. Then with two days of life remaining, he returned to being loquacious, even arrogant.

At 7 a.m. on 11 July 1958, Manuel heard Mass and took Holy Communion in a separate, unoccupied condemned cell alongside his own. An altar had been set up. The details of his confession remain unknown.

A few moments before 8 a.m. Manuel was given a glass of whisky. He drank it and told his wardens to get it over with. The hangman led him to the execution chamber. Less than 30 seconds later, Peter Manuel, Scotland's most notorious killer, was dead.

CASE FILE: MANUEL, PETER THOMAS ANTHONY

BACKGROUND

Peter Thomas Anthony Manuel, who was christened after saints, was born in the Misere Cordia Hospital in Manhattan, New York, on 15 March 1927. He was the second of three children born to a Roman Catholic couple, Samuel and Bridget Manuel, who had emigrated to the United States to seek a better life during the Depression of the 1920s.

The Manuel family tried to settle in Detroit, Michigan, where Samuel found work in a car factory. Bridget worked as a domestic servant but, after Samuel became ill and the family got poorer and poorer, the Manuels decided to return to

Scotland. In 1932, they settled in Motherwell but moved to Coventry, in England, five years later. Peter Manuel, then aged ten, was a dark-haired boy with an American accent who did not fit in well at school.

In 1938, at the age of 11, Manuel broke into a chapel and stole from the offertory box. In October 1938 he was put on probation for shop-breaking. Five weeks later, he faced the same juvenile court for housebreaking and was sent to an approved school.

Punished

From then until the age of 18, Manuel lived mainly in approved schools and Borstal institutions for a string of thefts and burglaries. He managed to escape on ten occasions, but was always recaptured. During one brief spell in the outside world, when he was 15, Manuel committed his first known act of criminal violence. After breaking into a house and stealing a sleeping woman's purse, he struck her on the head with a hammer.

On recapture, Manuel was confined in Leeds Prison. But his rage remained ungovernable. After being returned to an approved school in Yorkshire, he broke out and indecently assaulted a woman in December 1942.

By this time, Samuel and Bridget Manuel had lost their home during the war-time bombing of Coventry in 1941 and had moved to Lanarkshire. Their son joined them in 1946, after his release from Borstal. He was 18 years-old, below middle height but well built.

Imaginative

He was a slick talker with a vivid imagination. Manuel could fantasize or lie in detail at a moment's notice – usually when confronted by suspicious police officers – but his imagination was founded on a clear memory of places, people and events.

Manuel developed a certain skill at sketching with pencil. His drawings showed the attention to detail on people's faces that his piercing dark eyes suggested. He also began writing short stories on the typewriter at his parents' home, but these yarns could not fulfill the lust that crime aroused.

On 16 February 1946, Manuel broke into a bungalow in the Sandyhills area of Lanarkshire. The police were alerted and Detective Constable William Muncie searched the building.

Manuel hid from him in the basement and walked out after Muncie had gone. By chance, Muncie had to return and caught Manuel.

The Lanarkshire police had not previously heard of Manuel, the son of a respectable former district councillor, but soon learnt of his lengthy criminal record south of the border. Awaiting trial on bail, Manuel committed three assaults on women. One, an expectant mother, was raped.

At Glasgow High Court on 25 June 1946, Manuel was sentenced to eight years' imprisonment for rape. He was praised by the judge for the skill with which he had conducted his own defence. He had already been sentenced to 12 months in jail for a total of 15 burglaries.

Manuel served his sentence at the tough Peterhead Prison, where guards carried rifles. He won remission and was released in the summer of 1953.

Back to crime

Manuel, now 26, returned immediately to crime. His style was unchanged. He hunted at night, usually alone, with a cunning stealth. Manuel was seldom spotted by witnesses in a vicinity, but could be clumsy with forensic clues, such as traces of soil. After a crime, he would desecrate the scene by emptying tins of food and stubbing out cigarettes.

But he could not resist drawing attention to himself – as he did when speaking to PC Marr during the Knielands inquiry.

PSYCHOLOGICAL PROFILE

Peter Manuel was a killer who achieved a morbid thrill of power from the act of murder. This sensation of power was so important to him that savage violence, as a means of achieving it, became self-justifying. Manuel only once expressed the slightest remorse for his crimes, begging a detective to accept that he had shot and killed an 11 year-old 'wee boy', Michael Smart, only because he thought he was an adult.

All-male company

There is little in Manuel's very early life which sheds light on his condition. By the age of 11, he was a sneak-thief and, from there, his criminal career proved uncontrollable.

While other youths were finding their way through school,

learning a trade and mixing with girls, Manuel was caged in all-male company inside approved schools and Borstal institutions.

By the time he emerged, Manuel was incapable of patience, or applying himself to anything. He needed to escape from the humdrum streets around him, but never settled down to gradually working his way out of them.

Manuel grew impatient with his sketching and short-story writing because they gave him no immediate sense of power and conquest. In his book, *Rebel Without A Cause*, Robert Lindner writes:

'The psychopath, like the child, cannot delay the pleasures of gratification; and this trait is one of his underlying, universal characteristics. He cannot wait upon erotic gratification which convention demands should be preceded by the chase before the kill he must rape. He cannot wait upon the development of prestige in society: his egotistic ambitions lead him to leap into headlines by daring performances.'

Gifted

Some writers have observed that Manuel did not come from a disturbed background. His parents were sound, deeply religious people. Manuel himself had the natural gifts and intelligence to be able to work his way to better things. His father Samuel, however, was over-protective, and even allowed himself to be charged with receiving stolen goods, rather than abandon his son.

Very few people ever seem to have subdued Manuel's violent lust for power. On 30 July 1955, the day on which he had been due to marry Anne O'Hara, his one-time fiancée, Manuel attacked a 29 year-old woman, Mary McLauchlan, in a field near his home in Birkenshaw.

Miss McLauchlan, though terrified, acted coolly. She lay still at knifepoint while she and Manuel listened to police officers following the sound of her screams. After an hour the search ended and Manuel told her he was going to kill her. Miss McLauchlan suffered his molestation, but not rape, and eventually asked kindly if he was in trouble.

Lucky escape

'I'm drunk. I don't know what I'm doing. I just felt I had to murder somebody,' Manuel replied. They then sat talking in the dark for a long time. Manuel told her a version of his broken-off engagement. Miss McLauchlan skilfully relaxed Manuel, who eventually drew the knife out of his pocket, balanced it on his fingers, and finally threw it aside. 'There, it's away,' he said.

With unwitting irony, Manuel offered to see her home. 'If you like, I'll come along to the police station with you now,' he said, 'and tell them what I've done. I've never done anything like this before.' Miss McLauchlan said she had no intention of going to the police. The ruse worked. She got home safely and went to the police the following day. Manuel, smartly dressed and articulate, defended himself in court and was acquitted of the attack.

What prevented Manuel finding friends to divest himself of his troubles is unclear. But he was a nocturnal creature. Dark surroundings soothed him, and the long discussion with Miss McLauchlan took place at night in a field.

Manuel seems not to have used burglary to achieve wealth. He settled for tiny hauls, sometimes only a few pounds. It was being noticed that mattered to him. He wanted to be patted on the head for being so clever in having police officers chase around after his crimes.

In the end, Manuel's need to parade his power – his taunts to police, his confessions, and the conduct of his own defence in court – destroyed him.

Chapter 4

KENNETH BIANCHI & ANGELO BUONO

THE HILLSIDE STRANGLERS

In the winter of 1977, a series of young women were found murdered on the hills above Los Angeles. Then the killings stopped. Suddenly, in 1979, police picked up the scent again – it led them to two cousins, one of whom claimed to be not one person, but many.

The small town of Bellingham, in Washington State, looks out on one of the most beautiful views in the American northwest: the pine-covered slopes of San Juan and Vancouver Islands, and the Strait of Juan de Fuca.

With a population of only 40,000, violent crime is a rarity. So when the Chief of Police, Terry Mangan, was told one Friday morning that two girls were missing, his first thought was that they had left for a long weekend. Their names were Karen Mandic and Diane Wilder, students at Western Washington University.

First fears

Karen's boyfriend, however, always insisted that she would not go away without telling him, and when Mangan learned that Karen had left her pet cat unfed, he began to fear the worst.

On the previous evening, 11 January 1979, Karen had told her boyfriend that she and Diane were going on a 'house-sitting' job. It was at the home of a couple who were travelling in Europe. Apparently its security alarm system had failed, and Karen merely had to wait in the house for two hours while the alarm was taken away and repaired. Moreover, she would be paid $100 for the inconvenience caused to her.

The man who had offered her this job was a security supervisor called Kenneth Bianchi. Mangan checked with Bianchi's boss, Mark Lawrence, who owned the Coastal Security agency. Lawrence declared that Bianchi was a young man of excellent reputation, and a conscientious worker. He lived with a local girl called Kelli Boyd. They had a baby son, and Bianchi was known to be a devoted father. But he had no authority to offer Karen a house-sitting job.

This was soon confirmed by Bianchi himself. He told his boss that he had never heard of Karen Mandic, nor offered anyone a house-sitting job. He had spent Thursday evening at a Sheriff's Reserve meeting.

Armed guards

The detectives began to learn more details. Karen had told her boyfriend that the man who had offered her the job had sworn her to secrecy. He had also telephoned the woman who lived next door to the house and went in to water the plants, to warn her not to go near it that evening. He explained that armed guards would be on patrol.

Police were despatched to the empty house, in the expensive Bayside area. A locksmith opened the front door, and the detectives entered cautiously.

Everything seemed to be in order. The house was neat, and there was no sign of a struggle. But on the kitchen floor, the searchers found a single wet footprint. It was that of a man. Since it was still wet, they calculated that it must have been made within the previous 12 hours or so.

At noon that day, the local radio station broadcast the first descriptions of Karen's car – a green Mercury Bobcat. At 4.30 p.m., the description was heard by a woman who had seen such a car that morning, parked in a nearby cul-de-sac. She rang the police, and officers were sent to investigate.

Detective Bill Geddes approached the car and glanced through the rear window. He saw the corpses of the two missing girls huddled together, as if thrown into the vehicle. Both were fully clothed. They had been strangled and then sexually assaulted.

Bianchi was the chief suspect. A warrant was issued for his arrest, but he was out somewhere driving his security truck. His boss, Mark Lawrence, agreed to set a trap.

Contacting Bianchi by radio, he asked him to go to a guard shack on the south side of town to receive instructions. Half an hour later, the police car arrived. But the good-looking young man merely looked surprised, and surrendered without protest. Bianchi seemed so free of guilt that Detective Terry Wright, who made the arrest, began to suspect that this was all a mistake. Either Ken Bianchi was innocent, or he was a superb actor.

Back at the police station, Bianchi denied knowing Karen Mandic. He said there must have been an impostor using his name. The interrogators were inclined to believe him. They were even more convinced when Kelli Boyd, his common-law wife, arrived at the station.

Gentle lover

She was horrified at the idea that Ken Bianchi might be a murderer. To her, he was a gentle lover and adoring father, incapable of violence. When the police asked permission to search their home, both gave it without hesitation.

The search revealed that, whether Bianchi was a murderer or not, he was certainly a thief. Hidden in the basement, there were several expensive telephones and a brand new chainsaw. These items had been reported as stolen from places where Bianchi had worked as a security guard. Bianchi was charged with grand theft, and taken to the county jail.

A search of Bianchi's security truck produced more evidence – the keys of the Bayside house, and a woman's scarf. Diane Wilder's friends reported that she had a passion for scarves.

But the most convincing evidence came from examination of the bodies. Both girls had been strangled by some kind of ligature applied from behind, and its angle indicated that the murderer had been standing above them, as if walking downstairs.

On the stairs leading to the basement of the Bayside home, detectives found a single pubic hair. Two more fell from Diane Wilder's body when it was lifted on to a sterile sheet. Semen stains were found on the underwear of both girls. Carpet fibres found on their clothing, and on the soles of their shoes, matched the fibres in the empty house.

It became possible tentatively to reconstruct the crime. Ken Bianchi had telephoned Karen Mandic and offered her the house-sitting job. He had made her acquaintance when he was a security guard in the department store where she worked, which proved he was lying in saying he had never heard of her.

Bianchi had sworn her to silence but Karen had told her boyfriend. She had also told another friend, a security guard at the university. The friend had been slightly suspicious about the size of the remuneration.

Lying in wait

At seven o'clock that evening, in the police theory, Karen and Diane had driven to the Bayside house. Bianchi was waiting for them in his security truck – local residents had noticed it. Karen parked her car in the drive, outside the front door. Bianchi had asked her to accompany him inside to turn on the lights, while Diane waited in the car.

When he reappeared a few minutes later, Diane had no suspicion that her friend was now lying dead in the basement. Like Karen, she was strangled on the stairs. As far as could be determined, the killer had not raped either girl.

He had carried both bodies out to Karen's car, and driven to the cul-de-sac, wiped the car clean of fingerprints, and walked back to the Bayside house where his own truck was parked, disposing of the ligature on the way. The baffling thing about the crime was that it seemed pointless.

No memory

The case against Bianchi looked conclusive, even though he continued to insist that he had no memory of the murders. While he was held in jail, the police began checking on his background. He had been living in Glendale, a suburb eight miles north of downtown Los Angeles, before his move to Bellingham the previous May.

A detective rang the Los Angeles County Sheriff's Department. The call was taken by Detective Sergeant Frank Salerno of the Homicide Division. When Salerno was told that a former Glendale resident called Kenneth Bianchi had been booked on suspicion of a double sex-murder, his attention was riveted.

For the past 14 months, Salerno had been looking for a sex killer who had committed up to 12 similar murders in Los Angeles. The newspapers had dubbed him the Hillside Strangler. The last murder had taken place shortly before Bianchi left Los Angeles for Bellingham.

LOS ANGELES NIGHTMARE

The corpse lay sprawled on a hillside near Forest Lawn cemetery, south of the Ventura freeway. The girl was tall and black, and had been stripped naked. It seemed probable that her body had been removed from a car and tossed down the slope.

It was the morning of 17 October 1977. The girl's body temperature indicated that she had died the previous evening. Identifying her proved unexpectedly easy. Her fingerprints were on police files. She was a prostitute called Yolanda Washington, who worked around Hollywood Boulevard.

The autopsy showed that sexual relations had taken place and had involved two men. One of these was a 'non-secretor', a man whose blood group cannot be determined from his bodily fluids. But the men could simply have been clients, and had nothing to do with her murder. She had been strangled with a piece of cloth while she was lying down, with the murderer above her.

Second body found

The crime aroused little interest in the news media. Nor did the death of a second woman, found on the morning of 1 November. She lay close to the kerb in Alta Terrace Drive in La Crescenta, a town near Glendale, and it looked again as if the victim had been dumped from a car. As in the case of Yolanda Washington, the body was naked, and death was due to strangulation with a ligature. The victim was little more than a child – 15 years-old at most.

The autopsy disclosed a possible link with the murder of Yolanda Washington. The girl had been subjected to sexual intercourse by two men, one of them a non-secretor. The position of the body also suggested that she had been carried by two men, one holding her under the armpits and the other by the knees. Now the police were sure that they were looking for two killers.

This time the victim's fingerprints were not on file. The investigating officer, Sergeant Frank Salerno, had no definite starting point. A hunch led him to ask questions in Hollywood Boulevard, and to display a police artist's sketch of the dead girl to the area's floating population of drug addicts and prostitutes.

Several 'street people' said that she resembled a girl called Judy Miller, who had not been seen recently. It took Salerno another week to track down her parents. They lived in a cheap motel room, and one of their two remaining children slept in a cardboard box. At the morgue they identified their daughter from photographs. Judy had run away from home a month before. Salerno already knew that she had made a living from prostitution – but in a half-hearted, amateurish way. She had offered sex free to a casual boyfriend only an hour before she was last seen alive.

Repeated pattern

By the time Salerno located Judy's parents, there had already been another murder on the pattern of the first two. On 6 November, a jogger near the Chevy Chase Country Club in Glendale discovered the body of a woman lying near the golf course. She had been strangled with a ligature and subjected to a sexual assault.

Identification was made quickly. Soon after a news broadcast about the discovery, a man telephoned the police to say that his daughter had been missing for two days. She was a 20 year-old dancer called Lissa Kastin who had recently been working as a waitress. An hour later, Lissa Kastin's father identified her from television pictures.

Glendale was outside Salerno's jurisdiction, but he went to view the body. The ligature marks around the neck, and lines around the wrists and ankles, suggested that the stranglers had been at work again. As Frank

Salerno looked down at the body, the third in three weeks, he thought that this might be the start of an epidemic.

Even Salerno, however, was unprepared for what happened in the last three weeks of November 1977. Seven more strangled corpses were found, six of them naked. One, 18 year-old Jill Barcomb, discovered on 10 November, was a prostitute. Her body was found at Franklin Cyn Drive and Mulholland. Kathleen Robinson, 17, differed from the other victims in being clothed when her body was found at Pico and Ocean Boulevards on 17 November, so doubts were raised that she was a victim of the same killers.

But the day that shocked the news media into taking notice of the 'Hillside Strangler' was Sunday, 20 November, when three naked bodies were found, two of them schoolgirls. These were Dollie Cepeda, 12, and Sonja Johnson, 14, who had been missing since the previous Sunday evening. Their bodies were discovered on a rubbish dump in an obscure street called Landa, near Stadium Way. The nine year-old boy who found them thought they were discarded mannequins from a department store.

Autopsy

The girls' autopsies revealed that both had been raped and sodomized. Earlier that day, another nude body had been found on a street corner in the hills that separate Glendale from Eagle Rock. A missing person report helped to identify her as Kristina Weckler, a 20 year-old art student who lived in an apartment building in Glendale.

The next victim was found on 23 November, in some bushes off the Golden State freeway. She was identified as a 28 year-old Scientology student, Jane King, who had been missing since 9 November. The last victim of this month of 'spree killing' was found in some bushes in Cliff Drive, Glendale, on 29 November.

Her parents identified her as Lauren Wagner, an 18 year-old student, who had failed to return home the previous night.

Ten sex murders in six weeks was a grisly toll even by the standards of Los Angeles, where there are several murders a day. The 'Hillside Strangler' featured in television reports all over the world. But the police took care not to publicize their certainty that they were looking for two men – the less the killers knew about the investigation, the better.

City in fear

Women were afraid to go out alone at night. By the time Lauren Wagner's body was discovered, Los Angeles was in a state of panic. The police department responded by creating a combined task force from members of the Los Angeles Police, the Glendale Police and the Los Angeles Sheriff's Office, for which Salerno worked.

Despite the frustrating lack of clues, the investigation made progress. On the evening that the two schoolgirls disappeared, a boy had seen them go up to a car and speak to someone on the passenger side. This meant there were two people in the car. The girls were generally nervous about speaking to strangers but one was known to admire policemen. So it was possible that the killers had posed as police officers. Under hypnosis, the boy was able to say that the car was a large two-colour sedan.

Police lead

There was also a promising lead in the Lauren Wagner case. On 29 November, the day she disappeared, her father had seen her car across the street. The door was open and the interior light on. The car was parked in front of the home of a woman called Beulah Stofer, who described how she had seen Lauren abducted. As Lauren's car had pulled up, a big dark sedan with a white top had halted alongside, and two men had got out.

There was an argument, then Lauren had got in the other car and been driven away. Mrs Stofer had heard her say, 'You won't get away with this.' She was able to describe the men. The older one had bushy hair and was 'Latin-looking', while the other, taller and younger, had acne scars on his neck. Beulah Stofer had been alerted to the incident when her dog had barked.

Telephone threats

When Detective-Sergeant Bob Grogan interviewed Mrs Stofer later that day, she was close to collapse. The telephone had just rung, and a male voice with an East Coast accent had asked if she was the lady with the dog. When she confirmed this, the voice warned her to keep quiet about what she had seen, or she was as good as dead. The stranglers had obviously realized her evidence could be crucial.

Yet, undeterred, the Hillside Stranglers found another victim two weeks later, on 14 December. The naked body of a 17 year-old prostitute, Kimberly Diane Martin, was found, sprawled on a vacant lot on Alvorado Street, within sight of City Hall. This time there were more clues, for she had been sent by a call girl agency to the Tamarind Apartment building in Hollywood. A man had called the agency, asking for a blonde in black underwear, for whom he would pay $150 in cash.

When the agency asked for the caller's telephone number, he had assured them he was at home, although a later check on the number revealed it to be that of the public library. The girl was despatched to the Tamarind Apartments, and disappeared.

The police interviewed everyone in the apartment building, and one tenant – a personable young man called Kenneth Bianchi – said that he had heard screams. At the Hollywood public library, a woman described how a bushy-haired man had followed her around and glared at her.

During the remainder of 1977, there were no more murders, and the Los Angeles police hoped fervently that the stranglers had moved elsewhere. On 17 February 1978, that hope was dashed when someone reported the sighting of an orange Datsun halfway down a cliff below a lay-by on the Angeles Crest Highway, north of Glendale. In the boot was another woman's naked body. She was identified as Cindy Hudspeth, 20, a part-time waitress at the Robin Hood Inn. The medical evidence indicated that she had been raped, and by two men.

Then, at last, the murders ceased.

BATTLE FOR CONTROL

When Sergeant Frank Salerno heard that Bianchi had been arrested for a double sex killing in Washington State, he lost no time in travelling to Bellingham. Within hours of arriving, he was certain that one of the Hillside Stranglers had been found. Jewellery found in Bianchi's apartment matched items taken from victims in and around Los Angeles locations.

In custody, Bianchi continued to behave like an innocent man. He was highly co-operative. He told the police that his only close friend in Los Angeles was his cousin Angelo Buono, an automobile upholsterer who owned a house in Glendale. An undercover agent carried out a check on Buono. He had bushy hair, and was 45 years-old – Ken's senior by 17 years. Like Bianchi, Buono had been born in Rochester, New York, and Buelah Stofer, the woman who had received the threatening telephone call, had thought the caller had a New York accent.

When Bianchi's face appeared in the Los Angeles newspapers, a school-teacher who had interrupted the abduction of a girl in the Birbank district in February 1977 came forward again and told her story. One of the men, who had bushy hair, had warned her: 'God will get you for this.' Her description of the two men sounded like Bianchi and Buono.

Information about Buono also came from a wealthy Hollywood lawyer. In August 1976, he had telephoned a call girl agency and asked for a woman to be sent over to his Bel-Air home. The 15 year-old girl, Becky Spears, looked so miserable that the lawyer asked her how she came to be working as a prostitute when she obviously hated it. Her answer was that a girl called Sabra had lured her from her home in Phoenix, Arizona, to work for a man called Angelo Buono.

Degrading acts

Buono and his cousin Bianchi had terrorized the girl. They told her that she would be killed if she tried to run away. Buono subjected her to degrading sexual acts.

Horrified by this story of cruelty, the lawyer bought Becky Spears an air ticket back to Phoenix. Buono had then threatened him on the telephone – until the lawyer sent a well-muscled bouncer to warn Buono off. After that, the lawyer heard no more from Buono or his call-girl agency.

Beatings

The lawyer was able to give Sergeant Grogan the addresses of Becky Spears and the other call girl, Sabra Hannan, in Arizona. They were brought to Los Angeles, and confirmed that Buono and Bianchi had offered them jobs as 'models', then forced them to work as prostitutes, beating them and threatening them with death.

As the detectives delved into his background, it became clear that Buono was a highly unsavoury character. He had been married four times and fathered eight children. All four wives had left him because of his brutality. He was proud of his sexual stamina, and some of his girlfriends were in their early teens.

Frank Salerno and Grogan had little doubt that Buono and Bianchi were the Hillside Stranglers. Buono was the dominant one. Bianchi, for all his charm, was something of a weakling and a drifter. Even his girlfriend, Kelli Boyd, was fed up with his immaturity – she had left him in Los Angeles to rejoin her family in Bellingham, but Bianchi had followed her there.

Pimps

Salerno and his colleagues also thought they were beginning to understand how Buono and Bianchi had developed into serial killers. Their activities as pimps had made them accustomed to dominating and beating women. From an experienced professional prostitute, they had purchased a list of men who liked to have girls sent over to their homes. The list had been duly delivered, but turned out to be only of men who wanted to visit prostitutes in their rooms.

Buono had been enraged at the trick played on him. He had no means of locating the prostitute who had sold him the useless list. But he knew where to find one of her friends, another prostitute who had been with her when the list was delivered. The name of the friend was Yolanda Washington – the stranglers' first victim.

The case appeared to be virtually tied up. Bianchi looked certain to be convicted of the Bellingham murders. In Washington State, that would probably mean the death penalty. Faced with that prospect, Bianchi would prefer a trial in Los Angeles, where he could expect a life sentence. It would be in his interest to confess to the Hillside murders, and to implicate his cousin. At that stage, the evidence against Angelo Buono was slim but, with Bianchi's co-operation, it could be made impregnable.

Buono had by now been interviewed a number of times, and his attitude had an undertone of mockery. He seemed to enjoy the thought that the police had no real evidence against him. All that, Salerno reflected with satisfaction, would change when his cousin returned to Los Angeles.

And then, suddenly, the case threatened to collapse. Doubts were raised about Bianchi's sanity and, as a result, his responsibility in law for the crimes of which he was accused. Moreover, the doubts involved one of the most complex of all mental disturbances – multiple personality. In layman's language, this means a Jekyll-and-Hyde character whose normal side is totally aware of the existence of an alter ego, or separate personality.

Suicide threat

Ever since his arrest, Bianchi had been insisting that he remembered absolutely nothing of the evening on which he killed Karen Mandic and Diane Wilder. The police viewed this as a ploy to evade responsibility. But Bianchi's lawyer, Dean Brett, was impressed by his apparent sincerity, his protestations of horror at the thought of killing two women, and his hints that he was contemplating suicide.

In February 1979, Brett called in a psychiatric social worker, John Johnston, who was equally swayed by Bianchi's charm, gentleness and intelligence. If his claims of amnesia were genuine, then there was only one possible conclusion: Bianchi was a multiple personality.

Brett followed up this initial diagnosis by having Bianchi examined on 9 March 1979, by a forensic psychiatrist, Dr Donald T. Lunde of Stanford University, the author of *Murder and Madness*. Lunde recommended that Bianchi accept a course of hypnosis under expert supervision.

This began on 21 March 1979 and was conducted by Dr John G. Watkins, a specialist in multiple personalities and hypnosis from the University of Montana. Bianchi professed himself eager to co-operate. Within a few minutes of being placed in trance, Bianchi was speaking in a strange, low voice, introducing himself as Steve.

'Steve' came over as a highly unpleasant character with a sneering laugh. He told Dr Watkins that he hated 'Ken', and that he had done his best to 'fix him'. Then, with a little more prompting, he described how Ken had walked in one evening when his cousin Angelo Buono was murdering a girl. At that point, Steve admitted he had taken over Ken's personality, and turned him into his cousin's willing accomplice.

Frank Salerno and his deputy, Sergeant Pete Finnigan, listened quietly from a corner of the room. In his notebook, Salerno wrote down a single word: 'Bullshit'. But he knew that the investigation was in trouble. If Bianchi could convince a judge that he was a multiple personality, he might escape with a few years in a mental hospital. And since the testimony of a mental patient would be inadmissible in court, Angelo Buono would be beyond the reach of the law.

MOCKING THE LAW

Back in Los Angeles, the investigation looked slightly more promising. The boyfriend of Judy Miller, the second victim, had identified a photograph of Angelo Buono as the client who had enticed Judy into his car on the evening she disappeared. Beulah Stoffer identified the pictures of both suspects as the men who had pushed Lauren Wagner into a car. But without Bianchi's testimony, it would be a weak case.

Violent background

It was clear that Buono was brutal, violent and dangerous. He had hated his mother, and in later life made obscene references to her and to women in general. From the time he left school he had been in trouble with the police, and had spent his 17th birthday in a reform school. His hero was Caryl Chessman, the 'Red Light Bandit' of the 1940s, who held up women at gunpoint and assaulted them sexually.

At 20, Buono married a 17 year-old he had made pregnant. He left her within weeks. After a short period in jail for theft, Buono married again, and fathered four more sons. But his violence led to his second and third wife filing for divorce. A fourth left without a divorce.

After that, Buono lived alone in his house at 703 Colorado Street, Glendale. A friend who had once shared an apartment with him described him as being obsessed by young girls. Buono had boasted that he had seduced his 14 year-old stepdaughter, and one of his sons had confided that his father had seduced him, too. Buono was a man who spent his days dreaming about sex.

Sexual appetite

Meanwhile, in the Whatcomb County Jail in Washington, Ken's sinister alter-ego 'Steve' was also telling stories of Buono's insatiable sexual appetite, and of his habit of killing girls after he had raped them. These stories tended to contain certain anomalies – almost as if Steve wished to minimize his own part in the murders. The same applied to his later confessions to the police, but the general picture was clear. The first victim was the prostitute Yolanda Washington, killed for revenge and raped by both men. They had found the experience so pleasant that two weeks later they had picked up 15 year-old Judy Miller, a part-time prostitute.

Pretending that they were policemen and that she was under arrest, they had taken her back to Buono's house and raped her. She would have been glad to submit to sex for a payment of a few dollars. Then, with Bianchi kneeling on her legs, they had strangled her and suffocated her at the same time.

According to Bianchi's 'Steve', the next victim was the out-of-work dancer Lissa Kastin. They stopped her in her car and identified themelves by showing a police badge. They said they were taking her to the station for questioning. Back in Buono's house, she was handcuffed and strangled. The description provided by 'Steve' suggested that Buono had been over-whelmed by a loathing of women. It also indicated that Bianchi had savoured a feeling of holding absolute power of life and death. They dumped Lissa Kastin's body near the Chevy Chase golf course, in Glendale.

Four days later, on 9 November, their killing resumed. Bianchi saw an attractive girl waiting alone at a bus stop and began a conversation. She told him she was a Scientology student. During the conversation, Buono drove up, pretending he had not seen Bianchi for months, and offered him a lift. Jane King made the mistake of accepting a lift home. She, too, died in Buono's house. They were surprised to read later in a newspaper that she was 28 – she had seemed younger.

Four days after this, according to 'Steve', Bianchi and Buono saw two schoolgirls, Dollie Cepeda and Sonja Johnson, boarding a bus in Eagle Rock Plaza. They followed the bus, and when the girls disembarked near their home beckoned them over to the car. Bianchi again posed as a police-man, saying that a dangerous burglar was in the neighbourhood.

The schoolgirls were vulnerable. They had just stolen a hundred dollars worth of costume jewellery from a department store, and were not disposed to argue with the police. At Buono's home, both were subjected to violation and murdered. Their bodies were dumped on a rubbish tip. The police had reasoned correctly, that whoever had dumped the bodies there must have known the area intimately.

The next victim was an art student Bianchi had known when he lived in East Garfield, in Hollywood. Kristina Weckler had once spurned Bianchi's advances. Now they knocked on her door and Bianchi said, 'Hi, remember me?' Bianchi said he had joined the police reserve, and that someone had crashed into Kristina's car. Downstairs, she was bundled into Buono's car, taken to his house, and killed. Once again, 'Steve' described horrific details.

Redhead

The Thanksgiving killing spree was almost over. On Monday, 28 November 1977, they followed a redheaded girl in her car. When Lauren

Wagner pulled up in front of her parents' home, Bianchi flourished his police badge and said they were arresting her. While she protested – and a dog barked loudly in a nearby house – they bundled her into their car and drove her away. Realizing their purpose was rape, she pretended to be co-operative. She behaved as if she enjoyed it but her ploy failed. She was strangled.

Three weeks later, they summoned Kimberly Diane Martin, a call girl, to the Tamarind Apartments, and took her back to Buono's house. After raping her they dumped her body in a vacant lot.

The final Hillside killing was almost unplanned. On 16 February, Bianchi arrived at Buono's house to find an orange Datsun parked outside. A girl named Cindy Hudspeth had called to ask Buono to make new mats for her car. The two men spreadeagled the girl naked on the bed, tied her wrists and ankles and raped her. After that, they strangled her. They pushed her Datsun off a cliff with her body in the boot. The entire series of killings had now been recounted by 'Steve' during the sessions with hypnotists.

After the final killing Bianchi was twice questioned by the police in routine inquiries. He was only one of thousands, but Buono was becoming nervous and irritable. He was tiring of his cousin's lack of maturity, his naivety and carelessness. So when Bianchi told him that his girlfriend had left him and moved back to Bellingham, Buono urged him to join her. At first Bianchi was unwilling – his admiration of his cousin amounted to worship.

But Buono finally prevailed. On 21 May 1978, Bianchi drove to Bellingham and rejoined Kelli Boyd and their newborn son. He found work as a security guard, and was soon promoted to supervisor. But the small town bored him. He longed to prove to his cousin that he had the makings of a master criminal. By the start of 1979, the craving for rape and murder became intolerable. Bianchi's mind went back to an attractive student called Karen Mandic, whom he had met while working in a store.

A week later he was under arrest, and the Hillside Stranglings were finally over.

HOPE AND DESPAIR

The news that Kenneth Bianchi had accused his cousin of being an accomplice in the Hillside killings aroused anger in Buono's neighbourhood. He began to receive threatening letters, but it looked increasingly unlikely that either he or Bianchi would ever stand trial.

On 18 April 1979, Bianchi convinced another expert, Dr Ralph B. Allison, author of *Minds in Many Pieces*, that he was a multiple personality. At Allison's request, 'Steve' revealed even his last name – Walker. At the time, this information went unnoticed, but it would later prove significant. In the May 1979 issue of *Time* magazine, America learned that Bianchi had been pronounced a multiple personality by two of America's most eminent psychiatrists. Ken was innocent. It was 'Steve' who had killed the girls.

The prosecution decided it was time to bring in their own expert. Dr Martin T. Orne, of the University of Pennsylvania Hospital, was a known authority on hypnosis. In May 1979, Orne began to study the hypnotic sessions with 'Steve', which had been recorded on videotape. But they failed to answer the question that most trouble him: whether Bianchi was hypnotized or shamming.

Acting

But he did notice that the character of 'Steve' seemed to develop in the course of the sessions. Although coarse and foul-mouthed from the outset, he seemed to slip deeper into his role as the sessions progressed. To Dr Orne, this suggested an actor rather than a true alter ego.

Later in May 1979, when Dr Orne interviewed him, Bianchi was his usual co-operative self. Under hypnotic suggestion, he quickly slipped into a trance. Orne now decided to experiment. Good hypnotic subjects can be made to hallucinate in the presence of another person. Orne told Bianchi that his defence lawyer, Dean Brett, was sitting in an empty chair. Bianchi immediately did something that Orne had never before seen in a subject – he leapt to his feet and shook the hand of the imaginary lawyer. At that moment, Orne was certain that Bianchi was only feigning hypnosis. Genuine hypnotized subjects are content to talk to their hallucinations. They never try to touch them.

Dr Orne tried one further experiment. He casually dropped the information that multiple personalities have more than one alter ego. At the next session, Bianchi immediately produced another 'personality', a frightened child called Billy. Asked if he knew Steve, 'Billy' whispered miserably: 'He's a bad egg.' Now Orne was convinced that Bianchi was feigning.

Trapped

But it was the detectives Frank Salerno and Pete Finnigan who made the discovery that finally destroyed Bianchi's claim. Listening to a recording of the session with Dr Allison, they heard 'Steve' declare that his last name was Walker. Suddenly, both recalled seeing the name Steve Walker somewhere in Bianchi's papers.

A search revealed a letter to the registrar at California State University, signed 'Thomas Steven Walker' in Bianchi's handwriting. It requested a diploma without the name filled in. Sleuthing revealed that the real Steve Walker was a graduate in psychology from California State University, and had answered an advertisement for a job by sending some of his academic papers.

The advertisement had actually been placed by Bianchi, who had then used Walker's name and papers to obtain a fake diploma in psychology.

The defence psychiatrists declined to be convinced that Bianchi was shamming and should not stand trial. Dr Martin Orne and his colleague Dr Saul Faerstein, who conducted a session with Bianchi on 1 June 1979, were insistent that Bianchi was a fraud. Their opinion carried the day at the sanity hearing on 19 October that year.

Sobbing

At that hearing, Bianchi pleaded guilty to the two Bellingham murders and to five murders in Los Angeles. In the dock he sobbed and professed deep remorse. Under Washington law the judge sentenced him to life imprisonment without the formality of a trial. But there remained five more murder charges to answer in Los Angeles. Bianchi agreed to plead guilty and testify against his cousin in return for life with the possibility of parole.

In interviews with Salerno and Finnigan, he described every murder with a precision of detail that left no doubt that Ken, not 'Steve', was guilty.

On 22 October 1979, Angelo Buono was arrested and charged with the Hillside stranglings. He was placed in the county jail, where Bianchi occupied another cell. But Bianchi was already reneging on his plea-bargaining deal, explaining that he had made it only to save his life, and that he was innocent. The reason was simple. The District Attorney's office had decided to drop the other five Los Angeles murder charges, for which Bianchi could have been sentenced to death. He now had nothing to lose by refusing to co-operate.

As far as the police were concerned, it made little difference. The jewellery found in Bianchi's house linked him to some of the victims, while a wisp of fluff on the eyelid of Judy Miller, the second victim, was found to be identical to a foamy polyester material in Buono's house. Strand by strand, the case against Buono was becoming strong enough to convict him.

The next development took everyone by surprise. In July 1979, the assistant District Attorney, Roger Kelly, proposed that all ten murder charges against Buono should be dropped. He argued that Bianchi's testimony was so dubious and self-contradictory as to be virtually useless. Buono, he said, should be tried later on the non-murder charges such as pimping, rape and sodomy, and meanwhile should be free on bail of $50,000. It meant that even if Buono was convicted on the other charges, he would serve only about five years in jail.

Judge George agreed to deliver his ruling on 21 July 1981. In the week beforehand morale among the police was at rock bottom. No one doubted that if the District Attorney's office was unsure of a conviction, the judge would agree to drop the charges.

On the day of the ruling Buono and his junior counsel, Katherine Mader, looked cheerful. But it soon became clear that their confidence was misplaced. Whether Bianchi was reliable or not, the judge said, the evidence of various witnesses, and the Judy Miller fibre evidence, made it clear that there was a strong case against Buono. The motion was denied. If, the judge added, the District Attorney showed any lack of enthusiasm in prosecuting Buono, he would refer the case to the Attorney General.

Buono had to cancel his plans for a celebratory dinner with his lawyers. The District Attorney decided to withdraw and two deputies from the Attorney General's office, Roger Boren and Michael Nash, were appointed to prosecute Buono.

Buono's trial for murder started at Whatcomb County Court House in Los Angeles on 16 November 1981 and lasted until 14 November 1983. It was the longest murder trial in American history. The prosecution called 251 witnesses and introduced over 1,000 exhibits. But, though the transcript was eventually to fill hundreds of volumes, the trial held few surprises.

It took until June 1982 to reach Bianchi's evidence – he was the 200th witness to testify – and, at first, he was vague and ambiguous. But when the judge hinted that he was violating his plea-bargaining agreement, and would be sent to the notoriously tough Walla Walla jail in Washington, he became less vague. Bianchi spent five months in the witness box. His testimony had damning results for his cousin.

The defence team pursued a tactic of trying to discredit witnesses and evidence, submitting that testimony obtained under hypnosis should be inadmissible. The judge ruled that Bianchi had been faking both hypnosis and multiple personality. More serious was a motion by the defence to dismiss the whole case because one of the prosecution witnesses – Judy Miller's boyfriend – had been in a mental home. This was also overruled. The defence was at fault, the judge said, for failing to spot the material in the files.

In the final submissions in October 1983, Buono's defence lawyer, Gerald Chaleff, argued that Bianchi had committed the murders alone, and that his cousin was an innocent man.

The judge rebuked Chaleff for implying that the whole case against his client was a conspiracy.

The jury retired on 21 October 1983. After they had spent a week considering their verdict, the defence began to feel gloomy and the prosecution optimistic. It emerged later that one juror, resentful at not being chosen as foreman, had been consistently obstructive. Finally, on 31 October, the jury convicted Buono of the murder of Lauren Wagner.

Guilty

During the next two weeks they also found him guilty of murdering Judy Miller, Dolores Cepeda, Sonja Johnson, Kristina Weckler, Kimberly Diane

Martin, Jane King, Lissa Kastin and Cindy Hudspeth. But, possibly influenced by the fact that Bianchi had avoided execution, they decided that Buono should not receive the death sentence. On 4 January 1984, the judge ordered that Kenneth Bianchi should be returned to serve his sentence in Washington. Judge George then sentenced Angelo Buono to life imprisonment, expressing regret that he could not sentence him to death. In his final remarks he told the defendants: 'I am sure, Mr Buono and Mr Bianchi, that you will probably only get your thrills reliving over and over again the torturing and murdering of your victims, being incapable, as I believe you to be, of feeling any remorse.'

Asked later whether such acts as Buono and Bianchi had committed did not prove them insane, the judge commented: 'Why should we call someone insane simply because he or she chooses not to conform to our standards of civilized behaviour?'

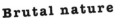

CASE FILE: BUONO, ANGELO 'TONY' & BIANCHI, KENNETH ALESSIO

BACKGROUND

Angelo 'Tony' Buono was born in Rochester, in New York State, on 5 October 1934, the grandson of Italian immigrants. He and his sister, Cecilia, ten, were taken to Los Angeles by their mother, Jenny – who had divorced Angelo Sr – when Angelo was five. They settled in Highland Park, on the southern edge of Glendale.

Brutal nature

Buono's academic record was poor. By the age of 14 he was stealing cars. Arrested for grand auto theft, he spent time in reformatories. At the age of 20, he married but his brutality led to divorce. Three more unsuccessful marriages followed, the last breaking up in 1972.

Three years later Buono set up his own car-body shop at 703 East Colorado, and became known as an excellent upholsterer – his customers included Frank Sinatra. Always oversexed, he slept with many young girls, including his sons' girlfriends. Long before Sylvester Stallone, he soon came to be known as 'the Italian Stallion'.

Killer: Kenneth Bianchi & Angelo Buono

Kenneth Alessio Bianchi was born on 22 May 1951, the child of a Rochester prostitute who gave him up at birth. He was adopted at three months by Frances Bianchi, the wife of a foundry worker. Her sister Jenny was the mother of Angelo Buono.

Compulsive liar

Kenny seemed a bright, normal boy, except for a tendency to compulsive and pointless lying. Darcy O'Brien in his book about the stranglers, *Two of a Kind* (1985), remarked that lying was not merely second nature to him but first as well. He was also a daydreamer, whose doctor suggested that his tendency to trance-like states might be due to mild epilepsy. A psychiatrist diagnosed him as overly dependent on his stepmother. At school he excelled at composition (what would now be called 'creative writing') but was a lazy and highly erratic student who pretended to be ill as often as possible. He was supported by his stepmother, who went out to work after Bianchi's stepfather died when he was 13.

Early marriage

Bianchi's charm and good manners made him a hit with the girls. He was married at the age of 18, but was quickly divorced after he came to believe that his wife had slept with someone else before they were married. The prospects of a second marriage, to a woman with two children, ended when she caught him with another woman.

In fact, Bianchi had a hankering to become a policeman. When the sheriff's department rejected him, he took a job as a security guard. But his tendency to steal led to frequent changes of job, although he was never actually caught and charged. Eventually, bored with Rochester and a sense of failure, he moved to California early in 1976.

Inevitably, he moved in with his cousin and was deeply impressed by the way Angelo bedded nubile teenagers and induced them to perform oral sex. One evening they called for a prostitute to come to the apartment but, instead of paying her, they stole her money. When her black pimp made threatening telephone calls and generally harassed him, Buono lost his nerve and demanded police protection. The threats finally stopped.

Immaturity

This contact with the police reminded Bianchi of his ambition to join the force, but both the Glendale and the Los Angeles police departments turned him down, possibly sensing his basic immaturity and untrustworthiness. Instead, Bianchi made plans to become a psychotherapist. He began reading textbooks but finally decided to take a short cut. He obtained a diploma by placing a fake job advertisement in an LA newspaper, then assumed the identity and qualifications of one of the graduates who answered it.

Buono, however, was getting exasperated with his weak-willed cousin and asked him to find a place of his own. Bianchi found work with a real estate company and rented an apartment. His next door neighbour was Kristina Weckler, an eventual victim of the stranglers.

Bianchi's former girlfriend visited him, but his extreme possessiveness led to rows. He sobbed with his head in her lap when she prepared to leave. After a more recent girlfriend left him for another man, Bianchi broke into her apartment and punched a hole in her diaphragm. He consoled himself with a new girlfriend, Kelli Boyd, whom he had met at the real estate company.

After losing his job when marijuana was found in his desk drawer, Bianchi rented an office and set himself up as a psychiatrist. When patients failed to materialize, his cousin Angelo had a brilliant suggestion: why not become pimps? At a party he told a 16 year-old girl from Phoenix named Sabra Hannan that he could guarantee her $500 a week as a photographic model. She declined, but changed her mind a few weeks later when she was broke.

Prostitution

When she moved into Angelo's house, the modelling jobs failed to materialize and Bianchi asked if she had ever considered prostitution. Sabra reacted indignantly, but later, after being beaten with a wet towel and ordered to perform oral sex on both men, she submitted. Buono told her that if she ran away she was a 'dead pussy'.

Sabra was the first of their 'stable' of prostitutes. The role suited both men. They liked to see themselves as macho superstuds who were born to use women.

PSYCHOLOGICAL PROFILE

What turned Angelo Buono, and Kenneth Bianchi from moderately successful pimps into serial killers? And why did Buono, who had no difficulty finding sleeping partners, risk life and liberty by embarking on the career of a sex killer?

The explanations almost certainly lie in the peculiar chemistry that existed between the cousins: Buono's macho brutality and Bianchi's almost feminine passivity. One psychiatrist suggested that there was a homosexual relationship, but this is almost certainly untrue. Both were too obsessed with women. Yet Bianchi's relation to his cousin was that of a besotted admirer, and when Buono pressed him to leave Los Angeles for Bellingham, he undoubtedly felt – as Darcy O'Brien remarks in his book, *Two of a Kind* – 'like a lover scorned.'

His murder of the two Bellingham co-eds was less a compulsive act than to have something to boast about next time he saw his cousin, an achievement for which he thought he would receive praise from Buono.

Moors murders

In England, the psychology of duo-killers can be studied in the case of Brady and Hindley, the 'moors murderers'. In America, it has emerged in numerous celebrated cases, the best known of which are Leopold and Loeb, the Chicago students who murdered a child 'for kicks', and Fernandez and Beck, the 'lonely hearts' killers.

In such cases, there is invariably a highly dominant partner and an accomplice of relatively low dominance. The high dominance partner experiences a deep craving to control the life of another person, to savour the 'will to power.' In fact, as the psychologist Abraham Maslow observed, persons of high dominance tend to look for a permanent sexual partner within their own high dominance group. Men of high dominance are willing to make sexual use of women of medium or low dominance but feel too contemptuous of them to form a permanent alliance.

Ian Brady, the moors murderer, ignored the adoring typist Myra Hindley for six months, finding her uninteresting. When he finally took her out on a date, he wasted no time in taking her virginity. He then lost interest in her sexually, but so enjoyed the 'master-slave' relationship that he set about converting her from Catholicism to atheism, then to admiration for the doctrines of the Marquis de Sade.

The inevitable next step was to enlist her aid in committing a series of particularly revolting rape-murders, in which she revelled. Without the relationship with Myra Hindley, it is unlikely that Brady would ever have committed a murder. The same pattern can be seen in the case of Leopold and Loeb, and Fernandez and Beck (although it was Martha Beck who was the dominant partner while her lover Raymond Fernandez was the 'slave').

Sexual prowess

This applies to the Hillside Stranglers. Buono was mildly contemptuous of his cousin, recognizing his weakness of character and craving to be liked and admired at all costs. Yet he also enjoyed Bianchi's hero-worship, which was based largely on Buono's sexual prowess.

Almost certainly, it was Buono who suggested that they should start pimping. Dominating a 'stable' of prostitutes was food for his ego. The loss of one of his 'sex slaves' – when a sympathetic customer put her on the next plane home – was a blow to his self-esteem, and being roughed up by a 'muscle-man' was an even greater blow. When, later, a prostitute sold him a useless list of clients, his bruised ego reacted with extreme outrage. One of the prostitute's friends – Yolanda Washington – was abducted and raped, then murdered.

Possession

Innumerable cases of sex murder reveal that the practice is addictive. The stranglers' second victim, Judy Miller, could have been raped and then just thrown out – the 15 year-old would have had no method of retaliation. But the murder of Yolanda Washington had made Bianchi and Buono feel that killing was the ultimate act of possession.

From then on, they revelled in murder. Prostitutes proved to be the least satisfactory victims. 'Respectable' girls, like Kristina Weckler, Lauren Wagner and Cindy Hudspeth, induced a far stronger sense of possession. So did children like Dollie Cepeda and Sonja Johnson, the schoolgirls they raped and murdered.

The partnership might have continued indefinitely had it not been for Buono's increasing dislike and distrust of his cousin. For Bianchi, the publicity aroused by the killings was almost as enjoyable as the crimes themselves. He revelled in the thought that he was in the spotlight.

Killing for Kudos

Buono, older and less psychologically unstable, regarded his cousin's attitude as both juvenile and dangerous. For him, Bianchi's departure for Bellingham was a relief. For Bianchi, it was a rejection, and he longed to prove his own enterprise and ruthlessness.

To kill not merely one but two girls struck him as a challenge, a way of proving that he had achieved the status of master criminal in his own right.

Chapter 5

DENNIS NILSEN

THE MUSWELL HILL MURDERER

Britain's most infamous mass murderer was a shy, retiring civil servant who lived a quiet life in a North London suburb. What made him commit such appalling crimes?

The drains at 23 Cranley Gardens had been blocked for five days when Dyno-rod sent a member of staff, Michael Cattran, to investigate. He arrived at the house in Muswell Hill, a northern suburb of London, at 6.15 p.m. on Tuesday, 8 February 1983. Jim Allcock, one of the tenants of the house let him in. Cattran quickly determined that the problem was outside the house, so he and Allcock walked round to the side and removed the manhole cover that led to the sewers. There was a 12ft drop with iron rungs down the side. Allcock shone a torch while Cattran climbed down.

At the bottom he found a thick glutinous 'porridge' made up of about 40 pieces of a greyish-white substance. The smell was nauseating. As he moved about, more fell out of the pipe that came from the house. Cattran told the tenants that the drains would have to be examined again in daylight. When he called his boss he told him he thought the substance might be human flesh.

At 9.15 the next morning, Cattran returned to the house with his manager and went straight to the manhole. To his astonishment the 'porridge' had totally disappeared. He knew that no amount of rainfall could have dislodged it, and he also noticed that the crack in the manhole cover was pointing in a different direction.

Cattran placed his hand inside a pipe and pulled out some pieces of meat and four small bones. Fiona Bridges, another tenant, told the men that she and Jim Allcock had heard footsteps in the night and suspected the man in the attic flat had been to the manhole. They decided to call the police.

Detective Chief Inspector Peter Jay arrived at 11.00 a.m. He immediately took the flesh and bones to Hornsey Mortuary for an opinion, then to Charing Cross Hospital to be examined by David Bowen, Professor of Forensic Medicine at the University of London and a consultant pathologist. Bowen confirmed that the flesh was human tissue, probably from the neck, and that the bones were from a man's hand.

Peter Jay soon found out that the occupier of the attic flat was Dennis Andrew Nilsen, an executive officer at the Jobcentre in Kentish Town. He lived in the flat alone with a mongrel bitch called Bleep and rarely spoke to the other tenants.

Nilsen had left for work at 8.30 that morning, after taking Bleep for a walk. Jay returned to the house with Detective Inspector McCusker and Detective Constable Butler, and waited for Nilsen to return home.

Wardrobe hiding place

At 5.40 p.m. that day, Dennis Nilsen walked up to the house. Peter Jay introduced himself, saying he had come about the drains. Nilsen said it was odd the police should be interested in drains and asked Jay if the other two men were health inspectors. Jay said they were police inspectors.

All four men walked up to Nilsen's flat and went into the back room, where Jay revealed that the drains contained human remains. 'Good grief!' Nilsen exclaimed. 'How awful!' DCI Jay told him to stop messing about and asked, 'Where's the rest of the body?'

There was a short pause before Nilsen answered. 'In two plastic bags in the wardrobe next door. I'll show you.' In the front room Nilsen pointed out the wardrobe, offering his keys. The overpowering smell was confirmation enough. Jay declined to open the cupboard just yet, but asked Nilsen if there was anything else. 'It's a long story,' he replied. 'It goes back a long time. I'll tell you everything. I want to get it off my chest, not here but at the police station.'

Peter Jay cautioned Nilsen and arrested him on suspicion of murder. Who exactly had been murdered, nobody knew.

Jay and McCusker took Nilsen by car to Hornsey Police Station. McCusker sat next to him in the back of the car. Both policemen had a suspicion troubling them, which McCusker was the first to voice. 'Are we talking about one body or two?' he asked.

'Fifteen or sixteen,' said Nilsen, 'since 1978.'

In the charge room at Hornsey, Jay was blunt. 'Let's get this straight,' he said. 'Are you telling us that since 1978 you have killed 16 people?'

'Yes,' replied Nilsen. 'Three at Cranley Gardens and about 13 at my previous address, 195 Melrose Avenue, Cricklewood.' He showed no emotion as he spoke.

That evening, Detective Superintendant Chambers accompanied Peter Jay and Professor Bowen to Nilsen's flat, where they opened the wardrobe and removed two large black plastic bags. They took these to Hornsey Mortuary, where Bowen opened them and conducted an examination of the contents.

In one bag he found four smaller shopping-bags. The first held the left side of a man's chest, including the arm. The second bag contained the right side of a chest and arm, the third a torso with no arms, legs or head, and the fourth a mixture of human offal. The bags had evidently been closed for some time, and the stench they released was scarcely bearable.

In the second black bag, Bowen discovered two heads, and another torso, with arms attached but hands missing. One head had the flesh boiled away, the other retained much of the flesh and some of the hair at the back, though the front hair and the lips had gone. It had recently been subjected to 'moist heat'. In fact, though the police were not yet to know, Nilsen had severed the head from the body only four days earlier and simmered it in a pot on the kitchen stove.

Identification

The head had belonged to Stephen Sinclair, a young drug-addict and social outcast whom Nilsen had met on 26 January 1983 and killed that same evening. Nilsen identified his victim in the first minutes of an interview with the police, which was to last a total of 30 hours spread over the coming days. He told them the flat contained the remains of three men. The second he called John the Guardsman, and the third he gave no name at all.

Nilsen suggested the police should look inside a tea-chest in the corner of his front room, and under a drawer in the bathroom. The bathroom contained Sinclair's legs and pelvis. In the tea-chest was another torso, a skull, bones, and mothballs and air-fresheners. It was now possible for the police to commence the grim task of assembling pieces of Stephen Sinclair on the mortuary floor.

On 11 February, Nilsen went with Jay and Chambers to 195 Melrose Avenue. He pointed out an area of the garden where they might find human remains. He had lived in the ground floor flat from 1976 to 1981, and during his final three years there, he said he had murdered about 12 or 13 men.

Sifting for evidence

The corpses had been cut into pieces and burnt on huge bonfires. A team of special police investigators sealed off the garden and began the laborious task of sifting through the earth for clues to the existence of people who had apparently disappeared without trace.

They found plenty of human ash and enough fragments of bone to enable forensic scientists to declare that at least eight people, probably more, had been laid to rest in the topsoil of a London garden. The police were entirely dependent on Nilsen's keen desire to co-operate, if they were to charge him before the statutory 48 hours had elapsed.

Sinclair was identified by fingerprints – since his prints were already on file for petty offences. It was for his murder that Nilsen was initially charged at 5.40 p.m. on 11 February, having agreed to be represented by a solicitor.

Ronald Moss agreed to take Nilsen as a client. The defendant appeared before magistrates at Highgate the following morning and was remanded in police custody for three days.

As the questioning continued, Nilsen indicated that he could not identify most of his victims. They were props to his fantasies rather than people, and he was not interested in who they were or where they came from.

There was one story in particular that made Moss and the police officers feel quite ill. Nilsen had strangled a young man three times, yet still his frail body clung to life. He then dragged him into the bathroom, plunged him into the bath, full to overflowing, and held him under water. The man had pushed himself up and pleaded for mercy, but Nilsen pushed him down again. He took the body back into the bedroom and lit himself a cigarette. Bleep his dog, began to lick the young man's legs, and Nilsen realized that the tiniest thread of life still protected him.

The young man could have been finally despatched in seconds, but instead Nilsen rubbed his legs to increase his circulation. He covered him with blankets, and effectively brought him back to life over the next day and a half.

The police were doubtful whether such a story could have any truth at all, but they were able to track the man down. His name was Carl Stottor. Without revealing why, the police asked Stottor to remember an incident two years before when he met Dennis Nilsen in a pub in Camden Town. Stottor told a story that entirely corroborated the one they had heard from Nilsen himself.

Nilsen's relentless account gave the police enough evidence to identify several victims. He was eventually charged on six counts of murder and three of attempted murder, and committed for trial. Ronald Moss, his solicitor, asked him one question as he went on remand to Brixton Prison, 'Why?'

Nilsen's reply was disarming. 'I am hoping you will tell me that,' he said. This sort of reply was to be typical of Nilsen. At times throughout the investigation and subsequent trial he appeared puzzled by his own actions over the years.

A FATAL OBSESSION

Dennis Nilsen woke up on New Year's Day 1979 to find the Irish teenager he had met the night before lying fast asleep beside him in bed.

They had met in a pub and then returned to Melrose Avenue where they had seen in the New Year together, drinking until they were insensible. After climbing into bed they fell asleep. No sex had taken place. Nilsen was afraid that when the boy woke up he would leave him, and he wanted him to stay. The boy's clothes were on the floor with Nilsen's own tie. He saw the tie and knew what he must do.

Straddling himself across the boy in bed, he placed the tie around his neck and pulled hard. Immediately the boy came to life and an almighty struggle ensued, as they rolled on to the floor and Nilsen pulled tighter. After about a minute the boy's body went limp but still breathed fitfully. Nilsen went to the kitchen and filled a bucket with water. He held the boy's head in the bucket until he drowned.

A strange night

Nilsen ran a bath and carried the dead body into the bathroom to be cleaned. He spent a long time drying it, to ensure it was spotless, and then dressed the body in fresh underpants and socks. For a while he lay in bed holding the corpse, then he placed it on the floor and he went to sleep.

The next day he wanted to put the body under the floorboards. but rigor mortis had set in and it got stuck. So he pulled it out again and decided to wait until the limbs could be worked loose after rigor mortis had lost its grip. He took the dog for a walk and went to work.

When the corpse could safely be managed, Nilsen undressed it again, cleaned it, masturbated beside it, and admired it. He expected to be arrested at any moment and was amazed when no one came to the door. The person whose life he had taken was, it seemed, not missed by anyone.

The experience, though it satisfied the now dominant needs of his fantasy, also frightened him, and he was determined it should not happen again. He decided to give up drinking. After a week living with the corpse, Nilsen put it under the floorboards. The body remained there for almost eight months.

Nearly a year elapsed before the second crime occurred, and the victim was to be the only one whose disappearance was widely reported in the press. Kenneth Ockendon was a Canadian tourist on a visit to England to look up family relations. He stayed in a cheap hotel near King's Cross station.

On 3 December 1979, he met Nilsen in a pub in Soho and they fell into chatty conversation, each buying a round of drinks. As Nilsen had leave from work that afternoon, they went on a tour of the sights of London, taking photographs. Ockendon agreed to go back to Nilsen's flat for something to eat. They stopped at an off-licence, sharing the bill, and returned to Melrose Avenue where they sat in front of the television eating ham, eggs and chips, and drinking rum, whiskey and beer.

Music and rum

As the evening wore on. Nilsen became uncomfortably aware that Ockendon would be leaving, and would go back to Canada soon. His feelings of imminent desertion were similar to those he had felt when he had killed the Irish boy. He knew he was going to murder Ken Ockendon in order to keep him.

It was late at night and they had both drunk great quantities of rum. Ockendon was listening to music through earphones. Nilsen does not recall putting the flex of the earphones around Ockendon's neck, but he remembers dragging him, struggling, across the floor, because he wanted to listen to the music as well.

The dog, Bleep, was barking frantically in the kitchen. Nilsen untangled the earphones from his friend's neck, put them on and listened to records as he poured another drink.

Later, he stripped the corpse naked and hoisted it over his shoulder, taking it to the bathroom to be cleaned and dried. Then he placed it next to him on the bed and went to sleep.

On waking the next morning, Nilsen placed the body in a cupboard and went off to work. When he arrived back at the flat that evening, he took the body out again and sat it on a kitchen chair while he dressed it in clean socks, underpants and vest. He took some photographs with a polaroid camera, placing the body in various positions, and then lay it next to him on the bed, as he settled down to watch television.

Without trace

Over the next two weeks, Nilsen would regularly sit in front of the television with Ockendon's body in an armchair next to him. Then he would strip off the socks, vest and underpants, wrap the body in curtains and place it under the floorboards for the night.

The disappearance of the Canadian tourist was a news item for several days. Nilsen thought there must have been several people who had seen them together in the pub, at Trafalgar Square, or at the off-licence. He waited for the knock on the door followed by questioning and, probably, arrest. But nothing happened.

House of no return

After this, the incidence of Nilsen's crimes became more frequent. Over the next 20 months that he was to remain the tenant of the ground floor at 195 Melrose Avenue, another ten men died, sometimes two within the same month. Murder had become a habit, a pleasure no longer tempered by inhibition or resisted through fear of discovery.

It seemed that people could walk through Nilsen's front door and never come out again without anyone noticing. Bodies accumulated on the ground floor while neighbours lived, unsuspecting, on the floors above.

There were far more casual acquaintances who went to Nilsen's flat and left unharmed, than there were those who died there. It was impossible to predict what might trigger a murderous impulse, although the encounter that might lead to one nearly always occurred in a pub, and especially one patronized by single, lonely, young homosexuals without a home.

Nilsen would engage someone in conversation, buy a few drinks, offer advice and good company. He had long experience of living in London and some of the men he met were wandering aimlessly in a strange city. They would gladly go back to Nilsen's flat for something to eat.

The method of killing was always strangulation, mostly with a tie. It was carried out when the victim was drunk and sleepy, or when he was actually asleep. Sometimes it would be completed by drowning.

Martyn Duffey was typical of the drifting youngster who is easily lured by a man like Dennis Nilsen. He came from Merseyside, had been in care and at school for the maladjusted. He had frequently run away from home and hitch-hiked to London, only to find there was nowhere for him to go once he got there. Social workers rescued him and paid his return fare.

Duffey had tried to settle down to a catering course, but after being questioned by police for evading a train fare, he relapsed into rebellion. He left home again, announcing his intention of living in New Brighton, Merseyside.

After turning up in London again, Duffey slept in stations. He met Dennis Nilsen shortly before his seventeenth birthday. Their shared experience of catering probably gave them something to talk about. Duffey went back with Nilsen, drank two cans of beer and crawled into bed.

In the pitch dark, Nilsen sat astride Martyn Duffey and strangled him. When he was limp, unconscious but still alive. Nilsen dragged him into the kitchen, filled the sink with water and held the boy's head under for about four minutes.

Nilsen describes in his own words what happened next. 'I then lifted him into my arms and took him into the room. I laid him on the floor and took off his socks, jeans, shirt and underpants. I carried him into the bathroom. I got into the bath myself this time and he lay in the water on top of me. I washed his body. Both of us dripping wet, I somehow managed to hoist this slipping burden on to my shoulders and took him to the room.'

89

Killer: Dennis Nilsen

Hiding places

'I sat him on the kitchen chair and dried us both. I put him on the bed but left the bedclothes off. He was still very warm. I talked to him and mentioned that his body was the youngest looking I have ever seen. I kissed him all over and held him close to me. I sat on his stomach and masturbated. I kept him temporarily in the cupboard. Two days later I found him bloated in the cupboard. He went straight under the floorboards.'

Billy Sutherland was 27 when he met Nilsen in a pub near Piccadilly Circus. He came from Edinburgh, was heavily tattooed and had served time in prison and at approved schools. He had a girlfriend and child in Scotland, but when in London he lived from day to day and was known to have slept with men for money.

Nevertheless, Sutherland always kept in touch with his mother, and it was she who alerted the police and the Salvation Army when contact with him abruptly ceased.

Sutherland was one of the few of Nilsen's victims to have been reported missing, but since there were 40 men on the missing persons list with the name Billy Sutherland, it is small wonder that his disappearance was never traced to Dennis Nilsen. He may have escaped his fate had he had somewhere to live, for he was an uninvited guest at Nilsen's home.

The two men spent the evening pub-crawling, ending up near Trafalgar Square. Then Nilsen got fed up with walking and said he was going home. He went to Leicester Square underground station and bought himself a ticket. Turning round, he found Sutherland standing behind him. Sutherland said he had nowhere to go, so Nilsen, reluctantly, according to his own account, bought another ticket and took him back to Melrose Avenue.

Sutherland died because he was a nuisance. Nilsen has no precise recollection of killing him, apart from remembering it was strangulation from the front, and that there was a dead body in the morning.

The death of Malcolm Barlow was even more casual. He was 24 years old and entirely alone. His parents were dead, there were no firm friends, and he had spent much of his life in care or in hospitals for the mentally handicapped.

Chance meeting

Barlow suffered from epilepsy and was in every way a difficult young man, disruptive and ungrateful. He turned up all over the country, living in hostels or with anyone who picked him up in the street.

On 17 September 1981, he was slouched on the pavement in Melrose Avenue, his back against a garden wall, when Nilsen left his flat a few doors away on his way to work. As he passed the young man, he asked if he was all right. Barlow said it was the pills he was taking and his legs had given way.

Nilsen told Barlow that he should be in hospital and, supporting him, took him back to the flat and made a cup of coffee. Leaving him there to watch the dog, Nilsen went to a telephone kiosk and called for an ambulance. It arrived within ten minutes and took Barlow off to Park Royal Hospital.

Barlow was released from hospital the following day and signed on at the local DHSS Office. Then he made his way back to Melrose Avenue and sat on the doorstep waiting for Nilsen to return from work. When Nilsen saw him, he expressed surprise. 'You're supposed to be in hospital,' he said. When Barlow said that he was all right now, Nilsen told him, 'You'd better come in.'

Alcohol and pills

Nilsen cooked a meal for Barlow and sat with him to watch television. Nilsen poured himself a drink. Barlow asked to have one as well, but Nilsen said he should not mix alcohol with pills. Barlow insisted that one or two little drinks would do him no harm, so Nilsen relented. 'Be it on your own head,' he said. Barlow had two rum and cokes, and fell into a deep sleep on the sofa.

After about an hour Nilsen tried to rouse him, slapping his face, but he was too comatose to move. Nilsen thought he would have to call an ambulance again, but he could not be bothered. He strangled Barlow because he was in the way, then carried on drinking until he was ready for bed.

In the morning, not being in the mood to prise up the floorboards where six corpses already lay, he stuffed the body under the kitchen sink and went off to work at the Jobcentre. Barlow was the last person to die at Melrose Avenue. 'I'm sorry that he managed to find me again,' wrote his murderer.

Several other victims who preceded Malcolm Barlow have never been identified. There was a long-haired hippy, an emaciated young man, and a skinhead with the words CUT HERE tattooed around his neck.

The death of one other nameless victim in 1981 is recalled by Nilsen in stark detail. 'I was squeezing his neck and remember wanting to see more clearly what he looked like. I felt no struggling ... I got on the chair and pulled his warm, limp, naked body in my arms. His head, arms and legs hung limply and he looked asleep.

'I could feel his warmth against my skin. I began to have an erection and my heart began to beat fast ... I tucked the body into bed and lay beside him naked on top of the bedclothes ... Getting up in the morning I put him sitting naked in the cupboard and went to work.

Killer: Dennis Nilsen

Cynical remarks

'I never thought of him again at work until I came home that evening. I got dressed into my jeans, ate, and turned on the TV. I opened the cupboard and lifted the body. I cleaned him up. I dressed him and sat him in front of the TV. I took his hand and talked to him, mixing my comments for the day with cynical remarks about the TV programmes ... I remember being thrilled that I had full control and ownership of this beautiful body ...

'I was fascinated by the mystery of death. I whispered to him because I believed he was still really in there ... I would hold him close often, and think that he had never been so appreciated in his life before ... After a week I stuck him under the floor.'

FINDING TIME, FINDING SPACE

Sharing a flat with several dead bodies did not bother Nilsen. It only became a problem when there was no space left for a fresh corpse. His first victim was burnt on a bonfire in the garden at Melrose Avenue, after seven and a half months under the floor.

By the end of 1980, he had accumulated another six bodies. Some lay under the floorboards and others had been dissected and stuffed into suit-cases, which he kept in the garden shed. Nilsen prised open the floorboards, laid the bodies out on the kitchen floor and, after a couple of stiff drinks, began the task of cutting up the corpses and placing the parts into carrier bags.

The internal organs were the easiest to dispose of. Nilsen poured them on to the ground between two fences at the side of the garden and within a couple of days they had disappeared – eaten by flies, rats and birds.

At the beginning of December 1980, Nilsen made an enormous bonfire and placed the various parts of corpses, wrapped in pieces of carpet, in the middle of it. An old car tyre was placed on the top to disguise the smell of burning flesh. The fire burned all day with Nilsen occasionally throwing on extra wood. Local children gathered round to watch the mass cremation.

Nilsen was to have one more bonfire at Melrose Avenue before leaving for his new flat, and a new life, at 23 Cranley Gardens at the end of 1981. He thought the move augured well for the future, as the flat was in the attic of a house. He could hardly continue killing people if there were no floor-boards to place them beneath, nor any garden to burn them in.

No strings attached

Shortly after the move Nilsen rescued a young man who was about to be picked up by the police in London's West End. He took him home, fed him and gave him a bed for the night – and saw him off again in the morning. He said he felt 'elated' that nothing had gone wrong, and indeed entertained several casual encounters before resuming his murderous career.

The first to die at Cranley Gardens was John Howlett, whom Nilsen refered to as John the Guardsman, a man he had met once before and who walked up to him in a pub to reintroduce himself. Nilsen strangled him with an upholstery strap, but Howlett put up such a fight that the murder took a very long time, and had to be completed by drowning.

Nilsen went to bed utterly exhausted, and admitted that he had thought Howlett might get the better of him. 'For a week afterwards, I had his finger marks on my neck.'

The omelette man

Graham Allen died as he was eating an omelette cooked by Nilsen, who had no recollection of having killed him, but assumed he must have.

Stephen Sinclair was the final victim, whose body Nilsen was busily dissecting the weekend before his arrest, though the flesh that blocked the drains of the house was most likely Graham Allen's.

Sinclair was another drifter – a punk, a drug-addict, a would-be suicide and a petty criminal. He toured the streets of London looking for the chance to find enough to survive through another day. Nilsen met him on the evening of 26 January 1983.

Dennis Nilsen felt sorry for Sinclair so he bought him a McDonald's hamburger and took him home. The account he wrote of Sinclair's death is the most vivid and upsetting, for it was the one of most recent memory.

The last victim

Sinclair was slumped in a chair, stupefied by drink and drugs. Nilsen fetched a piece of string from the kitchen, but it was not long enough, so he hunted for his last remaining tie and fastened it to the string. He told Bleep to go into the other room. 'Looking back I think she knew what was about to happen,' he wrote. 'Even she had became resigned to it.

'I was relaxed. I never contemplated morality. This was something which I had to do ... I thought to myself, all that potential, all that beauty, and all that pain that is his life. I have to stop him. It will soon be over ... I did not feel bad. I did not feel evil.

'I walked over to him. I removed the scarf. I picked up one of his wrists and let go. His limp arm flopped back on to his lap. I opened one of his eyes and there was no reflex. He was deeply unconscious. I took the ligature and put it around his neck. I knelt by the side of the chair and faced the wall. I took each loose end of the ligature and pulled it tight.

'He stopped breathing. His hands slowly reached for his neck as I held my grip. His legs stretched out in front of him. I held him there for a couple of minutes. He was limp and stayed that way. I released my hold and removed the string and tie. He had stopped breathing. I spoke to him. "Stephen, that didn't hurt at all. Nothing can touch you now." I ran my fingers through his bleached blond hair. His face looked peaceful. He was dead.'

Two weeks later, the police found Sinclair's dismembered body in Nilsen's flat.

SURVIVING EVIDENCE

Nilsen was remanded in custody and sent to Brixton Prison, south London. He was a Category A maximum security prisoner, which meant he had to spend almost 24 hours a day confined to his cell with only half an hour for supervised exercise. He resented this status. In his view, he had co-operated with the police and should, therefore, be given good treatment.

He was given 56 days' punishment for assaulting prison officers when his slop bucket had not been emptied. At times he fell into deep depression, but his friendship with another inmate, David Martin, boosted his morale and helped him pass the days and months that he waited on remand.

In the dock

The trial of Dennis Andrew Nilsen on six charges of murder and two charges of attempted murder opened at No. 1 Court in the Old Bailey, on 24 October 1983, before Mr Justice Croom-Johnson. There was no dispute that Nilsen had killed. What was being questioned at the trial was Nilsen's state of mind during the murders.

Allan Green, prosecuting counsel, proposed that Nilsen had killed with full awareness and deliberation, and was, therefore, guilty of murder. Ivan Lawrence, for the defence, said that Nilsen suffered from such abnormality of mind as to substantially reduce his responsibilty for his acts, and should, therefore, be guilty only of manslaughter.

Murder or manslaughter?

Prosecution and defence both agreed that Nilsen had an abnormality of mind. But whereas the defence affirmed that it was 'substantial' and inter- fered with his responsibility, the prosecution maintained that it was not sub- stantial enough to so interfere. In the end, the jury had to decide what weight to give to the word 'substantial', as required by the Homicide Act 1957.

94

Originally, Nilsen had intended to spare them all this by pleading guilty. The trial might then have been finished in a day. The police evidence, which was to make members of the jury look aghast and disbelieving, need never have been heard, and, the relatives of Nilsen's victims would have been spared the detailed knowledge of exactly how their sons and brothers had died.

When Nilsen changed his solicitor he was also advised to change his plea. After considering the evidence, Mr Ralph Haeems felt that there was a case for 'diminished responsibility', due to a mental disorder in Nilsen. This meant that all the evidence as to Nilsen's state of mind had to be heard.

Sparing the jury

Mr Allan Green gave some relief to the jury by promising them that they would not be shown police photographs taken inside the flat in Cranley Gardens after Nilsen's arrest, and at Hornsey Mortuary. Green also conceded in advance that he would not claim the murders were homosexual – that the men had died because they rejected sexual advances from the defendant. It was coincidental that some victims had met their killer in pubs frequented by homosexuals.

Mr Green made much of Nilsen's confession, taking the jury through all 15 killings and pausing over the death of John the Guardsman, which he described as 'chilling'. He also made sure the jury felt a proper sense of horror at the notion of dustmen carrying away parts of people in the household rubbish.

The witnesses

Three witnesses were called to give evidence that Nilsen had tried to kill them. They were Douglas Stewart who had reported Nilsen's attack on him to police, Paul Nobbs and Carl Stottor. Stewart's evidence was dispensed with fairly quickly, but when Paul Nobbs went into the box the atmosphere changed dramatically.

Here was a young university student, nervous but precise, who explained how he had been rescued by Nilsen from the unwanted attentions of another man, how they had gone to Foyles' bookshop together and then back to Cranley Gardens.

A friendly companion

Under questioning, Nobbs revealed that it was he who had approached Nilsen and not the other way around, hence Nilsen could not be be depicted as a 'stalker'. Nilsen was genuinely a friendly and helpful companion. He did not force him to drink, nor prevent him from twice telephoning his mother to say where he was. He had not pestered him for sex and was not violent.

Nobbs slept at Cranley Gardens and had woken up at 2 o'clock in the morning with a splitting headache. He went back to sleep and woke again at 6 a.m. He then saw himself in the mirror. His eyes were completely bloodshot, with no white visible. There was a red mark around his neck and he felt sore and sick. Nilsen told him that he looked awful and that he should go to a doctor. They parted as friends.

Later, Paul Nobbs was told at the hospital that he had been strangled. He had to assume that his attacker was Nilsen, but he did not report the matter to the police. He was afraid that he would not be believed, and that the police would be unsympathetic to what they would see as a homosexual squabble.

Giving evidence in a quiet, tentative voice. Nobbs made it clear that he had neither said nor done anything to provoke an attack, and that Nilsen's behaviour the next day gave no indication that anything untoward had happened. He agreed under questioning, that the attack must have occurred before 2.00 a.m and yet he had been left to sleep unmolested for another four hours, when he might easily have been despatched without mercy.

Murderous impulses

The defence used Nobbs' testimony to illustrate how Nilsen could behave perfectly normally one minute and yet be possessed of murderous impulses the next. In other words, Nilsen was not sane.

The next witness, Carl Stottor, told an incredible story in an almost inaudible voice, which pointed to the same conclusion – that Nilsen was unpredictable.

Stottor explained how he had been feeling miserable and suicidal over a broken love affair when he met Nilsen in a pub in Camden Town. Nilsen had comforted him, tried to cheer him up, and told him that he must not think of suicide at his age. 'He seemed a very nice person, very kind, talking to me when I was depressed,' Carl Stottor had declared.

They went home to Cranley Gardens, holding hands in the taxi by way of comfort rather than any sexual feelings – Nilsen had promised not to touch him. Stottor went to bed. When asked what he could remember of events that night, he told his nightmarish tale. 'I woke up feeling something round my neck. My head was hurting and I couldn't breathe properly and I wondered what it was.'

Losing consciousness

'I felt his hand pulling at the zip at the back of my neck. He was saying in a sort of whispered shouting voice, "Stay still, stay still." I thought perhaps he was trying to help me out of the sleeping bag because I thought I had got caught up in the zip, which he had warned me about. Then I passed out.'

Stottor paused, struggling to control emotion as the pain of recollection in such a public place affected him. The court was so quiet one might have heard an ant walking. The judge allowed him to compose himself, and he continued. 'The pressure was increasing. My head was hurting and I couldn't breathe. I remember vaguely hearing water running. I remember vaguely being carried and then I felt very cold. I knew I was in the water and he was trying to drown me. He kept pushing me into the water.

'The third time I came up I said, "No more, please, no more," and he pushed me under again. I just thought I was dying. I thought this man was killing me and I was dying. I thought, "You are drowning. This is what it feels like to die." I felt very relaxed and I passed out. I couldn't fight any more.'

Canine saviour

Carl Stottor passed in and out of consciousness. He was amazed to feel the dog licking his face as he lay on the couch, and Nilsen rubbing him to make him warm. There was an ugly mark around his neck and broken blood vessels all over his face. Nilsen walked him to the underground station and wished him luck.

This evidence demonstrated again that Nilsen behaved normally both before and after the attack, and that he 'saved' Carl Stottor, whom he could easily have killed as he lay exhausted after the struggle.

Counsel for the defence was establishing that Nilsen was at best insane, at worst diabolically possessed and not in control of his own actions. Was the defendant calm and concerned after the event, 'as though he was unaware he had done anything to harm you?' asked Mr Lawrence.

'Yes,' replied Stottor.

'How odd that was,' mused the QC as he sat down.

Detective Chief Inspector Jay gave evidence of Nilsen's behaviour during his confession, which he said was relaxed, co-operative and matter-of-fact. He agreed that it was very unusual for a man accused of such heinous crimes to be so forthcoming in giving information to his accusers. He also admitted that there were moments of humour, which the police found a necessary respite, to the catalogue of horror that unfolded before them. One example was when a constable told him to throw his cigarette end down the lavatory. 'The last time I did that,' Nilsen said, 'I got arrested.'

Killer: Dennis Nilsen

Nilsen's confession

Detective Chief Superintendent Chambers then spent the whole of one afternoon and the following morning reading out the transcript of Nilsen's confession at Hornsey Police Station. The vivid description of decapitations, boilings and dissections – told in a voice unmodulated by any recognition of the content of what it was uttering – brought a chill to the courtroom.

One member of the jury looked as if she were going to be sick, another repeatedly sank his head into his hands. A woman looked down upon Nilsen in the dock with pure hatred pouring out of her eyes. It was the moment of Nilsen's most vulnerable nakedness, but he spent the time checking his copy of the transcript to make sure there were no mistakes.

BEHIND BARS

The mood in court changed dramatically when two psychiatrists were called by the defence to give their view of whether Nilsen was sane or insane. It was not the first time that antagonism and mutual distrust between lawyers and psychiatrists had erupted in a courtroom.

Ivan Lawrence, defence counsel, had reminded the jury that they must not give way to feelings of revulsion, but must seriously consider the point put before them: namely that Dennis Nilsen was so abnormal mentally that he was incapable of forming the specific intention of murder and could not be held responsible for his acts.

Dr MacKeith said that Nilsen had difficulty experiencing any emotion apart from anger, and that he tended to attribute to others certain feelings without checking whether or not they were real. Nilsen, he said, showed many signs of maladaptive behaviour, and their combination in one man was lethal. He did not treat people as people, but as components of his fantasy. This he called 'depersonalization.'

Cross-examining, Mr Green was not so gentle. He told MacKeith that he really should make up his mind what he thought, and proved to the satisfaction of many present that Nilsen was, contrary to what MacKeith implied, cunning, resourceful and intelligent. He mentioned in particular the murders of John the Guardsman and Malcolm Barlow. In the latter case, Nilsen had pondered for 20 minutes before deciding to kill Barlow, an unconscious epileptic who was in the way. MacKeith agreed that in this particular instance there was no evidence of 'depersonalization'.

'And yet,' Green said, 'you say his responsibility was diminished at the time? Oh come, doctor. Face up to my question.'

Tension in the court mounted. When defining a case, barristers and doctors tend to speak different languages and define experience in different terms. This invariably leads to confusion and frustration in both camps. It was the same with the next witness, Dr Gallwey, who went so far as to describe Nilsen's condition as 'Borderline Disorder'. The judge no doubt reflected the jury's bewilderment when he expressed impatience with this professional jargon.

Malice aforethought?

Dr Gallwey attempted to explain by suggesting that Nilsen combined paranoid and schizoid elements, which made it impossible for him to respond to people as individuals. They were objects to him, and they muddled his private world. It was also crucially important to recognize that Nilsen did not have normal feelings.

'I cannot see how he can be guilty of malice aforethought if he is entirely without feeling, since feeling is an integral part of a person's intent and motivation,' he said – only to be told by Mr Justice Croom-Johnson that he was trespassing on interpretation of law, which he should leave to others.

The point was an essential one, which came up again and again under cross-examination from Green. 'He knew exactly what he was doing,' Green would say with conviction.

'Leaving aside emotion, yes,' Gallwey retorted. 'But his emotional condition is vital.'

'You in no way dispute that he was intellectually aware of what was going on.'

'No.'

'He knew what he was doing.'

'I don't agree with that. The distinction between intellectual and emotional awareness is not a trivial matter. If his emotions were removed, then he would behave like a machine.'

'Did he know the nature and quality of his acts?'

'No. He knew the nature of the acts only, he did not know the quality of them.'

Prosecution witness

The case for the defence having been completed, allowance was made for the prosecution to bring forward a 'rebuttal' witness – that is a third psychiatrist who would offer a diagnosis different from the two called by the defence. Dr Bowden could find no evidence of abnormality of mind as defined by the 1957 Act. He suggested, in fact, that Nilsen simply wanted to kill people, and said he felt sympathy for him, but could make no excuses in psychiatric terms.

Interestingly, he was the only one of the three doctors to say he thought Nilsen had shown remorse, and had once stood before him with tears in his eyes. But on the central issue of responsibility, Dr Bowden was unmoveable. 'In my experience,' he said, 'the vast majority of people who kill have to regard their victims as objects otherwise they cannot kill them.'

Summing up

Dr Bowden's brutally clear commonsense struck a chord with the jury. On the other hand, his obstinate refusal under cross-examination to admit there was anything wrong with Dennis Nilsen struck them as flying in the face of the obvious. It was left to the judge to disentangle these conflicting strands.

The prosecution had insisted that the defendant knew exactly what he was doing; the defence had said he was capable of knowing what he was doing. Croom-Johnson took four hours to sum up.

He guided the jury through the intricacies of the law, and also introduced some questionable concepts of his own. 'There are evil people who do evil things,' he said. 'Committing murder is one of them.' Later he added, 'A mind can be evil without being abnormal.' The concept of evil has a place in moral philosphy, and has been debated by thoughtful men for centuries.

Doctors never address themselves to evil, as it is outside their scope. Lawyers are careful not to use the word too glibly. But in Nilsen's case, the judge determined it would help the jury form a decision if he used layman's terms.

On the matter of Nilsen's personality, the judge was similarly simplistic. 'There must be no excuses for Nilsen if he has moral defects,' he said. 'A nasty nature is not arrested or retarded development of mind.'

The judge was making clear to the jury that, in his opinion, Nilsen was evil and not insane. The jury should, therefore, find him guilty of murder.

The jury retired in the late morning of Thursday, 3 November 1983. In spite of Croom-Johnson's summing-up advice, they were unable to reach a decision that day, and spent the night at an hotel. On Friday, they were still unable to agree on Nilsen's state of mind at the time of each of the murders, so Mr Justice Croom-Johnson said he would allow a majority decision. At 4.25 p.m. on 4 November, after a trial lasting two weeks, the jury returned verdicts of guilty on the six counts of murder, by ten votes to two, and guilty on one count of attempted murder by ten votes to two. On the second count of attempted murder, that of the young Paul Nobbs, they returned a unanimous verdict of guilty.

The judge condemned Dennis Andrew Nilsen to life imprisonment, with the recommendation that it should mean no less than 25 years. Nilsen was led away from the dock in the knowledge that it was unlikely that he would ever be released.

CASE FILE: NILSEN, DENNIS ANDREW

BACKGROUND

On a bleak autumn day, in the small coastal town of Fraserburgh in the northeast of Scotland, Betty Whyte gave birth to her second child, Dennis Andrew Nilsen. It was 23 November 1945. The father, Olav Magnus Nilsen, was a Norwegian soldier who came to Scotland after the German invasion of Norway in 1940. He met Betty Whyte, a pretty local girl, outside a café and married her in 1942.

The marriage was not a success, and the Nilsens never set up home together. Betty continued to live with her parents, Andrew and Lily Whyte, in whose modest house her three children by Nilsen were raised. Dennis hardly saw his father, who rarely came to visit. A few years later the marriage ended with a divorce.

Dennis grew up with his mother, elder brother and younger sister, but the strongest influence was that of his stern, strict and loving grandparents. They were fisherfolk, from generations of sea-faring men. These families from the fishing villages of Aberdeenshire were fatalistic in their approach to the world; most had lost some member of the family at sea.

Mental problems

Families were also deeply in-bred. After centuries of marrying within the small community there was a frequent occurrence of mental instability. Some of Dennis Nilsen's ancestors on his mother's side suffered from mental problems, and there were instances of suicide.

Dennis Nilsen also inherited the proud radicalism of these people, their blunt, argumentative nature and their stubborn independence. Both his grandparents were pious. His grandmother would not cook on the Lord's Day, so all Sunday dinners had to be prepared the day before. She did not approve of the radio, or of any self-indulgent pleasure. Grandfather Andrew never drank alcohol and never went to the cinema – he regarded both as devilish plots sent to lure the soul off its proper course.

Lonely childhood

Dennis Nilsen spent his childhood surrounded by an atmosphere of religious fundamentalism. He was curiously withdrawn, sullen and untouchable. He sank into an intensely private world that nobody could penetrate, apart from his grandfather.

Andrew Whyte was Nilsen's hero. He would regale the little boy with tales of the ocean waves, carry him aloft on his shoulders for long walks along the sandy coast, and carry him home in his arms when he fell asleep. When grandfather came home from sea, the whole family knew he was coming home to Dennis.

Andrew had a heart attack at sea in 1951. His body was brought by train to Fraserburgh and from there to the family home, where he lay in a box on the dining-room table. Dennis was not told his grandfather was dead. He was invited to 'come and see Grandad', and at the age of six he had his first view of a corpse. From that moment the images of death and of love fused in his mind. He wanted to be with his grandfather. He wanted to be dead.

The boy withdrew even more into the secret world of his imagination. He had few friends and did not consider himself worthy of those that he had. As he grew into puberty he was aware of being attracted to other boys, and thought this marked him out still further as being different.

Strong feelings

He left school at 15 and went straight into the army, where he trained in the catering corps. He learnt how to use a carving-knife and the principles of neat dissection. Life in the army took him to the Middle East and Europe, always in catering, and he became an amusing and articulate companion, though never a close friend. There was one soldier he admired in particular. Nilsen would persuade him to pose for photographs in the fields, lying down as if he had just fallen in battle.

Nilsen left the army after 11 years, in disgust at the British Government's treatment of the Irish, and joined the police force instead. He fulfilled his duties well as a junior police officer and had appeared to enjoy it, but his private life was gradually disintegrating into unhealthy fantasy. His obsession with the idea of death assumed bizarre manifestations. He would pretend to be a corpse himself, lying in front of a mirror and taking elaborate steps to simulate death, smearing blue on his lips and making his eyes bloodshot and his skin white with talcum powder.

While the fantasy remained private, it was safe enough, but the inner pressures to make real the experience of death were growing.

Dedicated worker

After two years in the police force, Nilsen joined the Civil Service, where he interviewed applicants for work at the Jobcentre off Charing Cross Road in London's West End. His work was much admired, as he was always on the side of the employee and regarded the employer's position as inherently exploitative. He soon rose to prominence as a branch secretary of the civil service union; he picketed frequently and was deeply upset by the apparent apathy of his colleagues.

In the evenings, he would go alone to pubs in Soho and Camden Town where he might meet a man for sex or conversation, the latter being by far the more important. He was lonely and craved company. He wanted an audience for his increasingly radical political views and someone to share a drink with.

Nilsen did not make promotion easy, for he was argumentative and uncompromising, but eventually he was appointed an executive officer and moved to Kentish Town. Still his colleagues would not join with his passionate trade union principles. He was a meticulous worker and frequently on a day off he would turn up at the office with his dog. To his workmates he could be short tempered and woundingly sarcastic, but he was often docile, generous and kind. Everyone agreed, however, that he was secretive and erratic.

New companion

Nilsen yearned for the security of a lasting relationship. One evening in 1975 he met a young man, David Gallichan, outside a pub and the next day they decided to set up home together. The pair moved into the garden flat of 195 Melrose Avenue, and with a dog and a cat, formed some semblance of a family. The relationship lasted two years.

PSYCHOLOGICAL PROFILE

If the law ever changes its attitudes to a murderer's mental state, the Nilsen case may well be remembered as a turning point. The eminent psychiatrist Dr Anthony Storr, among many other experts, believes that people of his profession should not be called as witnesses for the prosecution or defence. He proposes that the Court should simply find the defendant guilty or not guilty; then, if the verdict is 'guilty', psychiatrists would be used as independent assessors to guide the Court in its decision on what to do with him.

State of mind

In the case of Dennis Nilsen, there was never any doubt as to his guilt. He had confessed almost immediately when confronted by the police, talked freely, and even sketched his victims. But was he insane? The lengthy exchanges at the trial concerning 'mental disorder' and 'abnormality of mind' proved very little.

If anything, they merely showed that the legal system is ill-equipped to define a murderer's state of mind when the system depends on adversarial tactics between defence and prosecution. It is comparatively easy for any competent counsel to make a fool of an expert medical witness. Dr Bowden, the witness called for the prosecution, fared no better than Doctors MacKeith and Gallwey for the defence.

It is convenient to believe that any person capable of committing Nilsen's crimes is obviously insane. However, that view does not help in grasping what went on in his mind before, during and after the killings. To attempt to understand that, it is necessary to return to Nilsen's childhood, and in particular to the critical incident of his grandfather's death.

By the age of six, the only truly loving relationship that Nilsen had formed was with his grandfather. At a formative stage of his mental development the young Dennis was confronted with his beloved grandad's body. It is little wonder that love and death became inextricably linked in Nilsen's mind from that moment on.

A man apart

It is common for young people with homosexual tendencies to believe that they are 'the only one'. In the small, tight-knit community from which he came, it would have been almost impossible for Nilsen to articulate his feelings, or his worries about them. In the Army, where homosexuality is a crime, he would have been driven still further from expressing his complete personality. During his time in the civil service, his militant trade union principles again set him apart from his workmates.

The influence of alcohol must also be taken into account. The traditional refuge of the lonely and inarticulate, alcohol not only loosened Nilsen's tongue, it also made him uninhibited enough to kill, once the pattern of his mind had made murder a probability.

Love had fused with death in Nilsen's mind. He was incapable of forming relationships. He was drinking heavily. Is this enough to make a man a killer? Nilsen believed that the perfect relationship was only possible in death. The only model he had for a perfect relationship was the brief and far-off adoration for his grandfather, and that had ended – shockingly for Nilsen – in death. By the time he had given up even trying to relate to society in an ordinary fashion, death was equated with love, not only in his mind but also in actuality.

Dennis Nilsen killed not for the conventional motives of the murderer – money, sex, ambition. Quite literally, Nilsen had killed for company.

Chapter 6

DAVID BERKOWITZ
SON OF SAM

I n July 1976 the first of a series of murders was committed that would bring terror to the streets of New York City. But it took police nine months to find enough evidence to connect the crimes to a single serial killer who preyed on young women.

The 13-storey red building at One Police Plaza is New York's equivalent to London's New Scotland Yard. The crowd of crime reporters that gathered in its press conference room on the afternoon of 10 March 1977, knew there was something important in the air, but few of them had any idea what it might be. No one suspected that the Police Commissioner was about to explode a bombshell that would cause the greatest wave of mass hysteria in the history of New York City.

Commissioner Mike Codd's voice sounded calm as he read his prepared statement. It began with the announcement that ballistics experts had discovered a positive link between the murders of a girl called Donna Lauria, shot to death on 29 July 1976, and Virginia Voskerichian, shot two days before the conference.

Killer on the loose

He went on to say that the same .44 calibre revolver, a Charter Arms Bulldog, had been identified as the weapon used in three other shootings in the Bronx and Queens districts of New York.

As the commissioner sat down, cameras flashed amid the uproar as journalists pressed for more information. One of the first reporters to make himself heard wanted to know if the police were seeking an individual or several individuals. The reply was that they were seeking a white male, 25 to 30 years-old, 6ft tall, medium build, with dark hair.

The following day, headline writers had made sure that everyone in New York had heard about the '.44 killer'.

The murders had started on a hot midsummer night the previous year. On 29 July 1976, two young girls, 18 year-old Donna Lauria, and 19 year-old Jody Valente, were sitting in Jody's car at 1 a.m. outside Donna's home. They were chatting about boyfriends.

A few minutes later, Donna said goodnight to Jody, and opened the passenger door to get out. As she did so, she noticed a young man standing on the curb a few feet away. Before the door was fully open, he had reached into a brown paper bag, pulled out a gun, and dropped into a crouching position. 'What does this guy want?' Donna said, puzzled rather than alarmed. Then a bullet struck her in the right side of the neck.

First victim

The passenger window shattered. As Donna raised her hand to protect her face, another bullet entered her elbow and travelled down her forearm. Donna fell out of the car and hit the pavement. Jody screamed as a bullet tore into her thigh, and fell forward on to the horn, which began to blare loudly.

Mike Lauria, Donna's father, was already on his way downstairs, taking Donna's poodle for a walk, when he heard the shots. He ran the rest of the way, and found Jody leaning against the car, her hand still on the horn, screaming, 'We were shot!' Meanwhile his wife, in a state of shock, stood by the kitchen window, too stunned to move.

Mike Lauria accompanied his daughter to the hospital in the ambulance, begging her not to die. But she was already dead.

Jody was taken to the hospital, suffering from hysteria. She was nevertheless able to give the police a clear description of the killer, a clean-shaven white male with curly dark hair, about 30 years-old. She was certain she had never seen him before, and equally certain – since she knew Donna well – that he was not some rejected boyfriend.

Neighbours had noticed a yellow car parked a few spaces behind Jody's car, but it had gone by the time the police arrived.

Contract killing

The North Bronx, where the Laurias lived, is a predominantly Italian area, and the immediate suspicion of the police who investigated the murder was that it was connected with the Mafia. It sounded like a contract killing that had gone wrong, a case of mistaken identity. The bullets revealed that the murder weapon was a .44 Bulldog revolver, a five-round handgun whose sole purpose is killing people. At close quarters it has the power to blow a large hole in a door, but it has a powerful recoil, and at more than half a dozen yards, tends to be wildy inaccurate.

The next shooting took place so far away from the North Bronx that nobody suspected that there might be a connection. While the Bronx has a reputation for toughness, the borough of Queens, on the other side of the East River, is the bastion of New York's middle class. It was 12 weeks after the murder of Donna Lauria, that a young couple left a bar in the Flushing area of Queens, and drove to a quiet spot where they could be alone. The car belonged to 18 year-old Rosemary Keenan, a student at Queens College. Her companion was Carl Denaro, a 20 year-old record salesman, who was about to join the Air Force, and who had been celebrating his last days as a civilian when he met Rosemary.

Carl had shoulder-length brown hair, and was sitting in the passenger seat – two factors that may have saved Rosemary Keenan's life. For the man who crept up on the red Volkswagen assumed that the person in the passenger seat was a girl. This time, the .44 calibre revolver was tucked into his belt. He pulled it out and fired five times through the passenger window. The recoil of the gun made his aim inaccurate and only one bullet ploughed through the back of Carl Denaro's skull as he leaned forward to avoid the flying glass.

Shattered career

In spite of the wound, Carl Denaro had been lucky. The bullet had not entered the brain but had blown away a portion of his skull. In hospital, this was replaced by a metal plate, and he recovered after two months of treatment. But his dreams of a career in the Air Force were at an end.

The next shooting again occurred in Queens. Around midnight on 27 November 1976, two schoolgirls, 18 year-old Joanne Lomino and her 16 year-old friend Donna DeMasi sat on the steps of the front porch of Joanne's home on 262nd Street. The girls decided to call it a night. But as Joanne stood up and reached into her bag for her house keys, the girls' attention was caught by a man walking on the opposite side of their road.

Suspicious action

What startled them, as they would later testify, was the stranger's sudden change of direction when he spotted them in front of the house. After crossing the corner of the street, he headed straight toward Joanne and Donna. Both stood their ground, thinking that he was coming to seek directions. 'Say can you tell me how to get to,' he said, then pulled a gun from his waistband and without a word began firing at the girls. Both turned towards the door, Joanne groping frantically for her key. The first bullet struck Joanne in the lower spine, the second went through the base of Donna's neck. The girls stumbled into the bushes, while the gunman fired the remaining three bullets – all of which missed. A neighbour saw the gunman running down 262nd Street, still clutching the gun in his left hand.

In Long Island Jewish Hospital, doctors discovered that Donna was not badly injured, it would take her three weeks to recover. Joanne was less fortunate, the bullet had shattered her spine, and she would spend the rest of her life in a wheelchair.

This time, investigating detectives considered the possibility that the attacker might be the same man who had killed Donna Lauria and injured Judy Valente. But it seemed unlikely, for both Joanne Lomino and Donna DeMasi described their assailant as having long, fair hair. The neighbour who had seen him fleeing said the same thing. Jody Valente, on the other hand, was quite certain that the Bronx gunman had curly black hair.

Terror in the night

On 29 January 1977, a young couple went to see the film *Rocky*, then went for a late night meal at the Wine Gallery in Austin Street, Queens. Just after midnight, they left the bar and strolled several blocks to their parked car. John Diel was 30 years-old and Christine Freund 26 years-old. They had been lovers for several years and they were about to announce their engagement. As they sat in their Pontiac Firebird, both were thinking of getting home, the temperature outside was below freezing and their breath had fogged up the windows. John kissed Christine, and then began to start the car. Without warning, the passenger window dissolved into fragments and a roar of gunfire filled the car. When it stopped, John reached over to Christine. She was slumped forward and bleeding. She died a few hours later in St John's Hospital of a bullet wound in the head.

Killings are linked

It was when ballistic examination established that the bullet that had killed Christine Freund had been fired from a .44 Bulldog revolver that police first linked the four shootings – including that of Carl Denaro. Yet the descriptions of the assailants differed so widely that no one was yet thinking in terms of a solitary madman.

That finally happened six weeks later, on 8 March 1977. A 19 year-old Armenian student, Virginia Voskerichian, was returning to her home in Exeter Street, Queens, after a day at Columbia University in Manhattan. It was 7.30 p.m. when she politely side-stepped to allow a young man to pass her. Instead, he raised a gun to her face. Virginia tried to protect herself with the books she was carrying, but the bullet tore through them and went into her upper lip, knocking out several teeth, then lodged itself in her skull.

A witness who saw the man running away said that he was about 5ft 8in and young – about 18 – and was wearing a ski balaclava. Virginia Voskerichian, whose body was now lying in some bushes at the side of the road, had died instantly.

The spot in which she had died – in Forest Hills – was not far from the place where Christine Freund had been shot six weeks earlier. On the day after the murder, ballistics experts discovered that the riflings on the bullet that had killed her were the same as the one that had been fired at Christine Freund.

Whether the descriptions of the gunman tallied or not, there could be no doubt that the same gun had been used to shoot seven people, and that the .44 killer was choosing his victims at random.

THE WHITE ENVELOPE

The announcement of a police task force – known as *Operation Omega* – to trap the murderer did little to restore public confidence. In fact, as tip-offs flooded into the police switchboards, the Omega group, under Deputy Inspector Timothy J. Dowd, found itself faced with the impossible task of pursuing around 300 investigations each day. The Omega team were aware that their chances of catching a lone killer in the streets of New York City were remote.

At the time the police announced the formation of the new task force, the man they were searching for was writing the police a letter. It was written in block capitals, and took two days to complete. Now all the killer needed was an opportunity to deliver it. There was always the postal service, of course, but that would have been an anticlimax.

On the evening of 16 April 1977, another young couple spent an evening at the cinema, then went on to a party. At 3 a.m. the following morning, their borrowed Mercury Montego was parked by a wire fence in the Bronx, not far from the place where the first victim, Donna Lauria, had been shot. Eighteen year-old Valentina Suriani was sitting on the knee of her boyfriend, 20 year-old Alexander Esau, with her legs stretched out over the passenger seat. Their long goodnight kiss was broken by the bullets that shattered the passenger window. The first two bullets went into Valentina's skull, killing her almost immediately. The next two went into the top of Alexander Esau's head as he tried to dive towards the passenger door. He would die within two hours.

One of the first policemen to arrive at the scene noticed a white envelope lying a few feet away from the car in the middle of the road. It had been placed where no one could miss it, and it was addressed to Captain Joe Borelli, Timothy Dowd's deputy.

Deadly promise

The letter made one thing clear – the .44 killer was insane or, at least, he wanted to be thought insane. He believed he was being ordered to kill by his father, Sam, who was a vampire. Despite the apparently lunatic ramblings of the letter, however, it was clear that although he professed to love the people of Queens, particularly the women, he intended to kill more of them.

Unfortunately, by the time the letter reached the fingerprint department, it had been handled by several policemen. And even when their fingerprints were eliminated, the investigators were no better off. The author of the letter had held it by the very tips of his fingers, so there was not enough of a print on the paper to identify the sender.

For the time being, the existence of the Borelli letter was kept a secret. A journalist named Jimmy Breslin was one of the few who was allowed to see it, and he dropped a few hints about it in his column in the *Daily News* – such as the murderer's habit of spelling 'women' so that it rhymed with 'demon'. This may explain why, on 30 May, the .44 killer posted a letter addressed to Breslin into a mailbox in Englewood, New Jersey. With an eye on its circulation, the *Daily News* withheld the text for six days, contenting itself with tantalizing hints and quotations. Finally, when the suspense threatened to evaporate, they printed the complete letter. It was something of an anticlimax, being as incoherent and as cryptic as the Borelli letter.

One page of the Breslin letter was withheld from publication at the request of the police. The reason for this was the reference to NCIC (National Crime Information Center), the existence of which the police did not want revealed. It was in this section of the letter that the author had written a list of bizarre names suggesting that they may help police investigation: the Wicked King Wicker, the Twenty-Two Disciples of Hell, and John 'Wheaties', who was described as a rapist and suffocator of young girls.

Looking for clues

It seemed that these names were an invention of the author's imagination, yet it was odd that the author had written the name 'Wheaties' in quotation marks as if it was the nickname of a real person. But the police drew a blank. The letter did little to provide them with a clue to the killer and if the mad ramblings in the letter were some kind of code, no one possessed the key to crack it.

At least the letter provided journalists with a nickname for the .44 killer. He became known as Son of Sam.

Three weeks after publication of the Breslin letter, a 17 year-old Bronx schoolgirl named Judy Placido – who had attended the same school as

Valentina Suriani, and been a mourner at her funeral – celebrated her graduation by spending the evening of 25 June at a discotheque called Elephas, in Queens. There she met a good-looking young man called Salvatore Lupo, a petrol station attendant. When Judy said it was time to go home, Salvatore put his arm round her shoulders.

It was as they were talking about Son of Sam that the nightmare became reality, and the side window of the car dissolved under the impact of the bullet. It struck Salvatore in the wrist, then went on to pass through the flesh of Judy's neck. The next bullet was aimed at her head but did not penetrate the skull. The next pierced her right shoulder. Salvatore, stunned and unnerved, flung open the car door and ran back towards the discotheque for help. But the shooting was over, the attacker had fled.

Like so many of the victims, Judy was unaware that she had been shot, and was amazed to see her reflection in a rear-view mirror with blood covering her face. She jumped out of the car and ran towards the lights of the disco. She collapsed before she had covered more than a few yards.

In hospital, Salvatore was treated for a shattered wrist and a wound made by flying glass in his leg. Judy Placido, incredibly, had survived without serious injury. Neither had a clear view of their assailant. But three blocks away, a witness saw a 'stocky white male' running away.

The .44 killer may have been bad for New York's discos and restaurants, but he was undoubtedly a godsend to newspaper owners, who sold out edition after edition on the day following the latest shooting. The papers also had cause for anticipation. The Breslin letter had contained the phrase 'Tell me Jim, what will you have for July twenty-ninth?' That was the date of Son of Sam's first murder – the shooting of Donna Lauria. Did he intend to 'celebrate' the anniversary with another killing? Mayor Abraham Beame – who was preparing to fight an election – announced that he was assigning even more policemen to the Omega task force. On the evening of the anniversary of Lauria's murder, every other car on the streets of New York seemed to be a police patrol car. But the night of Friday, 29 July passed without incident.

GRISLY ANNIVERSARY

In the hot summer of 1977, on 31 July, two sisters from Brooklyn calculated that their chances of becoming Son of Sam's next victims were several million to one, and decided to spend the evening in a restaurant. Twenty year-old Stacy Moskowitz and her 15 year-old sister 'Ricki' were still waiting to place their order when a good-looking youth walked over and asked if he could join them. He introduced himself as Bobby Violante. When they separated, Stacy agreed to meet him the following evening to go to a film.

Lovers' lane

The film – *New York, New York* – was a disappointment, but the couple were enjoying each other's company and went for a bite to eat before heading for a quiet spot where they could be alone. At about 1.45 the following morning, Robert Violante had pulled his car into a spot under a streetlamp on Shore Parkway, just opposite a playground and softball park – a kind of urban lovers' lane.

In fact, another young couple – Tommy Zaino and Debbie Crescendo – had only just vacated that spot, feeling the streetlamp made them too conspicuous. As it was, the full moon made the Parkway almost bright as day. Because it looked romantic, Bobby Violante suggested a walk in the park.

They strolled over a bridge, spent a few minutes on the swings, then walked back to the car. As they passed the public toilets, they noticed a man in jeans – a 'hippie type' – leaning against a wall. But by the time Bobby and Stacy returned from their walk, the man had moved on.

Back in the car, they kissed. But Stacy said. 'Let's move on.'

'Just a few minutes more.' Bobby replied, and kissed her again.

Kiss of death

The kiss was interrupted by a roar of gunfire. Violante did not hear it, the impact of two bullets in the face had caused his eardrums to implode, so he was only aware of a humming sound. But he could feel Stacy jerking violently in his arms. And when she collapsed forward, he was unable to see her. The bullets had blinded him.

A few yards in front of them, Tommy Zaino had observed it all in his rear-view mirror. He had seen the man, a stocky type with stringy, fair hair, approach the car from behind and pull out a gun. Then he crouched, and fired four shots through the open passenger window. Zaino guessed immediately what was happening. As his girlfriend asked, 'What was that?' he shouted, 'Get down. I think it's Son of Sam.' Moments later, the gunman was running out of the park. The time was exactly 2.35 a.m.

Stacy Moskowitz died 38 hours later in hospital. Bobby Violante survived, but he remained blind.

This time, at least, the police had a witness, and an accurate description of the man. The moonlight and the light of the streetlamp had given Tommy Zaino a very clear view of the killer. But Detective John Falotico, who took the statement, realized immediately that there were problems. Jody Valente, the survivor of the first shooting, had described the gunman as having curly black hair. But Donna DeMasi and Joanne Lomino, the two schoolgirls who had been shot on the lawn, described him as having long, fair hair. Either there were two gunmen, or the dark-haired killer was wearing a blond wig.

Killer: David Berkowitz

In fact, there were many witnesses who had been in the region of the park at the time when Stacy and Bobby had been shot. Several people had observed a yellow VW parked in the entrance to the playground. A young girl on a bicycle had been followed by a small yellow car, and had pedalled frantically until she got home. A beautician and her boyfriend, seated near the entrance to the park, had heard the shots and saw a man in a denim jacket, with what they thought might be a cheap nylon wig, jump into a light coloured car and drive off. 'He looks like he just robbed a bank,' she commented to her boyfriend.

Obscenity

A nurse heard the shots and looked out of the window, in time to see a yellow VW speeding away. It was being driven so fast and so carelessly that it almost collided with another car at the first intersection, and the driver screamed an obscenity out of the window. The other driver was so incensed that he pursued the yellow VW for several blocks before losing it. He described the driver as having stringy brown hair.

At that stage, the most important witness of all decided to come forward. She was Mrs Cacilia Davis, a 49 year-old widow, and her motive in remaining silent was, quite simply, fear of retribution from Son of Sam.

On the night of the Moskowitz shooting, Mrs Davis had returned from an evening out with a male friend. Soon after 2 a.m. their car had pulled up outside Mrs Davis's apartment, two blocks from the softball park, and they sat and talked for a few minutes.

On the alert

Since they had been forced to triple-park in a one-way street, Mrs Davis remained alert for other cars, and kept glancing both ways. She noticed a police car not far ahead of them and at some distance behind them, a pale yellow car parked close to a fire hydrant – an offence in most cities in America. As Mrs Davis watched, a young man walked up to the yellow car – a Ford Galaxie – and irritably removed a parking ticket from its windscreen. The ticket had been placed there only a few minutes earlier by the two officers patrolling in the police car.

Mrs Davis invited her friend in for coffee. He declined, pointing out that it was already 2.20 a.m. At that moment, the police car drove off, and the Ford Galaxie pulled up behind the car Mrs Davis was in, and hooted angrily to indicate that he had no room to pass. Mrs Davis hurried out, and as she did so, noticed that the driver of the Galaxie was a young man with dark hair. Mrs Davis stood and watched as her friend drove off, followed by the young man, who quickly overtook her friend, and continued to speed behind the police car.

Nervous

A few minutes later, Mrs Davis left her apartment to take her dog for his late night walk in the park. There she noticed three parked cars – that of Bobby Violante, that of Tommy Zaino, and a VW van. On her way back home a few minutes later, she saw a dark-haired man in a blue denim jacket striding across the road away from the cars. He glared at her, making her nervous, so she hurried back to her apartment. The man was walking with his right arm stiffly at his side, as if carrying something up his right sleeve. She noted that he was similar to the man she had seen earlier driving the Ford Galaxie.

It was not until two days after the shooting – on Tuesday, 2 August 1977 – that Mrs Davis told two close friends about what she had seen on Sunday morning, and about the dark-haired young man who had crossed her path and glared at her. She had decided not to go to the police because she was afraid that Son of Sam might decide to eliminate a key witness. She had reason to be nervous.

But when Mrs Davis told her friends about the parking ticket on the Galaxie, they realized that she might have a vital clue to the identity of Son of Sam. Besides, she might already be in danger. If the young man who had glared at her was Son of Sam, then he would know that he had been seen by a lady walking a small, white dog.

Brave witness

Eventually, Mrs Davis was persuaded, and her friends rang the police. The result was that Detective Joseph Strano visited Mrs Davis, and took her statement. He was deeply interested in the young man who had glared at her, but less so in the yellow Galaxie and its driver. After all, it seemed unlikely that the Son of Sam had hooted his horn in a built-up neighbourhood – a minor offence – and then roared off behind a police car. Besides, the shooting had taken place after Mrs Davis had left the park at 2.33 a.m. The Galaxie had driven off about 15 minutes before she left the park. And Tommy Zaino had described the killer as a man with stringy, fair hair, while the Galaxie driver had short, dark hair.

This is why, when Strano filed his report, there was no great excitement on the Omega task force. But Mrs Davis was becoming more and more agitated. She had talked to the police because she was afraid that Son of Sam might come looking for a woman with a small, white dog. And they were apparently ignoring her.

When Strano interviewed her a second time, she threatened to contact the media anonymously. Strano countered that, according to the local police, no tickets had been issued that evening. When she insisted, he brought along a police artist to make a sketch of the man, and took her on shopping expeditions to find a denim jacket similar to the one the man had been wearing.

It was important to find out whether any summonses had been issued that night. If they had, then it would prove that Mrs Davis had been in the area at the right time, and that her description of the young man deserved to be taken seriously.

The search for parking tickets continued. But there was no sense of urgency – after all, the killer was a fair-haired man who drove a yellow VW, which had been parked two blocks away from the Galaxie. It was on 9 August – ten days after the shootings – that the missing parking tickets were finally located.

Three of the four cars were quickly eliminated – they were not yellow Ford Galaxies. The fourth, number 561-XLB, proved to be registered to a man called David Berkowitz, who lived at 35 Pine Street, Yonkers.

Breakthrough

A detective named James Justus was asked to check on Berkowitz. He rang the Yonkers police headquarters, and spoke to a switchboard operator called Wheat Carr. When he told her that he was working on the Son of Sam case, and that he was checking on a man called David Berkowitz, he was astonished when the girl shouted, 'Oh no, oh no!'

'Why?' asked Justus. 'Do you know him?' He was even more astonished when the Yonkers operator told him that Berkowitz was the man she believed to be Son of Sam.

DEMON VOICES

The family of Wheat Carr had reason to know David Berkowitz. He had written them anonymous letters, fire-bombed their home, shot their dog, and accused them of being satanists.

Two months earlier, on 10 June 1977, Wheat Carr's father, Sam, received a phone call from a man in New Rochelle, on Long Island Sound. The man's name was Jack Cassara, and he wanted to know why Sam Carr had sent him a get-well card, commiserating with him for falling off his roof. Mr Cassara had not fallen off his roof, nor even been on it.

Sam Carr professed himself equally mystified, and invited the Cassaras to come and discuss it. The Cassaras drove to Carr's house at 316 Warburton Avenue, Yonkers – a 20-minute car ride away and introduced themselves to the small, bald Mr Carr. When Sam Carr had studied the note, he told them that he had also been receiving some strange letters. They had complained about his dog, Harvey, a black labrador.

On 27 April of that year, someone had entered Sam Carr's back yard and shot Harvey. The dog had recovered, and the police had failed to trace the anonymous notes. In the previous October, someone had tossed a Molotov cocktail through Sam Carr's window but he had extinguished it before it could do any damage. A neighbour had also received abusive telephone calls and letters and on Christmas Eve 1976, someone had fired a number of shots through their window, and killed their German shepherd dog. Oddly enough, the get-well card had a picture of a German shepherd on it.

Alarmed and still mystified, the Cassaras drove back home. But when they told their son what had happened, he had a suggestion. In the previous year, a man called David Berkowitz had rented a room above the Cassaras' garage. He had also complained about the Cassaras' German shepherd, and had left abruptly after a few weeks, not even bothering to reclaim his $200 deposit.

Mrs Cassara looked in the local phone directory, and found a David Berkowitz listed at 35 Pine Street, Yonkers. She rang Sam Carr. 'Is Pine Street anywhere near you?' Mrs Cassara asked.

'Right round the corner,' Carr replied. Now certain that David Berkowitz was the fire-bomber and killer of dogs, Sam Carr notified his local police station. But when they asked if he had any concrete evidence, he had to admit that he did not. The police explained that, without evidence, they could not act on suspicion alone.

Abuse

Another of Berkowitz's neighbours had also complained to the police about abusive anonymous letters. He was a county police officer, Craig Glassman, who lived in the apartment directly underneath Berkowitz. On 6 August 1977 – a week after the Moskowitz killing – someone set light to a pile of rubbish outside Craig Glassman's door. He extinguished it before it caused damage, and notified the police. He also showed them two anonymous letters he had recently received. The writer seemed to think that Glassman was a spy who had been placed in his apartment block by Sam Carr, and accused Glassman and the Carrs of being part of a black magic group that was out to get him. The policeman who examined the letter immediately recognized the handwriting as that of the man he had been investigating – David Berkowitz.

In any other city but New York, all the evidence pointing to Berkowitz would have led to his arrest on suspicion of being Son of Sam. But New York has an unusually high percentage of paranoid psychotics, and any one of them might have been the .44 killer, which explains why there was a delay in informing Omega task force about the odd behaviour of David Berkowitz of Yonkers.

Even when Omega detectives were informed – by Detective Justus – there was no mad rush to arrest Berkowitz. They were looking for a man with stringy fair hair who drove a yellow VW, and the Yonkers police were able to tell them that Berkowitz did not fit that description. It was not until halfway through Wednesday, 10 August 1977, that detectives Ed Zigo and John Longo were finally despatched to Yonkers to check on him.

It was Zigo who spotted Berkowitz's Galaxie parked outside the Pine Street apartment block and peered in through its rear window. On the back seat was a duffel bag with the butt of a rifle protruding from it. There was nothing illegal about this – in New York, rifles do not even require a licence – but Zigo nevertheless opened the door and examined the semi-automatic Commando Mark III, a formidable piece of killing apparatus that would not normally be found in the possession of the average law-abiding citizen.

Next, Zigo looked into the glove compartment, and found an envelope addressed to Deputy Inspector Timothy Dowd, who was in charge of the Omega task force. It proved to contain a letter threatening a shooting attack on Long Island. Zigo rushed to the nearest telephone. 'I think we've got him,' he told Sergeant James Shea of the Omega task force.

'I'm Sam'

It was six hours later when David Berkowitz – a plump, dark-haired man with a cherubic face – walked out of the apartment block at 35 Pine Street and climbed into his Ford Galaxie.

Moments later, someone knocked on the car window, and Berkowitz found himself looking down the barrel of a pistol. 'Freeze!' shouted Detective William Gardella. 'We're the police.' Berkowitz, apparently unalarmed, gave him a beaming smile.

On the other side of the car. Detective John Falotico opened the door, held his .38 calibre revolver to Berkowitz's head, and ordered him to get out. Berkowitz clambered out of the car and placed both hands on the roof. 'Who are you?' Falotico asked.

Berkowitz turned his childlike smile on the detective. 'I'm Sam,' he said.

Back at One Police Plaza. Berkowitz confessed cheerfully to all the Son of Sam shootings and to being the author of the letters. He explained that he had been ordered to commit the murders by his neighbour, Sam Carr, and that these orders were transmitted to him by Carr's demon dog, Harvey. Demon voices had accompanied him when he went out hunting for victims, and told him what to do. He was so obliging and forthcoming that the questioning only took half an hour. After 12 months, the Omega team had their man.

Berkowitz pleaded guilty to all the murders and was sentenced to 365 years in prison.

Sergeant Joseph Coffey, who had conducted the initial interrogation summarized his feelings with the words. 'I feel sorry for him. The man is a fucking vegetable.'

SATANIC CLUES

The Son of Sam case seemed to be over. The police had caught the killer who had cost them so much effort and manpower. And Berkowitz had confessed to acting alone. Yet if that was so, the evidence against him was full of contradictions. The witness of the final shooting – Tommy Zaino – had described the killer as a man with stringy, fair hair. Berkowitz had short, dark hair. Mrs Cacilia Davis, who had identified Berkowitz as being the man she had seen near her apartment building, had encountered him only minutes before the shots rang out in the park two blocks away. At that time he was walking away from the park. Then there was the fair-haired man who had leapt into the yellow VW and almost collided with another car at the intersection. And if Berkowitz had been wearing a wig for some of the attacks, he was much taller than the description witnesses gave of the fair-haired man.

These anomolies were noticed by a young investigative journalist named Maury Terry in the newspaper accounts of the killer's arrest. Terry had been born in Yonkers, and so studied the Son of Sam killings with avid interest. As far as he could see, it would have been impossible for Berkowitz to have shot Stacy Moskowitz and Bobby Violante unless Zaino and Mrs Davis were mistaken. Terry went to interview them both, and both confirmed their original stories.

New story

Mrs Davis also told him something that had not been reported. This was the strange story of how she and her male companion had seen Berkowitz drive out of the area, honking his horn, a quarter of an hour before she saw him for a second time near her apartment. It seemed unlikely that a man carrying a wanted Bulldog .44 revolver would draw attention to himself in such a foolhardy manner.

Terry interviewed the witnesses who had seen the yellow VW and its fair-haired driver. They all confirmed their original accounts. It was as if there were two men, and that Berkowitz had a companion who carried out the shooting of Stacy Moskowitz and Bobby Violante. Of course it was possible that the witnesses were mistaken, and most of the people to whom Terry voiced his doubts believed this to be the case. Yet the more Terry looked into it, the more he became certain that Berkowitz had not acted alone.

There could be no doubt that Berkowitz was the man who killed the first victim. Donna Lauria – Jody Valente's description made this clear. But he was nothing like the stringy, fair-haired hippie, or the man in the ski balaclava who had been seen shooting the two schoolgirls on the lawn. Berkowitz's confession was full of inaccuracies.

There was another curious problem. According to Berkowitz, he had never actually met Sam Carr, the man whose 'demon dog' had ordered him to commit the murders. Sam Carr confirmed this. Although his house was visible from Berkowitz's sixth floor room, he had never heard of Berkowitz until the Cassaras had told him about their eccentric ex-tenant. Yet Berkowitz was apparently so obsessed by Carr that he chose to call himself 'Son of Sam'.

In fact, Sam Carr had two sons. John and Michael, both of whom hated their father. When Terry learned that John Carr's nickname was 'Wheaties', he remembered where he had seen the name before – in the 'Son of Sam' letter to journalist Jimmy Breslin. 'John "Wheaties", rapist and suffocator of young girls.' John Carr was obviously a witness who might be able to throw some light on this tangled affair. Terry's desire to interview him became doubly urgent when he learned that Carr was 'hippie' looking with stringy fair hair.

It was at this point that Terry learned something that made him shudder. Berkowitz seemed to have an obsession about dogs, especially German shepherds. In Walden, New York – only an hour's drive from Yonkers – 85 skinned German shepherds and Dobermans had been found in the year of the Son of Sam murders. More had been found in the Yonkers area, in Untermeyer Park. The teenager who told Terry about the latter added that a devil-worshipping group met and held ceremonies in the desolate woods there. Terry had already been studying various 'satanic' clues in the Son of Sam letters, and this latest evidence seemed to suggest that Berkowitz may have taken part in the blood rituals of a satanic cult.

Obsession

The police, like everyone else he talked to, dismissed the idea. Terry became more obsessed than ever with finding the elusive John 'Wheaties' Carr and in October 1978, finally learned of his whereabouts. But it was too late. Carr was dead. He had been found shot to death in a little town called Minot in North Dakota. The eventual verdict was suicide – Carr had been shot through the mouth with a rifle in his girlfriend's bedroom – but the Minot police were more inclined to view it as murder.

On the skirting board beside his body some letters had been scrawled in his blood – they looked like S.S.N.Y.C. But a man who had blown off the top of his head with a rifle dies immediately. It looked as if Carr had been battered to the ground while his killer – or killers – went to find the gun, and he had scrawled the message on the wall before they came back to shoot him in the mouth. The letters S.S.N.Y.C immediately suggested the words 'Son of Sam, New York City'.

Figures in blood

When Terry heard that the figures 666 had been printed on Carr's hand in blood, he had no further doubt that he was dealing with a satanic cult. The

666 symbol stands for the number of the prophesied Beast in Revelation, and was also used as a pseudonym by the famous exponent of Black Magic, Aleister Crowley.

The Minot police investigation also revealed that John Carr had connections with an occult group, and that he knew David Berkowitz. His girlfriend reported that when the news of Son of Sam's arrest flashed on to the television screen, Carr had remarked, 'Oh shit.'

By now, Terry's investigations, at first dismissed as the publicity stunt of a muck-raking journalist, were attracting serious attention. The District Attorney of Queens, John Santucci, was so impressed that he announced that he was re-opening the case. Terry tracked down people who had known Berkowitz, and soon realized that the 'mad monster' was by no means a loner. He had a surprisingly wide circle of acquaintances.

Occult

In 1975, the year before the killings began, David Berkowitz had lived in an apartment in Barnes Avenue, in the Bronx. One evening, as he was lounging outside, he had fallen into conversation with a young drug addict who was obsessed with the occult. This was Michael Carr, John Carr's brother. He invited Berkowitz to join him at a party in the building. The guests at the party included members of a witchcraft coven. John Carr had also been a member of this coven – The Twenty-Two Disciples of Hell, referred to in the Breslin letter. This is why, in due course, Berkowitz had moved to Yonkers, within 200 yards of Michael Carr's residence.

So now Michael Carr became the focus of the investigation. The problem was to find him. But once again, Terry was too late. In the early hours of 4 October 1979, Michael Carr's car ran into a streetlamp at 75 miles an hour as he drove towards Manhattan. There were no skid marks, and his sister, Wheat, was convinced it was murder. It looked as if he had been forced off the road or that a tyre on his car had been shot out.

At this point, the most unexpected witness of all came forward to add his testimony. Soon after Michael Carr's death, and Santucci's announcement of the re-opening of the case, David Berkowitz wrote a letter to a preacher in California:

'I really don't know how to begin this letter, but at one time I was a member of an occult group. Being sworn to secrecy or face death, I cannot reveal the name of this group ... This group contained a mixture of satanic practices which included the teachings of Aleister Crowley and Eliphaz Levi. It was (and still is) blood oriented ... These people will stop at nothing, including murder.'

Like most of Berkowitz's letters written from prison, this one sounds remarkably sane. In fact, in February 1979, Berkowitz had summoned reporters to announce that his stories about Sam Carr's dog and demon voices had been invented. But that, of course, is no proof he was sane. Far more convincing were letters he wrote to Maury Terry, containing statements that could be checked. He claimed that the state of his room at the time of his arrest – the mad letters, the hole in the wall – had been carefully planned, to support his insanity hoax.

A week before his arrest, Berkowitz had removed from his apartment his bed, sofa, bureau and expensive Japanese stereo system and a dinner service, as well as his extra clothing. The furniture was loaded into a hired van (Berkowitz described the location of the garage it had been rented from) and dumped the furniture in front of the Salvation Army warehouse in Mount Vernon. Berkowitz even specified the cost of the rented van. He knew the deposit required, and said the ravings on the wall were written on the same occasion.

Verified facts

Most of these claims could be checked, and Terry did so. The rental garage was where Berkowitz claimed it was, the prices given were correct, as was the description of the owner. The next-door neighbour verified that the hole had been knocked in the wall two days before Berkowitz's arrest, cracking the plaster in her apartment.

The ravings on the walls were all written with the same marker. The Salvation Army warehouse was where Berkowitz said it was, and although they now had no record of assorted furniture being left more than two years ago, they verified that it was a fairly frequent occurrence.

Berkowitz made another interesting claim. Shortly after the murders began, he went to be interviewed for a job in a dog pound. The pay was bad, but 'there was another way in which I was getting paid,' he said, 'somebody needed dogs! I guess you understand what I'm trying to say.' Again, Terry's checks revealed that Berkowitz was telling the truth.

But perhaps the most significant – and sinister – remark in Berkowitz's letters was as follows: 'Call the Santa Clara Sheriff's office (California) ... Please ask the sheriffs ... what happend [sic] to ARLISS [sic] PERRY.'

The answer, Terry discovered, was that on 13 October 1974, a girl called Arlis Perry had been horribly murdered in the Church at Stanford University. The body was naked from the waist down, and spreadeagled in a ritualistic position, with an altar candle inserted into the vagina. Her arms were folded across her chest, and between her breasts was another candle. Her jeans were so arranged across her legs that the result was a diamond pattern. She had been beaten, choked and stabbed with an ice pick behind the ear.

Terry's investigations quickly revealed that Berkowitz knew things about this little-publicized murder that had never appeared in print. Moreover,

Berkowitz had sent a female correspondent a picture of another girl, cut from a newspaper. with the comment she looked like Arlis Perry.

This happened to be true, but the only pictures of Arlis Perry that had appeared in newspapers were taken in her college days, when she had looked quite different. It is thought that Berkowitz had seen a 'death photograph' of Arlis Perry, and therefore knew who had killed her. It was, Terry claimed, a west coast satanic group with which Charles Manson had also been associated.

All Terry's new evidence fitted a pattern. It indicated that David Berkowitz had committed only three of the Son of Sam murders, those of Donna Lauria, Alexander Esau and Valentina Suriani. Terry had noted that some of the shootings were ruthlessly efficient, while others – like those of Carl Denaro, Donna DiMasi and Sal Lupo – were oddly incompetent. According to one informant, the killer in the ski balaclava, who had shot the two school girls, was a woman member of the coven. Donna Lauria had been killed because she knew about the coven. Christine Freund because she had upset one of its members. The killer of Stacy Moskowitz was John Carr, and the murder had been filmed by a video camera as a 'snuff movie' – this is why the killer chose a car parked under a lamp rather than Tommy Zaino's car, which was in a dark spot. Tommy Zaino had been lucky. He moved his car to a darker place 30 minutes before the shootings.

Satanic cult

Terry was even able to name the leader of the satanic cult in New York, Roy Alexander Radin, a 'showbiz' tycoon who moved to California in 1982. But once again, Terry learned all this too late. Roy Radin was murdered in California on Friday 13 May 1983 and his body had been dumped in Death Valley – Charles Manson's old stamping ground – with a defaced Bible lying open nearby.

Maury Terry's evidence, described in his book *The Ultimate Evil*, makes a strong case that David Berkowitz did not act alone. It also makes it clear that, although John Carr, Michael Carr and Roy Radin are dead, most of the other members of the 'Twenty-Two Disciples of Hell' are still at large. Terry's book ends with a description of some recent killings that suggest the coven is still active.

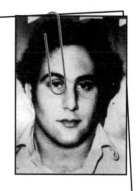

CASE FILE: BERKOWITZ, RICHARD DAVID

BACKGROUND

Richard David Berkowitz was an illegitimate child whose mother decided to give him up for adoption. His mother was Betty Broder, the daughter of Jewish parents. She had married an Italian American called Tony Falco, when she was 19. Six years later, he left her for another woman. In 1947, she began an affair with a married man, Joseph Kleinman, who was in the real estate business. But when she told him she was pregnant, he replied that if she wanted to continue seeing him, she had to get rid of the child.

David Berkowitz was born on 1 June 1953, and was immediately adopted by a Jewish couple, Nathan and Pearl Berkowitz who were unable to have children of their own.

When his foster mother died of cancer when David was 14, he was deeply upset. In 1969, he and his father moved into the Bronx's Co-op City, a supposedly, middle class area. But the area became dangerous, with gangs of youths terrorizing the neighbourhood.

No direction

David's school grades plummeted and he seemed to lose all sense of direction. As a teenager, he was shy and tongue tied with girls. Nat Berkowitz remarried in 1971. David resented his new stepmother and step sister, and decided to join the army.

His father was upset when his son returned from the army – in 1974 – denouncing Judaism and bursting with his new religious faith. Life became so uncomfortable in Co-op City that David soon moved out to his own apartment at 2151 Barnes Avenue, in the Bronx. Loneliness led him to search for his real parents. The Bureau of Records revealed that his real name was Richard Falco of Brooklyn. Through an old telephone directory he was able to trace his mother and elder sister. He dropped a card in his mother's mail-box, and a few days later, she called him.

They had an emotional reunion. He also met his sister Roslyn – who was by that time 37 years-old – and quickly became a welcome guest in the home she shared with her husband and children. David had found a family and seemed to be perfectly happy.

Worried

In the first half of 1976, his visits to his mother and sister became increasingly infrequent and brief. His sister was worried about the headaches David complained of. In February he had moved to the home of Mr and Mrs Cassara in distant New Rochelle. Only two months later he left the Cassaras' home equally unexpectedly to move into Pine Street in Yonkers.

On 29 July, Donna Lauria, the first Son of Sam victim, was killed by Berkowitz, in a car outside her family's Bronx apartment.

PSYCHOLOGICAL PROFILE

As a child, David Berkowitz acquired a reputation as a spoilt brat and a bully, though at school he was shy and himself the victim of bullying. He was big, strong, and an excellent baseball player, but he preferred to play with children younger than himself. One friend remembers David asking him if he would like to join a 'girl haters club'.

One of the keys to Berkowitz's psychotic behaviour was his sexual frustration – he was probably still a virgin when he was arrested. He always found it difficult to interest girls.

Warm

The only girl he ever dated was a neighbour in Co-op City called Iris Gerhardt. She liked his warm and obliging nature, and said of him, 'Dave was a guy who would do anything for you,' but the relationship remained platonic. Berkowitz commented, 'After a while, at Co-op City, there wasn't one girl who was a virgin,' but he always seemed to miss out. When his young friends began to smoke marijuana, David remained aloof, too inhibited to participate. 'I wanted to help people be important,' he said. As with so many serial killers, he was possessed by a powerful craving to exert power over other people.

When his father remarried, Berkowitz felt rejected. The craving to 'belong' led him to join the army. Later, the same craving led him to join the Baptists and spread the faith.

Alienation

Back at home in New York, it alienated him from his father, who remembers David standing in front of a mirror and pounding his head with his fists. Nat Berkowitz's departure for Florida seemed to be the closing of yet another door.

Since he was seven, David had known he was an adopted child, and knew the name of his natural mother. After his father left New York, David spent a year tracking down his real mother. But by then, it was too late. According to Berkowitz's later statements to psychiatrists, he was already hearing 'demon voices'. His father by this time was convinced that David needed psychiatric help. According to the investigative journalist Maury Terry, it was at around this time that he met Michael Carr and was drawn into the satanic coven that believed in human sacrifice.

Voices

In his book on the case, *Son of Sam*, Lawrence D. Klausner, accepts Berkowitz's story, that he was driven to kill by demonic voices. Berkowitz himself called a press conference after his sentencing to announce that the 'voices' story had been a hoax. Whether a hoax or not Berkowitz's shooting of girls was consistent with his sense of sexual frustration.

If there is any truth in the story that he became a member of a witchcraft coven, this would also be consistent with that lifelong craving to 'belong'.

Chapter 7

GRAHAM YOUNG
THE POISONER

If any murderer can be said to have been born evil, it was cold, calculating Graham Young. From the age of 11, this withdrawn young man was consumed by a single passion: poisons and their effects. Anyone he came into contact with – his family, friends or workmates – risked agonising illness and even death from his deadly experiments.

Everyone was puzzled by Chris Williams' illness. The 13 year-old complained of cramp in his chest and legs and severe headaches. The pain would peak, ease off, then start again a few days later.

The family doctor, Dr Lancelot Wills, examined Chris several times during 1961 but could not find any cause for the pain.

Finally, Dr Wills sent Chris to Willesden Hospital, north London, where a young intern diagnosed migraine, the severe headaches which can produce nausea. But Chris' cramps and vomiting continued and his mother wondered if he was 'simply playing up', as she called it.

It troubled Mrs Williams that there seemed no pattern to her son's attacks. They had begun about a year before, some on schooldays, some at weekends. There had even been an acute seizure after Chris and a schoolfriend had been to London Zoo one Saturday in the spring.

Unknown to Mrs Williams, the same mysterious symptoms were breaking out at the home of that same schoolfriend of Chris. His name was Graham Young, an intent, gauche 13 year-old who had a strange, formal way of speaking.

The Young family lived at 768 North Circular Road, Neasden in west London. Graham's 38 year-old stepmother, Molly, began to suffer stomach pains during 1961, though at first she dismissed them.

Her husband, Fred Young, a 44 year-old engineer who had lost his first wife soon after Graham's birth, was concerned for Molly and when he too

Killer: Graham Young

fell prey to severe cramps, he wondered if his son's chemicals might have got into the kitchen pots.

Fred had never been close to Graham, whose fascination with Nazism, poisons and black magic disturbed him, but he had encouraged his son's interest in chemistry.

In the summer of 1961, Graham's sister Winifred became ill and, soon after, it seemed that the bug had afflicted the whole family when Graham began vomiting during a visit to his Aunt Winnie, who lived nearby.

Winnie became worried. She was fond of her nephew, whom she had brought up as a baby, but confided to her husband, Jack Jouvenat, that she suspected Graham and his chemicals of causing the illnesses.

One morning in November 1961, Molly made tea. Winifred found hers sour, but emptied the cup and left for work. During the journey, she collapsed. Passengers helped her off at Tottenham Court Road underground station, close to her work, and a colleague took her to the Middlesex Hospital in Goodge Street.

After making tests, a surprised doctor concluded that Winifred had taken belladonna, a poison extracted from deadly nightshade plants.

Winifred had heard enough, 'It wouldn't surprise me if it was Graham messing about with his experiments,' she told her father. Fred Young searched the house while Graham sobbed in his room. The search revealed no trace of poisons and Winifred, embarrassed at accusing her brother without proof, apologized.

In the weeks that followed, Molly's condition deteriorated. Her looks aged and she became bowed over with backache. Early in the new year, she began to lose weight. 'She seemed to be wasting away before our eyes,' one friend was to say.

On Easter Saturday, 21 April 1962, Molly woke in her weakest state yet. Besides the usual pains, her neck was stiff and her hands and feet prickly.

At lunchtime, Fred returned home to find Graham in the kitchen, staring with great concentration through the window. Fred looked out and saw his wife suffering a convulsion on the lawn, writhing in pain. At Willesden Hospital the doctors had no time to find the cause of her illness. That afternoon, Molly Young died.

While the family was too upset to think clearly, Graham nagged them about the need for cremation, not burial, talking in his formal way about the latest techniques. His distraught father gave in. The ceremony took place at Golders Green Crematorium the following Thursday, 26 April. At the reception later at the Youngs' home, one of Graham's uncles began vomiting after adding pickle to his sandwich.

Soon afterwards, Fred Young told Winifred and Graham that the mortgage had been paid off and the house would pass to them on his death. A few days later, his own stomach pains and headaches returned.

Once again, the doctors at Willesden Hospital could find no organic problem, but kept Fred in for observation. Each day, Graham would watch his father coldly, then correctly forecast to the family what the symptoms would be the following day. Soon, Fred instinctively shunned his son. 'Don't bring Graham with you any more,' he told Aunt Winnie.

Fred returned home but was soon back in hospital. The specialists made progress, but were perplexed by their diagnosis: Fred had been poisoned with antimony, a rare metallic substance. One more dose would have killed him.

Aunt Winnie confronted Graham, who self-righteously denied feeding poison to his father. He spoke openly about his father's illness at his school, John Kelly Secondary, where a science teacher, Geoffrey Hughes, had long been troubled by Young's obsession with poisons.

One evening, Hughes went through Young's desk, finding bottles of poison, drawings of men dying in pain, and essays in Graham's handwriting about poison and murder. Hughes and the headmaster discussed the illnesses in the Young family with a doctor and arranged for a psychiatrist, posing as a careers guidance officer, to examine Graham.

The interview took place at the school on 20 May. The psychiatrist encouraged Young to talk about his favourite subject of poisons, flattering him about his expertise. Young went home elated. The psychiatrist went straight to the police.

Detective Inspector Edward Crabbe of Harlesden CID visited 768 North Circular Road the next day, 21 May, while Young was at school. Looking through his bedroom, he found enough poison to kill 300 people. There were also copies of *A Handbook on Poisons, Sixty Famous Trials* and *Poisoner in the Dock*, an account of notorious murderers. When Young got home, DI Crabbe told him to remove his shirt. A phial of antimony and two small bottles fell out. Young called the phial 'my little friend' but lied that he did not know what the bottles contained. It was found to be thallium.

At Harlesden police station, Young was questioned for many hours but constantly denied poisoning his family. That evening, his Aunt Winnie visited him. 'Oh, Graham, why did you do it?' she said. Young, pale and frightened, stood in silence until he was led away. The next morning, 22 May, he admitted everything.

At Ashford Remand Centre, he underwent tests, but informal moments proved just as revealing. 'I miss my antimony,' Young told a doctor. 'I miss the power it gives me.'

At the Old Bailey on 6 July 1962, Young pleaded guilty to poisoning his father, sister and his schoolfriend Chris Williams.

Mr Justice Melford Stevenson ordered that Young be detained in Broadmoor, a psychiatric hospital for the criminally insane, and that he should not be released for at least 15 years, and then only with the authority of the Home Secretary of the day.

Killer: Graham Young

A TEENAGE INMATE

Inside Broadmoor, Graham Young was given a small room to himself in the reception block of the gaunt Victorian building, whose redbrick walls sealed off its 750 inmates from the villages of Berkshire.

The window in his room was barred and the bed was screwed to the floor which was bare except for a rug. The 14 year-old was awoken each morning at 7 a.m. and the lights in the block were put out at 8 p.m. In the intervening hours, he and other inmates of the block made rugs and were allowed to read and play games such as snooker and billiards.

Young was one of the three youngest males sent to Broadmoor this century. His notoriety had spread throughout the prison-hospital, and his family felt that it was important not to abandon him.

Fred Young tried gamely to conceal his revulsion and anger but, after a few visits, the pair would sit in brooding silence and Fred never again returned. His son had not only poisoned Molly, but left Fred Young with a painful liver complaint.

Winifred and Aunt Winnie, however, made regular visits. So did Frank Walker, the uncle who had become ill at the reception after Molly's funeral. Young constantly asked Frank to bring him matches. His uncle obliged, until he learnt that they contained phosphorus, which can create poisonous effects.

Educational classes were given by part-time teachers at Broadmoor, but no one was obliged to attend them. The authorities searched for a private tutor who could draw Young's interest away from poison and Nazism, the only subjects he talked about, but the hospital was rejected by everyone it approached.

On 6 August 1962, one month after Young's arrival, an inmate called John Berridge suffered convulsions and died within a few hours. A post-mortem traced the cause to cyanide poisoning. An inquiry found that there was nothing containing this lethal poison inside Broadmoor but that laurel bushes, from which it can be extracted, grew alongside the building.

Several prisoners came forward and confessed to murdering Berridge. The authorities, aware that disturbed people often admit to crimes of which they are innocent, investigated each confession closely and were unconvinced that any was true. The case was left open.

But many inmates and some of the nursing staff were privately convinced by one of the confessions. It was made by Graham Young, who spoke in reverent scientific tones of the method for extracting cyanide from the plants.

Young's room in Broadmoor was soon covered with pictures of Nazi war leaders. He grew a clipped moustache in Hitler's style and spent long periods reciting his hero's war speeches. On the tins provided for tea and sugar, he drew skulls and cross-bones and wrote the names of poisons on the labels.

The library at Broadmoor was freely available to Young. He selected medical books, from which he broadened his knowledge of poisons and general medicine.

Young also read William Shirer's *The Rise and Fall of the Third Reich*, one of the standard works of Nazism, as well as Dennis Wheatley's chilling novels about the occult and Bram Stoker's *Dracula*.

Occasionally, Young would wander down to the sports field but never played, and used the handicrafts centre mainly to build swastikas. He wore one on a chain around his neck, sometimes kissing it like a cross purely to upset people.

The superintendent of Broadmoor, Dr Patrick McGrath, and a senior resident psychiatrist, Dr Edgar Udwin, jointly handled Young's treatment. The South African-born Dr Udwin, who ran his own clinic for mentally handicapped children, worked hard to help Young believe that his life was not written off and that he might even go on to study at university.

The nursing staff were torn between its suspicion of Young and a wish to avoid making him an outcast among outcasts. He was given a job in the kitchen. It was a risk, a gesture of trust they felt Young needed.

Shortly afterwards, the nurses' coffee was served looking unusually dark. It was found to contain toilet cleaner. No one was harmed, but the nurses learnt to joke with troublesome inmates: 'Unless you behave, I'll let Graham make your coffee.'

Late in 1965, after only three years in Broadmoor, Young applied for release. His father told the authorities that his son should 'never be released again' but Young's case was weak anyway, and was rejected. Soon after, a tea urn was found to contain an entire packet of sugar soap. Young was sent to the maximum security block, known as the 'cooler'.

Finally defeated, Young moodily came to realize that he had to co-operate if he was ever to be released. Dr Udwin noticed gradual changes in Young after his release from the cooler and for the next three years, Young showed signs of becoming steadier, more responsive to others.

Young talked less and less to Dr Udwin about poisons, although the psychiatrist was aware that the youth continued to admire the Nazi policy of exterminating Jews. It is not known if Young realised that Dr Udwin was himself a Jew.

The years passed slowly. Young weathered jibes from other inmates that he was the doctors' 'blue-eyed boy' and, even before his release was considered, applied for work in the police forensic laboratories, and for a place on the Pharmaceuticals Society training scheme. Both applications were met with terse rejections.

Young then wrote to the National Front, a fascist political movement, and was accepted as a member. He was entitled to his views, however right-wing, and in June 1970, after Young had been in Broadmoor for eight years, Dr Udwin reported to the Home Office that Young had undergone 'profound changes', and that his obsession with poison and violence had passed.

Killer: Graham Young

Young, nearing his 23rd birthday, was delighted and, on 16 June, he wrote to tell Winifred, now married and living in Hemel Hempstead, that 'the estimable Edgar' hoped to discharge him later that year.

None of the family knew a release was being considered but they understood that the Home Office could overrule the original sentence on psychiatrists' recommendation.

Fred Young, now living in Sheerness, Kent, was dismayed but Winifred and her husband, Dennis Shannon, were assured by Dr Udwin that her brother was cured.

On 21 November, Young began a week's stay with them. It passed well and, in a quiet moment, Young expressed remorse for what he had done. He returned at Christmas, bringing presents and a card stating that their dog had received psychoanalysis and was well again. It was signed 'Sigmund Freud.'

Early in 1971, the Home Office agreed to release Young, providing he accepted conditions about treatment and a fixed address. On 4 February, Young walked free, only a few weeks after telling a nurse, 'When I get out, I'm going to kill one person for every year I've spent in this place.'

BACK TO WORK

Graham Young arrived without warning on his sister Winifred's doorstep in Hemel Hempstead a few hours after leaving Broadmoor. She knew that his release was imminent, but no one had given her a date and her 23 year-old brother had not telephoned first.

Winifred took Young in, and wrote to their father in Sheerness, Kent, with the news. Young had four days to spend with Winifred before moving to Slough to attend a Government Training Centre. He passed the time drinking, and defending Hitler. On Monday, 8 February, he began training in Slough as a storekeeper. Three days later, a new friend, Trevor Sparkes, 34, complained of severe abdominal pains and a loss of control of his legs, but his doctor could find nothing wrong.

'This might help,' Young said, offering Sparkes a glass of wine that evening. Sparkes drank it and immediately suffered vomiting, facial swelling and near-convulsions which recurred throughout April.

Earlier that month, Fred Young received an official visitor from Broadmoor, who explained that his son's release was under consideration. Given that Graham had already been released and had had a frosty meeting with his father, Fred was outraged at the bureaucratic incompetence at Broadmoor and the stupidity of his misinformed visitor.

In mid-April, Young saw an advertisement for a storekeeper at a firm in Bovingdon, Hertfordshire, a village only a few miles from his sister's home. The company, John Hadland Ltd, specialized in high-speed photographic and optical equipment. 'I previously studied chemistry, organic and inorganic, pharmacology and toxicology ...' Young wrote in his application letter.

When Young arrived for his interview on 23 April, the managing director, Godfrey Foster, had received the Slough centre's glowing report on the young man, who was eager to talk about science. Foster, however, was more curious about the obvious gaps in Young's history.

Young said that he had suffered a nervous breakdown after his mother had died in an accident, but that he was now fully recovered. Foster, still unsure, said he would be in touch when he had made a decision. He then wrote again to Slough asking for a personal reference from Young's psychiatrist.

On 26 April, the centre forwarded Dr Udwin's report. It was not written on Broadmoor or Home Office stationery, but did not conceal the seriousness of Young's disturbance.

'This man has suffered a deep-going personality disorder which necessitated his hospitalisation throughout the whole of his adolescence,' Dr Udwin's letter began. 'He has, however, made an extremely full recovery and is now entirely fit for discharge, his sole disability now being the need to catch up on his lost time.'

Dr Udwin, certain that Young was cured did not mention the conviction for poisonings in 1962. To have done so would have ruined Young's prospect of a worthwhile job. Foster duly accepted the report and offered £24 a week to Young, who was dressed smartly in suit and tie when he turned up for work at 8.30 a.m. on Monday, 10 May.

The Hadland's staff welcomed him. Some quickly felt protective towards the rather solitary, absent-minded young man. The 59 year-old storeroom manager, Bob Egle, tried to take Young under his wing, as did Fred Biggs, who was head of the Work In Progress unit.

Another storeroom worker, Jethro Batt, drove Young back to his digs every night, but others among the 75 employees at Hadland's found the new recruit a bit obsessive. He seemed at peace only when discussing his beloved Adolf Hitler.

Young seemed keen to reciprocate the goodwill. He handed around his rolled-up cigarettes and offered to fetch tea for his colleagues in their personal mugs from the trolley. This was left each morning and evening at the end of the corridor outside the storeroom where Young worked.

Initially, he stayed with Winifred and Dennis in Hemel Hempstead but soon moved into a bed-sitting room at 29 Maynards Road in the town for £4 a week. No cooking was allowed and Young ate most of his evening meals at a nearby Wimpy bar. Twice a week he visited Winifred.

On 3 June, the storeroom manager, Bob Egle, became ill and spent a few days in bed with an upset stomach. On 8 June, soon after drinking his tea from the trolley, Ron Hewitt, a 41 year-old storeman who discussed science with Young, suffered considerable stomach pains, diarrhoea, and a burning feeling in his throat.

Hewitt's doctor diagnosed food poisoning and prescribed accordingly but the symptoms persisted. Hewitt was back at work by 15 June, still shaken and weak, and his attacks continued for the next three weeks.

Egle also felt fragile and took a week's holiday in Great Yarmouth with his wife Dorothy from 18 June. Since Fred Biggs was on his scheduled summer holiday, the storeroom was short-staffed and Young became a little bit bossy.

Egle was back by 25 June, apparently recovered. 'Nothing like a bit of sea air,' he said. The next day, his fingers went numb, his back ached and he could move only with pain. All night, he lay awake moaning.

In the morning, Egle's doctor had him taken to West Herts Hospital, which soon transferred him to the intensive care unit at St Albans City Hospital. The numbness spread through his body until he was virtually paralysed. He retained his hearing but was unable to speak.

The specialists twice revived him when his heart stopped but finally there was nothing they could do. On Wednesday, 7 July, with his wife at his bedside, Bob Egle died.

Two days later, after a post-mortem examination, death was recorded as the result of broncho-pneumonia and polyneuritis. Throughout Egle's final weeks, Graham Young had constantly asked Godfrey Foster's secretary about his condition, and had once shown her a medical article about polyneuritis, saying the symptoms were similar to those Egle was suffering.

Foster chose Young to represent the storeroom staff at Egle's cremation at Amersham on 12 July. Young spent the entire journey in Foster's car talking about polyneuritis, specifically the Guillain-Barre syndrome which Egle was judged to have suffered.

Foster, knowing of Young's long confinement, was deeply affected by his breadth of medical knowledge. Recalling Egle's service in World War II, Young said sagely: 'It's very sad that Bob should have come through the terrors of Dunkirk, only to fall victim to some strange virus.'

In the autumn, Young was put in charge of the storeroom for a trial period. He had become a more outgoing person, but irritated some staff by talking constantly about the much-mourned Bob Egle. Young managed his new responsibility badly, and his obsession with the Nazis was another source of his growing unpopularity.

Meanwhile, he kept up contact with his family. Besides the visits to Winifred and Dennis, he visited his cousin Sandra in St Albans and quite often went to Sheerness where Fred and Aunt Winnie were cheered by his relative success at work. The family heard about Bob Egle, but realised that men approaching 60 were susceptible to pneumonia.

Early in September 1971, Fred Biggs began to suffer violent stomach cramps and vomiting. On 20 September, Hadland's import-export manager, Peter Buck, had a cup of tea with Young and a clerk, David Tilson. A quarter of an hour later, Buck went down with stomach pains and nausea.

On 8 October, Tilson felt ill after a tea-break and two days later felt his legs going numb. The following Friday, 15 October, Young and a 39 year-old fellow storeman, Jethro Batt, were working late together.

'Do you know, Jeth, it is quite easy to poison someone and make it look like natural causes?' Young asked, prattling about something he called a 'recipe for death'. While Batt was out of the room, Young made some coffee. Batt found the first mouthful bitter and threw the rest away.

'What's the matter?' Young asked. 'Do you think I'm trying to poison you?' They both laughed. Twenty minutes later, Batt was sick. Over the weekend, his legs throbbed with pain.

On Monday, 18 October, Tilson was admitted to St Albans City Hospital suffering pains throughout his body. Within a few hours, his hair began to fall out. Batt, in bed at home, felt the pain up to his chest.

During the week at the factory, Young handed a mug to a woman colleague of 39 called Diane Smart. 'This is your coffee, Di. Drink it up.' Minutes later, she vomitted and cramp spread through her hands, legs and stomach.

Jethro Batt, meanwhile, was so tormented by pain at home that he told his wife he wanted to die. He suffered hallucinations and his hair, like Tilson's, began to fall out. Pills brought no relief.

By Thursday, 21 October, Batt could scarcely move. A week later, Tilson left hospital but returned in distress on 1 November. The doctors had last seen him with long hair. Now he was almost bald. On 5 November, Batt entered hospital, also without a hair left on his head.

Young went in to work on Saturday, 6 November, to catch up on work and was joined by Fred Biggs, whose latest attack had only just passed. Young made tea for Biggs, but Godfrey Foster cancelled his own request when told the work was done. The next day Biggs had a relapse.

Foster suspected that a well-known recurring local virus, known as the Bovingdon Bug, was causing the outbreak. Some employees wondered about the radioactive experiments on a nearby disused airstrip. Others feared the water was somehow contaminated.

The doctors treating the Hadland's staff were perplexed. Biggs was examined by seven doctors after entering West Herts Hospital on 4 November, but they were unable to pinpoint the cause of his suffering. On 11 November, he was moved to the Whittington Hospital, which specialises in viral complaints, but rather than getting better, his skin began to peel off.

On the same day, at Foster's request, the factory was examined by Dr Robert Hynd, the Medical Officer of Health for Hemel Hempstead, and a team of factory inspectors. They found nothing amiss. Hynd returned the next day to question the anxious staff separately about any illnesses in their families.

Fred Biggs was then transferred to the National Hospital for Nervous Diseases in London, but to no avail. On Friday, 19 November, he died. 'I wonder what went wrong,' Young told Diane Smart. 'He shouldn't have died. I was very fond of old Fred.'

Killer: Graham Young

With the workforce close to panic, the proprietor, John Hadland, summoned the firm's GP, Dr Iain Anderson, to address everyone in the canteen. Dr Anderson explained that there was no radioactive contamination from the airstrip and there was no heavy metal poisoning. Thallium, a heavy metal chemical, was sometimes used in making high refractive lenses, but not by Hadland's. He said there must have been an unusually virulent outbreak of the local virus and that intense efforts were being made to trace its origin. He pleaded for calm.

Hadland invited questions. 'Why had heavy metal been ruled out?' someone asked from the back. It was Graham Young.

Dr Anderson repeated what the factory inspectors had decided. He privately suspected that some heavy metal might still be found to be the cause, but did not wish to create alarm. Young continued to ask probing questions about the symptoms.

Eventually, Hadland declared the meeting closed. Dr Anderson casually went to see Young in the storeroom and flattered him on his knowledge. As always, Young warmed to appreciation and took the opportunity to parade his knowledge of toxicology.

Dr Anderson quietly reported back to Hadland. Both were reluctant to take action without proof. But, when left alone, Hadland thought matters over and telephoned the police.

EVIDENCE UNEARTHED

Detective Chief Inspector John Kirkpatrick of Hemel Hempstead police drove to Bovingdon immediately after John Hadland's call and began to compare the dates when the illnesses began with the movement of staff.

Hadland had mentioned no names over the telephone, but Kirkpatrick soon noticed that Egle and Hewitt had developed symptoms only a few weeks after Young had begun work. He telexed a list of several employees, Young included, to Scotland Yard's Criminal Record Office.

The next day, Saturday, 21 November, he contacted Detective Chief Superintendent Ronald Harvey, head of the Hertfordshire CID, who was attending a luncheon in London for forensic scientists.

After taking the call, Harvey returned to his seat and described the symptoms to the two scientists with whom he was sitting: Dr Ian Holden, a consultant to Scotland Yard and Dr Keith Mant. They listened and then both spoke almost at once with the same verdict: thallium poisoning.

The name was unknown to Harvey. When he reached Hemel Hempstead, Scotland Yard had replied that it had no record of any of the Hadland employees on the list. Kirkpatrick asked them to check again on one of the newest employees, Graham Young.

Harvey, meanwhile, was looking for a copy of a rare medical work, *Prick's Thallium Poisoning*, mentioned by Dr Holden and Dr Mant. Soon, a copy was dispatched in a squad car at high speed from the police forensic science laboratories in Cheshire. Scotland Yard had now located Young's record and Hadland and Foster were told the chilling news that Graham Young was a convicted poisoner.

From Winifred, Young's sister, police learnt he was spending the weekend with his father and aunt in Kent. Three detectives went to search his bedsitter and recoiled with disgust.

The walls were covered with pictures of Hitler and several other Nazi wartime leaders. Bottles, phials and tubes lay on tables, shelves and even the window sill. There were drawings of skulls, crossbones, tombstones and emaciated figures, some holding their hands to their throats, others clutching ominous looking bottles.

It was 11.30 p.m. when the Kent police silently surrounded the house in Alma Road, Sheerness where Young's family lived. Two officers rang the doorbell. Fred Young opened the door and sensed at once why they had come.

'Is Graham Young here?' asked one of the officers. Young could be seen making a sandwich in the kitchen. Fred said nothing, but pointed. One officer handcuffed Young, the other said he was wanted for suspected murder. Young went white as a sheet.

'Graham, what have you done?' Winnie said, coming into the hall.

'I don't know what they are talking about, Auntie,' he replied.

As Young was led out, Fred heard him ask the officers, 'Which one are you doing me for?' After the police car drove away, Fred went upstairs, took out Graham's birth certificate and every other document relating to his son and tore them to pieces.

By 3 a.m. the next day, Sunday, 22 November, the police at Young's bedsitting room had found empty ether and other chemical bottles, various powders, and books on forensic medicine. Under the bed they also found what looked like a poisoner's diary. It was entitled 'A Student's and Officer's Case Book.'

Detective Inspector Kirkpatrick and Detective Sergeant Roger Livingstone arrived at Sheerness police station soon after 3 a.m. Young's clothes had been taken away for tests and he had blankets for covering.

'I am arresting you on suspicion of murder,' Kirkpatrick said flatly.

'Yes, I know, but didn't you say murders, plural?' Young asked.

'No, I didn't,' Kirkpatrick replied.

On the drive to Hertfordshire, Young persistently questioned the detectives in his formal manner, despite being under arrest and wearing only blankets. Kirkpatrick said there was work to be done before the charges would be clear.

'I appreciate that is so in a case such as this,' Young said.

Kirkpatrick asked what he meant.

'We won't go into that now,' Young said. When Kirkpatrick revealed that the inquiry concerned the death of Fred Biggs, Young said, 'I shall want to know more than that, Inspector.'

Young lectured the two officers that he was innocent until proven guilty. Pleased at gaining the initiative, Young then coolly boasted to them that he had once committed a perfect murder: in 1962 he had killed his stepmother and she had been cremated. Kirkpatrick invited him to get matters at Hadland's off his chest.

'The whole story is too terrible,' Young said. Kirkpatrick asked him to save the lives of Tilson and Batt. Young obligingly spelt out the names of the antidotes needed to save them.

At 6.35 a.m. they arrived at Hemel Hempstead. DCS Harvey had been studying the 'case book' found in Young's room, which described various poisonings of people referred to by their initials.

'They are figments of my imagination,' Young said, dismissing the matter when asked about it.

'Did you give any of these people poison?' Harvey asked.

'Absolutely not.'

Young then lectured Harvey on how to conduct the investigation. 'These people offered you friendship,' Harvey pleaded. 'They tried to help you.' The strange young man again turned the tables. 'As you say, these people are my friends. So where is the motive?' he asked.

Young was allowed to sleep and fresh clothes were brought to him. The interview was resumed at 4.45 p.m. Just as in 1962, Young had suddenly decided to be co-operative.

Harvey went through the initials in the diary, identifying the victims. Young confirmed that he had poisoned them and repeated his boast about the perfect murder of his stepmother. He talked volubly about his fascination with poisons, describing their effect on human beings in minute detail, but laughed mockingly when Harvey asked for a written statement of these activities.

Final proof

The following day, Monday, 23 November, after a post-mortem examination failed to disclose proof that Biggs had died of any poison, his body was moved to the forensic laboratories at Scotland Yard for further tests. Undeterred, Harvey charged Young at 10 p.m. that night with the murder of Biggs. 'I have no wish to say anything,' Young replied, although the next day he was to say, 'It's over. The charade is over.'

The ashes of Bob Egle were exhumed in Gillingham, Norfolk, and also analysed at the police laboratories. The forensic officer handling the case, Nigel Fuller, conducted exhaustive analyses before announcing his conclusive results: both men had died of thallium poisoning.

On 3 December, Young was charged with murdering Egle. It was the first time in British legal history that the exhumation of cremated ashes had led to a murder charge and there were no previous records in British crime of murder by thallium.

A MACABRE MIND

The trial of Graham Young for murder opened at St Albans Crown Court on Monday, 19 June 1972 before Mr Justice Eveleigh and the usual jury of 12 men. Young's counsel, the former Solicitor-General, Sir Arthur Irvine QC, had taken the brief only days before.

Young was charged with the murders of Bob Egle and Fred Biggs, the attempted murder of David Tilson and Jethro Batt and the malicious poisoning of Trevor Sparkes, his Slough colleague, and Ronald Hewitt, Peter Buck and Diana Smart from Hadland's. Young denied all the charges laid against him.

Soberly dressed in a dark suit, he listened with composure as John Leonard QC, prosecuting, described the spate of grotesque illnesses at Hadland's, the evil findings in Young's diary and the evidence that Biggs and Egle had both died from thallium poisoning.

Under the law protecting defendants, the jury could be told nothing about Young's convictions in 1962 or about his eight years in Broadmoor, since this was well-known as a criminal as well as a psychiatric institution.

Leonard spent 20 minutes reading the diary to the jury. If accepted as a factual record, it indicated not only an intent to murder, but a methodical mind capable of seizing opportunities.

Young's taunting of the police that a motive had to be demonstrated was ill-founded. Where clear proof of murder exists, a prosecuting counsel does not have to discuss motive at all.

The diary was the centrepiece of the prosecution's case. The forensic proof of death by thallium, Young's lair of poisons and macabre drawings and his informal statements to police might not alone prove that he had systematically poisoned the Hadland's staff.

Young's explanation was simple. The diary was a work of fiction, based on the mysterious events taking place at the factory in Bovingdon.

His evidence began on the sixth day – Monday, 26 June. Young declined an invitation to sit down in the witness box, and stood with one hand in the left trouser pocket of his dark pinstripe suit, the other resting on a rail.

It was a meticulous performance. Young sipped water, asked for and was granted adjournments, and reverted to his hair-splitting way of speaking, which at times sounded like satire on the experts in court.

The diary, Young explained, was an 'exposition of a theory I outlined, somewhat fancifully, for my own amusement.' He had 'postulated someone with homicidal tendencies.'

The diary described R (Robert Egle) as 'the most logical choice' but

Young dismissed this as 'padding' and said he had needed a theme to fit his chemical interests.

'If I may say so, Mr Young, you display during the course of your evidence a remarkable calmness,' Leonard told him.

'I do not feel particularly calm, Mr Leonard, but I am not a person who manifests a great amount of emotion,' Young replied.

He was asked about a drawing which showed two left hands pouring poison into a cup with four heads. Two of these were bald, the same number as Hadland's employees who had lost their hair. Young called it a 'fantasy of my imagination.'

The jury were shown the drawings. Leonard said that figures on them corresponded to fatal doses of thallium and that the victims had 'the classic look of shock for a horror comic.'

Leonard probed Young's mask of innocence. 'Your expressions of regret at Mr Biggs' death were pure hypocrisy?' he said. 'His death satisfied you.'

'No,' Young replied. 'I can see very little satisfaction to be derived from a death like that.' His confessions had been a 'fake' in order to be allowed clothes, food and sleep, he said.

Leonard asked why, if the poison had been purchased for scientific tests, Young had almost no equipment to perform such tests. The defendant replied that he had done 'as much as I could' and had also tested thallium on 'wayside weeds'.

'You administered the thallium to four people, killing two of them and seriously harming two others,' Leonard said.

'I administered thallium to no one,' Young said. 'I performed the tests to satisfy my own curiosity about certain chemical problems.'

Leonard continued to challenge Young over the diary. 'As a work of fiction it jumps into the middle of the story pretty quickly, doesn't it?' he asked.

'Yes, but diaries often do.'

'Did you intend the diary for publication?'

'No ...' Young said. 'I was writing for my own amusement.'

'You have great confidence, Mr Young, in your ability to escape detection in the first place, and in the second place to escape conviction.'

'That is your opinion, Mr Leonard, you can hardly expect me to agree with it.'

Young made the fatal error during cross-examination of trying to match his interrogator point for point, wit for wit. Often, he nimbly outscored Leonard, leaving the prosecutor exasperated, and at no stage did Young crack or show the anguish of the falsely accused person. But this cool arrogance did not impress the jury.

Leonard read out a comment in the diary, 'Is someone setting up in opposition to me?!!!' and asked if that was a flippant remark in what Young claimed was a serious work of fiction.

'Since when, Mr Leonard, have poisoners been noted for their absence of humour?' Young replied.

'I don't know, Mr Young. I've never met any.'

Young bowed theatrically. 'Thank you, Mr Leonard,' he said.

Each counsel took only an hour over their closing speeches. Awaiting the verdicts on Thursday, 29 June, Young told his wardens that, if convicted, he would break his own neck on the dock rail. When the jury returned after an hour and a half's deliberation, Young's guard was doubled to four wardens.

He had been found guilty of murdering Bob Egle and Fred Biggs, of attempting to murder Jethro Batt and David Tilson, and of poisoning Ron Hewitt and Diane Smart. He was acquitted of poisoning Peter Buck and Trevor Sparkes.

Young said nothing as the judge sentenced him to life imprisonment. Downstairs, he asked to see Winifred and Aunt Winnie. His sister thought that his 'look' was now missing. 'Forget all about me,' Young told them. 'I'm sorry for all the trouble I have caused you.'

CASE FILE: YOUNG, GRAHAM FREDERICK

BACKGROUND

Graham Frederick Young was born in Honeypot Lane Maternity Hospital in Neasden on 7 September 1947. His mother Margaret had contracted pleurisy during pregnancy and died of tuberculosis when he was three months old.

Graham's father Fred, a machine setter, sent his eight year-old daughter Winifred to live with her grandmother in nearby Links Road, while Graham was brought up by Fred's sister Winnie Jouvenat and her husband Jack at 768 North Circular Road, a comfortable, modern terraced house with a garden.

Graham was close to the Jouvenats, whom he called Aunty Panty and Daddy Jack, and showed affection to their daughter Sandra. A chubby, freckle-faced little boy, he was fondly nick-named Pudding.

Fred Young re-married on 1 April 1950. His second wife Molly was an attractive, younger woman who played the accordion at a local public house. The family was soon reunited. Fred, Molly and Winifred joined Graham at North Circular Road while the Jouvenats went to live at Links Road.

At the age of five, Graham followed Winifred and Sandra to Braintcroft Junior School in Warren Road, Neasden. He was always a gauche, solitary child who had an uncomfortable relationship with his father, but he seemed fond of his stepmother and sister and the family budgie 'Lemon'. His family had no serious concern until bottles of chemicals, even Molly's nail varnish, began to fascinate him at the age of nine.

Young passed the 11-plus examination and was rewarded with a chemistry set by his father and a place at John Kelly Secondary school in Willesden. He acted well as the Ugly Sister in a pantomime, but was increasingly bored by any subject outside his own obsession. He told other boys that his stepmother was strict, mean with money and made him sit outside the pub while she played the accordion inside.

'Plain daft'

By the age of 11, Young was regularly borrowing library books on poison and medicine. Molly once found a bottle of acid hidden in his school jacket and Graham also enjoyed sniffing ether. When questioned, he told Molly that he had stolen both from a chemist's dustbin.

He read books on Adolf Hitler and the Nazi movement and liked to wear the Nazi swastika symbol. 'None of us took this obsession too seriously,' his sister Winifred was to write in her book, *Obsessive Poisoner* (1973). 'We just thought he was plain daft.'

Young was soon spending his pocket money on poisons, telling a local chemist, Geoffrey Reis, that he was 17 years old, the minimum legal age. In April 1961, he bought 25 grains of antimony, enough to kill several people. 'I was convinced by his knowledge that he was older than he appeared,' Reis was to say.

Power lust

Young later moved his custom to another chemist signing the poisons register 'M.E. Evans' and began carrying a bottle of antimony with him at school. 'It gave him a sense of security,' one classmate, Clive Creager, recalled. 'He was dangerous. He was evil and I was afraid of him.'

Young's lust for secret power led him to read about black magic and experiment with gunpowder extracted from fireworks. One day, his stepmother found in his jacket a wax model bristling with pins, a symbol of malicious will.

Both family and classmates recall his sinister drawings. 'I would be hanging from some gallows over a vat of acid,' Creager said. 'Graham would be holding a flame to the rope. He liked drawing people on gallows with syringes marked "poison" sticking into them.'

By early 1961, Young had become an expert on poisons, their effects and symptoms. He kept poison bottles at school, and books on poison and crime at home which he read and re-read avidly. 'Graham was totally obsessed,' Creager said. 'He had no normal school life, no interest in anything else.'

PSYCHOLOGICAL PROFILE

Graham Young was always trying to be a good boy. He wore neat clothes, disliked dirty jokes and spoke more like an adult than a young teenager. After poisoning his stepmother, the tender concern he showed her was exemplary.

Inside, there was a calculating murderer who could watch transfixed while his stepmother had convulsions on the lawn. However, it was not the pain which fascinated Young, but the symptoms. To him, these were the code of a private power he held over other people: 'I miss my antimony,' he told a psychiatrist when he was in Ashford remand centre after his first arrest. 'I miss the power it gives me.'

Guinea pigs

The psychiatrists who examined Young in 1962 had no doubt that he would always depend on poison as an instrument of survival, and Young left them feeling that his victims were mere guinea pigs.

One of the psychiatrists said Young 'had no grievances' against his relatives or the friend he had poisoned and indeed thought he loved them quite well. It just seemed, they were the nearest people to hand for his purpose'. This view was echoed by his sister Winifred, who wrote. 'He killed as though conducting experiments on rats.'

Young was imprisoned by his own gloom. The loss of his mother soon after birth, a sense of distance to his father, then the move away from his aunt who had brought him up must have left him without any anchor in life, searching for unwavering loyalty in others.

Young challenged his schoolboy friend Chris Williams to a

fight after Williams became friendly with another boy. Young lost and threatened to kill him. At home, he drew tombstones with the words 'Mum' and 'Dad' when his poisons or dead rats were taken away from him. To Young, this was betrayal.

His sexual development, wherever it might have led, was thwarted. It was no coincidence, that his first round of poisoning began just as he reached puberty, for he had no resources for coping with the turmoil of this experience.

At Hadland's Diane Smart noticed that Young had the smallest man's hands she had ever seen. When she said that hers would make two of his, Young replied, 'You'd be surprised what these hands can do for you, Diana.'

On another occasion, she asked Young if he ever went out with girls.

'I've had girlfriends,' he replied.

'Oh, so you're a woman hater then?' she asked.

'No, I wouldn't say that,' he replied, nettled. Inside, Young was again reaching for the one strength that sustained him: his fatal fascination with poisons. Like a child, he would react defensively to teasing; and like a child could never keep a secret.

After his arrest in 1962, he told his Aunt Winnie about poisoning his stepmother, with which he had not been charged, and in 1971 bragged half-naked in a police car about having committed a perfect murder nine years earlier.

The day after being charged with Fred Biggs' murder, Young revealed to a figure of authority, DCS Ronald Harvey, as much as he ever did to anyone except doctors, reciting a passage from Oscar Wilde's *The Ballad of Reading Gaol:*

Yet each man kills the thing he loves,
By each let this be heard.
Some do it with a bitter look.
Some with a flattering word.
The coward does it with a kiss,
The brave man with a sword.

After a pause, Young added, 'I suppose I could be said to kiss.' When Harvey mentioned remorse, Young replied, 'That would be hypocritical. What I feel is in the emptiness of my soul.'

Chapter 8

THE KRAY TWINS

THE GODFATHERS OF CRIME

In the 1960s, Ronnie and Reggie Kray became the most notorious gangland bosses in London's underworld. Their key to success was an appetite for violence that silenced rivals and bred loyalty through fear. Taken to the extreme of murder, however, violence ultimately led to their downfall.

On 9 March 1966, George Cornell perched on a stool in the Blind Beggar's saloon bar on the Whitechapel Road. At 8.30 p.m. on a midweek evening, the place was almost empty. Two other men were drinking at one of the tables, and an old man sat alone in the public bar.

Twenty-four hours earlier, Cornell had been a leading member of a south London gang run by two brothers, Charlie and Eddie Richardson. The previous night, they had raided a pub in Catford, south-east London. The raid had turned into a full-scale shoot-out. A man called Richard Hart had been shot and killed. Others, including Eddie Richardson, were wounded. With abundant evidence to work on, the police swooped.

Gangland feud

By the following day, only Cornell had escaped the dragnet. But for reasons known only to himself, instead of going to ground he decided he needed a drink. Strangely, instead of choosing a pub in south London, where the Richardsons had ruled supreme, he headed north of the Thames to Bethnal Green – the heartland of the Richardsons' greatest rivals, Reggie and Ronnie Kray.

For several months the two gangs had been engaged in a bitter struggle, and although the raid on the Catford pub had not directly concerned the Krays, Richard Hart had been a member of their gang. Revenge was called for, and this alone singled out Cornell as a marked man.

But Ronnie Kray had even more reason to want him dealt with. Shortly before Christmas 1965, the Krays had met the Richardsons at the Astor Club off Mayfair's Berkeley Square, ostensibly to discuss how their gangs could co-exist without confrontation. The talks broke down almost immediately, but not before Cornell had called Ronnie 'a big, fat poof'.

Wrong place, wrong time

When Cornell took his seat in the Blind Beggar, Reggie and Ronnie were drinking in another pub with various members of their gang (better known as the 'Firm').

Soon a startling piece of news arrived along the East End grapevine – George Cornell was drinking on their territory.

Ronnie announced he was going to drink elsewhere. He called for his driver, Jack Dickson, and his minder, Scotsman John 'Ian' Barrie, and asked to be driven home to Vallance Road, Bethnal Green. There he collected his 9-mm Mauser automatic, and told Dickson their next destination was to be the Blind Beggar.

When Ronnie Kray and Barrie walked through the saloon bar door, the barmaid was in the act of putting on a record, ironically titled 'The Sun Ain't Gonna Shine Any More' by the Walker Brothers.

'Well look who's here,' said Cornell. No more words were spoken. Barrie fired two shots into the ceiling and the barmaid ran down into the cellar. Ronnie then shot Cornell in the forehead and watched him slump down on to the bar.

The pair turned and walked from the pub. They got into their car and drove off. For Ronnie, this was the moment of triumph. He had finally committed the ultimate crime without fear and in the open.

The news spread fast, and soon everyone in the East End – including the police – had heard about the murder. Ronnie revelled in the sensation. 'I had killed a man,' he later wrote, 'and everyone knew I had killed him ... Now there was no doubt I was the most feared man in London. They called me the Colonel because of the way I organized things and the way I enjoyed battles. It was a name that I loved. It suited me perfectly.'

But despite the fact that everyone knew who had murdered George Cornell, no one would speak to the police. All four witnesses in the Blind Beggar were visited by members of the Firm and warned of the consequences of opening their mouths. And with no evidence beyond the corpse itself, the police were powerless.

In killing Cornell, Ronnie did more than demonstrate an ability to stretch violence to its limits: he also got one up on his twin brother. For the next 18 months, he kept on reminding Reggie that until he too had killed they could not be regarded as equals.

Failed assassin

By the autumn of 1967, the Firm was having increasing problems with one of its hangers-on, a small-time crook called Jack McVitie, known as 'the Hat' because of the headwear he wore to hide his baldness. An immensely strong man, and once a fearless brawler, McVitie had gradually been consumed by drink and drugs.

Occasionally the twins offered McVitie a spell of employment. In the summer of 1967, he cheated them of some money. To prove his loyalty, he was told to shoot Leslie Payne, a former business associate of the Krays. He was given a gun and an advance of £100, with another £400 to follow on completion of the job.

McVitie never did kill Payne, but he kept the Krays' money. When Reggie tried to smooth matters over, by lending McVitie another £50. Ronnie taunted his brother that he was turning soft. Matters grew worse when McVitie got drunk and, armed with a sawn-off shotgun, went to the Regency Club in Hackney claiming he was going to shoot them. His threats soon reached the ears of the Krays.

On Saturday, 28 October 1967, the twins arranged a party for their mother and friends in a Bethnal Green pub. During the course of the evening, Reggie received word that McVitie was due to turn up at the Regency later on that night.

After drinking himself to the point of numbness, Reggie took leave of his guests and arrived at the Regency just before 11 p.m. McVitie was nowhere to be seen. Frustrated, Reggie left his .32 revolver with Tony Barry, one of the two brothers who managed the club, and left to join his brother at a party in nearby Cazenove Road.

Fatal party

When Reggie arrived. Ronnie was disappointed – his brother had failed him once again. Resolving on action, Ronnie dispatched his cousin Ronnie Hart to the Regency to retrieve the gun, insisting it had to be delivered by Tony Barry himself. Then he sent out Anthony and Christopher Lambrianou, two half-Greek brothers, to track down Jack McVitie.

Hart returned first, Barry handed over the gun and disappeared into the night. Shortly before midnight the Lambrianous came back. With them was Jack the Hat.

Completely drunk, he walked into the room shouting. 'Where's the birds and the booze?' Reggie was waiting for him behind the door. He put his gun against McVitie's head and pulled the trigger. The killing should have been as simple as Ronnie's, but the gun failed to fire. Reggie grabbed McVitie, but he managed to struggle his way free and tried to throw himself through the window. He was hauled back in by his legs.

'Be a man, Jack,' said Ronnie.

'I'll be a man,' said McVitie, by now in tears, 'but I don't want to fucking die like one.'

With McVitie's arms held behind his back by Ronnie, Reggie took a carving knife and plunged it into his face just below his eye. He then stabbed him repeatedly through the chest and stomach until he was dead. The house was cleaned up, and the corpse disposed of. At last Ronnie could be proud of his brother.

With no witnesses other than members of the Firm, it was a while before the police got wind of McVitie's disappearance. His wife reported him missing, but with no body, there seemed little reason to suspect foul play.

Even when rumours of McVitie's killing reached the police, there was little they could do. For the second time the twins had killed in cold blood, but sheltered by the barrier of the East End wall of silence, for the time being they managed to remain impregnable.

FIGHT TO THE TOP

In the spring of 1952, Reggie and Ronnie received their National Service call-up papers, requiring them to join the Royal Fusiliers at the Tower of London. This proved a watershed in their criminal careers.

A few hours into their army career, the twins turned and walked towards the door. A corporal asked where they thought they were going. Home, they replied, to see their mother. The corporal caught hold of Ronnie's arm. Ronnie punched him on the jaw, knocking him out, and with his brother strolled through the door.

In the tower

The following morning the army came and collected them, and they returned without a struggle to their barracks, where they were sentenced to seven days in the guardroom.

They immediately decided to desert again. In the guardroom they met Dickie Morgan, a former Borstal boy from Mile End. As soon as their seven days were up, the three of them walked out of the Tower and headed straight for Morgan's home near London's docklands.

For the first time, the twins encountered a world where crime was regarded as a way of life. Through Morgan, they began to drink in clubs and bars frequented by criminals, and by the time the army caught up with them once again, they had opted to forgo the possibilities of boxing for a life of full-time villainy.

From then on, the army and the law actively aided them. A month in Wormwood Scrubs (for assaulting a policeman) and nine months at the Shepton Mallet military prison (for striking an NCO and going absent without leave) only served to introduce them to a wide range of criminals from across the country.

With their sentences completed, the army discharged the twins, leaving them with the problems of earning a living. They spent a large part of the day in the Regal snooker hall in Mile End. The place had seen better days – gangs had their fights there, fireworks were thrown at the manager's alsatian, the baize on the tables was slashed. When the manager resigned, Reggie and Ronnie stepped in with an offer to rent the hall for £5 a week.

Keeping the peace

Immediately, the trouble stopped. As Reggie later explained. 'It was very simple: the punters, the local tearaways, knew that if there was any trouble, if anything got broken, Ron and I would simply break their bones.'

Apart from maintaining order, the twins redecorated the hall, moved in 14 second-hand tables and began to earn some reasonable money. Their aim, however, was not merely to secure an income. With the Regal they had found themselves a base from which to operate. One of their first tasks was to see off threats from potential rivals. When a Maltese gang appeared to demand protection money, the twins went after them with knives. Word started to circulate about the newest arrivals in the East End underworld.

With a headquarters and a growing band of regulars who found the twins' patronage useful, the twins started to flaunt their violence. In the late evenings, Ronnie would frequently stand up and announce it was time for a raid. Then, accompanied by Reggie and a crowd of followers, he would set off for a pub, dance hall or club to engineer a brawl. At the same time, small-time crooks began to find the Regal a useful place to meet and discuss and plan possible ventures.

The twins also began to operate protection rackets – pension and nipping lists as they were known – whereby pubs, cafes, illegal gambling joints and bookies would be obliged to hand over goods or money in return for protection from rival gangs.

But although the income had begun to flow on a regular basis, the twins were still very much local villains, criminals from the East End who worked the East End. If they were going to break from their ghetto they needed an introduction to the wider world of organized crime in the West End.

In 1955, it appeared as if their break had finally arrived. The joint bosses of the London underworld were two men called Billy Hill and Jack Comer, better known as Jack Spot. Between them they had overseen the West End's drinking, gambling, prostitution and protection rackets for more than a decade. But they fell out with each other and after being badly cut up in a fight, Spot decided he needed some extra muscle. He called on the Krays.

Preparing for war

This was the invitation the twins had been waiting for – and immediately they embarked on large-scale preparations for a gang war with Spot's enemies. They collected weapons, called up their followers and established a base in Vallance Road.

They heard that the opposition was meeting in a pub near Islington. After assembling their army at the Regal, the twins set off for north London. When they arrived, they found the place empty – Billy Hill had got wind of the impending battle and ordered his men to pull out.

What the old-timers such as Spot and Billy Hill had long since learned was that power was wielded not through violence itself but by the credible threat of violence. The twins dealt in the real thing. Frustrated by the Islington fiasco, they sought a confrontation elsewhere. They chose a social club in Clerkenwell Road which was the headquarters of a gang of Italians.

Arriving shortly after 10 p.m., Ronnie entered alone and challenged the men inside to a fight. A bottle was thrown at his head, but no one said anything. In response he pulled out a Mauser and fired three shots into a wall. Still no one reacted, so Ronnie turned around and walked out.

Clearly he had made his point – the twins meant business. But no one wanted to do business with them. Even Spot tired of their antics and retired to run a furniture business.

Ignoring the twins, however, would not make them go away. Despite their failure to win full acceptance, they were no longer mere East End hoodlums, and it was only a matter of time before a major opening into the London underworld turned up. In the summer of 1956, the owner of a West End drinking club called the Stragglers approached the Krays to help stamp out the fighting that plagued his bar.

The next few years were to be ones of increasing prosperity. Ironically, one of the major reasons for this success was the fact that in November 1956, Ronnie received a three year prison sentence for grievous bodily harm. Having installed themselves in the Stragglers, the twins became involved in a dispute between the club's proprietors and a rival Irish gang. Ronnie thought the gang should be taught a lesson, and, after raiding the pub where the Irishmen met, participated in beating a man called Terence Martin to near death.

Although the separation from Ronnie was a great emotional blow to Reggie, it gave him free rein to manage the twins' business interests. Without his brother's continual demands for violent retribution at the faintest hint of an insult or competition, they flourished. One of his first moves was to open a legitimate club of his own – the Double R on the Bow Road, which soon became the East End's premier night spot. At the same time, he moved into minding and protecting the illegal gambling parties held at smart addresses in Mayfair and Belgravia.

Meanwhile, Ronnie appeared to accept his prison sentence at Wandsworth Prison with equanimity. Armed with his reputation and copious supplies of tobacco from his brother, he had little difficulty ensuring he was treated with due respect by his fellow inmates, many of whom he already knew. But, unexpectedly, because of his good behaviour he was transferred to Camp Hill prison on the Isle of Wight.

Isolated from both his friends in Wandsworth and his family, Ronnie's mind began to collapse with amazing speed. Just after Christmas 1957, he heard that his favourite aunt had died. After spending the night in a straitjacket, Ronnie was certified insane the following morning.

Planned escape

Transferred to Long Hill, a psychiatric hospital close to Epsom in Surrey, Ronnie's condition rapidly improved. Little attention was paid to strict security, and every Sunday visitors could come and see their friends or relatives. Reggie, naturally, was a regular visitor. But while he could see that Ronnie was on the road to recovery, he knew that if the hospital continued to regard his twin as insane they could postpone his release date indefinitely. Ronnie had to escape.

The plan was simplicity itself. Reggie entered the hospital wearing a light-coloured overcoat and while the ward attendant looked elsewhere, Ronnie put on the overcoat and walked through the door to freedom. By the time it was realized that the remaining twin was Reggie, Ronnie was on his way to a caravan in Suffolk.

Although his mind again deteriorated rapidly in the isolation of the countryside, the scheme worked. He remained free long enough for his certification of insanity to expire. Reggie then handed him back to the police, and he completed his sentence in Wandsworth Prison.

Strength to strength

Released in the spring of 1958, he could finally start to enjoy the riches Reggie had been accumulating for the last two years. Ronnie was soon back to his old ways, planning gangland battles and expanding the twins' operations through threats and violence. Then the twins undertook their biggest and most profitable venture to date – Esmeralda's Barn.

Esmeralda's Barn was a successful casino in Wilton Place, in London's wealthy Belgravia. Tipped off that it was effectively owned by just one man, Stefan de Faye, the twins' accompanied by Ronnie's financial adviser Leslie Payne, paid him a visit in the autumn of 1960. Payne outlined the twins' proposition that de Faye should sell his controlling share in the casino for £1,000. The prospect of falling foul of Ronnie and Reggie was enough to persuade de Faye to accept the offer. Overnight the twins were set up for the Sixties with one of the most lucrative casinos in the West End.

KINGS OF GANGLAND

With Esmeralda's Barn, the twins gained far more than a West End foothold. Its gaming tables alone earned them around £1,600 a week, and Reggie was soon busy at work adding protection money from the other clubs and casinos that had proliferated with the legalization of gambling in 1960. At least ten of them were handing over £150 weekly by 1962.

At the same time, the twins continued to open their own clubs. In March 1962, they opened the Kentucky, a bigger version of the Double R, in Stepney. Two years later, they bought into another club, the Cambridge Rooms on the Kingston by-pass, and invited the world heavyweight boxing champion Sonny Liston to the opening night party.

Celebrity status

Increasingly Reggie and Ronnie were meeting on social occasions with the rich and famous, who were unaware of their illegal activities. They all seemed to enjoy being photographed with the Krays.

The pictures resemble a 'who's who' of the Sixties smart set, ranging from actors and showbusiness celebrities such as Judy Garland, George Raft, Diana Dors and Barbara Windsor to sports personalities like football manager Malcolm Allison and the boxer Ted 'Kid' Lewis.

But although the first half of the decade was an era of expansion, the twins failed to capitalize fully from either their legitimate or illegal business interests. Largely responsible for this was their inability to give up the habits that got them where they were, but which also proved a liability.

As fast as the Krays added a new concern to their empire, an old one crumbled off. The Double R had its licence revoked after Reggie refused to give the police information on the whereabouts of Ronnie Marwood, wanted for the stabbing of a policeman. Esmeralda's Barn, which should have kept the twins in a regular source of income for years, soon began to run at a loss once Ronnie started handing out credit to gamblers who could not repay their debts. In 1964, the Krays received a tax demand from the Inland Revenue that they were unable to meet. The Barn went out of business.

Strangely, the twins never appeared to be in crime for the money – they took it as a mark of success, but once they had secured a reasonable return for their efforts, they became bored.

Novelty began to grow more and more important. Ronnie in particular continually produced one extraordinary scheme after another. Later, that same year, he plunged into one of the twins' most bizarre ventures.

Ernest Shinwell, son of the veteran Labour peer, Manny Shinwell, proposed they invest in a project to build a new town at Enugu in eastern Nigeria. The twins immediately put in £25,000, later followed by a lot more. The investment yielded no return whatsoever, although Ronnie did get one or two trips to Nigeria, where he was driven round in a Rolls-Royce and stylishly entertained.

If the Krays spent money easily, there appeared to be no potential shortage of sources of new funds. In 1965, the twins spread their net wider as they began to develop a working relationship with the American Mafia.

Big bucks

Their first chance to prove themselves in the field of international crime came with the theft of $55,000 worth of bonds from a bank in Canada. Too hot to be laundered through North America, some of the bonds were offered to the Krays for sale in Europe. Soon the trade was flourishing.

In the same year, the Krays' criminal career suffered a setback. Hew McCowan, the son of a baronet and owner of a Soho club called the Hide-a-way, told the police the Krays were demanding half his profits. Reggie and Ronnie were arrested, and after 56 days in custody appeared at the Old Bailey charged with demanding money with menaces.

By the time the trial took place, however, they had dug up enough information about McCowan's history as a police informer to throw doubt on the reliability of his evidence. The trial was halted before the summing-up speeches and the twins were released. The very same day, they celebrated their acquittal by buying the Hide-a-way, renaming it El Morocco and throwing a victory party.

Reggie weds

For Reggie, the good times looked set to continue. On 20 April, he married the woman he had courted for three years, 21 year-old Frances Shea. The wedding was celebrated in typical Kray style, with Rolls-Royces, David Bailey as the official photographer, celebrities such as boxer Terry Spinks in attendance and congratulatory telegrams from Judy Garland, Barbara Windsor and many others.

But beneath the veneer of upward mobility, the violence which had been the twins main asset in getting them to the top began to turn sour on them. Instead of settling down to enjoy the proceeds of their protection rackets, clubs and casinos, Ronnie in particular became obsessed with proving himself to be the unchallenged boss of London's underworld.

Over the years, his suits became slicker, he began to wear ostentatious jewellery, and more and more he regarded himself as a Godfather figure. But while he adopted the appearance of a smart crook, moving with the times and mingling with the jet set, his mind was slowly disintegrating.

Ronnie cracks

Ronnie's bouts of depression worsened, and he started to regard almost everyone around him with suspicion. His fears would give way to sudden bouts of pathological violence. It did not take much to set him off. One old friend who tried to borrow £5 was slashed in the face. Another had his cheeks branded after starting a brawl in Esmeralda's Barn.

Ronnie, however, wanted more than random attacks and knifings. Ever since the days of the Regal billiard hall, he took a great pride in his organizational abilities, assembling gangs to beat up rival gangs, and building up an armoury of weapons that included machine guns. Time after time, however, his dream of releasing his forces on competition worth attacking had been thwarted.

Only with the emergence of the Richardson brothers and their gang did the Krays look as if they finally had an enemy powerful enough to demand their full attention. The fact that the Mafia was now dealing with the twins added an extra piquancy.

Ronnie found himself in his element. After the meeting when Cornell called him a 'fat poof', he had a double grudge to bear, and when a car ran down a man who resembled Ronnie in Vallance Road it looked like a gang war was starting. Later Ronnie recalled, 'I was loving it. Fighting, scrapping, battling – that's what I'd come into it for in the first place.'

Gang shoot-out

Unhappily for Ronnie, the excitement was shortlived. When the two Richardson brothers became involved in a shoot-out with another gang at a pub in Catford, it looked as though they had destroyed themselves without any help from the Krays. Ronnie once again felt he had been cheated of the opportunity to prove himself through violence.

And instead of revelling in this stroke of luck that left the twins as the undisputed rulers of London's gangland, Ronnie's pathological urge for revenge overpowered him. Within 24 hours he had murdered George Cornell.

As usual, it fell on Reggie to ensure all the loose ends were tidied up and his brother kept out of jail. The two of them took a three week holiday in Morocco, only returning when the local police began to harass them.

They arrived back in London to find a distinctly uneasy atmosphere. Some of the protection money had dried up, and a few members of the Firm had made themselves scarce. It did not take long for the twins to reassert their authority, but it needed a bit more to raise morale.

Freeing the axeman

Soon the twins hit on the perfect scheme – springing Frank 'the Mad Axeman' Mitchell, an old friend of Ronnie's, from Dartmoor Prison.

The idea was much simpler than it sounded. Mitchell had become a trusted prisoner allowed to work outside on the moors. His warder let him wander off by himself. He visited local pubs and even had a mistress for a while, making love in a deserted barn. In any case, the purpose of freeing him was not to secure his liberty permanently, but to draw attention through the press to the fact that he had been incarcerated without a release date.

On 12 December 1966, everything ran smoothly to plan. Even before the prison authorities realized Mitchell was missing, he had been driven to a safe flat in Barking in east London, and there he stayed for the next 12 days. He sent letters to *The Times* and the *Daily Mirror*, both of which were published, but as the days passed he grew more and more frustrated at finding himself cooped up with even less freedom than he had when he was at Dartmoor.

As Christmas approached, matters reached a head. Mitchell steadfastly refused to give himself up, threatened his minders with violence and demanded to see his family. For the Krays it was a crisis: if he escaped, he could wreck the organization by implicating them all in his escape.

To calm Mitchell down, they told him on 23 December that he would be taken to a place in the country the following day. The van arrived at 8.30 p.m. on Christmas Eve, Mitchell got in. He was never seen again.

The Krays have always maintained that Mitchell was smuggled out of the country and set up with a new identity abroad. They have refused to specify where.

But Albert Donaghue, the man who drove the van, said in court that Mitchell was shot repeatedly by Freddie Foreman, an old friend of the twins, and two other men after leaving the flat in Barking.

If the aim of freeing Mitchell had been to raise the Firm's spirits, it clearly backfired. Even if he did leave Britain, the rumours and the lack of proof counted against the twins.

Nonetheless they survived. The police apparently had made no progress with the Cornell investigation, and there was even less evidence to connect them with the disappearance of Mitchell. Ronnie's mental problems seemed to have stabilized, while Reggie remained as calm as ever.

Then, in the early summer of 1967, Reggie's world fell apart. Despite the extravagant celebrations of his marriage to Frances, the marital bliss had proved shortlived. He had refused to allow her to work, forcing her instead to sit alone in their flat while he was constantly out and about managing the twins affairs. Barely two months after the wedding, Frances found the strain too much and moved back to her parents' home. Her mental condition deteriorated, and by the autumn she was receiving her first treatment for acute depression.

Various attempts were made to patch up the marriage, all without success. Then, in June 1967, Frances committed suicide with an overdose of barbiturates. His wife's death shattered Reggie and changed him forever. He began drinking heavily, started taking pills and gradually grew as sadistic and violent as his brother.

When he heard that a friend Frederick had disliked his wife, Frances, he drank himself into a frenzy and, with two members of the Firm, drove to Frederick's house at around 7 a.m. Screaming abuse, Reggie started shooting, and hit Frederick in the leg. Shortly afterwards another man received the same treatment at a club in Highbury for refusing to give Reggie £1,000. He also slashed the face of a former boxer at the Regency Club.

At the same time, he had to endure the continual taunts of his brother: Ronnie had grandiose plans for expansion, Reggie was content with milking the easy money they were already receiving. Ronnie, despite his preference for boys, was the hard man, Reggie, with his taste for women was soft. Ronnie had killed a man. Reggie had not.

Topping the hat

The strain eventually proved too much. As the problems with Jack 'the Hat' McVitie grew, Ronnie began to talk of having to kill him himself. Reggie was left with no choice – if his brother was planning once again to prove his superiority in the field of violence, then he had to get his blow in first. And so, on a Saturday night in October 1967, he finally did.

CRACKING THE CASE

In the aftermath of the Hew McCowan case, the twins found themselves in a strong position. If the police harassed them, or worse still failed in another attempt to bring them to justice, they could claim they were being victimized.

As long as they remained discreet, it looked as if their long-term future was secure, especially as virtually no news of McVitie's murder had leaked out. The police had heard little more than that some immigrant crooks had been involved.

In 1967, however, Scotland Yard decided it was time the twins were permanently put out of circulation. The head of the operation was the twins' old adversary, Leonard 'Nipper' Read. To prevent leaks, his team of 14 detectives moved into Tintagel House, a block of government offices on the south bank of the Thames, which was isolated from all but the most essential contact with Scotland Yard.

Here Read began the long and painstaking task of sifting through all the known information about the twins. Progress was slow. Reggie and Ronnie soon discovered detectives had attempted to interview many of their victims and associates, and warned them to keep silent. It looked as if once again the wall of silence would see the twins through.

What Read needed was a break. It came from the unlikely source of Leslie Payne, the man who had masterminded the acquisition of Esmeralda's Barn and organized many of the 'long firm' frauds, and was triggered by the twins' use of gratuitous violence.

In a belated attempt to test McVitie's loyalty before Reggie stabbed him, Ronnie had dispatched him to murder Payne. Although McVitie bungled the attempt, Payne came to the conclusion that it was either his life or theirs.

He decided to talk to the police, and in December 1967, he spent three weeks in a Marylebone hotel giving Nipper Read a statement that eventually ran to some 200 pages. It contained everything he knew about the twins' activities, from Esmeralda's Barn to their Mafia connections.

The task now was to verify Payne's claims. Read's solutions involved attaching a safety clause to all the statements his team gathered, whereby they would never be used unless the twins had first been arrested.

Continuing confidence

Despite the secrecy of Read's operation, the twins' network of sources soon let them know he was on their trail. They were not unduly disturbed – as Reggie later said. 'We didn't think we would go down. We underestimated the cunning of the police.' They contented themselves with buying two pythons and naming them Nipper and Gerrard (after the detective involved in the McCowan case). Ironically, the snakes proved too hard to handle. One escaped, and the other was returned to its seller.

At this point, Alan Cooper, a financier, began to play a more important role in the Krays lives. Cooper had helped the twins dispose of some stolen Canadian bonds. Although Reggie favoured caution until the police hunt had died down. Ronnie was growing ever more obsessed with establishing himself as the Godfather figure of the London underworld. This called for more contact with the Mafia, and in Cooper he thought he had found the contact who could help him.

Despite the fact that Ronnie had a criminal record. Cooper said he could arrange an American visa for him through Paris, and once in the United States, various meetings could be arranged with the Mafia. Ronnie leapt at the opportunity. Cooper was as good as his word and in April 1968, the two of them flew into New York for a few days' discussions with a Mafia representative called Frank Ileano.

To Ronnie, it looked like another step up the ladder. After returning to Britain, he warmed to Cooper's suggestion that the Mafia would appreciate the killing of George Caruana, a Maltese club-owner, as a display of the Krays' strength. The two of them decided to put a bomb in his car. Cooper said he knew a man who could supply the explosive. He dispatched an assistant to fly to Glasgow to collect four sticks of dynamite from a contact in the centre of the city.

As he boarded his return flight, the man was arrested. Under questioning he named Cooper as his boss. Nipper Read hauled Cooper in, only to discover both to his surprise and irritation that Cooper had been operating as an agent of the United States Treasury Department and with the knowledge of Read's superiors at Scotland Yard.

According to Cooper, his task was to implicate the twins in attempted murder. With the dynamite courier arrested, this now became impossible, so Read decided to use Cooper as bait to get the twins to incriminate themselves. He installed Cooper in a private hospital with a microphone beside his bed. He then got him to invite the twins round.

A certain strangeness in Cooper's manner on the telephone alerted Ronnie and Reggie, and instead of going themselves they sent one of Reggie's friends. He refused to commit himself in front of Cooper and once again the twins had escaped Nipper Read.

It seemed that the police had walked into another cul-de-sac. The twins tightened their organization, and opted for a low-profile approach to running their empire. With the Richardsons in jail and the deaths of Cornell and McVitie fading into the past, it looked as if they would weather the storm.

Nonetheless, the strain of endless vigilance had begun to tell. Although the money continued to flow in from the clubs and casinos, with no major deals on the go life had lost some of its excitement. One evening in early May 1968, Ronnie decided that what the Firm needed was a good 'knees-up'.

Last night out

He told everyone to collect their women and head for Mayfair's Astor Club. Outside the club, there was the usual gaggle of photographers snapping pictures of everyone who entered. Maybe there were more than usual, and Reggie, visibly irritated, shouted at them to stop. No one noticed that they were never offered the rapidly developed prints as souvenirs later in the evening.

Through the early hours of the morning, the twins carried on drinking, their troubles forgotten. Ronnie was enjoying the company of a young man he had brought along for the evening, and Reggie had a young lady. At 5 a.m., they left the Astor and returned to their flat at Braithwaite House, on City Road, Finsbury.

They had barely had time to fall asleep when the front door was crashed off its hinges with a sledgehammer. Ronnie and Reggie awoke to find themselves surrounded by armed policemen. At their head was Nipper Read, clipping handcuffs around their wrists and reading aloud the standard arrest statement.

Banged up

Simultaneously across the East End, other groups of armed police swooped on 24 addresses. Only two of the men on Read's wanted list escaped the raids. With the twins picked up, the safety clause on the statements already collected could be activated. And although the evidence was not as strong as he would have liked – there was nothing pinning either of the murders on Reggie and Ronnie – if Read could demonstrate that now he held the upper hand, then maybe others would talk.

Read was playing a risky game – failure now would probably put the twins beyond the reach of the law forever. But if the wall of silence could be made to crack, then it might pay off.

THE EMPIRE CRUMBLES

Even locked up in Brixton Prison, the twins were confident they could still escape justice. Every day their mother brought them lunch, usually cold chicken and a bottle of wine, while friends would drop by with news from the outside world. With their cousin, Ronnie Hart, and Ronnie's minder, Ian Barrie, still at large, most people who knew them thought they could continue to ensure that no one would talk. Even when these two failed to escape Nipper Read's net, the Krays still believed the wall of silence would hold strong.

Slowly, however, the first seeds of doubt crept into their minds as the messages reaching them grew more pessimistic. Their fears were confirmed at the preliminary hearings held at Old Street Magistrates Court on 6 July 1968. To generate as much publicity as possible, the twins asked for all press restrictions to be lifted. 'We want the world to see the diabolical liberties the law has been taking,' Reggie said.

Journalists were delighted – the trial would be the biggest they had witnessed for years. The twins were less happy when into the witness box stepped Billy Exley who had guarded both Vallance Road after the killing of George Cornell and Frank Mitchell after his escape from Dartmoor.

For the first time Reggie and Ronnie began to look vulnerable. Exley was followed by the Blind Beggar's barmaid. As she stood to begin her evidence. Nipper Read could not resist a smile – he knew his assistant Superintendent Mooney had persuaded her to reveal the threats she had received after the killings of George Cornell.

Breathing space

With the completion of the preliminary hearings, the twins were held in Brixton Prison for five more months. This gave Read the breathing space he needed to convince more members of the Firm to take the witness stand and testify against Reggie and Ronnie.

The actual trial opened at the Old Bailey on 7 January 1969. Reggie and Ronnie were both charged with murder and being an accessory to murder. Public interest was intense. Seats in the public gallery were sold on the black market for £5, and celebrities such as Charlton Heston were in attendance. The twins' old friend Judy Garland sent them a good-luck telegram (prompting Ronnie to remark to the judge, 'If I wasn't here now I'd probably be having a drink with Judy Garland').

It soon became clear that almost all the twins' Firm had deserted them. Ronnie Hart was the principal prosecution witness. Along with John Dickson, the man who had driven Ronnie and Ian Barrie to the Blind Beggar, he turned Queen's evidence in return for freedom from prosecution. Altogether 28 criminals gave evidence against the twins.

Spirited defence

With the odds weighing so heavily against them, the twins had no chance of escape. They elected, however, to go down fighting. When Ronnie stepped into the witness box, he embarked on a spectacular course of denial. Not only were he and George Cornell friends, but he had never even been to the Blind Beggar on the evening in question. Reggie likewise refused to concede a thing. In their own eyes, they behaved with dignity and integrity throughout the trial, while their former accomplices and friends had betrayed their loyalty.

On only two occasions did the twins lose their composure. Ronnie called the prosecuting counsel 'You fat slob!' after hearing how the police had confiscated his grandparents' pension books. And when the court was hearing about the circumstances surrounding Frances's death and funeral. Reggie screamed. 'The police are scum.'

In one respect, however, they disappointed the press and public. Many people hoped that there were secrets to reveal about the celebrities and politicians who knew them. But again, according to the twins, this was a matter of honour. Members of their Firm may have grassed on them, but they were not going to stoop to their level. 'We never informed on anyone,' said Ronnie. 'We believe that two wrongs do not make a right. We believe we are better off than the rats who deserted our ship.'

Only three men remained loyal throughout the trial. Ian Barrie, who received 20 years for his role in the murder of Cornell, the twins' elder brother, Charlie, and a friend of his, Freddie Foreman, who were both sentenced to ten years for disposing of McVitie's corpse.

After the longest criminal trial in legal history – 61 days in all – the jury retired. They took 6 hours and 54 minutes to find the twins guilty. Just after 7 p.m., on 8 March 1969, the judge, Mr Justice Melford Stevenson, finally pronounced sentence, 'I am not going to waste words on you. In my view society has earned a rest from your activities. I sentence you to life imprisonment, which I recommend should not be less than 30 years.'

The Krays had finally been broken. They were both 34. By the time they left jail, they would be almost ready to draw their pensions.

Law of the jungle

A few other matters remained to be cleared up. The twins were tried for the murder of Frank Mitchell. Although they pleaded guilty to harbouring him, there was insufficient evidence to convict them of his death. The charges concerning their criminal business activities were left on file.

They had lived by the law of the jungle, on the principle that only the fittest had the right to survive. Now the Krays were behind bars, fit only for study as one of nature's oddities.

CASE FILE: KRAY, REGGIE & KRAY, RONNIE

BACKGROUND

Reggie was the first of the twins to be born, late on 24 October 1933. Ronnie followed him less than an hour later. Their mother, Violet, was delighted, even though twins would strain the family's finances. They already had a four year-old son Charlie.

Their birthplace, Hoxton, was one of the poorest areas in Britain. It was even looked down upon by people from other poor parts of East London. Traditionally the only ways of escaping its poverty were either boxing or crime.

Their father, Charlie Kray 'pestered' for a living – persuading people to sell him clothes, silver and gold for resale at a profit. His work, travelling across England, kept him away from home a lot, and from the very start Violet was the dominant figure in Reggie's and Ronnie's lives.

Throughout their childhood, she doted on them, always taking care to treat them with scrupulous equality. In a world where no one owned much of value, she found in her twins something that made her stand out, and they became the pride of her life.

Despite the twins' identical appearance, as they grew from babies into young boys, various differences in their character began to emerge. Reggie was slightly brighter and more outgoing. Even at an early age he found it easier than Ronnie to talk to people. Ronnie found ways to compensate – either by sulking or screaming to gain attention, or trying to outdo his twin in over-blown displays of love for their mother.

Each twin would pay close attention to every move the other made. Fiercely loyal to each other, they were also the greatest of rivals. If one started a fight, the other had to join in. And soon Ronnie learned how to turn this to his advantage: by beginning a fight and drawing Reggie in they became equal partners in misbehaviour with no chance of Reggie becoming the golden boy.

Shortly before the outbreak of World War II, the Kray family moved from their house in Hoxton to Vallance Road in Bethnal Green. Although Violet took her three sons to live in the comparative safety of the Suffolk countryside early in the war, to escape the German bombing, she missed London and her family too much, and they soon moved back.

Fighting thrill

Amid the devastation of the Blitz, the twins discovered the excitement and thrill of fighting. On the bomb sites and in burned out buildings, they fought with rival gangs of boys, and quickly earned a reputation as the toughest of scrappers.

The war also gave the twins practical experience at outwitting the law. In 1939, their father had received his military call-up papers, but preferring to keep his business going he went on the run. He would occasionally return home to visit his wife and children, however.

Twice when he was in the house, the police arrived to try and apprehend him. The first time, old Charlie Kray hid beneath the table, sheltered from view by the tablecloth, while the twins were questioned about his whereabouts.

On the second occasion, Charlie dived into a cupboard. With a policeman poised to open its door, Ronnie called out, 'You don't think my dad would hide in there, do you?' The constable shrugged, and went to search elsewhere.

Teenage boxers

Rapidly the twins were learning the art of survival – outwitting the forces of law and order, and making use of their taste for fighting. For a while, however, it looked as if they might direct physical prowess into legitimate channels.

Their elder brother, Charlie, had joined the Royal Navy during the war, and soon established a promising reputation as a forces' boxer. While on leave, he started to teach the twins a few tricks, hanging a canvas kit bag from the ceiling of a bedroom at Vallance Road to use as a punch-bag.

The first time the twins stepped into a boxing ring was at a fair held in a local park. One of the main attractions was a booth where hardened fighters would take on challengers who wanted to go a few rounds. If the challenger survived the allotted number of rounds, he stood to win a few pounds.

On one occasion, none of the fair-goers were eager to take a chance, despite the exhortations of the ringside manager. Suddenly Ronnie shouted he was game for a try. Laughter broke out around the booth, while the manager joked that there was no one small enough to fight him. At this point, Reggie called out that he was prepared to take on his brother.

The two of them stepped inside the ring and, cheered on by the audience, they attacked each other for all they were worth. After three rounds, the match was halted, and they were paid half-a-crown (12½ pence) each.

Their potential as fighters caught the eye of a local coach, and the twins embarked on a strict regime of training. In pursuit of a career in boxing, they went without cigarettes and drink, and began to win bout after bout.

Different styles

Reggie was the more promising of the two. In 1948, he won the London Schoolboys Boxing Championship, and after turning professional at the age of 16, he won all seven of his bouts. Ronnie was not far behind him, but whereas his brother had the technique of the true professional. Ronnie would wade in to overwhelm his opponent through sheer power.

But the twins big problem was an inability to confine their violence to the ring. Their first serious brush with the law came in 1950, when they beat up a 16 year-old fellow East-Ender in a Hackney alley.

Two witnesses had seen the fight, and named the Krays as the attackers. Their evidence was backed up by the victim, and Reggie and Ronnie were remanded in custody for trial at the Old Bailey.

Before the trial took place, however, both the witnesses and the victim were reminded of the dangers they ran if they repeated what they had seen in court, with the result that when the case came up it was rapidly dismissed for lack of evidence. Already the twins had learned the power of threats backed by violence, and how easy it was to gain immunity from the law by instilling fear in victims and witnesses.

Assault charges

A year later, in the summer of 1951, the twins were charged with another assault. They had been standing outside a cafe on the Bethnal Green Road, when a policeman pushed Ronnie in the back and told him to move along. Ronnie turned round and punched him in the mouth, knocking him to the pavement. The brothers made their escape, but within an hour they were stopped by two officers and Ronnie was arrested.

Although he had nothing to do with the original incident, Reggie felt he had let his brother down badly. As a matter of honour, he went back to the Bethnal Green Road in search of the policeman Ronnie had hit. When he found him, he tapped him on the shoulder. As the policeman turned round, Reggie punched him on the jaw and laid him out for the second time that afternoon.

On probation

A few days later, the twins appeared before a magistrate, but once again the Krays escaped serious trouble. With the help of a local priest who pleaded on their behalf, they received nothing more serious than probation.

By now, Ronnie and Reggie had stumbled on the combination of binding loyalty and rivalry that would both carry them forward and protect them in the adult world. Where one led the other had to follow – and the one who pushed the hardest would be the one in control.

PSYCHOLOGICAL PROFILE

One of the puzzles behind the Kray story is why the twins believed they had to go as far as murder to consolidate their criminal empire. The deaths of George Cornell and Jack 'the Hat' McVitie eventually finished their careers and earned them prison sentences of 30 years each.

Even taking into account the code of silence that was supposed to protect them, the risks they took were unnecessary and ultimately ruined them.

Ronnie Kray's reason for murdering George Cornell in March 1966 was to prove to the south London Richardson gang that the Krays were prepared to confront any opposition and eliminate it. They did not need to. Two days earlier, the Richardson gang had effectively destroyed themselves in an abortive shoot-out with a smaller gang.

Deadly revenge

Eddie Richardson had been wounded and the police had enough evidence to convict the Richardsons for the shooting. When Ronnie Kray walked into the Blind Beggar and shot Cornell, he achieved nothing except to provide further proof of what everyone already knew about the Krays – that they were capable of unrestrained violence.

Eighteen months later, Reggie Kray stabbed Jack 'the Hat' McVitie to death because he had insulted and challenged the Krays in public. The twins persuaded themselves that if they did not respond to these threats, their integrity would be damaged. Jack McVitie was nothing more than a small-time East End hard-man, given to bouts of drinking and violence.

He posed no real threat to the Krays and did not come from a rival gang that would be likely to do so.

True motive

The reason for the two murders had more to do with the twins' obsession with their image as gangsters. Violence was the tool that had been used to bring them success and, far more than their skills at corruption, protection, extortion and fraud, it was their willingness to use violence that had earned their reputation.

As their empire expanded and they began to reap the financial benefits, the Krays still remained restless and dissatisfied – fame, or notoriety seemed to matter more than wealth.

This applied particularly to Ronnie Kray. He was fascinated with the world of Al Capone and the Chicago gangsters of the 1920s. He heard that the Mob bosses of the time used to have their private barbers and so he arranged to have one himself. He had his suits specially made for him. He enjoyed being nicknamed 'the Colonel', because it fitted his own image of a tough, semi-military leader, completely in charge of events.

He was also intrigued by the power of fire-arms and explosives. He had bought his first gun when he was 16 and as the Kray empire expanded, so did his armoury. By the time the twins were mobilizing for 'war' against the Richardsons, he had obtained two Browning machine-guns and was trying to buy Mills bombs and limpet mines.

Meeting the Mob

Ronnie Kray's other obsession was with the Mafia. He was intrigued by the possibility of forming an alliance with them and helping them to establish a foothold in London. His visit to America to make contact with them was more like the fulfilment of a childhood fantasy than the business trip it was intended to be. He returned to London with very little achieved, but seemed satisfied to have rubbed shoulders with his senior cousins in crime.

Ronnie Kray failed to use violence as a means to an end. As his career developed it became clear that it was an end in itself. In order to prove that he was a master of his chosen profession he had to commit the ultimate act of violence – to kill a man. By shooting George Cornell he felt he could stand shoulder to shoulder with the Americans he so respected – he had 'got his button,' to use their own terminology and that was reason enough to have carried out the act.

It was different for Reggie Kray. Without the overpowering influence of his brother, it is very likely that he would have been happy to consolidate their position without resorting to murder.

Money deals

While Ronnie Kray organized campaigns against his enemies. Reggie preferred to set up deals that would bring in more money. Reggie was quite capable of using violence but, unlike his brother, he understood that it should be used for a purpose.

It was the special hold that the two brothers had over each other that eventually led to Reggie's murder of Jack McVitie. As twins they had always formed a united front, acting with a common purpose that gave them a sinister advantage over their opponents. The strength that this solidarity gave them was perhaps the key to their success, and it formed a dependance on each other that proved unbreakable.

By murdering George Cornell, Ronnie Kray had established a psychological advantage over his brother. Reggie was made to feel that until he too had killed a man, he was letting down Ronnie and becoming a dangerously weak link in their partnership.

The ultimate act

Reggie resisted the pressure from his brother until the end of 1967, when Jack McVitie began to take unacceptable liberties with the twins. It also coincided with a time when Reggie was at his most emotionally vulnerable, in the months that followed the suicide of his wife Frances.

Against his better judgement, but with a cold-bloodedness that went beyond his brother's murder of George Cornell. Reggie murdered Jack McVitie and rejoined Ronnie on an equal footing of brutality.

Chapter 9

ALBERT DESALVO
THE BOSTON STRANGLER

For three years the Strangler stalked the streets of Boston, leaving a macabre trail of terror in his wake. As conventional methods failed them, the police resorted to desperate measures to ensnare him – psychic detection, hypnosis, even a truth serum.

On Thursday, 14 June 1962, a few minutes before 7 p.m., Juris Slesers drove up and parked outside 77 Gainsborough Street – a red-bricked house in an attractive tree-lined road in the Back Bay area of Boston. He got out of the car, went up to the third floor and knocked on the door of apartment 3F where his mother, Anna Slesers, lived.

There was no reply. He knocked again, more loudly. She loved music, perhaps she had the radio or hi-fi on too loud and could not hear him? There was still no answer. Juris knocked again, puzzled. She was, after all, expecting him.

By 7.30, Juris was convinced that something must be wrong. Perhaps, she had been taken ill and collapsed inside, unable to call for help. At 7.45, Juris broke down the door of the apartment. As he entered, he almost fell against a chair placed in the middle of the hallway. He went into the bedroom and found that the dresser drawers had been left open.

Finding no sign of his mother, Juris strode down the hallway, towards the kitchen and bathroom. He found his mother, lying on her back on the kitchen floor. Her legs seemed to have been forced wide apart, with her right leg bent at the knee. Her housecoat had been left open at the front, so that she was naked from the shoulders down. The blue cord of her housecoat had been knotted tightly around her neck and tied into a clumsily-shaped bow.

Seeing that his mother was probably dead, Juris phoned the police, who arrived four minutes later. A few minutes after eight o'clock, Special Officer James Mellon and Sergeant John Driscoll from the Homicide Division arrived. A visibly shaken Juris explained how he thought his mother must have been depressed and committed suicide. But Inspector Mellon's impression as he glanced round the room was quite different.

The bath next to the body was one-third full of water, as if Mrs Slesers had been about to have a bath. This and other clues pointed to the much more likely explanation that she had been interrupted by an assailant who had murdered her.

Neat disarray

There was something else, too. Mellon had been struck by the general neatness of the hall and living room. Yet a wastepaper basket had been left in the kitchen with odds and ends strewn around it. The drawers of the dressing table in the bedroom had all been pulled open, and their contents disturbed.

Mellon's suspicions were soon to be confirmed. The autopsy revealed that Anna Slesers had suffered head injuries, either from a fall or a blow, but had undoubtedly been strangled. Although there was no evidence of rape, she had been sexually assaulted.

By now, the generally held opinion of the police was that an intruder had broken into the apartment intent on robbery. He came across Mrs Slesers undressing for her bath and was seized by an uncontrollable urge to assault her. He panicked and strangled her from fear of being identified.

There were still two things that puzzled them, however. The first was the method of entry into the apartment. There were no signs of a break-in, which led to the obvious conclusion that Mrs Slesers must have let her assailant in. But she was a shy, retiring woman who had never been seen in the company of a man. It seemed even less likely that she would open a door to a stranger, particularly while wearing only a bathrobe and without her dentures in.

No motive

The second question that troubled the police was motive. The ransacking of the apartment had suggested burglary. Yet a small gold watch and other pieces of jewellery had been left untouched.

Even more curiously, there had seemed to be some method in the disarray, suggesting a leisurely examination of the victim's possessions, rather than a frenzied random ransacking.

Few of the details of the crime were made public, although over the next few days more than 60 people were questioned, to no avail. Indeed, it seemed for a short time that Anna Sleser's murder might be just one more Boston crime statistic. Then, on 30 June, just two weeks later, the body of another elderly woman, 68 year-old Nina Nichols, was found in almost identical circumstances. She had been strangled with two of her own nylon stockings (again knotted into a bow) and her housecoat and slip had been pulled up to her waist so that she lay naked and exposed.

Orderly chaos

As in the Slesers case, the apartment superficially bore all the signs of ransacking. Nina Nichols' bags had been torn open and their contents thrown about. Her clothes and other possessions had been tossed in all directions, and a photo album had been ripped apart, its pages scattered everywhere.

But again, robbery could not be considered a motive – an expensive camera worth at least $300 had been left – and the same orderliness existed in the midst of chaos. There was no sign of a forced entry, and no clues in the character of the victim. A widow for many years, Nina Nichols was known to have no male companions.

The Boston police were now faced with a situation in which two elderly women had been sexually molested and strangled within two weeks of one another. Police Commissioner Edward McNamara, newly appointed to supervise the Boston police force, called a conference of department heads for Monday, 2 July.

But even before the conference had ended, he received news of a third strangling. Helen Blake, a retired practical nurse of 65 years of age, was found in her apartment at 73 Newshall Street in Lynn, a town several miles north of Boston.

Similar pattern

She was discovered in much the same circumstances as the first two victims, almost naked, and strangled with a nylon stocking with a bra looped through it. The bra straps had been knotted under her chin in the form of a large bow. Like Anna Slesers and Nina Nichols, she had been sexually assaulted, though not raped, and her apartment had been searched, and its contents left disturbed.

Helen Blake had been dead for a few days by the time she was found. The autopsy revealed that she had been murdered on 30 June, the same day as Nina Nichols, although the time of death had been unspecified. The killer had now struck twice in the same day.

The pattern and frequency, of the killings was now becoming too strong to be ignored, and the police began to realize that they were not dealing with isolated killings carried out by separate people. They were now forced to admit that the murders could well be the work of one person – a serial killer with abnormal sexual tendencies. Feelings were best summed up, perhaps, by McNamara's comment on hearing of Helen Blake's death: 'My God, we've got a madman loose.'

MOSAIC OF MURDER

The news of Helen Blake's death brought a swift reaction from McNamara, as the Boston police were mobilized into the greatest manhunt the city had ever known. All leave was cancelled, and every available detective drafted to the case.

The 18 to 40 age group had been singled out by psychiatrists assisting the police. The killer was, in their opinion, a youngish man who was suffering from delusions of persecution and a hatred of his mother – hence his attacks on older women. Checks were made on all known sex offenders and men released from mental institutions.

As suspects were rounded up and records were checked, the police appealed to women to keep their doors locked, and to be especially vigilant. A 24-hour emergency hotline number – DE 8–1212 – was published in all newspapers and mentioned in every radio and television news broadcast.

Fear of panic

McNamara appealed to the press, requesting that they reveal as few details about the murders as possible. The fear of panic in the streets was upper-most in his mind.

Meanwhile, he sought help from every quarter. Fifty hand-picked detectives were chosen to attend a special seminar given by a specialist in sex crimes from the FBI, who had also offered its assistance. Among them were Detective Lieutenant Edward Sherry, Lieutenant John Donovan, Chief of Boston's Homicide Division, James Mellon and Detective Phil DiNatale – all later to form the backbone of the police investigations into the case. Immediately after the lecture, they were re-assigned to the stranglings, in the hope that their new-found knowledge would point them in the direction of as yet unrecognized clues.

Same hallmarks

More than a month passed with no reports of similar killings. Then, on 21 August, Ida Irga, a quiet, retiring woman of 75, was found strangled in her locked apartment at 7 Grove Street, a five-storeyed apartment house in Boston's West End. She had been dead for about two days.

The crime bore all the hallmarks of the previous killings, with one grim variation. The victim had been left with her legs apart, a pillow had been placed under her buttocks, and her ankles locked into position between the vertical rungs of the backs of two chairs. In short, the body had been left in what one journalist described as a 'grotesque parody of the obstetrical position'.

There was one other appalling detail. In what could only be described as a mocking act of defiance, the body had been placed so that it would be the first sight to greet whoever entered the room – in this case, the 13 year-old son of the building's caretaker.

These details were not made public, partly because they were considered too shocking to print, but also because the police wanted certain facts to be known only by them and the killer. That way, they hoped, they might catch the killer out through a blunder in a conversation – a slip of the tongue, perhaps, revealing a detail that only the guilty man would know.

Calm hysteria

Three days after Ida Irga was found, the *Boston Herald*, in a well-intentioned attempt to calm the city, published an editorial on the statistical unlikelihood of becoming a victim of the 'Mad Strangler', as sensationalist newspapers now called him. Entitled 'Hysteria Solves Nothing', the article read, 'If it may be fairly said the police are looking for a needle in a haystack, it may be said with equal validity that a given person's chances of becoming a victim of the killer or killers are almost nil.'

Six days later, on 30 August, in what seemed a cruel mockery of this piece, Jane Sullivan, a 67 year-old nurse who lived alone, was found strangled in her first-floor apartment at 435 Columbia Road, Dorchester – the other side of Boston from Ida Irga. The time of her death was estimated about ten days earlier – 20 August – which meant that she and Ida Irga had been strangled within the same 24-hour period.

The police redoubled their efforts. A Tactical Patrol Force was set up, consisting of 50 hand-picked men, all specially trained in karate, quickdraw shooting and laboratory procedures. In three-man units, they would comb the city by night, ready to handle any situation that could not be dealt with by ordinary patrol cars.

In early September, Dr Richard Ford, Chairman of the Department of Legal Medicine at Harvard University, gathered together state and Boston law enforcement officials, medical examiners and psychiatrists to try and put together a profile of the killer.

The possibility that a woman might have committed the murders had been ruled out at a very early stage because of the enormous strength required to move the victims. For most of the psychiatrists, the mental picture that seemed to be emerging was of a nondescript man, possibly with a routine nine-to-five job, whose safety lay in his very anonymity: a man who, externally at least, seemed quiet and well adjusted but in reality was just the opposite.

Nondescript killer

What Ford and his associates were looking for, he explained, was a 'common denominator', to be found perhaps 'in how and when these women met their deaths, or in something about the places in which they lived, or in something relating to their mode of living.'

Any hopes of finding a clue to the killer's identity in the pattern of the crimes was to be dashed, however, by the next group of murders, which broke the mould of the previous killings.

The first was of Sophie Clark, on 5 December 1962. Although she was killed in the same way as the other victims, and her apartment had been ransacked, the differences in the crime were striking. Unlike the other victims, Clark was young, just 20 years old. She was also black, and did not live alone. And, unlike the other victims, she had been raped.

Clark's murder was followed, on 31 December, by that of Patricia Bissette, a 23 year-old secretary and on 6 May 1963, by the death of Beverly Samans, a 23 year-old student from Cambridge, who, although strangled, was believed to have died from stab wounds in the throat. Both women had been raped.

Impossible task

The police were now completely baffled. The change in the age group of the victims seemed to irrevocably rule out the psychiatrists' earlier suggestion of a 'mother-hating psychotic'. It now seemed possible that the theory that more than one person was involved might, after all, be correct. The task before the police began to seem more impossible than ever.

As the public outcry increased, and people demanded an investigation into the seeming police ineptitude. McNamara helplessly cited statistics. The police had checked over 5,000 Massachusetts sex offenders, screened every inmate at the Centre for the Treatment of Sexually Dangerous Persons at Bridgewater State Hospital, interviewed thousands of persons, and questioned over 400 suspects.

No real clues

Yet, the fact remained that there had now been eight stranglings, and not a single conclusive clue had been found by a force of nearly 2,600 men working 12 and 14 hours a day. No woman in Boston, whether young or old, living alone or in company, could be considered safe.

Two more strangling victims were to be found that year – Evelyn Corbin, aged 58, on 8 September 1963, and Joann Graff, on 23 November. This last date was one of particular significance in American history. On 22 November 1963, President John F. Kennedy had been assassinated in Dallas, Texas. The next day was one of national mourning.

That the murder had been committed when the nation, and Boston in particular, was in mourning, was later to be described by one psychiatrist as 'the greatest act of megalomania in the history of modern crime'.

Turning point

The eleventh and final strangling, on 4 January 1964, was to prove a final turning point in the case. The victim, Mary Sullivan, aged 19, was the youngest to date, and the details of her murder the worst of all. In the words of the police stenographer's report, she was found propped up on her bed, 'buttocks on pillow, back against headboard, head on right shoulder, knees up, eyes closed, viscous liquid (seminal?) dripping from mouth to right breast, breasts and lower extremities exposed, broomstick handle inserted in vagina . . . seminal stains on blanket.'

Sense of outrage

Tied around her neck were a stocking, and two brightly coloured scarves, knotted in a huge bow under her chin. Between the toes of her left foot had been placed a brightly coloured New Year's card, reading 'Happy New Year'. At the same time, police found a tiny sliver of tinfoil, like that used to wrap film, suggesting that the Strangler might have photographed the scene to record his artistry, before departing from Mary Sullivan's apartment.

Boston's sense of outrage at the crime was overwhelming. The youth of the victim and the awfulness of the crime, details of which had filtered through to the public, somehow struck a chord that none of the other murders had approached.

New measures now became imperative. Two weeks later, Attorney General Edward W. Brooke, Jr announced that the Attorney General's Office of the Commonwealth of Massachusetts, the highest law enforcement agency of the state, was taking over the investigation of all the stranglings in and out of Boston. He was appointing Assistant Attorney General John S. Bottomly to take charge of the operation. 'This is an abnormal and unusual case and it demands abnormal and unusual procedures,' he declared.

FALSE TRAILS TO NOWHERE

As John Bottomly sat in his office at the State House, Beacon Hill, he surveyed the monumental task before him. It had been made quite clear, on his appointment, that this was not to be a take-over from the police but, rather, a co-ordinating operation. Nevertheless, it was evident that the situation he had inherited was one of total chaos and confusion.

In the 18 months since the stranglings had begun, five separate police departments and three district attorneys had become involved. The scattered location of the various departments had inevitably led to difficulties in communication. To add to the confusion, the different police departments had kept some details of the crimes from the public, and some from each other – either to minimize the risk of leaks or out of a misplaced sense of competition.

What was needed, Bottomly realized, was a central 'clearing house' of information. All the data from every police department in Boston, Cambridge, Lynn, Lawrence and Salem, where the crimes had been committed, had to be assembled in one place, then somehow analysed.

Bottomly acted quickly: copies were ordered to be made of every report on the stranglings in the files of every police department where the crimes had been committed – a staggering 37,500 pages in total. The information was processed and fed into a digital computer.

At the end of January 1964 came the most extraordinary development in the case to date. Some weeks before, a retired businessman had suggested that Bottomly (with the help of the businessman's own private funds) enlist the help of Peter Hurkos, a 52 year-old Dutch psychic.

The bizarre chapter that followed would have been worthy of the most fantastic of fiction stories. On 29 January, Hurkos and his bodyguard, Jim Crane, arrived at Lexington, 15 miles from Boston itself.

The next day in a small motel bedroom, the psychic began to construct an image of the Strangler.

First, he said, he would like to get an impression of the Strangler's victims. A detective, Julian Soshnick, handed over a batch of photographs and laid them face down, in neat piles, on the bed. Hurkos gently touched them, and within minutes, his hand came down on one stack. 'This one, this top one, show dead woman, legs apart, I see her,' he said, in his heavy Dutch accent. 'Here I show you.'

Exact position

He then lay on the carpet and demonstrated exactly how the victim in question had been arranged by the Strangler. When Soshnick turned the photograph up, it was of the Strangler's first victim. Anna Slesers, found in exactly the position that Hurkos had just demonstrated. Before his incredulous audience, Hurkos then repeated the process with the other victims.

Hurkos's 'radar brain' (as he liked to call it) then started generating images of the killer himself. Soon he was describing a slight man, 5ft 7in or 8, weighing between 130 and 140lb, with a sharp nose and a scar on his left arm. There was also something wrong with his thumb. Then, inexplicably, came the comment. 'He loves shoes.'

Hospital connection

Later that night. Hurkos drew a pencil line on a local map, round an area in the suburb of Newton, which contained Boston College and St John's Seminary, and claimed that this was where the killer had lived. As the party sat open-mouthed, he cried. 'I see priest . . . no, he is not priest, he doctor from hospital.'

The next morning. Hurkos and his retinue drove to Boston to discuss matters with Bottomly. As the car passed along Commonwealth Avenue, and No. 1940 in particular. Hurkos became increasingly agitated: 'Terrible, awful, terrible thing happen here.' This was where Nina Nichols, the third victim, had been killed.

During his sleep that night, Hurkos talked aloud. He began with a series of statements in Portuguese, a language he did not know, about someone called Sophia. (Sophie Clark was the ninth victim, and her father was Portuguese – a fact that Hurkos could not have known.) Then, abruptly, the psychic broke into two voices that began an argument with each other – Hurkos in his normal Dutch accent, and Hurkos playing the killer in a soft, high-pitched effeminate Boston accent.

A week before Hurkos had arrived, a former student at Boston College had written a strange letter to its school of nursing. The man claimed to be a professional writer, interested in writing an article on the school's graduate class of 1950. He also expressed an interest in meeting nurses, suggesting that 'friendship might lead to the altar'.

Possible suspect

In view of Hurkos' revelations. Bottomly now ordered a check on the man, who, it emerged, had been on the Strangler suspect list. He had a history of mental illness, was 5ft 7½in tall, weighed 130 lb and had a very sharp nose. He had once attended St John's Seminary, and was a door-to-door salesman of ladies' shoes.

On physical examination, the shoe salesman was found to have scars on his left arm, and a deformed thumb. Hurkos had been right in every detail, but the investigation came to nothing. The salesman clearly had no knowledge of the crimes, and could not be connected with any of the victims.

Hurkos left Boston on 5 February, a week after he had arrived. His involvement in the case was to end as strangely as it had begun. On 8 February, in what was seen by many as a police attempt to discredit the Attorney General, he was arrested on a charge of impersonating an FBI agent.

Meanwhile, all efforts on the investigation were redoubled. The reward for the Strangler was increased from 5,000 dollars to 10,000 dollars a strangling. In addition, more members were to be recruited to the Medical-Psychiatric Committee, which had been appointed at the beginning of the year.

Two stranglers?

On 29 April, nearly four months after the Mary Sullivan strangling, the committee met with representatives from the police. The major question they had been asked to consider was whether the same person who had killed the earlier, older victims, had also killed the younger women: in short, one murderer or two?

The general consensus among most was that the 'old women' had been killed by one man, and the 'girls' by one or more men who had tried to make their crimes resemble the stranglings of the older women. The younger victims' killers were, they felt, to be found amongst the girls' friends, probably 'unstable members of the homosexual community'.

This was now seeming more and more likely. Homosexual killings might well explain the degrading positions the women had been left in – the final mockery, perhaps, from a woman-hater. In addition, many of the victims had had connections with homosexuals in some way. The Back Bay area in which Sophie Clark and Patricia Bissette lived, and Beacon Hill where Mary Sullivan lived, were both frequented by homosexuals, and Evelyn Corbin's apartment house was not far from such an area.

New hope

By the end of the year, the frustration among the police force was almost unimaginable. For many, the hunt for the Strangler had acquired the status of a personal crusade. Anxious not to overlook any possibilities, they had doggedly pursued every lead that came their way.

It was amid this background of low morale, dashed hopes, false trails and unutterable frustration that Detective Lieutenant Donovan received a phone call on Thursday, 4 March 1965. The caller was Lee Bailey, a brilliant young attorney who had recently made his name in Boston. Now he was claiming to know someone with information about the Strangler. Bailey could not yet reveal his informant, but asked Donovan to give him some questions to ask the man to check that he was telling the truth. The man's name was Albert DeSalvo.

CAPTURED BY CONFESSION

In February 1965, an unusual encounter took place between two inmates at Bridgewater State Hospital. One of the men involved was George Nassar,

Killer: Albert DeSalvo

a 33 year-old violent criminal who was under observation pending trial for a particularly brutal murder. The other was Albert DeSalvo, a mild-mannered 34 year-old petty criminal, known mainly for his bragging and sexual boasting.

Early in November 1964, he was arrested for the sexual assault of a number of women in Massachusetts and Connecticut. (The assaults were known as the 'Green Man' crimes because DeSalvo always wore green work clothes.) Sent to Bridgewater for observation, he found himself sharing the same cell as George Nassar.

One day DeSalvo broke off from his sexual boasting to ask Nassar a tantalizing question. 'George, what would happen if a guy was sent up for robbing one bank when there were really 13 banks robbed?' Nassar replied dismissively and DeSalvo walked away. A few days later, he approached Nassar again, saying, 'You thought that was a nutty question. Well . . .'

The exact details of the conversation that followed were never known, but they were enough to convince Nassar that DeSalvo was the Strangler. Swayed by this conviction – and, no doubt, the inducement of a 110,000 dollar reward – he contacted his lawyer, Lee Bailey. Although initially reluctant to get involved, Bailey was persuaded by Nassar's insistence that DeSalvo wanted to see him, and agreed to a meeting.

Informal confession

On 4 March, unsure of what to expect, Bailey went to Bridgewater to meet DeSalvo for the first time. The man who greeted him was around 5ft 8in tall, with dark hair and a sharp, beak-like nose. His voice was thin and high-pitched, and his manner sincere and charming. His engaging style, combined with an otherwise totally forgettable appearance, made him, in Bailey's opinion, a likely suspect for the stranglings. It was not difficult to understand how this man might have talked his way into women's apartments murdered them, then slipped away in total anonymity.

In the recorded interview that followed. DeSalvo confessed not only to the 11 known murders by the Strangler, but also to an additional two killings the police had not known about – Mary Brown, beaten and stabbed in her Lawrence apartment on 9 March 1963, and an 80 year-old woman, who had apparently died of a heart attack in his arms. DeSalvo could not remember her name or the date of her murder. (Later investigations would reveal her as Mary Mullen, killed on 28 June 1962.)

In a calm, almost matter-of-fact voice, DeSalvo gave detailed descriptions of the crimes, including facts that had never been made public. (He was able, for example, to state correctly that Patricia Bissette's door opened outwards.) He drew exact sketches of the 13 apartments where the crimes had taken place, and also talked about the Strangler's knot, explaining that it was the knot he always tied and that he had used it when tying the removable casts on his daughter Judy's crippled hip. He liked to tie a big bow to make her smile.

With the exception of one or two mistakes, DeSalvo's descriptions of the crimes were almost faultless, Bailey – certain that he had found the Strangler – telephoned Lieutenant Donovan, and invited him to come and listen to the recording. As soon as he heard the tape, Donovan immediately contacted the Attorney General's office.

The investigators were in a dilemma. Despite the accuracy of DeSalvo's accounts – and his obvious anxiety to confess – there was no real legal evidence to convict him. The Strangler left no fingerprints that could be matched up to DeSalvo's, nor had there been any eye-witnesses. The only survivor of his attacks – a German waitress – proved unable to identify him, and none of the victims' neighbours recognized him from photographs.

Interrogation

In the absence of any evidence, DeSalvo's guilt would have to be proved. Up until then, his confessions had been made on a purely informal basis, and no one had ever been sure whether or not he was telling the truth. It was now decided that DeSalvo should undergo a proper interrogation by Bottomly on all 13 murders, with the assurance that nothing he said would be used against him in court. Police officials and detectives in each suburb would check every statement he made. If he was found to have been telling the truth and ruled competent to stand trial, psychiatrists would examine him to determine his state of mind when committing the murders.

If found sane, he would make a formal confession to be used in court, where he would plead not guilty in the hope of being committed to a mental institution. If he was ruled sane (which would mean execution), there would be no confession and all proceedings against him would stop. His immunity assured, DeSalvo agreed.

Through the spring, summer and autumn of 1965, DeSalvo met Bottomly weekly in the presence of a third party as witness. He poured out his stories of the killings – eager to confess, it seemed, in the hope that this would help him understand himself. Painstakingly, he tried to record each strangling in detail.

Most of the murders occurred at weekends, he explained, because 'I could always get out of the house Saturday by telling my wife I had to work.' Once out of the house, DeSalvo described how he would drive around aimlessly in his car, a 1954 green Chevrolet coupe, until what he described as 'the urge' to murder came over him. There was no plan to his actions at all.

He would pick a building at random and ring any buzzer with a woman's name on it. He found no difficulty in talking his way into the apartments with the excuse of having to do building or decorating work.

Killer: Albert DeSalvo

Irresistible urge

After a few minutes' conversation, DeSalvo would be seized by an irrational and irrepressible urge to murder, which seemed to come over him when the victim turned her back on him. He described this in detail in the case of Nina Nichols, 'as her back was turned to me and I saw the back of her head . . . I was all hot . . . everything built up inside of me. Before you know it I had put my arm around her and that was it.'

One recurring theme in the confessions was DeSalvo's total mystification at his own behaviour. 'There was nothing about Anna Slesers to interest any man . . . why did I do it?' When asked why he had ransacked the apartments, he could not give a satisfactory answer. 'That's what I'm trying to find out myself,' he said. He was similarly confused as to why he had left Ida Irga with her legs through the chair slats. 'I just did it,' he said, by way of explanation.

In many of his descriptions DeSalvo would distance himself totally, as if talking about someone else. A typical example of this was his account of how he had nearly murdered a girl before Anna Slesers. 'I looked in a mirror in the bedroom and there was me strangling somebody. I fell on my knees and crossed myself and I prayed. "Oh God, what am I doing? I'm a married man. I'm the father of two children. Oh God, help me." It wasn't like it was me . . . it was like it was someone else I was watching. I just took off.'

When talking about Patricia Bissette – the only victim to have been found covered up, and not exposed – he explained. 'She was so different . . . I didn't want to see her like that, naked . . . She talked to me like a man, she treated me like a man . . . I remember I covered her up all the way.'

Similar regrets were also expressed about the youngest of the victims, Mary Sullivan. 'Why? I say to myself, it could of been my daughter, too.'

At times, DeSalvo showed a marked reluctance to even discuss the crimes. At other times, he was totally calm and unmoved, as in his description of his actions after Joann Graff's murder. 'I had supper, washed up, played with the kids until about 8 o'clock, put them to bed, sat down and watched TV.'

As DeSalvo's confidence and trust in Bottomly grew, he admitted that there had been a problem for some time. 'This thing building up inside me . . . all the time . . . I knew it was getting out of control.' He explained that he had only decided to confess on reading a statement by Governor Peabody that the Strangler would not be executed but sent to a mental institution for treatment.

DeSalvo's extraordinary confessions came to an end on 29 September 1965. Police investigations had revealed that time and time again he had been right, and had known things that had never been made public. They now had little option but to believe that the tearful man before them was indeed the Boston Strangler.

180

As they surveyed their files, the ironies of the case must have been apparent to them. After the massive manhunt they had conducted, the killer had finally turned out to be someone who had been on their files all along, but had been missed because of his listing under the category of breaking and entering rather than sex offences.

Lee Bailey found DeSalvo's case a tremendous challenge. He did not want him freed. Neither did he want him to go to the electric chair, but rather placed in a mental hospital where doctors could study him and help him.

In his opinion, a trial would be the only way of establishing judicially that DeSalvo was the Strangler. It was only if this happened, he believed, that DeSalvo would receive proper medical attention and analysis.

He was, however, faced with a legal difficulty. Psychiatrists had now ruled that DeSalvo was insane when he had committed the murders, but under new Supreme Court rulings (not helped by the fact that Bottomly had now resigned), the prosecution was no longer willing to allow DeSalvo to confess pleading insanity.

Legal history

In a brilliant legal move, Lee Bailey decided to allow DeSalvo to stand trial for the Green Man offences. Psychiatrists could then testify to his insanity without this bearing any direct relation to the crime he was being tried for. He could still be found legally insane without being executed.

The case was almost unprecedented in legal history. The onus would be on the defence to prove guilt. As Bailey himself was later to say, 'We found ourselves before a really unbelievable situation. It was up to us to prove he was the right man – and to do it without giving the State one single piece of legal evidence. Albert had to get by that electric chair.'

ESCAPING THE EXECUTIONER

On 30 June 1966, Albert DeSalvo attended a hearing at the Middlesex County Courthouse, East Cambridge, to assess his competency to stand trial for the Green Man crimes. Only by standing trial, and being found not guilty by insanity, Bailey believed, would DeSalvo eventually get the medical help he needed. The charges in question here, however, were armed robbery and indecent assault – the stranglings could be referred to implicitly but would have no bearing on the case.

After the testimony from the psychiatrists, whose opinions on DeSalvo's competency were divided. DeSalvo himself took the stand. Asked by Bailey if he wanted further psychiatric help, DeSalvo replied, 'What I always asked for was medical help, and I haven't received any.' Later questioned by the prosecuting counsel, Donald Conn, Assistant District Attorney of

Killer: Albert DeSalvo

Middlesex County, he stressed his wish to tell the truth about his past, no matter what. 'I feel that I couldn't live with myself . . . I wish to in my own way release everything that is inside me, the truth. And whatever may be the consequences, I will accept because I have always from the very beginning wanted to tell the truth.'

On 10 July, the presiding judge, Horace Cahill, judged DeSalvo to be competent to stand trial. The next day, he was brought before Judge George Ponte in the same courthouse where he pleaded not guilty. He was remanded, without bail to Bridgewater, for trial – as the Green Man – at a later date to be agreed.

Six months later, on 9 January 1967, the Green Man trial opened at Middlesex County Superior Court. DeSalvo was charged with ten counts of indecent assault and armed robbery. His plea was not guilty by virtue of insanity.

As in the pre-trial hearing, the prosecutor was Donald Conn. His main witnesses were four women who had been victims of the Green Man. Their identities were kept secret because of the intimate nature of the evidence involved. Reluctantly and with great embarrassment, the women told the court what the Green Man had done to them, describing how they had been tied up, raped and humiliated at knife point.

Judgement of sanity

Bailey's main witnesses for the defence were two psychiatrists, Dr Robert Ross Mezer of Boston and James Brussel. Although DeSalvo was being tried only for the Green Man offences, it was their task to bring up the stranglings as part of his psychiatric background. Bailey's whole case hinged on DeSalvo's diagnosis by the two psychiatrists as a schizophrenic. In his opinion, the jury, when told about the stranglings, could not fail to judge DeSalvo insane – even though these crimes were not directly a part of the trial.

Summing up the case for the prosecution, Donald Conn described DeSalvo as little more than a cunning criminal who was feigning symptoms of mental illness in the hope of being committed to a mental institution, and released within a few years. In a highly charged speech, he pointed at the jury, shouting, 'It's my duty to my wife, to your wife, to every woman who might conceivably be a victim of this man, to stamp his conduct for what it is – vicious criminal conduct. Don't let this man con you right out of your shoes.'

Wasteful and barbaric

Bailey's closing remarks were equally impassioned, as he made a plea that DeSalvo be found insane so that he could be remitted to a mental hospital

182

and receive proper psychiatric treatment. Not only for his own sake, Bailey pointed out, but also to achieve a better understanding of such crimes in the future. 'This man, Albert DeSalvo, is a phenomenon,' Bailey explained, 'a unique opportunity for study . . . We've never had such a specimen in captivity. He should be the subject of a research grant from the Ford Foundation or a similar institution.

'What I'm stating here is not a defence,' Bailey continued, 'it's a sociological imperative. Aside from the moral, religious, ethical or other objections to capital punishment, to execute DeSalvo is just as wasteful, barbaric and ignorant an act as burning the witches of Salem.'

In his summing up, Judge Cornelius Moynihan explained to the jury that they could find DeSalvo guilty, not guilty or not guilty by reason of insanity. Judge Moynihan also told the jurors that they should erase all accounts of the stranglings from their minds, with the remark. 'He is not on trial for homicide.'

On 18 January, the jury retired to consider their verdict. They were out for 3 hours 45 minutes. At 6 p.m., they returned a verdict of guilty.

Life sentence

When the jury's verdict was read out, Judge Moynihan considered carefully the question of sentencing. Bailey explained that it was DeSalvo's wish that he be incarcerated for life, saying. 'He wants society to be protected from him.'

DeSalvo was indeed sentenced to life imprisonment, and was sent back to Bridgewater Hospital, pending permanent assignment to a maximum-security prison. To Lee Bailey, James Brussel and many others interested in the case, the decision was a severe mistake. Despite its name, Bridgewater was in reality more like a prison than a hospital, and, with its inadequate staffing, there was little likelihood that DeSalvo would receive the attention he deserved.

Cry for help

As far as DeSalvo was concerned, there was no doubt that the escape from Bridgewater Hospital was a cry for help. He had left a note on his bed in his cell, apologizing for his escape and saying that he had left because he wanted help and nothing was being done for him.

Psychiatrist James Brussel, for one, was convinced that DeSalvo was telling the truth. In his opinion, DeSalvo was 'simply and honestly bewildered by his own nature and he wanted help in his search for explanations. His escape was a way of calling public attention to his plight.'

Despite hysteria among the press and public, DeSalvo gave himself up

Killer: Albert DeSalvo

voluntarily 38 hours after his escape, by walking into a clothing store 40 miles away, and telephoning Bailey's office with the alleged remark, 'It's over. Take me back.'

In an impromptu press conference after his arrest, DeSalvo explained his reasons for the escape. 'I didn't bother anybody and I never will. I didn't mean no harm to nobody. I did it to bring it back to the attention of the public, that a man who has a mental illness and hires a lawyer, and no one does anything about it.'

No escape

In a tragic mishandling of the case, Albert DeSalvo was immediately transferred from Bridgewater State Hospital to Massachusetts' maximum security Walpole Prison, from where there was no possibility of escape, and where he was to spend the rest of his days.

Six years later, the story of the Boston Strangler was to end as mysteriously as it had begun. On 25 November 1973, Albert DeSalvo was found dead in his cell at Walpole Prison. He had been stabbed six times through the heart – supposedly in a prison 'brawl'.

His killer was never found.

CASE FILE: DESALVO, ALBERT

BACKGROUND

Albert DeSalvo was born on 3 September 1931, the third of six children of Frank DeSalvo, a plumber and labourer, and his wife Charlotte, the daughter of an officer in Boston's Fire Department.

Frank DeSalvo was an alcoholic who beat both his wife and children. When Albert was just seven, he looked on as his father knocked his mother's teeth out then, one by one, bent her fingers back until they snapped.

Perhaps the most harrowing experience of Albert's early life – so much so that he was never able to talk about it in any detail – was being sold into slavery. His father handed him and his two sisters over to a farmer in Maine for a total of $9, where they remained captives for many months.

The family were always poor. The elder DeSalvo did little to support them, and they were on and off the welfare rolls for the whole of Albert's childhood.

Taught to steal

When he was not brutalizing his children, Frank DeSalvo was teaching them to steal. Albert was just five when his father first took him to a store and showed him what to take and how to do it. Albert progressed from shoplifting to robbery and then to breaking and entering.

Sex was a constant presence in the overcrowded apartment building in Chelsea – a working-class suburb of Boston – where Albert grew up. His father regularly brought back prostitutes and made his children watch when they had sex. Albert had his first sexual experience (with other children) when he was just six or seven. His unsual appetite and capacity for sex brought him many early conquests among neighbourhood girls, as well as the local homosexual community who were willing to pay him for his services.

Frank DeSalvo left home in 1939, and made no further efforts to support his family. Charlotte finally divorced him in 1944, marrying again a year later.

Young runaway

Throughout his childhood, Albert ran away to escape his father's violence. He slept beneath the wooden wharves of East Boston's docks, a favourite haunt of the city's young runaways.

A few weeks after leaving school in 1948, Albert enlisted in the army. In 1949, he was posted to join the army of occupation in Germany for five years.

In Frankfurt, he met and married Irmgard, the daughter of a middle-class Catholic family. He brought his wife back with him to the USA in 1954. He was then posted to Fort Dix, where his daughter, Judy, was born in 1955.

DeSalvo left the army in 1956 with an honourable discharge – a charge of sexual misconduct against a nine year-old girl that had been laid against him was not proceeded with – and he returned to Chelsea. Later he and Irmgard set up home in Malden, a Boston suburb, where their son, Michael, was born.

Although he had a job and a home, Albert occasionally found himself with no money and he turned to breaking and entering. He was twice arrested in 1958, and each time was given a suspended sentence.

PSYCHOLOGICAL PROFILE

DeSalvo always claimed not to understand why he had killed, though at times he blamed his wife, his upbringing, his overwhelming sexuality, even himself. His bafflement as to his motives was a recurring theme of his confessions, and he repeatedly claimed that his desire to understand his compulsions and be cured of them was the main reason why he had confessed. When he talked about the stranglings, he often used the third person, as if he had been a powerless observer of what was happening, rather than the man who was actually carrying out the murders.

Two killers?

Those psychiatrists who had attempted to provide a psychological profile of the Strangler before his arrest were just as confused as DeSalvo. Most felt that there were at least two murderers at work. One was a shy, introverted, under-sexed, possibly homosexual man who killed the older women to revenge himself against a dominant mother whom he hated. The other was a more conventional – if particularly brutal – rapist, a loner seeking power over women, motivated perhaps by sexual rejection.

The seducer

When DeSalvo admitted to the crimes, many theories about the killer evaporated. He was fond of his mother, though felt she had neglected him and failed to protect him from his father's violence, and far from being a loner, he was a family man. Besides, by his own admission, DeSalvo sexually assaulted some 2,000 women in his criminal career and seduced many more. This was not the biography of a man who killed out of frustrated lust.

The age difference of the two groups of women that had obsessed the psychiatrists was, according to DeSalvo, a matter of coincidence, as much coincidence as the other connections between the victims, hospitals and classical music. He had selected victims at random from the names on their doorbells.

Obsession

DeSalvo was obsessed with women in general, not young women, old women or pretty women, just women in general.

In all of his guises – Measuring Man, Green Man and Strangler – he entered women's apartments with the intent of making some kind of sexual contact with them. Only on 15 occasions, in a period of less than two years, did he attempt to kill. Once he had failed because he caught sight of himself in the mirror and could not go through with it.

The killings began soon after he was released from prison, after the Measuring Man crimes. This was at a time when Irmgard rejected him sexually, insisting that he had once again to prove himself to her. In this account of the killings on each occasion the trigger came when the woman turned her back on him. In doing so, they brought out in him feelings of hatred that he could not control.

The hatred came from feelings of rejection. In the case of Beverley Samans, one of the most savage killings, Albert described how her constant pleas of 'don't do it', reminded him of how his wife spurned him.

All his life he had attempted to better himself. He ingratiated himself with authority figures, both at school and in the army. He had married out of his class, but to no avail. He never felt accepted. He had treated his wife with respect, and she according to DeSalvo would 'make me feel like nothing . . . gave me an inferiority complex.'

New respect

Perhaps, in the end, the one characteristic all his victims shared, their middle-class respectability, was what cost them their lives. Certainly, when he talked of his career as the Measuring Man, he made much of the fact that he was an uneducated man who had managed to outwit and con college girls, saying 'they think they are better than me. They was all college kids and I never had anything in my life but I outsmarted them.'

Chapter 10

ROY FONTAINE
THE EVIL BUTLER

He was a connoisseur of fine wines, an expert in antiques and a consummate actor. After spending most of his life in prison for jewellery thefts, he planned one final haul that would set him up in comfort for his old age. But his willingness to kill destroyed him.

An elderly woman in tweeds was waiting by the ticket barrier at Carlisle railway station when an Inter-City express drew to a halt on Tuesday, 31 May 1977. She was Lady Peggy Hudson, a robust, bespectacled widow of 72 who owned Kirtleton Hall, a rambling estate about 25 miles to the north in the Scottish wilds.

Lady Hudson spent much of her time shooting in the countryside, and racing her greyhounds. But being a woman of impeccable manners, she had wanted to meet her new butler off the train. His name was Roy Fontaine. Lady Hudson had hired Fontaine through a reputable employment agency, paying a fee of £140. Fontaine's references had been glowing and Lady Hudson was surprised at being able to hire such a man for £20 a week.

When the train had halted, a smartly dressed man in his mid-50s stepped off with his hand luggage. He was on the short side, with receding dark hair, a portly bearing and a slightly arrogant smile.

Getting acquainted

Kirtleton Hall was a 200 year-old estate lying near the village of Waterbeck, along Kirtle Water, some 20 miles east of Dumfries. As they drove across the English border with Scotland, Lady Hudson and her new butler got to know each other. She explained that her late husband, Sir Austin Hudson, had been a Conservative MP, and a junior minister during World War II. He had died in 1956. Fontaine, who had a clipped Scottish accent, chatted easily about antique jewellery. He seemed particularly interested in silver and said that he had once been a dealer in antiques.

Lady Hudson was impressed by his suave manners and knowledgeable ways. Fontaine was settled into a furnished flat at Kirtleton Hall. Kirtleton, surrounded by rolling fields and set amongst trees, had a glass extension housing an indoor swimming pool under a domed roof. It soon became clear that Fontaine was also a connoisseur of wine and a voracious reader of literature.

Still curious, Lady Hudson invited Fontaine to make use of her own library, and asked why he did not work in London, where he could earn much more money. Fontaine replied that he preferred the country and was hoping to buy a small inn one day. In reality he was busy weighing up the possibilities of robbing Lady Hudson, deciding that she possessed enough valuables to make the risks worthwhile.

After a few weeks at Kirtleton Hall, Fontaine told Lady Hudson that he had received a letter from a young friend in Birmingham who was looking for work as a gardener. Accepting Fontaine's recommendation, Lady Hudson agreed that the young man, David Wright, could come to stay. She quickly came to like the 30 year-old Wright, a handsome, outdoor type who shared her love of shooting and fishing, and took care of her dogs.

Wright, who was short of money, noticed that Fontaine spent cash freely at the Kirtle Inn, in the local village of Kirkpatrick Fleming. Fontaine would buy rounds generously and put the change in the charity box.

Soon, Wright began to ask Fontaine for money, and the butler never refused. Whenever he asked, Wright received a £10 note, and sometimes even an entire week's worth of Fontaine's wages. It was understood that, if the gifts were not offered, Wright would mention to Her Ladyship where the two men had first met. This had been at Long Lartin jail in Worcestershire in 1974.

At that time, Fontaine had been serving a two-and-a-half year sentence for receiving stolen documents and illegally possessing a gun. The two men had become close. Wright knew that handling stolen documents had been an exception in the butler's career of crime. Fontaine was a professional jewel thief.

The missing ring

One day in late August or early September 1977, Wright suggested to the butler that they rob Lady Hudson. Fontaine, who had his own plans for a robbery at Kirtleton Hall, rejected the idea but, soon after, noticed that a ring worth several thousand pounds, an heirloom of his mistress, was missing from her jewellery collection. Wright denied all knowledge of it.

After making furtive inquiries, Fontaine retrieved the ring from a local girlfriend of Wright's and replaced it before Lady Hudson returned from a trip to London. Fontaine again confronted Wright, who stormed out of the kitchen in fury.

That night, Fontaine was woken up by the report of a rifle echoing round his room. A bullet had embedded itself in the headboard. Wright was standing drunkenly by the bed, holding a .22 rifle. 'I told you that we were going to rob Lady Hudson,' he said. To try to calm Wright, Fontaine suggested a robbery while their mistress was away. 'You're a bloody fool,' snapped Wright. 'She has her most valuable jewellery with her so we wait until she comes back.' He demanded half the haul.

Fontaine got out of bed and approached Wright who swung the rifle butt, catching him a blow on the nose. Stunned by the sight of Fontaine bleeding copiously, Wright threw down the rifle and began to moan, 'What have I done? What have I done?' When the older man, recovering from his shock, had stemmed the bleeding, the pair cleaned the bloodstains from the bed. Fontaine dug out the bullet, plastered the hole in the headboard, and covered the plaster with dark boot polish.

It was now dawn. Fontaine bundled Wright off to bed, and rang his sister Violet in Newcastle. 'He's trying to get me,' he said in a frantic voice, but did not name Wright. To the other servants, Fontaine explained that he had got his cuts and bruises by banging his head on the ladder of the swimming pool the night before.

The hunt

When Wright reappeared drowsily later in the day, Fontaine suggested they shoot some rabbits to feed Lady Hudson's dogs. In the gunroom, Wright chose a double-barrelled shotgun with six cartridges. Fontaine selected the .22 rifle used against him the night before and seven cartridges.

Deep in the woods, Wright fired off a round from each barrel, re-loaded, and went to collect a dead rabbit he had hit. Wright asked why Fontaine had not fired. 'I only go for big game,' the butler replied. Wright pointed to a rabbit and told Fontaine to shoot. Fontaine agreed, aimed at the animal, then swung the barrel towards Wright a few feet away. He fired four shots. The last of these killed Wright.

Fontaine dragged Wright into some bushes and covered the body with bracken. Returning to the house, he put back the rifles. He bought some champagne to replace some that had been stolen and drunk by Wright. After meeting Lady Hudson at Carlisle railway station, he explained that Wright had left after receiving a job offer in Torquay.

Concealment

After dinner that night, Fontaine slipped back to the woods, dragged Wright's body to a stream, and covered it with stones and rocks. He went back the next day to complete the job.

But Fontaine's story about banging his face in the swimming pool, and his explanation of Wright's sudden disappearance, did not satisfy Lady Hudson. She had become suspicious and, early in September, made an appointment to see the Chief Constable of Dumfries and Galloway, Alex Campbell. On the same day, quite by chance, both Lady Hudson and the local police received anonymous telephone calls warning them about a Mr Roy Hall. Checks were made, and Fontaine was fired from Kirtleton Hall with a month's wages on Wednesday, 7 September 1977.

Roy Fontaine had been unmasked as Archibald Thomson Hall, one of Britain's most notorious jewel thieves. But Wright's body had not been found. On 8 September 1977, Fontaine took a train to London and started looking for butler's jobs.

ENEMY WITHIN

On Sunday, 16 October 1977, Fontaine rented a cottage at Newton Arlosh, near Carlisle, for £40 a month. He told the owner, a local accountant, that he was divorced and needed somewhere to settle himself for a while. Fontaine moved straight in and for a few weeks was a regular customer at the local Joiners' Arms. But his expansive, high-spending manner was gone. Fontaine was brooding about Wright.

Towards the end of October, Fontaine answered an advertisement in *The Lady* magazine for a buttling position in London. His bogus references were again accepted, and Fontaine became the butler of Walter Travers Scott-Elliot, an 82 year-old former Labour MP, and his wife Dorothy, at Richmond Court in Sloane Street, Chelsea.

Hitting it off

Scott-Elliot and his new servant seemed to get on very well. Both were fussy about their personal appearance and enjoyed shopping trips to Harrods and other stores, as well as eating together in Italian restaurants. Fontaine was also able to appreciate Scott-Elliot's priceless collection of Indian antiques.

The Scott-Elliots enjoyed considerable wealth – Dorothy Scott-Elliot came from a rich family in Calcutta, while her husband had in his time been a successful merchant – and owned properties in France and Italy. They had the proceeds from selling a valuable estate near Langholm, Dumfriesshire, and held accounts in a number of international banks.

Inside job

Their penthouse at 22 Richmond Court was full of French furniture and heirlooms from both their families. The 60 year-old Mrs Scott-Elliot suffered from arthritis but was mentally alert. Her husband was prone to spells of tiredness and confusion. Fontaine immediately began to open the Scott-Elliot's post, and assess the value of the Indian antiques.

On 8 December Fontaine went out drinking with a small-time thief named Michael Kitto, whom he had met a few weeks before through a mutual friend, Mary Coggle. Kitto, 39, was on the run after stealing a pub's takings of £1,000.

Fontaine and Kitto had discussed a plan to defraud the Scott-Elliots, and Kitto was invited back to the flat that night to inspect the antiques. They arrived there at 11.30 p.m. Mr Scott-Elliot was asleep in his bedroom. His wife had been taken into a nursing home for treatment for her arthritis and Fontaine expected to find her bedroom empty. As he opened the door, Mrs Scott-Elliot confronted him, demanding to know what he was doing and why the second man, Kitto, was in the flat.

Fontaine knocked her to the ground. Alarmed by the commotion, Kitto tried to restrain and quieten Mrs Scott-Elliot, but her screams continued. Fontaine put a pillow over her face to muffle her shrieks and held it over her mouth for at least two minutes. Kitto assisted him. A few moments later Mrs Scott-Elliot became motionless.

The two men were stunned. After several minutes passed in silence, they carried Mrs Scott-Elliot's body to the bed and placed it between the sheets in a sleeping position. Mr Scott-Elliot had been woken by the noise. Fontaine heard footsteps and intercepted his employer at the bedroom door. After being told that his wife had had a nightmare but was now sleeping peacefully, Mr Scott-Elliot returned to his bed. Fontaine and Kitto went to the butler's room to make their plans.

The next morning, Friday, 9 December 1977, Fontaine and the badly-rattled Kitto collected their friend Mary Coggle, a 51 year-old cleaner, at a telephone exchange near King's Cross railway station. Coggle seemed unperturbed by the story of Mrs Scott-Elliot's death, but intrigued by the prospect of putting on her furs and jewellery. She agreed to help the two men dispose of the body.

Later that morning, Mr Scott-Elliot rose and asked Fontaine how his wife was. The butler replied that she had gone out early to shop and wanted to meet Mr Scott-Elliot at the Reform Club for lunch. Scott-Elliot left on time for the appointment, walking in his usual urgent, military manner.

Getaway car

While he was out, Fontaine and his accomplices hired a Ford Cortina in Victoria under assumed names. They asked for the silver-grey car to be delivered to Richmond Court. By this time Scott-Elliot had returned. He was weary and mentally unalert, and he made no mention of having failed to meet his wife. He obligingly signed the cheque for the vehicle. Scott-Elliot's condition was aggravated by drugs he took as medication.

In the evening, Fontaine, Kitto and Coggle took the body of Mrs Scott-Elliot, wrapped in a blanket, down the back staircase of the flat, and placed it in the boot of the Cortina. Fontaine again fobbed off his employer by saying that Mrs Scott-Elliot had gone out. After loading some small antiques from the flat into the car, Fontaine fed a double dose of sleeping pills to Scott-Elliot and told him they were all about to embark on a long journey.

It was dark outside when the drowsy Scott-Elliot was assisted into the rear seat of the car, where he believed his silver-haired wife was waiting. Kitto posed as the chauffeur. Fontaine sat alongside him. In the back, Scott-Elliot saw a woman in a mink coat. He looked at her with a confused expression but made no comment. The woman began talking easily to him about furniture and the home, and soon Scott-Elliot dozed off, unaware he had been speaking to Mary Coggle in a wig.

During the journey, Scott-Elliot woke from time to time, showing a remarkable power of recognition for the little towns and landmarks they passed. But he did not appear to realize that his wife was not sitting next to him.

The four reached Fontaine's cottage at Newton Arlosh very late. Scott-Elliot was helped into bed. In the morning of Saturday, 10 December 1977, they drove across the Scottish border, stopping in Lanark to buy a spade, and at Crieff in Perthshire, where they took lunch at the Drummond Arms Hotel. By this stage, Scott-Elliot seemed too confused to grasp what was happening.

Dumping ground

After leaving the hotel, Kitto drove the party west to Comrie, then turned south on to the B827. After a further 15 miles, near the village of Braco, he stopped the car at Fontaine's direction. A wall ran between the snow-covered ground and the deserted road. Kitto lifted the body of Mrs Scott-Elliot over the wall to Fontaine, who was standing in a ditch on the other side.

Using the shovel they had bought at Lanark, they dug a shallow grave, and covered the body with bracken, leaves and branches. While they worked, Coggle sat with Scott-Elliot in the car beside the road, feeding him pills.

MURDEROUS ALLIANCE

The village of Newton Arlosh in Cumbria, a few miles inland from Solway Firth, had a population of 350. Most were farming people. They knew Fontaine from his quiet days alone at Middle Farm Cottage before he joined the Scott-Elliot household, but probably had not noticed the arrival of Fontaine's party in the early hours of Saturday, 10 December.

But curious eyes did observe the same party return from its 300-mile round trip to Comrie in the afternoon of the same day. The elderly Scott-Elliot, heavily-drugged, had to be supported through the door of the cottage. Fontaine, Kitto and Coggle put him to bed and made dinner for themselves.

Forgery fraud

While eating, they discussed their plans for the fraud Fontaine wanted to carry out. He considered a robbery of the antiques less important than a series of forgeries that could net at least £100,000, and possibly twice that amount, from the Scott-Elliots' various bank accounts and shares.

By losing the chance to obtain Mrs Scott-Elliot's authentic signature, part of the planned fraud had to be abandoned. Fontaine also pondered how long the couple's friends would wait before becoming suspicious. On the journey back from finding a burial place for Mrs Scott-Elliot, the three had stopped at the Royal Stewart Restaurant in Crieff, drinking doubles of whisky and Bacardi. Their confidence returning, they had explained that the elderly gentleman in the car was their grandfather.

Scott-Elliot had relatives in Aberdeenshire, but Fontaine realized they would be over-curious about Mrs Scott-Elliot if he took the old gentleman there. By the end of the meal, he, Kitto and Coggle, who was by now wearing a blonde wig, had agreed on the next stage of their plan.

Drinking party

The group spent two days resting. Scott-Elliot slept in the cottage while Fontaine, Kitto and Coggle drank at the Joiners' Arms. The publican, Jack Fyrth, realized that Fontaine, drinking lager and whisky liqueurs, was the leader of the party. Fontaine had regained his affability and was buying the rounds. He told Fyrth he had once worked in catering, but now dealt in antiques.

On Tuesday, 13 December, Fontaine, Kitto and Coggle helped Scott-Elliot into the Ford. Kitto again took the wheel and drove north. Fontaine had planned a long route. It was dark when they reached the Tilt Hotel at Blair Atholl, Perthshire, after a 200-mile journey. Mary Coggle, in Mrs Scott-Elliot's mink coat, sauntered over to the reception desk to order rooms.

Three chalets were provided. Fontaine and Kitto, reverting to the roles of butler and chauffeur, helped Scott-Elliot into one chalet, and ordered him a meal. Then, with Coggle, they ate in the dining room, still playing the roles of servants. After Coggle had gone to bed, both men drank heavily, telling other guests that their employer was a former MP, and that Coggle was his wife.

The following morning, Wednesday, 14 December, the four took breakfast together in the dining room. Coggle, in her blonde wig, was restrained while Fontaine and Kitto addressed Scott-Elliot as 'Sir'. The elderly gentleman showed no signs of discomfort or protest to the staff waiting on the table.

Highland wilds

After breakfast, Scott-Elliot paid the bill of £61.20 with a cheque signed in the name of Scott. He thanked the manager, Malcolm McNaught, for a 'very nice stay' and the party drove away.

Kitto drove the Ford north to Inverness, where all four stopped for lunch at a pub, then cut south-west down the A831 route from Tomich until they reached the lonely highland wilds of Glen Affric, along Loch Affric. Scott-Elliot asked drowsily if he could leave the car to relieve himself. Kitto stopped the car by some dense woods.

Fontaine suggested to Scott-Elliot that he step over a stone wall bordering the road so that he would be unseen if another car passed. As he was on his way back to the car, Fontaine suggested that he have a rest. Agreeing, Scott-Elliot rested against a tree, asking where they were, and finally sat down.

The butler and the chauffeur grabbed Scott-Elliot at this point, and tried to pull him among some bushes. Scott-Elliot resisted, and Fontaine tried to strangle him with a scarf. But his employer, now fighting for his life, showed remarkable strength. Finally, Fontaine fetched a spade, and ordered Kitto to use it to kill Scott-Elliot. Kitto immediately obeyed.

Afterwards, Fontaine and Kitto dug a shallow grave in the same bushes a short distance from the road, and placed the body in it. They covered it with branches and leaves and returned to the car, where Mary Coggle had sat throughout the killing. They lit cigarettes and talked for a few minutes. The three drove to Inverness and then headed south, spending the night at a hotel in Aviemore, west of the Grampian Mountains.

Kitto and Coggle drank heavily during the evening and spent the night together, while Fontaine had been quiet and introspective, drinking alone in a separate bar. On the following morning, Thursday, 15 December, the three drove to Perth where they managed to find buyers for some of the Scott-Elliots' antiques. The following day, they disposed of more goods near Edinburgh.

Dressed to kill

Tension was building up between Fontaine and Coggle, who was now wearing Mrs Scott-Elliot's diamond rings and gold necklaces as well as the mink coat, and carrying her crocodile handbag. Coggle was over-dressed and Fontaine believed this posed a threat to their safety. Fontaine was also ashamed of her. Ever since he had taught his sister Violet how to behave like a lady, Fontaine had held strict views on the subject. At one point during the evening in Edinburgh, Fontaine and Kitto walked out of a bar without acknowledging Coggle when she entered.

By the time the three arrived back at Middle Farm Cottage in Newton Arlosh, on Friday, 16 December, the mood had worsened. Fontaine and Coggle argued over whether Mrs Scott-Elliot's mink and jewellery should be sold. Coggle was determined to keep them but Fontaine realized that people would start asking questions if she wore them in London. Kitto sided with Fontaine. They offered her the full proceeds of a sale. Coggle was willing to release the jewellery but not the mink coat.

In the early hours of the following morning, Saturday, Coggle asked Fontaine to make love to her on the mink coat. He obliged, hoping he could afterwards persuade her to part with the coat. Again, Coggle refused.

Later that day, Fontaine told her flatly that the mink must be sold or burnt. He turned on the electric fire in the living room of the cottage to show his determination. Coggle flew into a rage and Fontaine struck her with a poker, again and again, as Kitto held her. Coggle collapsed, still breathing. The two men suffocated her, then went to the Joiners' Arms for a drink.

On Sunday, 18 December, Kitto and Fontaine again drove north across the Scottish border. They found another deserted stretch of road, this time at Middlebie near the Dumfriesshire town of Lockerbie. They left the body of Mary Coggle in a stream known as Back Burn.

Over the next fortnight, the two men based themselves at Newton Arlosh, spending heavily at the Joiners' Arms, while making a series of trips south to the Scott-Elliots' flat. Fontaine had sent a telegram in their name to the friends in Aberdeenshire whom the couple were due to visit for Christmas. They removed everything further of real value at the flat, selling it to a series of contacts in London and the Midlands.

In between these journeys, they passed Christmas at the nearby home of his sister Violet and her husband, John Harvey. On Christmas morning, the body of Mary Coggle was found in the stream hundreds of miles to the north by a young man taking a stroll.

New trio

On Friday, 13 January 1978, Fontaine's younger brother Donald Hall was released from Haverigg Prison, Cumbria, where he had served a three-year sentence for housebreaking. Donald, 17 years younger than Fontaine, had turned to petty crime in his youth. Fontaine considered him uncouth, but he and Kitto collected Donald from Lytham St Annes, north of Newton Arlosh, on 14 January and drove him back to Middle Farm Cottage.

Fontaine and Kitto had returned the silver-grey Ford Cortina to the hire firm in Edinburgh, and from another company hired a Ford Granada with a registration number of YGE 999R. Fontaine was troubled by the figures 999 – the emergency police telephone number – and substituted a false number plate.

The three men spent the rest of the day drinking and eating out in Carlisle, discussing plans for a country-house robbery. Fontaine and Donald rang their half-sister Violet to wish her a happy birthday.

Years in prison had not helped Donald to learn tact. Back at Middle Farm Cottage on the Sunday evening, he plied Fontaine and Kitto with questions about their seemingly unlimited funds. He sensed they had recently completed a large venture.

When Fontaine mentioned that the next job they had planned would involve tying someone up, Donald boasted of his ability to secure a victim by binding only his thumbs. Fontaine, living with the strain of the killings he had already committed, saw the danger of allowing his brother into his plans.

Donald offered to demonstrate his foolproof system by posing as a 'tie-up' victim. Fontaine and Kitto humoured him until Donald was lying trussed on the floor of the cottage. Kitto then pressed a cloth soaked in chloroform against his nose and mouth until he died. This had the gruesome distinction of being the first chloroform killing in British legal history.

On the following morning, Monday, 16 January 1978, Fontaine and Kitto once more crossed the border into Scotland with a body in the boot of a car. By nightfall, they had booked two single rooms at the Blenheim House Hotel in North Berwick.

BODY SEARCH

The Blenheim House Hotel lies on the Firth of Forth, 16 miles east of Edinburgh. A stately stone building with a pillared entrance, the hotel stands on the seafront and caters mainly for golfers, walkers and swimmers. In the snow and rain of Monday, 16 January 1978, it had only one guest, a commercial traveller, when Fontaine's hired red Granada pulled up.

The hotelier, Norman Wight, who ran Blenheim House with his wife Margaret, watched Fontaine and Kitto at the reception desk. They were travelling light. Between them they carried only a hold-all, a hanger holding a jacket and shirt and an overcoat. Kitto signed the register in the name of Compton, giving an address in Mill Hill, north London.

Fontaine talked a lot and seemed in charge. He said they were completing a short tour of Scotland before emigrating to Australia, but seemed anxious to get the registration over with. Wight found the pair odd, but did not quite know why.

Wight discreetly observed his new guests while they drank brandy in the bar. He had always carefully studied the routine circulars issued by the police about wanted criminals. Neither of the two guests fitted anything Wight had read recently, but he remained troubled. The guests went into the dining room and ordered a meal. 'What do you make of them?' Wight asked his wife. Mrs Wight said she felt uneasy.

Wight slipped into his office and rang the local police. They had nothing under the name of Compton, but agreed to check the registration number of the Ford Granada. The number-plate bought by Fontaine, TUR 884R, belonged to a Ford Escort owned by a store in the south of England.

Number clue

While the guests finished their dinners and ordered desserts, two officers, Police Constables Michael Webster and Charles Turner, arrived from North Berwick police station and saw the original registration number, VGE 999R, on the tax disc on the windscreen. Further checks established the name of the self-drive company in West Lothian which had hired out the Granada.

Fontaine and Kitto were drinking brandy when the policemen approached their table. They explained that inquiries were being made about the Granada. Fontaine and Kitto were driven away in a police car.

Further south, events were in train which the officers at North Berwick were not yet aware of. Two days before, on Saturday, 14 January 1978, while Fontaine and Kitto were driving Donald Hall back to Newton Arlosh, Detective Constable Andrew Martin of Chelsea CID in central London had visited the Scott-Elliots' block of flats, in Sloane Street. Antique dealers had told police that silverware and other items, thought to belong to the couple, were being offered for sale.

The head porter at Richmond Court, Douglas Sutch, told Martin that the Scott-Elliots were probably in Italy, but had uncharacteristically left no forwarding address. Their butler had been coming to and fro.

Fake telegram

The friends of the Scott-Elliots in Aberdeenshire reported receiving a telegram from 'Walter and Dorothy', saying they would be spending Christmas in Rome. DC Martin, accompanied by Mr Sutch, forced the door of 22 Richmond Court, and called in forensic experts. Inquiries at the couple's banks failed to disclose any instructions about travelling abroad.

The Chelsea police investigation was still underway on Monday, 16 January when Fontaine and Kitto were taken to North Berwick police station. They gave their names as Roy Thomson Hall of Lytham St Annes, and John Blackman of Kilburn, north London. The Ford Granada was driven from the Blenheim House Hotel to the police station, but its boot remained unopened.

Fontaine was allowed to visit the toilet without an escort. Once inside, he slipped through the window, and hurried away on foot through the rain. Soon, he got a lift to the home of a local taxi-driver, John Hutchinson, after explaining to a passing motorist that his wife was ill.

Hutchinson drove Fontaine from hospital to hospital for three hours. Fontaine kept up a charade that his wife had been in an accident, and he had not been told which hospital she was taken to. Finally, they were stopped by a road block.

'They must be looking for someone,' Hutchinson remarked.

'It's nothing to do with me, son,' replied Fontaine.

A young officer, PC William Cowan, asked Fontaine his name. Donald Stewart, the passenger replied. Cowan and a colleague radioed a description of Stewart to Musselburgh police station, and were told to bring him in. One officer climbed into the taxi. When they reached Musselburgh, Fontaine insisted on paying the full fare.

Body in the boot

In the early hours of Tuesday, 17 January 1978, detectives told Fontaine that a body had been found in the boot of the Granada at 10.05 p.m. the previous evening. Fontaine was searched. His pockets contained £326 in cash, more than 60 silver Tudor pennies, and ten white tablets. Fontaine said that they were tranquillizers.

He asked his guards for water, and was brought a glass. Waiting until their eyes were turned, Fontaine, with a contortionist's skill, withdrew a number of powerful sedatives that he had concealed in his rectum and swallowed them in the water. He immediately lost consciousness. A convoy took him at high speed to Edinburgh Royal Infirmary, a few miles away. There, a stomach pump thwarted the attempt at suicide.

On the afternoon of the same day, 17 January 1978, Detective Chief Superintendent George MacPherson of the Lothian and Borders Police formed a large murder squad at his headquarters in Edinburgh. Officers were sent to Newton Arlosh. From London, the Scotland Yard police made a call about the silvery-grey Ford Cortina which Fontaine had hired in London but left on the forecourt of the hire firm's Edinburgh branch.

The Lothian police in turn mentioned the arrest of Fontaine, and the link to the Scott-Elliots was made. Soon, faced with the questioning of Detective Inspector Tom McLean, Fontaine and Kitto began to tell their stories. Forensic experts conducted extensive tests at Newton Arlosh, where traces of Mary Coggle's blood were found, and at Richmond Court.

Overwhelming forensic evidence soon emerged that Coggle and Donald Hall had died at Newton Arlosh. On the same day, 17 January, two dozen police officers searched the woods around Glen Affric for the body of Walter Scott-Elliot. It was found on Wednesday, 18 January.

Later that morning, a large party of police officers took Kitto to the Braco region to hunt for Mrs Scott-Elliot's body. Kitto proved unable to locate the spot. The hunt went on.

The next day, Fontaine made another attempt to kill himself in his cell. He had kept some sedatives concealed in his rectum, but his life was again saved at Edinburgh Royal Infirmary. Fontaine saw that he had nothing to lose by telling his full story. Two days later, he called detectives to his hospital bed.

'You might as well know about another one,' he told them. 'For starters, you had better ring Drumfries about one nobody knows about. It is a guy called David Wright and he is buried in the forest near Lady Hudson's estate. I shot him in the head.'

Fontaine offered to locate both Wright's body and that of Mrs Scott-Elliot. Doctors gave him permission to travel and, with the use of dogs, Wright's grave was quickly found on the same day, Saturday, 21 January. The following day, Fontaine guided police effortlessly to the exact spot on the B827, south of Comrie, where Mrs Scott-Elliot lay buried.

As her body was exhumed from the snow-covered ground, the police escort saw that Fontaine's face betrayed no feeling whatsoever.

GUILTY NORTH AND SOUTH

The trial of Roy Fontaine for the murders of Walter Travers Scott-Elliot and David Wright took place at the Edinburgh High Court on Tuesday, 2 May 1978 before Lord Wylie in a packed courtroom. The hearing lasted less than two hours.

Fontaine, charged under his real name of Archibald Thomson Hall, wore an expensive grey suit with a crisply pointed white handkerchief. He pleaded guilty to both charges. Kitto, seated alongside Fontaine in the dock, admitted assisting in the murder of Scott-Elliot. The deaths of Mrs Scott-Elliot, Mary Coggle and Donald Hall fell within English jurisdiction.

Colin McEachran, the Advocate-Depute and prosecuting counsel, told the court that the 54 year-old Fontaine had twice been certified insane in his youth. Two psychiatrists had examined him after his arrest in the Scott-Elliot case, McEachran said. They had concluded that he had a psychopathic personality. He felt no remorse over his victims, but was sane in law and fit to plead.

Outlining the killings, McEachran said that David Wright, Lady Hudson's gardener at Kirtleton Hall, had 'a record of violence'. Fontaine had told the police that, exhausted by Wright's blackmail, he had decided to settle matters when Wright fired a bullet at him while he was in bed. 'I decided then that I had to kill Wright,' Fontaine had said in the statement which was read out in court.

McEachran also disclosed that, while burying Scott-Elliot's body, Fontaine and Kitto had been spotted by a girl who later told police of seeing 'evil-looking creatures' in the woods. 'It may be she recognized some blood lust in their eyes at the time,' McEachran claimed.

Kitto's counsel, Donald Macauley QC, tried to depict his client as a helpless instrument in the hands of the dominating Fontaine. Macauley described how Mrs Scott-Elliot had made an 'unexpected appearance' at the flat, when Fontaine believed she was in a nursing home.

'The end result of that particular experience was that Mrs Scott-Elliot died,' Macauley said. Kitto's involvement had begun with only 'a simple burglary.'

However, the death of Mrs Scott-Elliot was not among the charges faced in Scotland, and Macauley's case was weakened by a statement about Mr Scott-Elliot's death given to the Lothian and Borders police by Kitto himself.

In this statement, read out in court, Kitto had openly admitted, 'We finally decided the old man had to go. We found a clump of bushes, got the old man out of the car and killed him.'

The passing of sentences by the judge was brief and undramatic. Lord Wylie sentenced both men to life imprisonment, the mandatory sentence for murder, and said that for Kitto he would not fix any minimum number of years that must be served before the prisoner could apply for parole.

'In the case of you, Hall [Fontaine],' Lord Wylie said, 'the circumstances seem to me to indicate that it would be appropriate to make a recommendation.' He ordered that Fontaine be detained for at least 15 years.

Fontaine, the man who loved style and attention, had ended his days of liberty without any touch of dramatic flair in the courtroom. He sought solace in trying to appear unaffected as he was led away in handcuffs, smirking at the press benches.

Kitto grinned at the reporters and said, 'Life begins at 40.'

On Wednesday, 1 November 1978, six months after the Edinburgh hearing, Fontaine and Kitto took their seats next to each other in the dock of the Old Bailey courtroom in London, as the English chapters of their murderous alliance were unfolded before the Recorder of the City of London, James Miskin QC.

Fontaine wore a three-piece suit in dark-blue, once again with a neat white handkerchief in his breast pocket. He had hoped to see his adopted sister Violet, his one consistently loyal friend, in the public gallery. But she was said to be too distressed to attend the trial.

In a quiet voice, Fontaine pleaded guilty to the murders of Mary Coggle and his brother Donald Hall. He denied murdering Mrs Scott-Elliot at her flat in Sloane Street. Kitto, dressed in a tweed suit, admitted murdering Mary Coggle and pleaded guilty to manslaughter, not murder, in the cases of Donald Hall and Mrs Scott-Elliot.

Silence in court

The prosecuting counsel, Michael Corkery QC, spoke for an hour to a hushed, sombre courtroom, as packed as the Edinburgh hearing had been. He described how Fontaine and Kitto had met, and planned a robbery of the Scott-Elliots' antiques. He moved on to the death of Mrs Scott-Elliot – one of the disputed charges – and then explained how Fontaine had bitterly argued at the cottage in Newton Arlosh with Mary Coggle.

'She wished to return to her old haunts around King's Cross, wearing a mink coat worth £3,000, which belonged to Mrs Scott-Elliot,' Corkery said. 'That was bound to attract attention and she refused to give it up.'

The death of Coggle formed the only murder charge heard at the Old Bailey to which both Fontaine and Kitto put in a plea of guilty. Corkery described the men's association with her in greater detail than he did the more complex issues of who was most responsible for the deaths of Mrs Scott-Elliot and Donald Hall.

Corkery told the court that the contested charges were to be left on file to avoid unnecessary public expense. The hearing had lasted three hours.

The judge, Mr Recorder Miskin, asked Fontaine and Kitto if they had anything to say.

'No,' each replied.

Dealing with Kitto first, the judge said he recognized that Fontaine had been the driving influence. 'Nevertheless, you played your vile part,' he said. Kitto was sentenced to life imprisonment, with a recommendation that he serve at least 15 years.

'Thank you, sir,' Kitto replied.

The judge turned his attention to Fontaine. 'Having regard to your cold-blooded behaviour and undoubted leadership in these dreadful matters,' the judge said, 'I have no hesitation in recommending to the Home Secretary that you shall not be considered for parole during the rest of your natural life save in the case of serious infirmity.'

The handcuffed Fontaine bowed at the judge. Escorted by warders, he turned to leave the dock and was heard to mutter 'Jesus Christ'. A moment later, with regained poise, he gave the press a mocking smile.

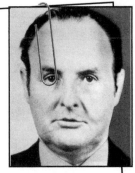

CASE FILE: FONTAINE, ROY

BACKGROUND

Roy Fontaine was born Archibald Thomson Hall in Glasgow on 17 July 1924. His parents, Archibald, a postal clerk, and Maisie, lived in a small tenement in McLean Street on the city's Southside. Archibald Jr went to infant school in the Jordanhill district, and the family eventually moved to the improved surroundings of Albert Street, close to Queen's Park.

Big brother

When Fontaine was seven, his parents adopted an infant girl, Violet. He grew into a protective older brother and, according to Violet, the family was close-knit in its early years. 'My brother bore his parents only one grudge – the fact that he had been christened Archibald,' she was to recall. 'He persuaded all our friends to call him Roy.' The second name was added later after Roy's favourite film actress, Joan Fontaine.

In his early teens, Fontaine enjoyed dressing his sister in flowers and silk from around the house, and adorning her in their mother's necklaces and brooches. 'He had a very strong artistic streak,' Violet said. 'When I was around seven or eight, he exercised infinite patience and hours of his spare time making dresses for my dolls.'

The youth loved all forms of elegance. He insisted on sleeping only in crisp fresh sheets and his fingernails were never dirty. Fontaine was also a fastidious housekeeper. Whenever his mother was ill, Fontaine would cook for the family, ensuring flowers were arranged throughout the house.

Dark side

However, a surreptitious side was developing to Fontaine's character. At home, he kept his stronger feelings to himself. Violet recalled that he usually appeared even-tempered. 'I can only remember having one quarrel with him,' she said. But at the age of 13, Fontaine got a ticking off from Glasgow magistrates after being charged with 'malicious mischief'.

The first serious discord between Fontaine and his father

began when he was 16. Fontaine had an affair with a married woman, 20 years older than him, who took her neat, spruce young lover out to the finest hotels in Glasgow.

In 1940, during the early days of World War II, the family lived briefly in barracks at Catterick, Yorkshire. One day, military police found stolen documents in Fontaine's room. On the walls were Nazi swastikas and pictures of Adolf Hitler. Fontaine unashamedly told the soldiers how he worshipped the German leader.

Sneak thief

Archibald Hall Sr, injured in action in France, was honourably discharged some months later. The family returned to Glasgow. Fontaine was by now a practised con-artist and sneak thief. On one occasion, he openly obtained a Red Cross collecting box, and helped himself furtively to another. He handed in the takings from a poor district, while pocketing the cash from the second box, collected in a wealthy neighbourhood. Later, he stole a medical bag containing dangerous drugs from a doctor visiting the family house, and was later found spending freely at a hotel. He refused to say what had happened to the drugs.

In May 1941, Maisie Hall gave birth to her second son, Donald. On 11 August in the same year, her elder son was sent to prison for the first time. Fontaine was sentenced at Glasgow Sheriff Court for theft and issuing a forged document. From then on, his working life was devoted to crime, despite a brief interlude selling antiques.

Loyal sister

Only Violet in his family had any hold on Fontaine's deeper loyalty. His parents, shamed by his constant arrests, continually moved rather than face their neighbours. But Violet stuck by her brother, in spite of his law-breaking, grateful for his teaching her how to behave like a 'lady', how to use cutlery and recognize good clothes. 'I know he has done some diabolical things,' she once said, 'but, strangely, he did like caring for people.'

PSYCHOLOGICAL PROFILE

Roy Fontaine was a professional jewel thief for some 35 years, with no record of violence until, at the age of 53, he was transformed into a savage killer of five people.

The connoisseur who could deeply appreciate a piece of carved silver showed no pity at the wretched sight of his victims' remains. The fastidious showman who loved dignified occasions, and companions with good taste, buried the people he killed in makeshift graves.

After his arrest, Fontaine's sister Violet and his stepfather John Wooton visited him in Saughton Jail, Edinburgh. They asked why he had suddenly resorted to murder. Fontaine refused to bare his soul. 'Well, it's fate isn't it?' he said with a shrug.

Delusions

Fontaine had once believed that he was a master-criminal. His conclusion seems to have been based on the number and ingenuity of the robberies he pulled off, rather than any ability to avoid arrest.

As a youth, he had adulated Adolf Hitler, probably as a symbol of superiority rather than for any political reason. In prison, Fontaine read exhaustively. Biographies of celebrities, works on etiquette, politics and modern thought, as well as antiques and craftsmanship, were his favourite reading. He coped with being a long-term prisoner by having affairs with a number of young men. Fontaine would play the dominant role, holding forth knowledgeably and having his lovers bring him snacks.

Fontaine had the gift of believing in his own fantasies. That was how he managed to impersonate William Warren-Connel at a royal garden party, and convince the management of a top hotel that he was an Arab sheik.

Soft spot

His family insisted that, as a boy, he was kind and considerate to others much of the time, with a soft spot for people down on their luck. In those days he relied on his wits, not violence, to survive.

Fontaine was also, for most of his criminal life, a loyal man by his own lights. He always refused to 'shop' his accomplices, and once campaigned strenuously on behalf of a young fellow-prisoner, convicted of violence, whom Fontaine thought had been treated unfairly.

But by the time Fontaine emerged from prison in the spring of 1977, much of his self-belief was collapsing. He had spent most of the previous quarter-century in prison, and had been deeply wounded by a male friend turning against him. Fontaine was 53 years old, with no wealth to show for his 'brilliant' crimes.

Getting careless

There were signs, too, that his fertile imagination and speed of responses were slowing down. During his time at Kirtleton Hall, he made little effort to act the part of refined butler when out drinking in the nearest village, and foolishly allowed a telephone call about a 'job' he was going to do to be overheard by an employer.

From then on, Fontaine fell prey to self-destruction. He had invited David Wright to Kirtleton Hall, even though he was opening himself to blackmail by a man he knew to be hard up and capable of violence.

Then he had brought Mary Coggle into the Scott-Elliot plot, when a moment's reflection would have told him that mink and jewellery would go to her head. He failed to ensure that Mrs Scott-Elliot was still away when he brought Kitto back to the Chelsea flat, and had taken brother Donald, whom he never trusted, to the cottage he rented at Newton Arlosh.

Finally, after years of successfully playing the part of a rich, cultured person in swanky hotels, Fontaine himself aroused suspicions at a small hotel in North Berwick. Although he escaped from the local police station, he soon resigned himself to complete failure, twice trying to kill himself and confessing to the murder of Wright when there was no suspicion that the gardener was dead.

At 53, Fontaine no longer believed in his own dreams. His vanity was in tatters and, with it, all his sympathy and pity for others.

Chapter 11

THEODORE ROBERT BUNDY
THE COLLEGE GIRL KILLER

He had an unlimited supply of young college girls who were easily charmed by his wit and good looks. He crossed America to escape the police, but he could never escape his urge to kill. Nobody knows the true death toll – Bundy look that secret with him to the electric chair.

Seattle is a pleasant city on the west coast of America. It has tree-lined avenues, vast expanses of water, and a relaxed and easy-going atmosphere. In relation to most cities of comparable size in the USA, its crime rate is small. One of the major problems facing its police force, however, is the high incidence of sexual assault.

Seattle is full of pretty university students, many living together in old fashioned clapboard houses with minimal security. But a sex crime that took place on 4 January 1974, struck the investigating officers as bizarre.

Sharon Clarke shared a house with a number of other students. When she failed to appear by mid-afternoon on 5 January, friends went down to her bedroom in the basement to see if she had overslept. They found Sharon unconscious, her face covered with blood. She had been hit over the head with a blunt instrument – a metal bar that had been wrenched from the bed-frame. She had not been raped, but the metal bar had been thrust into her vagina, causing lacerations.

After more than a week in a coma. Sharon recovered, but she was unable to provide the police with any useful information. The attack had left her with brain damage.

Peeping tom

The police reckoned that the attacker had watched Sharon undressing through her bedroom window, then found an unlocked door and made his way into her bedroom.

Four weeks later, a flatmate of 21 year-old Lynda Ann Healy went into Lynda's bedroom to see why the alarm was still buzzing at 8.30 in the morning. Lynda was a psychology student at the University of Washington. She also had a job at the local radio station reading the ski report on the early morning show. For this she had to get up at 5.30 a.m. When her flatmate saw that the bed had been neatly made up, she assumed that Lynda had gone out.

It was not until that evening, when Lynda's parents arrived for dinner, that someone pulled back the bed-clothes and found that the sheets and pillowcases were stained with blood. In the wardrobe, Lynda's nightdress, also stained with blood, hung on a peg. But there was no trace of Lynda.

Pleasure seekers

It looked as if the attacker had entered the basement and knocked her unconscious. He had then removed her nightdress – probably to put her clothes on – and remade the bed. If the intention had simply been rape, it could have been accomplished there and then. The inference seemed to be that this man wanted to take his time, to enjoy the pleasure of possession.

A few days later, an unknown man rang the police, and told them that Sharon Clarke's attacker was the same person who had abducted Lynda Ann Healey. According to the caller, the man had been seen outside both houses. The police never traced the caller.

Two weeks later, 19 year-old Donna Manson left her dormitory on the Evergreen campus, southwest of Olympia, on her way to a jazz concert. She never returned. Neither did Susan Rancourt, Roberta Kathleen Parks, Brenda Ball, or Georgann Hawkins. By mid June 1974, six girls had vanished. Georgann had disappeared during the short 100-yard walk from her boyfriend's student residence to her own.

As July started, police in Seattle were wondering who the seventh victim would be?

The answer came in a manner that would cause nationwide headlines. On 14 July 1974, two girls disappeared from the Lake Sammamish State Park. But this time, the abudctor had been seen by several witnesses. The park, 12 miles east of Seattle, was a favourite picnic spot. It was a hot day and the park was crowded. At about midday a girl named Doris Grayling was approached by a wavy-haired man with his arm in a sling. He asked her if she would help him lift his boat on to his car. She accompanied him to the car – a brown Volkswagen (VW) – but he then told her the boat was further up the hill. Unwilling to go further with a stranger, she excused herself and left.

Noted accent

Within an hour he had approached a pretty blonde named Janice Ott, who was living alone by the lake. When he asked her to help him with his boat, she invited him to sit down and talk. People sitting only a few yards away heard him introduce himself as Ted, and noted that he had an accent that might have been Canadian or even British. They talked for ten minutes about sailing and, in response to her saying, 'sailing must be fun. I've never learned how,' he offered to teach her. They set off together. She never returned to her place on the beach.

Only a couple of hours later, 18 year-old Denise Naslund left a group of friends, which included her boyfriend, and went to the ladies' lavatory. When she failed to return, they assumed she had met a friend for a chat. When she had still not returned after four hours, they reported her disappearance to a park ranger.

Same approach

Police investigating the case the next day learned that the young man with his arm in a sling had approached several girls with the same story about needing help with his boat. One girl was approached – and had refused – only minutes before Denise Naslund had disappeared.

Because Ted had been seen – and heard – by so many people, the Seattle newspapers were able to publish descriptions and artists impressions of the suspect. The police received many calls informing them that the man sounded like a University of Washington student, Ted Bundy. One of these calls was from an old friend of Bundy, crime reporter Ann Rule, another was from Meg Andrews, his girlfriend of four years standing.

But Bundy was only one of hundreds of suspects – the number swelled to 3,500 – and at first he seemed perhaps one of the least likely. He was apparently a decent, friendly young man who had been a political canvasser and had worked for the Crime Commission and also the Department of Justice Planning. On top of this, it seemed highly unlikely that a man who was about to abduct his victim would use his real name within the hearing of other people. Consequently, the Bundy file soon sank close to the bottom of the long list of suspects.

Human bones

On 6 September 1974, grouse hunters two miles east of Lake Sammamish Park found some human bones in the undergrowth. Dental charts identified them as those of Janice Ott and Denise Naslund. There was also a thigh bone belonging to a third body, but this one defied identification.

As the months went by, it began to look as if the Seattle murders had come to an end. By an odd coincidence, a similar series was about to begin in Salt Lake City. Ted Bundy had moved here to become a law student at the University of Utah.

DEATH IN UTAH

The good-looking man walked up to Carol DaRonch in the shopping centre in Murray, a suburb of Salt Lake City. It was a damp November evening in 1974 and the attractive 17 year-old was peering at a window display when the young man introduced himself as a police officer. He asked her whether she had left her car in the store car park, and she replied that she had.

After requesting and taking down the licence number he explained that he and his colleague had apprehended a man breaking into the car. He asked her to accompany him to it, to see if anything had been stolen.

The car park was some distance away, and as they walked towards it through the drizzle, Carol noticed that the police officer was allowing her to lead the way. She asked him for some identification. The man drew a wallet from his inside pocket, and opened it. In the semi-darkness, she could see something that looked like a police badge.

She was relieved to see that her car seemed to be undamaged, and that it was still locked. She opened the driver's door, and told him that nothing was missing. As the man bent over to try the passenger door, she noticed a pair of shiny handcuffs in the inside pocket of his green sports jacket.

He explained that his partner had taken the suspect to the sub-office on the other side of the mall, and asked Carol if she would mind going there with him to make a statement.

The policeman, who was about ten years older than Carol, seemed so serious and self-assured that she lacked the confidence to ask further questions. On the far side of the mall, they approached a small building, which the man identified as the sub-office. Carol was unaware that it was really a laundromat. The man tried the side-door, announced that his partner must have taken the suspect back to police headquarters, and told Carol that he would drive her there to sign a complaint.

She asked him for his name as they approached an old, battered-looking VW.

He told her he was officer Roseland of the Murray Police Department.

The vehicle certainly did not look like a police car. It was scratched and dented and, as she climbed in, she observed the back seat was torn.

In the enclosed space, she noticed alcohol on the man's breath. When he made a U-turn and went in the opposite direction to the police station, vague anxiety suddenly turned to alarm. Minutes later, the VW turned into a dark side street and screeched to a stop outside a darkened High School, the front wheel bouncing up the pavement.

It had taken Carol a long time to realize that she was being kidnapped, but as soon as she did, she made a grab for the handle and threw open the door. With terrifying speed, the man seized her wrist and snapped a handcuff on it. But as he tried to grab the other wrist of the screaming girl, he made a mistake and closed the handcuff on the same wrist. Then he pulled out a gun, pointed it at her head, and threatened to blow her brains out if she made another move.

Too terrified to care, Carol grabbed the handle, opened the door again, and fell out. The man was following her, with a metal bar in his hand, when they were illuminated by the headlights of an oncoming car. As Carol ran towards it, screaming, the VW accelerated away.

Half an hour later, the frightened girl told her story to a sergeant at police headquarters. He noticed a few spots of blood on the white fur trim of her coat – blood from scratches that Carol had inflicted on the face of her would-be abductor – and he clipped them off for forensic examination.

In Viewmont High School, a few miles north of Murray, an audience of students and parents was preparing to watch a comedy called *The Redhead*, presented by the school drama society. The drama teacher, Jean Graham, was similar in appearance to Carol DaRonch – tall, pretty, long brown hair parted in the middle. Minutes before the curtain was due to rise, Jean was walking towards the dressing rooms, when she was approached by a tall, good-looking young man who asked her if she would go to the car park and identify a car for him.

Deadly play

Jean Graham was in a hurry, so she told the man that she did not have time. But she took a good look at him, and observed that he had brown wavy hair and a moustache, and wore a well-cut jacket, dress-trousers and patent leather shoes.

He was persistent. In the first intermission, he was still there, and half an hour later, he again asked her to go with him to the car park. 'It will only take a few seconds,' he said. But she was still in a hurry and declined.

In the audience that night sat 17 year-old Debbie Kent, together with her parents. Debbie was not entirely happy, she had left her brother Blair at an ice rink, promising to pick him up after the play. But the play was overrunning, and Blair would be wondering what had happened to her. Debbie's father was recovering from a heart attack, and she was anxious not to worry him. So half an hour before the end, she decided to skip the rest of the play, to drive over to her brother.

Jean Graham was seated in the back row, glad the play was drawing to a close, when the door opened and the man came in and sat down in the seat opposite. He was breathing heavily, as though he had been running, and the people in front of him looked round irritably. When the curtain finally came down, he stood up and hurried out.

As the school slowly emptied, Debbie's parents waited nervously for her to return. Eventually, they decided to walk to the home of friends who lived nearby. It was only as they were crossing the car park that they saw their car was still there, and realized that their daughter had not made the trip to the ice rink.

The following morning, police investigating Debbie's disappearance searched the school grounds. Just outside the south door, not far from the car park, they found a handcuff key. Residents in a nearby block of apartments described hearing two piercing screams coming from the car park, some time after ten the previous evening. It was when the police discovered that the handcuff key fitted the cuffs taken from the wrist of Carol DaRonch that they began to piece together what had probably happened.

Carol's description of the policeman and Jean Graham's description of the persistent young man were too close for coincidence. After the failure to seize Carol, he had tried again. Debbie Kent had been grabbed as she walked into the car park. She had time to scream before she was rendered unconscious – with the iron bar.

Why did her attacker return to the auditorium? Probably because he knew that her screams had been overheard, and did not want to be seen driving away in his easily identifiable VW. If he had stayed where he was, any watchers in the apartment building would lose interest. So he went back into the school, waited until the play was over, then drove off with his unconscious victim. All this indicated exceptional coolness.

Practised abductor

In fact, Debbie Kent was the fourth girl to disappear in the Salt Lake City area in five weeks. The first had been a 16 year-old high school cheerleader, Nancy Wilcox. Nancy had quarrelled with her parents on 2 October, and accepted a lift in the VW. She had not been seen since. On 18 October, Melissa Smith, the 17 year-old daughter of the Midvale police chief, left a pizza restaurant late at night with the intention of hitch-hiking home. But she failed to get there. Nine days later, her naked body was found in Summit Park, violated and strangled, her face so battered that even her father failed to identify her at first.

On 31 October, another teenager, Laura Aime, set out for a Halloween party. She was six feet tall, and had a reputation for being able to take care of herself. Around midnight, she seems to have accepted a lift. Her body, beaten and violated, was discovered in the mountains four weeks later, on 27 November 1974.

Early in the morning of Saturday, 16 August 1975, Sergeant Bob Hayward drove slowly through a quiet neighbourhood of Salt Lake City, on the lookout for drunken drivers. In Brock Street, he turned on his head-lights, illuminating a parked VW. The car lurched into motion and took off at high speed. Since it was driving without lights, Hayward followed it, switching on his red spotlight. After jumping two red traffic lights, the driver, realizing that he could not outrun the police car, turned into an empty petrol station.

The tall, good-looking young man who climbed out and walked towards the police car was dressed entirely in dark clothes. When Hayward asked for identification, the man produced his driver's licence. It revealed him to be Theodore Robert Bundy of 565 First Avenue.

Asked why he had tried to evade a police officer, he explained, somewhat implausibly, that he had not realized he was was being followed by a police car. He had spent the evening, he said, at a drive-in movie – *The Towering Inferno* at Valley View. But Hayward recalled passing the drive-in earlier that evening, and had noticed that it was playing a triple bill of westerns. He asked Bundy if he could look inside his car.

Booked on suspicion

The passenger seat had been removed, and in the open bag on the floor beside it, Hayward discovered a brown knitted ski balaclava and a mask made out of ladies stockings with eye-holes cut in it. Nearby on the floor lay a steel bar, and in the boot of the car, he found a pair of handcuffs. Hayward turned and snapped handcuffs on the young man's wrists. 'You're under arrest,' he said.

DASH FOR FREEDOM

Three days after Bundy's arrest in Salt Lake City on 16 August 1975, a group of detectives sat down to their usual Tuesday morning meeting in the Temple of Justice. The detectives investigating the murder of police chief's daughter Melissa Smith reported no progress, as did those investigating the disappearance of Debbie Kent from the school play.

Detective Daryl Ondrak then described the arrest of Bundy the previous Saturday, and displayed the stocking mask and the iron bar. Bundy had now been freed on his own recognizances, but all agreed that it looked as if the suspect had been on his way to a burglary. Homicide Detective Jerry Thompson frowned when he heard the name Bundy – it seemed familiar.

Back in his office, he opened the suspects drawer, and there found what he was looking for – a thin file marked Bundy. A Seattle detective, Bob Keppel, had given him the information contained in the file. Bundy was a suspect in the 'Ted murders' of the previous year, and now he had moved to Salt Lake City. But Keppel had decided that he was clean – a hard-working law student with a degree in psychology from the University of Washington simply did not seem the sex maniac type.

The iron bar, the handcuffs and the stocking mask seemed to cast doubt on this diagnosis. At the same time, Thompson remembered something else – the attempted kidnapping of Carol DaRonch. She had also been hand-cuffed and threatened with an iron bar, and her abductor, like Bundy, drove a battered VW.

When Bundy was re-arrested five days later, he showed no sign of concern. He knew enough about the law to realize that the burgling-tool charge was only a misdemeanour that could not be made to stick.

The clear-up

Under questioning, he showed the coolness and casual self-confidence that would become familiar to the detectives trying to prove him guilty of murder. The stocking mask he wore when skiing to keep his face warm; he had found the handcuffs in a garbage can; the ice pick and the iron bar were part of his car tool-kit. As to searching his apartment, he gave his permission freely.

Naturally, the police found nothing suspicious – Bundy had had almost a week to clear up. But when Thompson noticed a number of holiday brochures about Colorado, he recalled that several girls had vanished there during the past year. Asked if he had ever been in Colorado, Bundy flatly denied it. The brochures and a map had been left in his apartment by a friend. In a drawer, Thompson noticed a bunch of credit card receipts, and slipped one into his pocket.

Back in his office, Thompson talked to the Colorado police about the disappearances there. The map, he told them, looked new and unused. But one of the ski brochures had a cross next to a hotel called the Wildwood Inn in Snowmass.

There was an exclamation at the other end of the line. 'A girl called Caryn Campbell disappeared from there in January. Her body was found a month later. She had been raped and battered to death.'

Suddenly, it was all looking far more promising. And if Carol DaRonch identified Bundy as her abductor, they would have a case. But Thompson met an unexpected setback. Carol had been so shattered by her experience that her memory was poor. Looking through a pile of mugshots, she agreed that the one of Bundy looked a little like her abductor, but that is as far as she would go. When they took her to see Bundy's VW, it was to discover that it had been recently resprayed.

On 1 October, Thompson's luck began to improve. Bundy was taken to the Hall of Justice for a line-up. The women who were there to identify the abductor were Carol DaRonch, Jean Graham and a student from Viewmont High School.

Headline maker

Although Bundy had shaved off his moustache, had his hair cut short, and changed the parting to the other side, all three identified him. Later that day, Judge Cowans signed a complaint charging Bundy with kidnap and attempted homicide.

Within 24 hours, the name of Ted Bundy was known to headline writers across the United States. By now, the bones of four more of the Seattle victims – Lynda Healy, Susan Rancourt, Kathy Parks and Brenda Ball – had been discovered on Taylor Mountain, 20 miles from Seattle.

The implications were horrible. Their abductor could have had only one purpose in taking them there – to be able to take as much time as he liked with his sexual assaults, before strangling or battering them to death. The implications of the double-disappearance from Lake Sammamish Park were just as bad. A man who abducts and rapes a girl would hardly be expected to abduct another girl a few hours later. Ted had wanted to experience the pleasure of violating two girls at the same time, possibly in front of one another.

Clearly, he was more than an ordinary sex killer, he was an almost inhuman monster. This is why the news that Bundy had been charged was worthy of nationwide headlines.

But within eight weeks, he was out on bail – his mother had borrowed the money. She, of course, had no doubt of his innocence. Nor had his student friends in Salt Lake City – they were convinced that the police were out to frame him. Two ex-girlfriends were less certain.

For the past five years, he had been more-or-less engaged to a girl in Seattle, but she had started to experience doubts when she saw the artist's impressions of 'Ted' in the newspapers. When she found plaster of Paris in his drawer, she had finally telephoned the police to relay her suspicions. A more recent girlfriend described how Ted liked to tie her up with nylon stockings before having sex.

Insubstantial evidence

Such behaviour would not prove that Ted was a killer. What did look more promising was the fact that Bundy's blood group was the same as that of the blood found on Carol DaRonch after her struggle with her abductor. Also strands of hair found in his car were virtually identical with those of Carol DaRonch and Melissa Smith. A decade later, after the discovery of genetic fingerprinting, the blood alone would have established Bundy's guilt or innocence. But in 1975, neither the blood nor hair evidence was conclusive. Neither was the fact that the credit card receipts proved that Bundy had been in Colorado around the dates when girls had disappeared.

When Bundy finally walked into court in Salt Lake City on 23 February

1976, another thing became immediately evident – most of the spectators assumed that the police had made a mistake. This decent-looking, clean-cut, obviously articulate man could not possibly be the serial killer, he looked more like a young executive. In spite of Carol DaRonch's identification, the case against Bundy looked thin and circumstantial. This was his main line of defence – he had been the victim of a series of incredible coincidences.

Bundy's case continued to look convincing until he stepped into the witness box on the fourth day. It was not that there was anything wrong with the way he presented himself – it was just that he seemed too plausible, too clever. Explaining why he had driven away from the police car, he told the court that he had been smoking marijuana, and had thrown it out of the car as he drove.

He seemed a little too smart and confident to be innocent. In his closing arguments, the prosecutor admitted that the evidence was circumstantial. But when he went on to point out the odds against such a body of evidence leading to the wrong person, everyone in court recognized the power of his argument. Even so, the prosecutor felt that the verdict was likely to go against him.

It was not until the following Monday, when Judge Stewart Hanson declared, 'I find Theodore Robert Bundy guilty of aggravated kidnapping,' that he knew he had won. Bundy sobbed and pleaded not to be sent to prison. The judge was unmoved, and sentenced him to between one and 15 years in prison.

One thing had become obvious, if Bundy was the man who had abducted Carol DaRonch, then he was also the man who had kidnapped Debbie Kent from Viewmont High School. This in turn meant that he was a leading suspect in the other Salt Lake City abductions. And since his credit card receipts revealed that he had been in Colorado several times in 1975 – when five young women had vanished – it began to seem highly likely that Ted Bundy was a mass sex-murderer.

In January 1977, Bundy was moved to prison in Aspen, Colorado. The Colorado authorities were beginning to build up a convincing case that he had been responsible for the abduction of Caryn Campbell.

Aspen trial

A man answering Bundy's description had been seen in the hotel on the evening of her disappearance. Also a third lot of hair found in Bundy's VW matched Caryn Campbell's, and the crowbar found in his car matched the depression found in Caryn's skull. A credit card receipt showed that he had been in the area when a girl named Julie Cunningham had vanished, and a petrol station attendant had identified him. Altogether, the new case against Bundy looked rather more convincing that the previous one in Salt Lake City.

In the Colorado jail, Bundy was a popular prisoner. His charm, intelligence and sense of humour convinced many of his fellow prisoners of his innocence. He had decided to act as his own defence counsel, and this led to the decision to allow him in court without manacles. District Attorney Frank Tucker described him as 'the most cocky person I have ever faced.' But Bundy was certainly becoming increasingly bitter, aggressive and dispirited as the time of his trial approached.

Bundy appeared in court in Aspen on 7 June 1977. He listened to the public defender arguing against the death penalty. During the lunch hour, he strolled into the library on the second floor. Minutes later, a woman saw a man land on the grass verge below the window and limp off down the street. She asked a policeman, 'Is it normal for people to jump out of windows around here?' Cursing, the officer rushed up to the library. Bundy was no longer there.

He was, in fact, already in a nearby river gorge, stripping down to his shirt and shorts to make himself look like a hiker. Then, with his clothes stuffed into his sweater, he strolled off along the road to Aspen Mountain.

Further up the mountain, he found refuge in an unoccupied cabin, where he hid for two days. But when he set out again, Bundy somehow managed to retrace his steps and wander in a circle. After stealing a Cadillac, he was spotted by police, and re-arrested only blocks from where he escaped eight days earlier.

For the next six months, legal arguments dragged on. The prosecution wanted to introduce evidence about other girls who had vanished in Utah. Bundy fought back, using endless delaying tactics.

At 7 a.m., on 31 December 1977, a guard in Garfield County Jail left the breakfast tray outside Bundy's cell and saw a figure asleep in the bunk. At lunchtime the tray was still there. The figure had been a pile of books and pillows. A hole in the ceiling showed how, with the aid of a hack-saw blade, Bundy had made his second escape. By the time the alarm was raised. Bundy was in Chicago.

THE CHI OMEGA MURDERS

Tallahassee, the state capital of Florida, lies around 2,500 miles from Seattle on the south eastern tip of the United States. In spite of the distance, Tallahassee and Florida shared the relaxed atmosphere of a pleasant university campus.

It was two weeks since Ted Bundy had escaped from Colorado, but the news had hardly penetrated this far south. In the students lodging house known as the Oaks, nobody paid much attention to a new arrival – Chris Hagen – who had taken a small shabby room for $80 a month. The few who had talked to him found him intelligent and charming, but he seemed to prefer to keep himself to himself. What no one guessed was that Chris

Hagen was almost out of money, and was stealing from supermarkets to keep himself alive.

At 3 a.m. on Sunday, 15 January 1978, Nita Neary said goodnight to her boyfriend and let herself into the Chi Omega sorority residence on the edge of the campus. Someone had left the lights on, and she turned them off. Then she heard the sound of footsteps on the stairs, and saw a man hurrying towards the front door. As she opened it, she saw that he was wearing a dark knitted cap, and was carrying some sort of wooden club.

Her first assumption was that one of the students had sneaked a man into her room. But there was something furtive about this man's bearing that worried her. She ran upstairs and roused her room-mate, then the two of them went to waken the sorority president. As they were talking, a door opened and a girl staggered out, clutching her head. They recognized Karen Chandler, and a moment later saw that her hair was soaked with blood. They rushed into the room Karen shared with Kathy Kleiner, and found Kathy sitting up groggily in bed, blood streaming down her face.

A savage killing

The police were there within minutes. They quickly discovered that two more girls – Margaret Bowman and Lisa Levy – had been attacked and that Margaret was dead, strangled with a stocking. Lisa Levy died on her way to hospital. Margaret Bowman's knickers had been torn off so violently that her skin had been grazed. One of Lisa Levy's nipples had almost been bitten off, and blood was running from the anus and vagina. The medical examiner also discovered a bite mark on her left buttock.

An hour and a half later, in a small house just six blocks away, Debbie Cicarelli was aroused by loud bangs apparently coming from the next room, occupied by Cheryl Thomas. Minutes later, she heard whimpering noises. She roused her room-mate, and they both listened to the sounds. Debbie tried dialling Cheryl's phone number. As the telephone rang, there was a bumping noise and a sound of running feet. Minutes later, the house was swarming with police who had rushed over from the Chi Omega residence.

Cheryl Thomas was semi-conscious, and the bloodstained bed-clothes had been pulled from the bed. A wooden club lay on the floor nearby. Cheryl, like Karen and Kathy, would survive the brutal beating, only after coming close to death.

The Chi Omega murders made nationwide headlines – although, no one thought of suggesting that Bundy might be in Florida. In the Oaks, Chris Hagen continued to keep himself to himself. He often seemed to be drunk late at night.

In fact, he was now living mainly on theft – of credit cards and items from supermarkets. He was also becoming an expert at stealing women's purses. Then, on 5 February 1978, he stole a white van from a car park, and drove off in the direction of Jacksonville.

Two days later, on Wednesday, 8 February, a sloppily dressed man with a two-day growth of beard approached 14 year-old Leslie Parmenter in a Jacksonville street and tried to engage her in conversation, but he seemed confused and unsure of himself. At that moment, her 20 year-old brother drove up – he intended giving her a lift home – and asked the stranger what he wanted. The man mumbled something and wandered off towards his white van. Danny Parmenter followed him and, as he drove off, noted down the number of the van.

Gym class

The following morning, Chris Hagen left the local Holiday Inn without paying, and drove around aimlessly until he found himself near the Lake City Junior High School.

Minutes into her first period gym class, 12 year-old Kimberly Leach realized she had left her purse in another room, and asked to be excused to go and fetch it. But it was not until two o'clock that afternoon that someone noticed she had not returned, and rang her mother.

That same afternoon, Chris Hagen was back in Tallahassee. The following evening, he took a girl out to dinner, using a stolen credit card, and behaved impeccably. But later that night, after a policeman had looked searchingly at the stolen van, he left the apartment by means of the fire escape, stole an orange VW in which the owner had left the keys, and headed west towards Pensacola.

In the early hours of the morning of Wednesday, 15 February 1978, Patrolman David Lee saw an orange VW driving erratically out of an alleyway. He radioed the licence number, and moments later, was told that it was stolen. When he flashed his lights, the car accelerated for a moment, then the driver pulled over.

Lee ordered the driver to get out and lie down. But as the suspect obeyed, he kicked the policeman's legs from under him, and took to his heels. Lee pulled out his gun and fired, the man collapsed on the pavement. But as Lee bent over him, the man hit him on the jaw. They struggled for a few moments, then Lee finally managed to snap the handcuffs on the man's wrists.

A gloomy outlook

As they drove off towards the police station, the handcuffed man remarked gloomily, 'I wish you'd killed me.'

Back at the station, the suspect insisted that his name was Kenneth

Misner, and supported his story with identification papers and a birth certificate. But the police soon learned that the papers had been stolen from a real Kenneth Misner in Tallahassee. It was another 24 hours before the Pensacola interrogators discovered – through overhearing the prisoner's phone conversations – that they had arrested a man named Ted Bundy. The name meant nothing to them.

In the early hours of the morning, a demoralized and exhausted Bundy talked into a tape recorder. His aim, he explained, was to try to make his interrogators understand his problem. It had all started, he said, when he had seen a girl riding a bicycle, 'I knew I had to have her.' And although she had escaped, his future course was now determined. 'Sometimes I feel like a vampire,' he said but denied responsibility for the Chi Omega attack.

Discovery of a body

It was nearly two months later, on 7 April 1978, that a highway patrolman looked into an old shed near the Suwannee River State Park and saw a foot wearing a sneaker. It was the naked, decomposing body of Kimberly Leach. Injuries to the pelvic region suggested sexual assault. The cause of death was 'homicidal violence to the neck region'. One sickened lawman declared. 'We're gonna send that Bundy to the electric chair.'

But Bundy's hour of weakness had passed. He was once again insisting on his total innocence, and that his apparent connection with a chain of sex murders was pure coincidence.

HIS OWN DEFENCE

Bundy was right about one thing. All the evidence against him was circumstantial – all, at any rate, except for the bite on Lisa Levy's left buttock.

Three weeks after Kimberly Leach's body had been found, policemen held the struggling Bundy down and took an impression of his teeth. This impression would finally convict Ted Bundy of Lisa Levy's murder.

Once again, Bundy had decided to act as his own defence lawyer, and his delaying tactics succeeded in getting the trial delayed from October 1978 to June 1979. At one point, he changed his mind, and decided to accept a defence team from the public defender's office. But when they made it clear that they wanted him to enter into 'plea bargaining' – agreeing to plead guilty to the murders of Lisa Levy, Margaret Bowman and Kimberly Leach in exchange for a guarantee that he would not receive the death sentence. Bundy sacked them.

It was the third major mistake of his criminal career. The first two had been the careless driving offences that had led to his two arrests. This third mistake would prove, eventually, to be the most serious of the three.

Losing ground

The trial began on 25 June 1979, and Bundy scored an initial success when his objections succeeded in having it moved from Tallahassee to Miami, on the grounds that Tallahassee jurors would be prejudiced. But from then on, it was clear that Bundy was losing ground fast. The evidence against him was damning. There was the girl, Nita Neary, who had seen him leave the sorority house, the stocking mask found in the room of Cheryl Thomas, which was virtually identical with the one found earlier in Bundy's car. Above all, the bite marks found on Lisa Levy's left buttock, which dental experts testified to be those of Bundy's own teeth.

Bundy scored a success when the judge ruled that the tapes of his confessions to the Pensacola police were inadmissible because his lawyer had not been present. But while Bundy himself continued to believe he was doing well, no one else in court could doubt that the case against him was overwhelming. Public defender, Margaret Good made a powerful speech in Bundy's defence, underlining every possible doubt.

On 23 July 1979, the jury took only seven hours to find him guilty on a long list of indictments. Asked if he had anything to say, Bundy put on another of his displays of injured innocence, and replied with tears in his voice. 'I find it somewhat absurd to ask for mercy for something I did not do.'

On death row

Judge Edward D. Cowart sentenced Bundy to die by electrocution, concluding, 'I bear you no animosity, believe me. But you went the wrong way, pardner. Take care of yourself.'

The first of many books on Bundy concluded with those same words. But the Bundy story was by no means over. From the Raiford Penitentiary, where he was placed on Death Row, Bundy continued to fight for his life. On 7 January 1980, he was tried in Orlando for the murder of Kimberly Leach.

Colour slides of the body were shown, and the medical evidence seemed to indicate that the girl had been raped in the van, dressed again, then taken to the hut, stripped and possibly sodomized. On 7 February 1980, Bundy was again found guilty. Once again, he burst into tears. Two days later he married a girl named Carole Boone, a divorcee with a teenage son. He had met her some years earlier and she had stuck by Bundy, after Meg Anders had left him. She continued to believe his innocence.

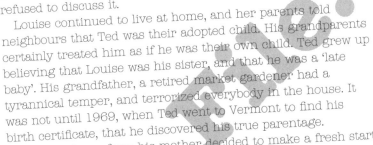

CASE FILE: BUNDY, THEODORE ROBERT

BACKGROUND

Theodore Robert Bundy was the illegitimate child of a respectable and religious young secretary, Louise Cowell. He was born in a home for unmarried mothers near Philadelphia on 24 November 1946. His mother chose the name Theodore because it means 'gift of God'. The identity of his father is unknown, and Louise always refused to discuss it.

Louise continued to live at home, and her parents told neighbours that Ted was their adopted child. His grandparents certainly treated him as if he was their own child. Ted grew up believing that Louise was his sister, and that he was a 'late baby'. His grandfather, a retired market gardener had a tyrannical temper, and terrorized everybody in the house. It was not until 1969, when Ted went to Vermont to find his birth certificate, that he discovered his true parentage.

When Ted was four, his mother decided to make a fresh start and went to stay with relatives in Tacoma (a town close to Seattle). At a church social, she met and later married a mild, easy-going southerner, John Bundy, who had just left the navy. He found a job as a cook in a veterans hospital, and remained there for the rest of his working life. Ted found his new father dull and uncultured, but showed no resentment towards him, nor to the half brother and sisters that later came along.

Habitual liar

Ted was an oversensitive and self-conscious child who had all the usual daydreams of fame and wealth. He fantasized about being adopted by the cowboy star Roy Rogers, and actually asked his uncle Jack, a professor of music in Tacoma, to adopt him. At an early stage he became a thief and habitual liar. He achieved fairly good grades at school, became an enthusiastic boy scout, and was a natural athlete. He later became an excellent skier, although the expensive equipment he used was almost certainly stolen.

As a first year student, he was lonely, silent and shy. The desire to be different led him to study Chinese.

In his late teens, Ted became heavily infatuated with a fellow student, Stephanie Brooks. She was beautiful, sophisticated, and came from a wealthy family. By now, Ted had already developed something of that charm and air of sophistication that made him attractive to women, and they became engaged.

To impress Stephanie and her family, Ted went to Stanford University to study Chinese. He was lonely there, emotionally immature, and his grades were poor. 'I found myself thinking of standards of success that I didn't seem to be living up to,' he said. Stephanie eventually wearied of his immaturity, and broke the engagement. He was shattered and deeply resentful. His brother Glenn commented, 'Stephanie screwed him up . . . I'd never seen him like this before.'

Ted took a menial job in a hotel dining room and became friendly with a drug addict. One night they entered an abandoned cliffside house and stole whatever could be carried. He found it a strangely exciting experience, and began shoplifting and stealing for thrills. On one occasion he walked openly into a greenhouse, removed an 8 ft palm, and drove off with it sticking out of the sunroof of his car.

He also became a full-time volunteer for Art Fletcher, the black Republican candidate for Lieutenant Governor. Ted enjoyed the sense of being a 'somebody' and mixing with interesting people. In 1972, he worked at a Crisis Clinic as a psychiatric counsellor. Later, he took a job working for the Crime Commission and Department of Justice Planning. In 1973, he began to study law, at the University of Puget Sound in Tacoma.

When Stephanie Brooks met him again, seven years after they split up, she was deeply impressed by the new high-powered Ted. They talked of marriage again and spent the Christmas of 1973 together.

Sweet revenge

Then Bundy 'dumped' her as she had dumped him. When she rang him to ask why he had not contacted her since their weekend together, he said coldly, 'I have no idea what you're talking about,' and hung up on her.

A few weeks later, as if his revenge had somehow broken some inner dam and inspired him with a sense of ruthless power and confidence, he became a rapist and murderer.

PSYCHOLOGICAL PROFILE

Bundy is an example of what has become known as 'the serial killer' – a form of violence which has grown steadily in recent years, particularly in America. Jack the Ripper in 1888, is probably the first modern example, with five victims over a period of ten weeks. The serial killer is a person in whom the normal inhibition about taking human life has broken down, and the motive in the majority of cases is sex. For such a person, killing has become simply a bad habit. Bundy also belongs to an alarming sub-department of serial killers, the high I.Q. killer.

On the day before his execution, Bundy talked frankly to Dorothy Lewis a New York psychiatrist, and certain important new insights emerged. Bundy's grandfather, who showered affection on him during his early years and was the only true 'father' Bundy ever knew, was a man of violent temper who sometimes beat up his gentle and patient wife. Bundy, himself possessed of a violent temper, felt from an early age that bursts of rage were justified. He could never understand why he had so much rage, much of which was directed towards his mother, with whom he admitted he had a very superficial relationship. As a highly intelligent teenager, he felt an outsider in the working class home with an unlettered stepfather and a repressed and religious mother.

Another basic drive in Bundy's case was a craving to be famous. But a streak of self-pity, the feeling that 'the world was against him', prevented him from making the kind of effort that might have brought him success. Killing girls and outwitting the law gave him a sense of real achievement. Bundy also enjoyed the challenge of luring the smartest, most beautiful female students to their deaths.

Craving violence

The ultimate key, is Bundy's immensely powerful sexuality. From an early age he had been a compulsive masturbator, and later became obsessed by sadistic pornography. He admitted to fantasizing about necrophilia. His long-time girlfriend Meg Anders described how he used to tie her up with stockings before sex.

Such acts could not satisfy Bundy's desire – like some legendary Caliph – to have total control of the sexual partner.

This gradually turned into a craving for violence. He later admitted that he often strangled the victim during the sexual act. Vaginas were stuffed with twigs and dirt, and the women were sodomized with objects such as aerosol cans.

Some of the bodies although partly decomposed, had freshly washed hair and eye make-up had been applied, indicating that he had kept them for acts of necrophilia.

One of the most difficult things to understand is Bundy's ability to switch from a charming conversationalist to an unfeeling killer.

Author Stephen Michaud asked Bundy whether he had much conversation with his victims. 'There'd be some,' he answered. Since this girl . . . represented not a person, but the image, or something desirable, the last thing we would expect him to want would be to 'personalize this person.'

The kind of inner-hardness and ruthlessness required to treat a girl as a throwaway must have been present in Bundy from a very early age, possibly from soon after birth.

Behavioural scientists now know that if an animal is deprived of mother love for the first few days of its life it becomes permanently incapable of forming bonds of affection. For two months after Ted Bundy's birth he was left at the nursing home without his mother, while his grandparents debated whether to give him up for adoption. This may have been the period that determined his career as a killer.

Dreadful reminder

Perhaps the most disturbing observation is the one Bundy made to Stephen Michaud, 'Somebody that was truly shrewd, with a little bit of money, could probably avoid detection indefinitely. It has always been my theory that for every person arrested and charged with multiple homicide there are probably a good five more out there.'

Chapter 12

JACQUES MESRINE
FRANCE'S PUBLIC ENEMY

The French dubbed him 'Public Enemy No. 1', but many people secretly admired his daring escapades from prison and cheeky mockery of the police. The legend was hollow. Jacques Mesrine was a vindictive, brutal murderer who felt no remorse for the victims of his private war against civilized society.

On the afternoon of 12 November 1967, a couple walked into the foyer of the Hotel de la Croix Blanche in the French town of Chamonix. The man was tall and powerfully built, with an air of confidence. His female companion was dark-haired with a good-looking, if slightly coarse, appearance.

They took up their reservation for a double room for 10 days and signed the register. The man gave his name as Jean-Jacques Moreau, a 33 year-old company director from Paris. It was an old habit of his not to sign his real name in hotels.

The couple planned to have a simple winter holiday and enjoy a good rest. But, while eating dinner in the hotel two days later, they saw a man at the reception desk who interested them. The guest was an Arab, in western clothes, and looked wealthy.

A waiter explained that the guest was Albert Setruk, who often visited the hotel and was rumoured to carry millions of francs in his briefcase. The couple noticed that while Setruk chatted to the receptionist, the briefcase stood on the floor by his feet. Later, discreet inquiries among the hotel staff revealed that Setruk was Tunisian and frequently visited the town's casino late in the evening.

The Tunisian and his aide, André Flery, went to the casino that very night, returning at about 2 a.m. on the morning of 15 November. The night receptionist was a dark-haired woman whom Setruk did not recognise. She escorted the two men to the lift, explaining to their surprise that their keys were in the doors to their rooms.

As the three emerged from the lift on the first floor, they were confronted by the tall fellow guest. In a moment, a gun was pointing at them. Assisted by the dark-haired girl, the man searched Setruk and Flery, taking their documents and about 7,000 francs. The two men were then pushed downstairs, gagged and bound, and left behind the desk, where they lay beside the trussed-up figure of the more familiar night receptionist.

The thieves cut the hotel telephone wires, loaded their cases into the car, called out a farewell to the three men they had tied up and drove off. Their names were Jacques Mesrine and Jeanne Schneider.

Financially, the robbery had not been a great success. Mesrine had found no money inside Setruk's briefcase when he broke into his room. But he was delighted that Schneider seemed to enjoy the sheer thrill of danger. The 29 year-old Mesrine had waited a long time to find a mistress with his own cool.

Showman

Throughout his career, Mesrine had enjoyed brazenly outwitting his opponents. He liked to be conspicuous to the point of flamboyance. In 1960, on his first known robbery, Mesrine had entered a block of flats with a splendid bouquet of flowers. Two years later, he used his father's car to execute a robbery at the home of a wealthy engineer, Robert Grussenbucher, in Normandy. He escaped with jewellery, paintings and cash.

Six weeks later, Mesrine had been arrested while recklessly driving the same car to a different robbery. Police found guns in the car. Mesrine was sentenced to three years' imprisonment. Although released on parole after less than 18 months, it rankled with him that he had not actually escaped from jail.

Now, driving away from Chamonix in the darkness, Mesrine felt that life was doing him justice. He had admired the way Jeanne Schneider had waved the gun in the faces of their victims and laughed when Mesrine had punched Setruk on the chin.

Mesrine and Schneider committed several more thefts over the following weeks. In some, Jeanne dressed as a man. Often, her presence seemed to inspire Mesrine to show off and take unnecessary risks. Their crimes took on a brutal, violent edge and Mesrine developed a habit of lingering too long at the scene of a crime, savouring his triumph.

In one of these, on 8 December 1967, Mesrine, a male accomplice and Jeanne, dressed as a man, bound and gagged a dressmaker named Madame Coudercy, and her daughter and son-in-law, inside her shop in the rue de Seze in Paris. Each of the gang was armed.

Killer: Jacques Mesrine

Slow torment

Mesrine spent much of the night drinking heavily and recounting his criminal exploits to his terrified victims. He toyed with the dressmaker and her daughter by waving a flick-knife close to their faces. Eventually, the robbers escaped with jewels and valuables worth millions of francs.

Mesrine's taunting violence inside the dressmaker's shop showed a new side to his criminal style, which had previously expressed itself as a combination of bravado and straighforward aggression.

The police in Paris and across France compiled detailed reports of Mesrine's bravado. He soon turned from a man merely under suspicion and wanted for questioning into a fugitive. After brief trips to Spain and Italy, Mesrine and Jeanne Schneider decided to escape from the pressure of a manhunt in their own country. Early in 1968, they caught a flight to Montreal in Canada. It was five years before Mesrine saw France again, and during that time his criminal career grew broader and deeper.

BREAKING OUT

Mesrine did not immediately resume his criminal activities in Canada. He took a job on a building site and, when this work finished, he found work as a chauffeur. He wanted to study the lie of the land before committing himself to risky ventures.

Mesrine's first crime in the New World owed more to opportunism and revenge than to planning for gain. On 7 March 1969, he and Jeanne had entered the service of Georges Deslauriers, a wealthy but crippled businessman who could walk only with the aid of crutches. Mesrine was to act as chef and chauffeur, while Jeanne was to be the housekeeper. The couple were housed in the lodge on Deslauriers' large, picturesque estate at Saint-Hilaire, on the outskirts of Montreal.

Sacked

There is no proof that Mesrine intended from the outset to rob his employer. However, following a violent quarrel between Jeanne and another of the servants, the French couple were asked to leave. Jacques was filled with resentment as he always was when dismissed or excluded.

The pair returned to Montreal, where Mesrine hatched a plan to kidnap Deslauriers and hold him to ransom. For this scheme, he enlisted Michel Dupont, a young Frenchman, and Jeanne drove them to the estate after midnight, an hour when the helpless landowner would be alone.

Deslauriers was bundled into the car and driven away. Mesrine delivered a ransom note to his brother, demanding 200,000 Canadian dollars, but the brother did not appear at the designated venue and the kidnappers, returning to their flat, found that their captive had escaped. The three fled to the port of Percé, some 800 kilometres (500 miles) away. Dupont was arrested when, foolishly, he returned to his home in Montreal.

While in Percé, the kidnappers stayed at the Three Sisters Motel, posing as Belgian tourists and befriending the owner, Madame Evelyne Le Bouthillier. She invited them into her room for drinks. On 29 June 1969, over a week after Dupont's departure, Mesrine and Schneider booked out of the motel and headed towards Quebec province. The next morning, Madame Le Bouthillier was found strangled.

Shortly afterwards, Mesrine and his mistress crossed the US border in a hired car and drove south. On Dupont's information, they were arrested just outside Dallas, Texas, and, on 23 July 1969, flown back to Montreal to face charges for both the Deslauriers kidnapping and the murder of Madame Bouthillier. Mesrine vehemently denied the murder charge, expressing outrage at being accused of killing a helpless woman.

Pending the trial, Mesrine was held in prison back in Percé and may well have decided that the comparative lack of security there presented some enticing opportunities.

Mesrine fashioned a rough knife out of the handle of an aluminium mug, sharpening it on a wall. On 17 August 1969, a guard was overpowered and locked in a cell. As only three warders were on duty during the evening shift, Mesrine had no difficulty in wandering round the jail until he found Jeanne Schneider. The couple even had time to steal food from the kitchens before escaping through the exercise yard.

It was outside the prison that they encountered real problems. The single feasible route lay through thick forests and, in the rain, they made slow progress. In the morning, a search party with tracker dogs hunted them down. Soon after, faced with overwhelming evidence, Mesrine and Schneider pleaded guilty to the kidnapping and were sentenced to ten and five years in jail respectively. The murder trial, which began on 18 January 1971, was more controversial. Defence lawyers were able to show inconsistencies in the evidence of some of the dead woman's relations. As a result of these witnesses' over-zealous attempts to incriminate Mesrine, he and Jeanne were acquitted, although the judge was clearly unhappy at this verdict.

Mesrine was taken back to the top-security wing of the St Vincent-de-Paul gaol in Laval to serve his sentence for the kidnapping. This was the showpiece of the Canadian prison system. It had been specially constructed in 1968, at a cost of 2.5 million dollars, to house inveterate would-be escapers. In the correctional unit, there were 65 warders guarding 62 prisoners. The place was reckoned to be escape-proof.

On 21 August 1972, Mesrine and four other men broke out of the prison during an exercise period. One was swiftly recaptured, but the others reached the nearby Highway 25, where they flagged down two passing cars and completed their getaway. The escape, which exposed the incompetence of the prison system, became front-page news.

Mesrine returned to Montreal, where he joined forces with Jean-Paul Mercier, another of the escapees. The two men had much in common. Although eight years younger than Mesrine, Mercier was a hardened criminal who had been serving 24 years for attempted murder and kidnapping. Like Mesrine, he already had one previous jail break to his credit.

High-speed risks

Only one week after the break-out, on 28 August, the two men robbed the Toronto Dominion Bank in Montreal, before embarking on a reckless scheme that carried Mesrine's signature. His stay in the correctional unit at Laval had fired his resentment at purpose-built, high-security blocks. He was determined to return to Laval and spring the remaining inmates from the correctional unit.

However, as Mesrine, Mercier and Mercier's girlfriend, Suzanne Francoeur, approached the jail, they saw that extra guards had been stationed both inside and outside the walls. Despite this, Mesrine opened fire on a nearby police car. Shots were returned and the two criminals fled ignominiously. This pointless act of bravado offered a tragic foretaste of the deadly crime to come.

On 3 September 1972, the three spent a pleasant afternoon in the large wooded area to the north of the city. They managed to find a remote spot, where they expected to be undisturbed, and passed the time in shooting practice, using paper targets pinned to the trees.

Late in the afternoon, on their way home, they were stopped for a routine check by two forest rangers, Mederic Côté and Ernest Saint-Pierre. Opening the boot of the car, the rangers were astonished to find an assortment of at least 12 loaded guns and asked the strangers to accompany them to the warden's office. Mesrine and Mercier refused.

Double murder

It was at this moment that the two rangers realized they had chanced upon serious villains. An instant later they had been gunned down. As they lay on the ground, Mesrine shot both victims in the head, to ensure that they were dead. The killers then stole the pistols from the rangers' holsters and a rifle from their pick-up truck. They covered the two bodies with leaves and left them on a nearby dirt track, where they were discovered two days later. They had been middle-aged men, used to dealing only with the occasional poacher.

Mesrine, Mercier and Suzanne drove back to Montreal but, despite the public outrage about the deaths of the forest rangers, did not leave the city immediately. Mesrine smuggled a message to Jeanne Schneider, offering to help her escape. But Jeanne had heard that police were circulating the names of Mesrine and Mercier as suspects in the forest killings, and chose to serve out her sentence.

A journey south

The two men did not lie in hiding for long. A few days after the shootings, they robbed a bank opposite their apartment.

Three days later, they robbed it again. This was exhibitionism by Mesrine, who had seen a cashier looking disgusted as they left the building after the first raid. On the second, it was she who was ordered to empty the tills. Mesrine warned her not to scowl as they left the bank or they would rob it a third time. He had felt slighted at being held in disdain by a minor employee of a bank over which he was demonstrating his superiority.

Finally, Mesrine and Mercier decided to drive south into the United States and, from there, to travel to South America.

They did not travel alone. Mercier was accompanied by Suzanne and Mesrine by his new 19 year-old mistress, Jocelyne Deraiche. She had met Jacques while he was masquerading under the alias of Bruno Dansereau, and soon she fell under the spell of his charm.

The foursome crossed the border and headed for New York. They remained there briefly while Mesrine made arrangements for them to settle in Venezuela. The Organisation de L'Armée Secrète (OAS) network helped him to procure the false papers he needed to establish a new identity.

New frontiers

In Venezuela, the group moved into a luxurious villa near Caracas. Mesrine and Mercier intended to 'commute' periodically into the United States to continue their bank raids. However, Suzanne required an operation and Mercier accompanied her back to Canada. Then, soon after, Mesrine learned that Interpol were on his trail and that he might not be safe in Venezuela. He was running out of places to hide, and so decided on a typically bold course of action. At some time in December 1972, Mesrine and Jocelyne flew to Spain, hired a car and quietly drove across the border into France.

CHASED IN PARIS

Mesrine's stealthy return to Paris, after nearly five years on the American continent, was like a homecoming. Undaunted at being an international

Killer: Jacques Mesrine

fugitive, he delighted in showing Jocelyne the sights, buying her new clothes and dining with her in the finest Parisian restaurants.

At the same time, he was keen to re-establish his old lifestyle as soon as possible. This meant finding new hideouts and stocking them with furniture, clothes and an array of guns. Whenever possible, Mesrine preferred to keep several bases, in case one hideout had to be abandoned at very short notice. This was expensive and Mesrine soon resumed a routine of armed robberies and hold-ups.

But things had changed during his absence. Mesrine was now a much bigger fish. Interpol was on his trail and his prolific activity – Mesrine committed more than a dozen crimes in the first two months of 1973 – meant that capture was inevitable.

On 5 March, Mesrine entered the 'Dixie' bar, near the Place de la Madeleine. During the course of a quarrel, Mesrine smashed bottles behind the bar and menaced customers with a Colt .45 pistol. A policeman tried to intervene and Mesrine fired, wounding the officer, whose two shots in return hit a door-frame.

Mesrine made good his escape by hijacking a taxi. But the police had already located his hideout by tailing a known accomplice from one of his bank jobs. Mesrine was staying at a flat that he had rented from a judge – the sort of comic gesture which he appreciated – and detectives kept careful watch on this for several days. On 8 March, they surprised Mesrine in the hallway as he returned from the shops. The operation was bloodless and efficient.

Mesrine's arrest was followed by a flowering in his public reputation. At his flat at 1, Rue Pierre Grenier, the police had uncovered a treasure trove of cash, travellers' cheques, false passports and firearms. Their astonishment mounted when, during his interrogation, Mesrine claimed to have committed 39 murders.

As soon as they started to investigate these 'killings', the police became sceptical. However, news of this boast filtered through to the press and, immediately, the name Mesrine was in the headlines. A myth was born. Mesrine wasted no time in consolidating the legend. As he was led off to La Santé prison to await trial, he turned to a policeman and asked: 'What do you bet me that I'll be free within 3 months?'

Mesrine had already completed checks on the courthouse in Compiègne, where he knew he would appear if ever arrested. On 6 June 1973, he was taken there to face a minor charge of passing dud cheques six years before. An accomplice had smuggled a Luger pistol into the lawyers' toilet. Mesrine retrieved it and took the magistrate hostage. The unfortunate man was dragged out into the courtyard, where a friend of Mesrine was waiting in an Alfa Romeo. Releasing his hostage, Mesrine sprinted to the car amid a hail of bullets. He was wounded in the arm, but his driver had been well briefed and got them to the isolated farmhouse chosen as their refuge.

Within a fortnight, Jocelyne had joined Mesrine and they moved into a flat in the seaside resort of Trouville. In a typical show of bravado, Mesrine selected an apartment that was only yards away from police headquarters and then rapidly befriended one of the local officers. His elaborate disguise made him virtually unrecognizable in short hair, a thick beard and the kind of casual clothes that ran counter to the debonair image presented of him in the press.

Mesrine enjoyed the summer, visiting the nearby racecourse and casinos, until Jocelyne flew back to Canada in September. Mesrine had by this time been returning to Paris to commit further robberies. He had developed the tactic of executing these in tandem, moving on directly from his initial hold-up to carry out a second.

On 27 September 1973, during one of these double robberies, the registration number of the getaway car was spotted as Mesrine and his accomplices were leaving a bank and the police located it while the second robbery was in progress. Mesrine escaped, but one of his men was wounded and the inexperienced driver, Pierre Verheyden, was arrested. He soon gave detectives a number of important clues.

Verheyden's information led police to Mesrine's hideout in the Rue Vergniaud. The specialist 'anti-gangs' unit, with its team of sharpshooters, was called out and the apartment was sealed off. The officer in charge, Commissaire Robert Broussard, ordered his men to move in. He called out to Mesrine to give himself up. Realizing that he was surrounded, Mesrine agreed after stalling for just long enough to burn some of the more incriminating evidence within his flat. Inside, he had laid out his armoury of guns and ammunition like a soldier's kit awaiting the inspection of a commanding officer.

The theatrical surrender was clearly designed to attract attention. Soon, stories about Mesrine monopolized the headlines. Many were highly fanciful and Mesrine tried to bring lawsuits against four papers for defamation of character. But it was to be three-and-a-half years before he stood inside a courtroom again.

Rich imagination

During the long wait, Mesrine wrote an autobiography in which he portrayed himself as a brutal, vengeful killer. Its contents were recognized as pure invention and the book was seen as a glorified press release.

Mesrine made other attempts to maintain public interest. In November 1975, he smuggled out a letter containing a death threat against a journalist named Jacques Derogy, who had written an article critical of the prisoner. At the same time, Mesrine developed his case for prison reform. He saw no contradiction in being both homicidal and philanthropic.

Overall, time weighed heavily on Mesrine. When, on 3 May 1977, his trial finally opened, he felt like a great actor making a triumphant comeback to the stage after a long absence. He played his part well, and the press and the public hung on his every word.

Applause in court

Newspaper correspondents noted how he had the cheerful, confident air of a military commander. Mesrine winked at journalists and flirted with a female lawyer. When the list of his false passports and identity papers was read out in court, Mesrine turned to Judge Charles Petit and told him that by the following morning he could have one made out in his name. His moment of triumph came when he removed, from the knot of his tie, a tiny plaster impression of the keys to his handcuffs, which he had bought from a guard. Joyfully, Mesrine threw the plaster cast into the crowd and the gallery erupted. The judge was less amused. Mesrine was sentenced to 20 years' imprisonment. But he was not too disheartened. He had decided not to serve the full term.

CLOSING IN

La Santé, the prison in Paris where Mesrine was confined, had the reputation of being escape-proof. No one had ever broken out of it. A new top-security wing had been built and this became Mesrine's home.

On the morning of 8 May 1978, Mesrine was led into an interview room in his wing for a routine meeting with Christiane Giletti, one of his lawyers. The guard was sent away to fetch some papers. In his absence, Mesrine leapt up on a chair and removed the cover from a ventilation duct. Concealed there were pistols, tear gas pellets, a knife and a length of blue mountaineering rope.

Outside, an accomplice, François Besse, had overpowered a guard and, with a third prisoner, burst into the nearby staff office. The warders there were relieved of their guns, papers and keys, and the three convicts swiftly changed into the navy blue uniforms of the prison guards.

In the courtyard, the bogus warders instructed some workmen to move their ladders to the outer wall of the prison. Ten days before the escape, Mesrine had spotted these builders fitting new grilles on to cell windows and had altered his plans to make use of their presence.

It was only when they saw 'warders' climbing up the outer wall with mountaineering gear that the perimeter guards realised something was amiss. Shots rang out. The third prisoner was killed, but Mesrine and Besse got clear. Still wearing their official uniforms, they flagged down the driver of a white Renault, forced him out, and drove off to a flat near Les Invalides.

Back at La Santé, the air duct in the interview room was found to contain another gun, a hand grenade and a dagger. Mesrine's grappling iron was hidden behind bookshelves in an adjoining room. Clearly, there had been considerable assistance from outside.

The press had a field day, but the police hierarchy was deeply worried and even President Giscard d'Estaing made known his displeasure. An intensive manhunt was launched.

At 11 p.m. on 27 May 1978, Mesrine and Besse strode confidently into the police headquarters at the Normandy resort of Deauville and, introducing themselves as policemen, asked to see the Duty Inspector. On being told that he was out, the pair left quietly, promising to call again. Mesrine judged that there would be few officers around at that time and that he and Besse would be able to seize some uniforms and guns.

From the police station, the two men walked directly to the casino. There, they used Ministry of Justice identity cards, which they had stolen during their escape from La Santé, to gain access to the Cashier's Office, where they demanded money at gunpoint. But someone sounded an alarm and, when Mesrine and Besse emerged from the casino, the police were waiting. The robbers tried to shoot their way out. Both men were wounded, Besse seriously. Two bystanders were also hit. Somehow, the gunmen managed to get away.

On the run

During a desperate chase through the Normandy countryside, their first getaway car broke down. They stole another. More shots were exchanged as they drove through a police roadblock. The second car, damaged by gunfire, veered off into a ditch. Mesrine and Besse staggered across the fields and sheltered under trees while police helicopters circled overhead. They took hostages at an isolated farmhouse, forcing their captives to drive them towards Paris. Finally, they completed their journey in a rowing boat and in yet another stolen car.

Mesrine was undeterred by the narrow escape and began planning his next crime. To attack a casino, he argued, was to attack the empire of vice. The only way to win against its bank was to use a gun. Similarly, Mesrine explained away his next big raid, on the Le Raincy branch of the Société Générale, as revenge. The Société Générale had been awarded substantial damages out of the earnings Mesrine had made from his book. At that time, Mesrine wrote angrily to its Director, accusing him of stealing his money and warning him to consider it only as a temporary loan.

Mesrine carried out the robbery while Besse held hostage the wife of a senior bank employee. Mesrine was tempted into trying his hand at kidnapping once more.

His victim was Judge Charles Petit, the man who had sentenced him to 20 years in jail. Mesrine planned to use the abduction of a prominent legal figure as a platform for airing his views on prison reform and the maximum security wings.

Besse wanted nothing to do with the scheme and Mesrine had to enlist the help of two raw recruits. Their inexperience proved crucial when the attack took place on 10 November 1978. One of the judge's relations was able to alert the police and Mesrine was fortunate to escape unscathed. His next kidnapping venture was more carefully planned. Mesrine needed money and so the victim was a rich industrialist, Henri Lelièvre.

Once again, on 21 June 1979, Mesrine and his henchman posed as policemen, requesting their aged target to accompany them to the local station to help with some routine enquiries. Instead, they drove him to a rented house near Blois. Negotiations over the ransom were complex and lasted over a month. The police efficiently foiled the first delivery of the ransom, almost capturing Mesrine's accomplice in the process. After renewed threats, however, Lelièvre's son Michael made a clandestine payment, with the result that the elderly gentleman was released. Only then did the police find out that Mesrine had been behind the plot.

Time running out

The ransom of six million francs gave him precious breathing space. During the summer of 1979, he travelled to Italy and, perhaps, further afield to Algeria. Newspaper reports claimed that he also went to Spain or England. However, Mesrine knew his freedom was only a brief interlude. The banknotes from the Lelièvre kidnapping had been marked and, once laundered, would only be worth a percentage of their face value. Returning to Paris in the autumn of 1979, Mesrine faced having to resume his fraught and increasingly dangerous career as a bankrobber.

The pressure of living on the run was unremitting and Mesrine's mood was darkened by the knowledge that there could only be one way out. He would never go to jail again.

LAST JOURNEY

At the beginning of August 1979, the French authorities took a decisive initiative. A special anti-Mesrine squad was formed under the leadership of one of the most senior police officers in France, Commissaire Maurice Bouvier. He was to co-ordinate the efforts of the three serious crimes units, and thus try to eliminate all the rivalries that usually existed between these separate departments.

The three squads were the OCRB (Office Centrale de Repression de Banditisme) headed by Lucien Aimé-Blanc, the BRI (Brigade de Recherche et d'Intervention – the so-called 'anti-gangs') under Commissaire

Broussard, and the BRB (Brigade de Repression de Banditisme), led by Serge Devos.

Within a month, the new unit had its first solid lead. On 10 September, a journalist named Jacques Tillier was found shot and wounded after a meeting with Mesrine in a cave, in the forest of Verneuil-en-Halatte. The latter even sent photographs of his victim to a Paris newspaper, explaining that he had punished the man for betraying him. This was a curious incident, as Mesrine was always keen to keep good relations with the press, and it seems likely that he believed Tillier to be a police informant.

In fact, Tillier did have police connections. In the past, he had been an inspector in the DST (Défense et Securité du Territoire), but his meeting with Mesrine had been arranged purely to write a story for his paper. Detectives were less than pleased to find that, not for the first time, a reporter had withheld vital information from them.

As Tillier was questioned thoroughly by the police, one important clue emerged. Mesrine had an accomplice. From Tillier's memory, it was clear that this man had also been an inmate in one of the high-security blocks and this, combined with his physical description, eventually led them to the name of Charly Bauer.

It took detectives a further month to track Bauer down. Finally, on 24 October, they found his car parked in the St Lazare district of northern Paris. Bauer's girlfriend eventually collected the car and, from that moment, their flat in the Rue St Lazare was under constant surveillance.

Exactly one week later, Bauer led them to Rue Belliard, an address in the Montmartre area. The surveillance team watched intently as, moments later, Mesrine came out from the flats with his current mistress, Sylvie Jeanjacquot. Mesrine was disguised as an elderly man, walking with the aid of a stick, but the police were convinced that they had found their quarry.

Eagerly they followed as Jacques and his friends went for a stroll up to the market in the Boulevard Ornano. There, they gazed at the window displays, paused to make some purchases at a furniture store and tried on some shoes in another shop, before returning to their base in the Rue Belliard.

The police were uncertain over how to approach Mesrine. They knew he would be armed. During his latest clandestine interview with the magazine *Paris Match*, he had deliberately allowed himself to be photographed with two revolvers stuffed into his belt. It was also known that he made a habit of carrying hand grenades.

Final vow

Moreover, Mesrine had repeatedly stressed his resolve never to be recaptured. 'The police must know that I'll never give in,' he had said in the interview. 'I won't go back to prison. I will shoot and it's too bad if innocent people get in the way. I won't shoot first, but I won't be the only corpse on the pavement.'

Much time and money had been invested in tracking Mesrine down. Many reputations were at stake. Now that he was cornered, it was imperative that no mistakes were made.

Accordingly, the building was staked out and a long wait began. Residents from the other flats were discreetly evacuated. Plain-clothes policemen and women masqueraded as road sweepers, gasmen, delivery boys, housewives and prostitutes. Everyone's nerves were on edge. A whole day passed and nobody came out. The police debated whether or not to storm the place.

Mesrine and Sylvie emerged just before 3 p.m. on Friday, 2 November. He was wearing a leather jacket and carrying a suitcase. She was clutching her white miniature poodle. They were going away for the weekend.

They climbed into a brown BMW saloon and set off. Soon, they turned into the Place de Clignancourt, near the Flea Market. A blue lorry, with a tarpaulin covering its load, signalled and cut across to turn right. Another lorry hemmed in the BMW from behind.

Suddenly, the tarpaulin on the blue lorry was thrown back, revealing a group of police marksmen. Without warning, they opened fire and a salvo of high-velocity bullets tore through the windscreen. Mesrine was killed instantly. His body slumped forward over the steering wheel. One hand dangled down, towards the black bag at his feet, which contained his hand grenades. A car pulled up alongside the BMW. A man leaned out and fired one single shot into Mesrine's head.

Sylvie Jeanjacquot was severely wounded. She stumbled out of the passenger seat and took a few uncertain steps before collapsing on the cobblestones. An ambulance took her to the nearby Boucicaut hospital, where her life was soon out of danger.

Into the streets

The small army of policemen and women involved in the operation surged forward from the surrounding streets. Swiftly, they cordoned off the area to hold back the gathering crowds. Their mood was one of jubilation, mingled with relief. Some officers embraced each other.

Mesrine's body remained in the car, sagging over his seat-belt for more than an hour. Nobody seemed to want to touch it. It was as if no one could believe that the hunt was finally over.

A crowd of 400 spectators built up around the barriers, jostling for a view. Mesrine's 18 year-old daughter Sabrina arrived and was led away in tears by a policeman. Finally, at 4.20 p.m., the police removed Mesrine's body. Broussard, his old adversary, helped to lift him from the car. A message was sent to the Paris Prefecture's headquarters: 'Mesrine has been killed. No casualties on our side.'

Detectives made a careful search of the flat at 35/7 Rue Belliard and found that Mesrine had equipped it to withstand a siege. In addition to the expected arsenal of guns, they also found eight gold bars and 200,000 francs in cash. Every radio and television station in the country had by this time interrupted its programmes to broadcast the sensational news of Mesrine's death.

In the evening, Maurice Bouvier chaired a press conference at the Place Beauvau. Already, there was some public criticism over the way the police had handled the affair, with no apparent attempt being made to avoid the bloodshed. Bouvier calmly explained that Mesrine was known to be carrying hand grenades.

Last words

Three days later, the news was released that a tape, recorded by Mesrine shortly before his death, had been discovered in his flat. It contained a farewell message for Sylvie. 'I know I am going to die and the cops will get me in the end. But I've led the life I wanted. I regret nothing and I shall sell my hide dearly.'

CASE FILE: MESRINE, JACQUES

BACKGROUND

Jacques Mesrine was born into a comfortable, middle-class family on 28 December 1936. His father, Pierre, ran his own business designing textiles while his mother, Monique, provided a warm home life for Jacques and his elder sister in their apartment in Clichy, on the northern outskirts of Paris.

In June 1940, at the outset of World War II, Pierre Mesrine entered the French army as Monique and the children joined the throng of refugees fleeing from Paris. They travelled south to Chateau-Merle, a village near Poitiers, where they stayed with relatives. Soon, Paris fell to the German army and Mesrine's father was held in a prison camp.

The boy Mesrine spent three rather solitary years in Chateau-Merle. After some time his mother had returned to occupied Paris to look for work and her son, though liked for his charm, often chose to play or wander by himself rather than join other boys. 'I have a nicer time on my own,' he told a concerned adult.

Inner conflict

The only men in their prime around the village tended to be full-chested German soldiers and the stealthy, conspiratorial members of the French Resistance who crept around the houses at night. These two extremes pre-figured Mesrine's own adult life – the strutting, show-off villain and the shadowy outlaw on the run.

The Mesrine family was reunited after the war in 1945 and settled once again in Paris. After being left much to his own devices in the countryside, the eight year-old Jacques found the discipline of school life constrictive. But he performed well enough and, at the age of 12, was sent to a boarding school in Juilly, some 50 kilometres (30 miles) away. Here, tempted by the freedom, he became a troublemaker and in the summer of 1951, he was expelled.

By this time, the family had bought an old farmhouse in Normandy for weekend retreats. Jacques borrowed a rifle from a neighbour and learnt to shoot, though he later declared that he shot mainly at trees or milk bottles. The youth loved animals and spent long, solitary hours studying the wildlife.

Fighting drudgery

These ruminative periods were in direct contrast to his life in the bustling city of Paris where he had signalled a need to be famous without a willingness to work patiently for success.

Reading the warning signs, Pierre Mesrine sent his son to a local school, Lycée Chaptal, but Jacques soon slipped into truancy, leaving his school books with a friendly café owner before going off to a cinema or to meet a girlfriend. When he did attend school, Mesrine often spoiled for a fight, apparently needing to test his strength or his sharp-wittedness in debate rather than to inflict pain.

The inevitable expulsion from Lycée Chaptal was followed by an abortive attempt to complete an electronics course at a technical college.

Menial jobs

Without any qualifications, Mesrine had no choice but to take menial jobs, which he hated. But during this period he met and married a beautiful girl called Lydia from Martinique in the West Indies. She was already pregnant, but Mesrine seemed unconcerned at becoming the father of another man's child. They moved into a tiny flat where Mesrine, already a gourmet, enjoyed having his own kitchen. He also enjoyed the company of Lydia's easy-going family, who did not make demands on him. But he was annoyed that Lydia gave up her university course in chemistry, because he had hoped to depend on her earnings.

Troubles at home

Lydia, in turn, resented Mesrine's growing disinclination to take on a proper job. The rows soon started and, when Lydia's child was born, Mesrine found that he resented having to provide for him. Soon the novelty of the new family started to wear off and Mesrine began to neglect his wife.

It was a relief to the young man, still only 19, when his army call-up papers arrived in the autumn of 1956. Very soon, he volunteered for active service in Algeria, the French colony where the army was fighting to quell a nationalist uprising.

PSYCHOLOGICAL FILE

After Mesrine's death, one newspaper described him as an unsavoury star who became the victim of his own inflated reputation. Certainly Mesrine had no desire to share the anonymity of most crooks, hiding away in some back-street dive to avoid being caught. He actively sought the limelight and, with his passionate interest in reading and collecting press-cuttings about himself, Mesrine was reminiscent of a temperamental actor fretting about his latest review.

Much of his criminal activity was motivated by a desire for attention. This may have been a legacy of the loneliness he felt when separated from his father during the war and, later, his boarding school years, or it may have been an attempt to recapture the praise he had won for his successful exploits in Algeria.

Party lover

Mesrine was naturally gregarious. All his favourite activities involved company – party-going, nightclubs, eating at fine restaurants, attending race meetings, gambling in casinos. They also required style. Mesrine was particular about the cut of his suit, the appearance of his women and the quality of his food and wine.

For his own security, he could not afford to trust or confide in many people. Yet he still possessed great personal warmth and magnetism. His prison guards and even the victims of his non-violent crimes remarked on his charm. From his friends, he commanded respect and unswerving loyalty.

Jacques' early grudge against figures of authority and his decision to concentrate his attacks on big institutions like the banks won him the unspoken admiration of many law-abiding citizens. Then, as his dramatic escapes made him more newsworthy, Mesrine's attempts to manipulate his own public image increased. There were theatrical gestures, such as offering champagne to the police. There were also defiant touches – introducing himself to his victims, lingering too long at the scene of a crime, walking into police stations – which courted disaster as well as column inches in the press.

Violent folly

Whatever his fantasies or secret following in France, the murder which Mesrine is known to have committed was characterized only by its meanness and stupidity. The middle-aged forest ranger, Mederic Côté, was armed but could never have out-drawn Mesrine, and could easily have been disarmed and tied up with his partner while the attackers made their escape.

It is possible that Mesrine felt resentful and belittled by the fact that two mere forest rangers – not police officers, and not even French forest rangers – tried to detain him. He saw himself as writ large, and arrest by a forest ranger old enough to be his father would have destroyed his image of himself.

Deep loathing

The two shots he fired into the forest rangers' heads before concealing their bodies indicates some deep well of loathing inside Mesrine. He was to claim that he wanted to ensure that the men were dead. As a criminal, Mesrine was bold but, as a man, he lacked the bravery to confront his own fears and depressions.

Significantly, Mesrine felt no remorse for either forest ranger, only for the 12 year-old son of one of them, Ernest Saint-Pierre, crying by his father's grave. The photograph so disturbed Mesrine that he asked aloud if the boy knew his father had been allowed to kill in the name of the law. Only by thinking of the ranger as an agent of society could Mesrine deal with his distaste for himself.

This distaste may have motivated some of his later, grand fantasies in which Mesrine saw himself as a campaigner for prison reform, a Robin Hood figure and a doomed romantic hero, preferring death to mediocrity. No one knows if he ever looked within and saw the shallow cruelty of his true nature.

Chapter 13

DR BUCK RUXTON
THE SAVAGE SURGEON

In 1935, Buck Ruxton, an Indian doctor living in England, murdered his wife and his children's nursemaid. The police knew he was guilty; their problem was to prove that the skilfully dismembered remains they found were those of the two women. The result was one of the most sensational murder trials of the century.

On 19 September 1935, Miss Susan Johnson was enjoying a quiet Sunday afternoon stroll near Moffat, a popular resort town in Dumfriesshire. As she walked across a bridge over a stream, she paused to look at the waters below. Her attention was attracted by an oddly-shaped object protruding from some sort of wrapping and caught up in undergrowth. She looked more closely and recoiled in horror when she realised it was a human arm. Hurrying straight back to the hotel where she was staying, she told her brother of her discovery. He returned to the stream and uncovered other parts of the human body wrapped in newspapers and pieces of a sheet.

The police were informed and the stream and its ravine were searched later during that afternoon by Sergeant Sloan from the local Dumfriesshire Constabulary. He discovered a further four bundles of human remains. Some were wrapped in clothing (including a blouse and a pair of child's rompers) and some in a pillowcase and another piece of the sheet.

An intensive search was then organized, and within a few days several other pieces of human flesh had been found in the stream – called the Linn – and the Annan, the river into which it flows. On 28 October a left foot was found at Johnstonebridge, some nine miles south of Moffat on the Edinburgh–Carlisle road. The final gruesome discovery – on 4 November – was that of a right forearm and hand found on the Edinburgh road south of the bridge over the Linn.

Together the discoveries comprised two heads, two upper bodies and shoulder blades, 17 limb portions and 43 pieces of soft tissue. All the remains were badly decomposed and infested with maggots. They were first examined at Moffat and then removed to the Anatomy Department of Edinburgh University. It was here that was undertaken much of the brilliant forensic work for which the case became famous.

At the beginning of their inquiries, the police were led to believe that one of the bodies was a man's. Stories to that effect appeared in the press before the forensic scientists realised that they were dealing with the quite skilfully dismembered remains of two women. Some of the remains had been found along the Linn and the Annan well above the level of the water and this suggested they had been washed downstream and on to the banks by heavy storms throughout 18 and 19 September. The Dumfriesshire police together with detectives from Glasgow CID and other forces therefore confined their inquiries to people who had gone missing before that date, but they drew a blank.

Given the proximity of the Linn to such a major road, the police turned their attention to any irregular journeys made by owners of cars registered in Dumfriesshire. However they were no more successful with this line of inquiry.

It was when the police looked more closely at the pieces of newspaper found with parts of the remains that they first made headway. Among them was part of the *Sunday Graphic* dated 15 September 1935, later identified as one of a special local edition issued only in the Lancaster and Morecambe districts. When no one in Morecambe appeared to have been reported missing, the Chief Constable of Dumfriesshire turned his attention to Lancaster, its 40,000 population swollen by numerous holiday-makers. On 9 October he contacted the Lancaster Borough Police.

The parents of one Mary Jane Rogerson had meanwhile become increasingly concerned for the safety of their daughter, who had disappeared on or around 15 September. Mary, who had never gone missing in this fashion before, worked as a nursemaid to the children of a Parsee doctor called Buck Ruxton, who lived in Lancaster. Despite Ruxton's various efforts to placate them, the Rogersons went to the police asking that her description be circulated.

One of the newspapers to pick up the story was Scotland's *Daily Record*. From its pages Detective-Lieutenant Ewing from Glasgow CID learned that the doctor's wife was also missing. He noticed the similarities between the approximate description of one of the bodies given by Professor Glaister and that provided by Mary Rogerson's worried father and stepmother.

Identifying the clothes

Now aware that both women had lived in the house of a doctor – which might have accounted for the way in which the bodies had been cut up – the police showed both the blouse and rompers to Mrs Rogerson. She was immediately able to identify the blouse by a patch she had sewn on it before giving it to Mary.

It was also through Mrs Rogerson that the police identified the rompers. She mentioned that her step-daughter and the Ruxton children had on occasions been given clothes by a Mrs Holme, who let rooms to visitors at Grange-over-Sands. Among her visitors had been the Ruxtons, who had stayed there in June 1935. Mrs Holme had no trouble identifying the rompers, having tied a distinctive knot in their elastic before giving them to Mary Rogerson for the children.

It was at this point that the Dumfriesshire police handed the investigation to the Lancaster Borough Police under Captain Vann, the Chief Constable of Lancaster. His overriding concern now was to look more closely into the life of one of the town's citizens – Dr Buck Ruxton.

TRAIL OF BLOOD

By the time the Lancaster police had decided to interview Ruxton, the doctor had perversely already contacted them, asking that discreet enquiries be made to find his missing wife. This and later attempts to react naturally to her disappearance, to the press speculation that surrounded it and to the ghastly findings at Moffat proved neither convincing nor consistent. Not only had he given conflicting details of the circumstances of her disappearance and her likely whereabouts, but his behaviour since the weekend of 14/15 September had been highly unusual, even for the impulsive, emotionally-charged man he was known to be.

Isabella was last seen alive on Saturday, 14 September, when she had gone to Blackpool in Ruxton's car to see the illuminations and visit her sisters, Mrs Nelson and Mrs Madden. She left to return to Lancaster at 11.30 p.m. The car was found at Lancaster the following morning, but of Isabella there was no sign.

Under normal circumstances, Mrs Elizabeth Curwen, a charwoman, would have called at the Ruxton house, 2 Dalton Square, that following Sunday morning to begin work at ten o'clock. However she had been told by Ruxton the previous Friday not to come to the house until the Monday morning. Mrs Agnes Oxley, another charwoman, was also expected, but stayed at home after her husband received an early morning visit from Ruxton. He told her that Isabella had gone on holiday to Edinburgh with Mary and that she would not be required until the following day.

Among the deliveries to be made at Dalton Square that morning – in addition to Ruxton's copy of the *Sunday Graphic* – were four pints of milk brought by another helper, Mrs Hindson. She normally carried them through to the scullery, but on this occasion Ruxton asked her to put them down on a table just inside the door. He told her that Isabella and Mary had gone away with the children. His hand was bandaged and he said he had jammed it in a door.

At about 10.30 that morning, Ruxton left in his Hillman car to buy two cans of petrol, later calling at a second garage to have four gallons put in the tank. Shortly before midday, he drove his three children to Mrs Anderson's, the wife of a Morecambe dentist he and Isabella knew well. He asked her to look after them for the day, and described how he had cut his hand on a tin of fruit while preparing their breakfast.

Just before 4.30 p.m. Ruxton called on a Mrs Hampshire, a patient who was prepared to do some housework and was later one of the prosecution's most important witnesses at his trial. The account he gave her of Isabella and Mary's absence differed again from previous versions. Mary he said had gone away for a holiday, while Isabella was in Blackpool. He explained that he needed her help about the house because he had cut his hand badly and was trying to prepare for the arrival of decorators the following morning in accordance with arrangements he claimed had been made some months previously.

When she arrived at the doctor's house, Mrs Hampshire found that the carpet had been removed from the stairs, which were very dirty. Straw littered some parts of the floor, and protruded from under the locked bedroom doors of Dr Ruxton and Isabella. In the doctor's waiting-room, she found rolled-up carpets, stair-pads and a badly stained suit. In the yard at the back of the house she came across two carpets from the landing and stairs, and some partly-burned towels.

Cleaning up as best she could while Ruxton made arrangements for the children to spend the night with the Andersons, Mrs Hampshire asked for her husband to be called to help. On Mr Hampshire's arrival, Ruxton told him that he and his wife could take away the stair carpets and suit.

The following morning, however, Ruxton called on the Hampshires, asking for the suit to be returned to him so that it might be cleaned. Inspecting the suit, he came across the name-tag and told Mrs Hampshire to cut it off and burn it. When the doctor had gone, Mrs Hampshire looked more closely at the carpets he had given her and found that they – like the suit – were stained, and that the stains looked suspiciously like blood. Twenty to thirty buckets of water later, the colour that ran off them was still that of blood.

Fictitious journeys

Returning to Dalton Square, Ruxton suggested to Mrs Oxley that Isabella and Mary had simply made up the story of their trip to Edinburgh. Mrs Hampshire was told later that same day that Isabella had, in fact, gone to London. Pressed by Mrs Hampshire on the subject, Ruxton claimed Isabella had gone off with another man, whereupon he broke down and started weeping.

Killer: Dr Buck Ruxton

During this period, Ruxton made several often clumsy attempts to cover his tracks, only to draw more attention to himself in doing so. On Tuesday, 17 September, for example, he called on Arthur Holmes, a decorator, asking his daughter why her father had not been to Dalton Square when all that had been agreed was that Holmes should call some time in September. Later the same day, Ruxton was involved in a road accident at Kendal, knocking a cyclist off his bicycle. His explanation for what he had done and how he came to be there was contrived and convoluted.

The various women who helped Ruxton in his domestic tasks could hardly avoid noticing that something peculiar was going on. Mrs Curwen found a heavily stained blanket being soaked in a bowl of water in a recess in the backyard. She and Mrs Oxley were offered what remained of the carpets as a gift.

When Mrs Smith arrived to continue stripping paper from the wall near the stairs, she noticed that the curtains of the window below the top landing had traces of blood on them. Ruxton's response when she took the curtains down was to tear off and burn the bloodstained portion, remarking that the police would soon be accusing him of murdering Mrs Smalley, a woman who in a totally separate incident had recently been found dead in Morecambe.

On Thursday, 19 September, Dr Ruxton parked his car close to the back door of the house, closed the kitchen door on Mrs Oxley preparing his breakfast and made several trips between the car and the upstairs rooms. After Ruxton had left, Mrs Oxley noticed that some of the upstairs rooms previously locked were now open and that an unpleasant smell came from the doctor's room.

Since the Tuesday of that week, Ruxton had instructed Mrs Smith and Mrs Curwen to keep fires alight in the backyard on which he had burned papers. On Thursday afternoon, while sweeping out the yard, Mrs Curwen noticed pieces of burned blue and red material, and a bloodstained swab of cotton wool. The material she found resembled a coat and an old-fashioned dressing gown that Mary used to wear.

On Friday, 20 September, Ruxton told Mrs Curwen to buy eau-de-Cologne to rid the house of its nasty smell. Later that evening, Ruxton arranged for the children to be taken out by Miss Bessie Philbrook, one of his patients who had known Isabella socially. While driving her over to Dalton Square, Ruxton asked if she had known that Mary was pregnant, the first of several attempts to stop enquiries being made concerning the maid's whereabouts by suggesting that Isabella had taken her away to have an abortion. Ruxton tried to convince Mary's parents of this story when he called the following Wednesday, claiming that Mary had been seeing a laundry boy, an explanation that totally failed to assuage their growing fears.

On Tuesday, 1 October – two days after the remains were found at Moffat – the Rogersons called on Ruxton. He told them that Isabella and

Mary had broken into his safe, taken £30 and would almost certainly return once they had spent it. Again they were not to be placated and told Ruxton they would inform the police of Mary's disappearance. Also unimpressed by Ruxton's explanations was Isabella's sister in Edinburgh, Mrs Nelson, with whom the doctor had been communicating by letter. Aware of the discoveries at Moffat and of Mary's disappearance, she asked him whether he had done anything to harm her, a suggestion the doctor denied furiously and at great length.

On 10 October Ruxton told Mrs Hampshire to burn the suit he had given her, together with the most badly stained of the carpets. The next day, becoming increasingly desperate, he made several visits to the police station in Lancaster to complain about what he claimed were the unwarranted press reports linking him with the Moffat discoveries.

Ruxton spent what he must have realized was to be his last day of freedom trying to distort certain individuals' recollections of events that had occurred about 15 September in order to support his own version of events. He first asked the Anderson's maid whether she could say he had called every day since his wife had gone away, a request with which she first felt able to comply but later rejected.

The charwoman, Mrs Oxley, was asked to amend certain details about arrival at work on the morning on 16 September, but refused. Ernest Hall, a patient and odd-job man, was asked to say that when he called at Dalton Square to repair a fuse on the night of Saturday, 14 September, the door had been opened by Mary Rogerson. Despite Dr Ruxton's encouragement, Hall pointed out that he had been ill in bed on that day.

At 9.30 p.m. on Saturday, 12 October, Ruxton went to the police station for the last time. Asked to account for his movements between 14 and 30 September, Ruxton produced an extraordinary document entitled 'My Movements', on which he had clearly been working for some time, and made a voluntary statement based on what he had written. After further questioning, and consultation with senior officers from the Scottish police, Dr Buck Ruxton was charged with the murder of Mary Rogerson at 7.20 on the following morning. 'Most emphatically not' was his reply 'Of course not. The furthest thing from my mind. What motive and why? What are you talking about?'

Remanded in custody after appearing in the Borough of Lancaster Police Court, he was further charged with Isabella Ruxton's murder on 5 November. He was committed for trial on both charges, but when additional evidence came to light, was eventually tried only for the murder of his wife. The police had little doubt that they had caught their man, but the burden of proving Ruxton's guilt fell more heavily than ever before on the practitioners of forensic medicine.

FORENSIC TRIUMPH

The first task of the expert medical team called on to assist the police in their inquiries had been to reconstitute the bodies from the varied remains found at Moffat. At first it was not certain how many bodies they came from and what sex they were. Despite the decomposition, it quickly became apparent how thorough the murderer had been in removing their identifying marks: facial features and virtually all the fingertips had been removed.

Markedly different in their size and form, the two heads were first designated Head Number One (later shown to be Mary Rogerson's) and Head Number Two (later revealed as Isabella Ruxton's). They formed the basis for the assignment of other parts in the reconstruction of the bodies. Professor John Brash of the Anatomy Department of Edinburgh University was able with increasing confidence to apportion parts to one or other of what it became clear were two bodies.

The pelvic trunk portion of Body Number Two, for example, could be seen to be part of the same body as the upper portion, since the latter had two lumbar vertebrae attached to it, while the other had three. Together, these two trunk portions completed the proper total of five vertebrae and, when placed together, articulated perfectly. X-ray examinations in which the bones could be compared exactly with regard to shape, size and texture confirmed the initial finding.

When the two bodies had been reconstructed as best they could be, Brash was joined by John Glaister, Regius Professor of Forensic Medicine at the University of Glasgow, and Dr Gilbert Millar, Lecturer in Pathology at the University of Edinburgh.

Determining the sex of the two victims did not trouble the experts unduly. In Body Number Two, female sex organs were still intact, while in the head of the other body, a small and obviously female larynx was discernible. Additionally, pieces of facial skin from Body Number One showed no signs of a beard.

The fact that the two bodies had been drained of blood and viscera on dismemberment – which delayed the usual process of decay – meant that some pieces of flesh could be identified under microscopic examination. Three pieces of flesh were found to be female breasts, although Glaister could not prove they belonged to either of the bodies.

Firm conclusions

The appearance of the bones enabled Glaister and his colleagues to reach fairly firm conclusions about the ages of the two women. In Body Number One, for example, sutures in the bones of the skull were not completely closed, calcification of the extremities of bones and teeth was not complete, and wisdom teeth had not erupted. All these features pointed to a woman considerably younger than the more mature Body Number Two.

Eventually Glaister and the other medical experts were able to compile rough descriptions of the two women whose bodies they had examined. They assessed Body Number One as being between 18 and 25 years old (Mary was 20) and between 4ft 10ins and 4ft 11½ins tall (she was 5ft). Body Number Two was estimated to be between 35 and 45 years of age (Isabella was 34) and about 5ft 3ins tall (she was 5ft 5ins). The fact that the vertebrae in Body Number Two had been separated relatively skilfully gave further weight to the notion that some medical knowledge must have been applied in the dismemberment of the two women.

This idea was further strengthened when Glaister and Millar investigated the causes of death. With Body Number One, it proved impossible to determine a cause, but in the other body, a broken hyoid bone in the neck and small haemorrhages in the lungs suggested asphyxiation. If strangulation was indeed the cause of death, it would have left certain indications at the point of the tongue, the eyes, the ears and the tip of the nose. All these parts of the body had been removed, in what appeared to be an attempt to destroy any means of determining the cause of death of the two victims.

The forensic team next considered the apparently indiscriminate mutilation of certain parts of the bodies. The legs of one body had been completely stripped of the soft tissues and skin, while those of the others remained intact. The tips of the fingers and toes of one body had been removed, but had been left alone on the other. Similarly, the skin had been removed on just one of the upper forearms.

It was only when a list of known identifying features of the two women was compared with the remains that a pattern became clear, namely that the mutilations coincided with the location of distinguishing marks. Isabella's legs, for example, had been nearly the same thickness from the knees to the ankles, hence the removal of the soft tissues. Her bevelled, squarish fingernails had also been distinctive, so they, too, had been removed. The removal of the skin on Mary's upper forearm had been to conceal her conspicuous birthmark. She had a squint in one eye, and both eyes had been removed.

One of the specialists whose findings were to prove of particular value to the Crown case was Dr Arthur Hutchinson, Dean of the Edinburgh Dental Hospital and School. He was able to determine from the sockets of missing teeth in the two bodies that while some had been extracted some time ago, others had been removed immediately before or after death. That it was possible to date the extraction of teeth from the conditions of the sockets and gums appeared to have been overlooked by the murderer. Mrs Ruxton had rather prominent teeth, which would have been a clear clue to her identity.

The two bodies having provided nearly as much evidence as could be hoped, Professor Glaister next made a characteristically thorough examination of various articles and parts of the house in Dalton Square. He was assisted by Dr Millar and Dr Frank Martin of the University of Glasgow.

The report they eventually compiled was extensive, since a great many articles were removed from Dalton Square for examination and the number and character of their bloodstains were described in painstaking detail. Among the objects taken back to Glasgow University were the carpets, wallpaper and skirting boards, together with the entire contents of the bathroom, and parts of its walls and flooring.

Despite Ruxton's efforts to clean the bathroom and his instructions to Mrs Hampshire and the other charwomen to help clean parts of the rest of the house, Glaister found plenty of bloodstains and bloodstained material. Some stains indicated that they had come from a small spouting artery.

Glaister later acknowledged in court that they might have been caused by the bleeding from Ruxton's cut hand, a wound either deliberately self-inflicted or sustained while using a knife to cut up the bodies of the two victims. The stains from blood that appeared to have run over the rim of the bath, down the sides and into less accessible places, he felt, were less easy to explain, as were the bloodstains on the suit.

Glaister's professional presentation in court of findings like these and his unflappable cool under cross-examination gave great dignity to a trial that could easily have become merely a ghoulish public spectacle.

TURMOIL IN COURT

The trial of Dr Buck Ruxton began in the High Court of Justice in Manchester on Monday, 2 March 1936, before Mr Justice Singleton. Counsel for the Crown were Mr J. C. Jackson KC, Mr David Maxwell Fyfe KC (later Lord Kilmuir) and Mr Hartley Shawcross. Appearing for the defence were Mr Norman Birkett KC (later Lord Birkett) and Mr Phillip Kershaw KC.

Interest in the grisly case was intense, fuelled by Ruxton's earlier appearance in court in Lancaster, which had not been free of incident. When he appeared on 5 November to answer the second charge of murder – that of Isabella – he had protested so vehemently that the court was adjourned for five minutes so he might be calmed down. 'It's all prejudice, I cannot bear the thing', he claimed in one of several outbursts. 'Is there no justice? Who is responsible for it? My home is broken up – my happy home.'

Nor had the excitement been confined to the court proceedings. In the scramble for seats when the court doors were opened on that occasion, a window was broken in the fray.

A watertight case

The trial was to last eleven days, chiefly because of the sheer volume of medical evidence to be heard. Ruxton, the defence's only witness, did not appear until the ninth day, by which time the prosecution had presented a near-watertight case against which even so skilful a barrister as Norman Birkett could make little impression.

The first surprise of the case was the prosecution's decision to attempt to secure a conviction for the murder of Isabella alone. Mr Jackson claimed that she had arrived back from Blackpool, where she had seen her sisters, and then been beaten about the head, and probably stabbed and then strangled by Ruxton for her supposed unfaithfulness. Mary Rogerson had witnessed the incident and was murdered by Ruxton to silence her. Her skull had been fractured by blows to the head, but she had been killed by some other means.

Painstakingly, Jackson set out the case against Ruxton, explaining how the doctor had put off the arrival of Mrs Oxley in order to be able to cut up the bodies in the bathroom and drain them of blood in the bath. He described how Ruxton had brought petrol to speed up the burning of the bloodstained carpets and other material, the numerous inconsistencies in the stories he told as to his whereabouts, how Mrs Hampshire had been unwittingly recruited to help clear the house of any incriminating evidence and how the doctor had called on her to retrieve the name-tag in the suit he had given her.

There were the bloodstains on the stairs, railings, balustrade and carpets, he went on, further attempts to burn bloodstained material in the yard, and the unpleasant smell in the bedroom where Ruxton kept the bodies until he could remove their dismembered remains. The doctor's attempts to pacify Mary's parents, including suggestions that she had been taken away by Isabella to have an abortion, were also discussed.

Jackson then dealt with the discovery of the bodies in the ravine at Moffat, outlining just how exactly their patterns of mutilation matched the known distinguishing marks of the women. There was also, he explained to the jury, the damning evidence of the rompers and the blouse found wrapped around the remains, which had been traced back to the Ruxton household.

The doctor had then tried to get people to tell lies, Jackson said. He reminded the jury that the prosecution had no need to provide evidence of a motive for the murders, but suggested they look no further than Ruxton's obsessive jealousy and violent temper.

The prosecution then called a long list of witnesses, examined by a combination of Jackson, Fyfe and Shawcross. They were tirelessly cross-examined by Norman Birkett, who seized on the slightest discrepancy in the evidence given and challenged the assumptions made by the medical and technical witnesses wherever he could.

Among the first prosecution witnesses called was Mrs Jeanie Nelson, Isabella's sister, who described some of the lower points in Isabella's relationship with Ruxton and the latter's jealousy of Bobbie Edmondson. Various police witnesses also appeared to give details of the occasions, dating from April 1934, when Ruxton had appeared at the police station, complaining of his wife's behaviour and threatening her with violence.

Emotional denial

Eliza Hunter, a former domestic servant at 2 Dalton Square, described how she had seen the doctor with his arms around Isabella's neck and found a revolver under his pillow. Bobbie Edmondson's testimony revealed how Ruxton had talked in a roundabout way of the former's relationship with Isabella, and his subsequent emotionally-charged denial of any accusation of impropriety.

As anticipated, the evidence given by Mrs Hampshire, and later Mrs Oxley, Mrs Curwen and Mrs Smith, created a significant impact and was difficult to refute, particularly with regard to the bloodstained suits and carpets, and the other bloodstained articles being burned in the backyard. It was Ruxton himself, however, who reminded Birkett of one of the few chinks in the prosecution's armour via a hand-written note when the evidence of Mrs Oxley and Mrs Curwen conflicted over the locked doors of the bedrooms. Ruxton followed the evidence given very carefully and handed a great many notes to Birkett throughout the course of the trial.

One of the first medical witnesses to appear was Dr Stanley Shannon, medical officer at Strangeways Prison, under whose care Ruxton had been since being taken into custody. He asserted that it would have been impossible for the doctor to have cut himself on the tin opener in the manner he described.

More serious still for the defence was the testimony of Fred Barwick, a textiles expert from the Manchester Chamber of Commerce. He examined the pieces of sheet wrapped around parts of the bodies in the ravine and compared them with a sheet from the double bed in Isabella's room at Dalton Square, finding a flaw in the strengthening section of each of them. The flaw, he said, was identical, indicating that the two samples of sheet came not only from the same loom but also from the same warp on the loom.

Among several police witnesses who next appeared to describe the various threats issued by Ruxton on his visits to the station was Henry Vann, Chief Constable of Lancaster. He told how Ruxton's voluntary statement had been made.

Professor Glaister was called shortly after Drs Leonard Mather and Frederick Bury testified that there had been no evidence of blood on the stairs when they called to attend to Isabella following her miscarriage in April 1932. Distinguished in appearance and unerringly precise in the way in which he gave his evidence, Glaister was in the witness box for the best part of two days.

The impact he created was so great that by the end of the trial, the popular press had credited him with almost superhuman powers. The *Sunday*

Dispatch had already claimed erroneously the previous November that he was capable of determining the age, sex and weight of a body from just a single hair. In fact, Glaister was at pains to point out the limitations of his work and the need to give the defendant the benefit of the doubt if any existed.

In due course, Glaister explained the significance of the mutilation of the bodies and their identifying features, how dismemberment and draining of the blood from the bodies would require special medical knowledge and several hours in which to do it and how he had estimated, after examining the remains on 1 October 1935, that death had occurred some ten to 14 days previously.

Glaister's clashes with Birkett were the most absorbing of the whole trial, the latter having sought specialist advice from Sir Bernard Spilsbury, probably the most famous of all forensic scientists. Glaister could on occasions give his cross-examiner's questions short shrift. 'Of course', Birkett said to him at one point, 'there are many, many occasions when blood is spilled in a bathroom. For example, you could cut yourself shaving and there would be blood?' Glaister coolly replied, 'I should be amazed if I cut myself shaving and subsequently found on the side of the seat what I saw in this case.'

The evidence of Professor J. C. Brash of the Anatomy Department of Edinburgh University was given in a similarly authoritative and lucid fashion. Brash devised a brilliant method of demonstrating photographically the overwhelming probability that the remains found at Moffat were those of Isabella and Mary. Less strikingly but equally convincingly, he made casts of the feet of the bodies and fitted them exactly into the shoes identified as Isabella's and Mary's.

There was still further damning proof. Detective-Lieutenant Bertie Hammond's work at the photographic and fingerprint department of the Glasgow police established that finger and palm prints taken from the hand of Mary's dismembered body matched impressions found on various articles taken from 2 Dalton Square.

Ruxton takes the stand

It was not until the ninth day of the trial that Ruxton took the stand. Agitated, fearful and sometimes in tears, he could do little but deny the prosecution's most damaging assertions. He slowly became more measured in his answers under cross-examination, but neither he nor his counsel could make much headway.

Asked about his relationship with Isabella, he added to his answer a quotation in French: 'Who loves most, chastises most.' Among his denials was his contradiction of the evidence of PC William Wilson, who claimed Ruxton had once said in the course of one of the disputes with Isabella. 'I will commit two murders in Dalton Square tonight.'

Mr Justice Singleton could find little to say in Ruxton's favour on summing up on the 11th day. 'If there is an avenue, let him walk down it to freedom,' the judge said, picking up an expression that Birkett had used earlier, only to add, 'But if there is not, he cannot.' He reminded the jury instead of the discrepancies in the testimonies of Ruxton and the witnesses, of the bloodstained suit and stair carpets and the doctor's attempts to persuade other witnesses to tell lies.

Referring back to the rompers, he added, 'If you are satisfied as to the identity of these remains, and if you are satisfied that those rompers were on one of the heads, does it not establish the case for the prosecution, as case was seldom established before on circumstantial evidence?' He reminded them, finally, of the significance of the *Sunday Graphic*, and of the flaw in the sheeting.

Birkett could only point to the circumstantial nature of some of the evidence and reminded the jury there was no real indication that Ruxton had gone out on the night of 16 September to dump the remains as the prosecution alleged: the night had been wet, but the car was found dry the next morning, unmarked by any traces of blood. The jury needed little over an hour to reach its verdict. Found guilty as charged, Ruxton was sentenced to death.

A HOPELESS CAUSE

After hearing the jury's verdict Ruxton politely requested to be allowed to appeal, an uncharacteristically restrained way to behave, given his excitable temperament. He even went so far as to thank the court for its patience and the fairness of his trial.

Mr Justice Singleton offered his thanks to the expert medical witnesses and, in particular, Professor Glaister, whose professionalism had clearly impressed him as much as it had millions of others through the reports in their daily newspapers. 'No one could sit in this court,' he remarked, 'and listen to the evidence of Professor Glaister, either in examination-in-chief, or in cross-examination, without feeling that there is a man who is not only master of his profession, but is scrupulously fair, and most anxious that his opinion, however strongly he may hold it, shall not be put unduly against the person on trial.'

Innocent sources

Ruxton's appeal was heard by the Lord Chief Justice (Lord Hewart), Mr Justice du Parcq and Mr Justice Goddard. Criticising the way in which some parts of the case had been dealt with in the judge's summing up, Birkett cited in particular the fact that, having been urged to think more carefully about the suit given to Mrs Hampshire, the jury had not been reminded of the possibility – mentioned by a prosecution witness – that the blood might in fact have come from completely innocent sources.

Birkett also came back to the point that the car in which Ruxton was alleged to have driven with the bodies to Moffat bore no trace of either mud (in spite of the rain that night) or of blood. The cumulative effect of all the matters raised amounted to such a substantial misdirection, Birkett asserted, that the verdict should not be allowed to stand.

The Appeal Court, however, was having none of it and in giving the judgement, the Lord Chief Justice said he could find nothing even remotely to suggest the possibility of misdirection on the part of the judge. His appeal dismissed, Ruxton was hanged at Strangeways Prison, Manchester, on 12 May 1936.

The intense public interest in the case continued even after Ruxton's execution. Women gathered outside his home in Dalton Square in the hope of being allowed to buy some macabre memento from his home. From his death cell, Ruxton offered Birkett a memento – a set of fishknives – in recognition of the skill with which he had conducted his defence.

Following Ruxton's execution, a Sunday newspaper published his confession to the murders, recorded initially a day after his arrest. The newspaper was reported to have paid some £3,000 for the confession, from which part of the costs of his defence were paid. This kind of deal between newspapers and people who had been accused of sensational crimes was fairly common at the time.

CASE FILE: RUXTON, BUCK

BACKGROUND

Buck Ruxton (original name Bukhtyar Rustomji Hakim) was born into a Parsee family of Indian French origin in Bombay on 21 March 1899. He had a respectable, middle-class upbringing and received a thorough education. An apparently thoughtful and sensitive youth, he studied at Bombay University, where in 1922 he qualified as a Bachelor of Medicine and later as a Bachelor of Surgery. Great things were foreseen by his family and associates for the young doctor in view of the first-class honours awarded him in medicine, midwifery and gynaecology.

From university he joined the staff of a Bombay hospital,

before later becoming Medical Officer to the Malaria Commission. On 7 May 1925 he married a well-to-do Parsee girl in Bombay. The marriage was short-lived, however. He came to England alone and concealed all evidence of it, fearful that it would affect his social and professional standing.

At the time of his marriage Ruxton was employed by the Indian Medical Service for which he had worked in Basra and Baghdad, as well as Bombay. By the time he came to England, he had also served as a ship's doctor. With the help of a grant from the Bombay Medical Service, he attended courses at London's University College Hospital, going under the name of Dr Gabriel Hakim.

Second 'marriage'

After a brief spell in Paris, in 1927 Ruxton moved to Edinburgh – a major centre of the medical world – where he studied to become a Fellow of the Royal College of Surgeons. He failed the entrance exam on three occasions, but was allowed to practise by the General Medical Council on the strength of his excellent Bombay degrees. It was while in Edinburgh that he met Isabella van Ess, then still married to a Dutchman but using her maiden name of Kerr.

A fairly tempestuous courtship followed, but one based on a genuine mutual affection, and when the doctor went south to work as a locum to a London doctor, Isabella followed shortly afterwards. By now, he had changed his name by deed poll to Buck Ruxton. This, he suggested to a friend, 'tripped off the tongue' and was more likely to prove palatable in sombre medical circles than his full name, which, like other aspects of his background, he jettisoned as inconvenient baggage.

In 1929, while in London, Isabella gave birth to a daughter, Elizabeth, the first of their three children. The following year, the family moved to Lancashire, where Ruxton acquired a substantial practice. They lived in a solid-looking terraced house in Lancaster's Dalton Square. In 1931 Isabella gave birth to a second daughter, Diane, and two years later, to a boy, Billie. Mary Rogerson was the maid taken on to look after them.

PSYCHOLOGICAL PROFILE

Dr Buck Ruxton was an emotionally unstable man; periods of calm and reasonableness were interrupted by bouts of wild behaviour, tearful self-pity and occasional violence. Allied to his excitable temperament was an obsessive jealousy, a potentially explosive combination. As Ruxton himself said in court of his relationship with Isabella, 'We were the sort of people who could not live with each other, or without each other.'

On many occasions after their frequent quarrels, Isabella would walk into his surgery and say warmly: 'I wonder how I could ever pick up an argument with you.' All too frequently, the rows were started by Ruxton with his groundless accusations of adultery, and on a number of occasions the police were called to Dalton Square to arbitrate in disputes between the warring partners.

Sometimes, as Captain Vann was to recall, the disputes were settled in his office at Lancaster police station. The police there described the doctor as acting like a madman, talking so fast and erratically as to be almost completely incoherent and bursting into tears. Vann later claimed in an article written on the case for the *Police Journal* that Ruxton had made Isabella run up and down the stairs fifty times barefoot as a penance after she had danced with another man at a local function.

Breaking point

Ruxton's behaviour had in the past pushed Isabella to breaking point. In 1932, for example, an urgent telegram brought her worried sister, Mrs Jeanie Nelson, down to Lancaster from Edinburgh. She was told by an angry Ruxton that Isabella – in the later stages of a pregnancy that was to result in a miscarriage – had tried to commit suicide by gassing herself. This Isabella had denied, claiming it was an accident.

Isabella had threatened to walk out on Ruxton on several occasions, but invariably felt constrained by her concern for the welfare of the children. In 1934, though, she got as far as Mrs Nelson's house in Edinburgh, bringing with her all of her baggage, only for a tearful Ruxton to follow her there and eventually persuade her to return.

Ruxton's suffocating jealousy can best be gauged by the events of the weekend before the murders of Isabella and Mary. On 7 September, she went to Edinburgh with some friends, Mr and Mrs Edmondson, together with their daughter and their son, Bobbie. Isabella had originally arranged to stay the night with her sister, but instead decided to stay with the

Edmondsons at the Adelphi Hotel, occupying a single room like the others.

Ruxton, meanwhile, had followed the party to Edinburgh, where he came to the conclusion that Bobbie Edmondson and Isabella were having an affair. No evidence for this or any other instance of Isabella's supposed infidelities ever came to light, but for a man of Ruxton's psychological profile, the trip provided all the ammunition he needed.

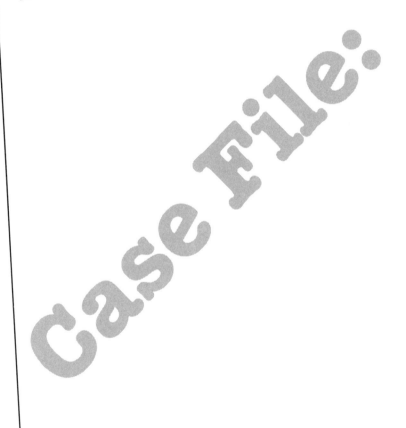

Chapter 14

CHARLES STARKWEATHER
THE REBEL KILLER

Self-styled rebel and dissolute teenager Charlie Starkweather dreamt of being a cowboy – a storybook villain. In 1958, he realized his fantasy and rode along the outlaw trail with his schoolgirl lover like a latter-day Bonnie and Clyde. In his wake he left 11 motiveless murders.

Charlie Starkweather never had a real girlfriend until he met Caril Fugate. He was not seen as much of a catch by most of the girls in his home town of Lincoln, Nebraska – at 5ft 5ins, with bow legs, a pug face and a hoodlum reputation.

Caril liked him, though. She liked his tough, rebel image, and did not care about his lowly origins and his dead-end jobs – she was poor herself. She also liked to listen to his stories in which he fantasized about being a cowboy or having the fastest hot-rod in town. He was always telling stories.

They met in the early summer of 1956. Starkweather's friend, Bob von Busch, was dating Caril's older sister, Barbara, and persuaded Starkweather that Caril, just turned 13, could easily pass for 18. The four went on a double date to a drive-in movie.

After that, Caril had one date with another boy. Starkweather went looking for him and threatened to kill him if he saw Caril again. The boy backed off, and Starkweather and Caril started going steady. It made Starkweather feel good to be wanted.

Neither set of parents cared much for the relationship. Caril's mother and step-father thought that Starkweather, at 17, was too old for her. Starkweather's parents thought Caril was leading him astray. This just brought the young lovers closer together.

Going steady

They went on dates to the movies, sometimes with Bob and Barbara, some-times on their own. Starkweather loved wild places, and whenever he could, he drove Caril out into the countryside around Lincoln. During the day they hunted together. In the evening they lay back, held hands, and looked into the starry black Nebraskan night. Sometimes they just drove round in Starkweather's pale blue 1949 Ford sedan, listening to the rock 'n' roll sta-tions on the radio.

Starkweather liked to buy presents for Caril. He bought her jewellery, including a locket with 'Chuck' – her nickname for Starkweather – and 'Caril' engraved on it, soft toys, a radio and a record player. It was not easy on the pittance that he earned, especially with rent to pay and a car to keep on the road. He thought there must be an easier way to make money, and felt he knew what it was.

For a long time Starkweather had fantasized about being a criminal, and he enjoyed detective comics and crime movies. Although he had been involved in a few adolescent scrapes, he had never been in trouble with the law. Now, needing money to keep Caril, it seemed time to start his criminal career.

Gun-loving boy

Charlie Starkweather was not interested in being a sneak thief. For him, crime meant armed robbery. Starkweather loved guns. He liked taking them to pieces, oiling and cleaning them, and he loved to shoot. Although he was short-sighted and had a habit of firing from the hip, he was a good shot.

He thought about sticking-up a bank, but decided to start small, and rob the Crest Service Station on the main highway just north of Lincoln.

He knew the station pretty well, knew its routines and how much money was kept there overnight. He used to hang out there, working on his car and living on Pepsi and chocolate bars from the vending machines.

Several times, when he had been locked out of his room for being behind with the rent, he slept at the station in his Ford. The attendant would wake him at 4.15 a.m. so he could get to work. He had taken a job as a garbage-man so he could be off work when Caril got out of school.

At 3 a.m. on 1 December 1957, Starkweather pulled into the Crest sta-tion with robbery on his mind. It was a bitterly cold night, well below zero, and a freezing Nebraska wind was blowing.

The attendant, 21 year-old Robert Colvert, was alone. He was new to the job, and barely knew Starkweather though he had annoyed Starkweather the previous day by refusing him credit on a soft-toy poodle that he wanted to buy for Caril.

Starkweather was nervous. He bought a pack of cigarettes and drove away. A minute or so later, he came back for a final check. This time he bought some chewing gum.

Third time lucky

The third time he was ready. He had tied a bandanna around his face like a cowboy, pulled a hunting cap down over his give-away red hair, and put on some gloves. He carried a canvas money-bag in one hand, and a shotgun in the other.

Colvert filled the bag with the loose notes and change from the till, just over $100 in all. He could not open the safe – not knowing the combination.

Starkweather ordered the young man into his Ford. Colvert drove while Starkweather sat in the passenger seat, keeping his shotgun trained on him. When they reached Superior Street, a dirt road outside the city limits that was used by Lincoln's teenagers as a lover's lane, Starkweather told his captive to get out of the car.

According to Starkweather, Colvert made a grab at the shotgun, which went off, blasting him into the road. When his victim began to struggle to his feet, Starkweather reloaded and finished him with a shot to the head.

Later that day, Starkweather said, he told Caril about the robbery, saying that an accomplice had done the actual shooting.

In the evening, he got rid of the shotgun, which he had stolen from Bob von Busch's cousin, Sonny, by throwing it into a creek. A few days later, he fished it out, cleaned it, and put it back in Sonny's garage. The gun had not even been missed.

In the next few days, Starkweather repainted his car black, spent nearly $10 in change on a selection of used clothes, and paid what he owed on the rent so that he could get back into his room.

Although the other attendants at the garage mentioned his name to the police, and the owner of the clothing shop reported his pocketsful of change, Starkweather was never questioned about the robbery.

Taste for killing

He stopped turning up for work on the garbage truck and was eventually fired. He was growing lazy now he had found a way of getting easy money. More than that, he had discovered that killing people did not bother him. Indeed, shooting Colvert had made him feel good.

Starkweather spent his days going to the movies, reading comics, playing records and working on his car. He spent hours practising his quick-draw technique in front of a mirror.

The proceeds from the robbery did not last long. He got behind on the rent again, and ended up sleeping in a garage he rented to work on his car.

On Sunday, 19 January 1958, he went to Caril's home at 924 Belmont Avenue, an unpaved road in the poor quarter of Lincoln. There was a terrible argument. Caril was putting on weight and her family were convinced that Starkweather had made her pregnant. According to Caril, she was so sick of the fighting and his wild, threatening behaviour that she told Starkweather she never wanted to see him again.

Whatever she said, Starkweather did not believe it. A week before, he had arranged to go hunting jack-rabbits with Caril's stepfather, Marion Bartlett, on 21 January, and he intended to keep the appointment.

In the morning, Starkweather helped out his brother Rodney, by working the garbage route for a while, then he went to his apartment building to check that his room was still padlocked. It was. His rifle was locked away in the room, and he borrowed one from Rodney before setting out for Belmont Avenue.

Nobody knows why Starkweather went there. It might have been an honest attempt to get back on good terms with the Bartletts, a desire to provoke some kind of show-down, or simple dumb obstinacy. He took with him, as a kind of peace offering, some rugs he had scavenged from his garbage route. Velda Bartlett, Caril's mother, had said she might like them.

The only person ever to give an account of what happened next was Starkweather. He gave several versions, differing in details – especially in the part Caril played.

Velda Bartlett was not particularly interested in the rugs. Her husband Marion Bartlet, remained in the kitchen, playing with their pretty 2½ year-old daughter, Betty Jean.

Starkweather sat in the living room on his own, cleaning Rodney's rifle to pass the time. Finally, Velda told Starkweather that Marion was not going hunting and that he was to leave and never come back. There was another argument and Velda, a short, slight woman, slapped him around the face two or three times.

Humiliated

Confused and hurt, Starkweather ran out, leaving the rifle behind. He came back for it a few minutes later. Marion Bartlett began haranguing him, then literally booted him out of the house.

Just after 2 p.m., Starkweather went down the block to a grocery store to use their telephone. He called the transport company where Marion Bartlett worked as a nightwatchman and said that Mr Bartlett was sick and would not be in for a few days.

Starkweather left his car at a relative's home nearby, then went back to 924 Belmont Avenue to wait on the back steps for Caril to come home from school. According to Starkweather, Caril was already in the house, arguing violently with her mother.

He went in. Velda accused him of getting Caril pregnant and hit him again. This time he slapped Velda back. Marion Bartlett grabbed him from behind and started wrestling him out of the house.

They fell to the ground. Marion broke off the fight and went looking for a weapon. Starkweather went into Caril's room and loaded his rifle. When Marion returned brandishing a claw-hammer, Starkweather shot him in the head.

He reloaded and saw Velda coming towards him with a kitchen knife in her hand. Starkweather shot her, then hit her twice with the rifle butt as she went down.

Caril's sister, Betty Jean, was screaming. Starkweather picked up the kitchen knife and threw it at the little girl. It hit her in the neck. He killed her with a blow to the head with the rifle.

Then he went back into the bedroom and finished off Marion Bartlett by stabbing him repeatedly in the throat with his hunting knife.

When it was over, Starkweather wrapped Mr and Mrs Bartlett's bodies in bedclothes and trussed them up with the washing line. He dumped Betty Jean in a cardboard box.

Mr Bartlett was dragged into the frozen back yard and hidden in a disused, dilapidated chicken-run. His wife and daughter were carried out and crammed in an outside toilet.

Starkweather mopped up the blood with rags, splashed perfume about to mask the smell, then went to watch television in the living room.

Conflicting stories

Starkweather later claimed that Caril was present during this frenzy of killing and that she even egged him on. She said that she had come home to find her family gone and Starkweather waiting for her with a gun.

She said that he had told her his gang was planning a bank raid. Marion and Velda had found out and they and Betty Jean were being held hostage in another house. Unless Caril co-operated, he would make one phone call and they would be killed.

ON THE ROAD

After the killing of Caril's family, Starkweather and Caril spent the next six days living at Belmont Avenue. Starkweather said it was the best week in his life. He said that they lived like kings with no one to push them around.

Whenever anyone came to the door, Caril told them that she and the rest of the family were sick and in quarantine, while Starkweather hid in a room off the hall with his gun cocked and ready to shoot.

Killer: Charles Starkweather

Tied up

Starkweather made occasional runs to the grocery store to stock up on Pepsi Cola, crisps, chewing gum and ice-cream. He paid for the items with money he had taken from Marion Bartlett. Caril claimed he had tied her up whenever he went out, but Starkweather always denied this.

They lived as man and wife and apart from the bodies in the backyard, theirs was a typical domestic set-up. They looked after the family pets – two parakeets, a dog called Nig and a puppy, Kim, that Starkweather had bought for Caril. They played cards and watched a lot of television. Starkweather used Marion Bartlett's tools to cut down the barrel of the dead man's shotgun.

On Saturday, 25 January, Caril's sister Barbara came to visit the family at Belmont Avenue, with Bob and their new baby. Barbara was worried that her mother had not been in touch. Caril shouted to her sister to stop before she had got half-way up the path. She called out that the whole family had the flu and the doctor had said no one was to come to the house.

Threats

When Barbara kept on coming, Caril screamed 'Go away! If you know what's best you'll go away so mother won't get hurt!' Something in Caril's tone scared her sister and she immediately retreated.

Later, Bob von Busch returned with Rodney Starkweather. Again, Caril sent them away, telling them her mother's life would be in danger if they did not leave. They went to the police, and a patrol car was sent out to the house that evening.

Caril told them the same story – that the family was quarantined with the flu. She claimed that her family did not get on with Bob von Busch and that was probably why he had called the police. The officers thought Caril calm and collected and left their inquiries at that.

Starkweather had been hiding in the bathroom while Caril told her story. After the police went, he left the house. He left Rodney's gun at the house of a mutual friend. He then called Barbara von Busch to leave a message telling her where the gun was and reassuring her that there was no need to worry: he had bought some groceries for her family. When Rodney picked up the rifle, he noticed the butt plate had been knocked off.

Disbelief

The only person who called at Belmont Avenue on Sunday was Starkweather's sister, Laveta, who was also a confidante of Caril. She refused to believe Caril's story about the flu, so Caril drew her close and whispered that Starkweather was in the back of the house plotting a bank robbery with another man.

When Laveta reported this story to her father, Guy Starkweather, he was sufficiently disbelieving to delay calling the police until the next day.

On the Monday morning, Caril's grandmother, Pansy Street, came to the house, determined to see her daughter. There was a note on the door saying, 'Stay a way Every Body is sick with The Flue', and signed 'Miss Bartlett'.

Mrs Street was not to be put off. She shouted until Caril made an appearance at the front door. When Mrs Street dismissed her story, the girl begged her to go away as her mother's life was in danger.

Mrs Street went straight to the police. While she was at the station, Guy Starkweather phoned in with the information his daughter had given him about his son. The police went to Belmont Avenue again. There was no answer at the house. They broke in and found everything neat and tidy, with nothing to excite their suspicions. They took Pansy Street home and let the matter rest.

At 4.30 p.m., Bob von Busch and Rodney Starkweather went over to Belmont Avenue to check things out for themselves. They found the bodies almost immediately, but the house was otherwise deserted. The hunt was now on for the two young lovers, but they had had several hours' start.

Pansy Street's first visit had convinced Starkweather that the dream period was over. It was time to get away. Caril packed a bag with some clothes and family snapshots. Starkweather wrapped his hunting knife, Marion Bartlett's shotgun and a .32 pistol he had found in the house in a blue blanket. They sneaked out the back way and went to get Starkweather's car.

Hitting the road

After picking up a couple of spare tyres at the garage Starkweather rented in the wealthy part of town, they stopped in at the Crest Station to buy petrol and maps. Then they set off for the open highway.

Starkweather headed south out of Lincoln across the flat, frozen, midwinter farmlands. He headed for the small community of Bennet, where he had often hunted in the past, usually on the land of an old family friend, August Meyer. Starkweather loved the woods around Bennet. It was the only place he felt truly alive.

They stopped at a service station to have some work done on the car. Starkweather bought some ammunition – readily available in hunting country – while Caril went to an adjoining cafe to buy four hamburgers. She waited there about ten minutes before Starkweather came in and paid with a $10 bill. They left together.

In Bennet, the recent heavy snowfalls had turned the dirt roads to mud, and when they turned into Meyer's mile-long drive, the car got stuck, next to what had once been a country school. All that remained of it was some scattered bricks and wood and a storm cellar, built so that the children could shelter from the tornadoes that raced across the plains in the summer. Starkweather and Caril went down into the cellar to warm up, then walked up the lane to the farm.

According to Caril, Starkweather asked to borrow Meyer's horses to drag his car out, then shot him as he went into his barn. Starkweather's version was that he and the old man argued about getting his car out of the mud. Meyer went into the house and came out firing a rifle. The rifle jammed, and Starkweather shot him as he turned to go back indoors.

Whatever the truth, August Meyer was killed by a blast in the head from a sawn-off shotgun at close range. Starkweather dragged his body to the wash-house and covered it with a blanket, then he and Caril ransacked the farmhouse, looking for money, food and guns. Their total haul was around $100, a pump-action .22 rifle, some socks, gloves, a sweatshirt, a new straw hat, some jelly and some biscuits.

Stuck

They trudged back up the land and, after an hour or two of freezing work, managed to dig the Ford out of the mud. Starkweather tried to inch it out of the lane, but it slid off into a ditch and, in attempting to back it out, he stripped the reverse gear.

They were rescued by a passing farmer, a neighbour of Meyer, who towed them out with a cable attached to his car. Starkweather insisted he take $2 for his trouble.

They bought some .22 ammunition at a service station, then returned to Meyer's farm, taking a more passable lane. Starkweather wanted to spend at least one night there. Caril became frightened. She was sure the body had been found, and insisted that Starkweather turned around. When he did, the Ford stuck fast again.

It was dark by now. Taking their guns, they abandoned the car and walked back to the road. They were headed for the storm cellar – or cave, as they called it – where Charlie had decided they should spend the night.

Innocent victims

Headlights cut through the darkness. Starkweather put out his thumb, and the car stopped. Inside the car were Robert Jensen, whose father ran the local store, and his girlfriend Carol King. Both were high school students from Bennet. When Starkweather explained his car trouble, Jensen offered them a ride to the nearest petrol station, where they could ring for help.

As they got in the back seat, Jensen turned and asked them for their guns – Charlie had the pump action .22 and Caril carried the sawn-off shotgun – Starkweather insisted they were not loaded.

The service station was closed, and Starkweather, who was feeling increasingly trapped, put his gun to Jensen's head and told him to drive them back to Lincoln.

They had not gone very far when Starkweather changed his mind. He ordered Jensen to turn back to the storm cellar. He said he was going to leave the teenagers there and take their car – a dark blue, souped-up 1950 Ford with whitewall tyres.

As they drove, Starkweather told Jensen to hand over his wallet. Caril emptied it and passed the money to Starkweather.

They parked the car at the entrance to the lane where they had stuck earlier in the day. Caril sat in the car, listening to the radio, as Starkweather marched his prisoners off at gunpoint. As Robert Jensen went down the steps, Starkweather shot him six times in the back of the head. He later claimed that Jensen had rushed at him.

Half naked

Carol King was killed with a single shot from behind. When she was found, she was lying on top of her sweetheart's body at the bottom of the cellar steps. She was naked from the waist down and her back was muddy and scratched as if she had been dragged across the ground. There was no conclusive evidence of rape – although Starkweather admitted to having been tempted – but she had been stabbed several times in her lower abdomen. The narrow puncture marks, from a rigid, double-edged blade, could not have been made with Starkweather's hunting knife. Starkweather claimed that Caril had attacked the girl's body out of mad jealousy.

When the killing was over, Charlie and Caril closed the heavy storm cellar door and went back to Jensen's car. It too was stuck in the mud.

They finally dug it out around 10.30 p.m. and set off towards Lincoln. Starkweather wanted to see if the police had discovered the Bartletts' bodies yet.

MURDERS AT THE MANSION

The Bartlett house was surrounded by police cars. Starkweather kept on driving out of town, heading west. His brother, Leonard, lived in Washington state, more than 1,000 miles away, and Starkweather thought that might be far enough.

By about 1.30 a.m. they had reached Hastings, Nebraska. Jensen's car was not running too well at this point, and Starkweather was tired and suffering from a streaming cold. He turned the car around and headed back to Lincoln, confident that the police would not be expecting them.

It was 3.30 a.m. when Starkweather and Caril arrived back in their home town. They parked in the wealthy section of town, where Starkweather used to collect garbage, and went to sleep.

Killer: Charles Starkweather

On the morning of Tuesday, 28 January, they cruised the area, looking at the houses of the rich. The plan was to hide out in one of them by day, resting, then to steal a car and make a getaway that night.

The mansion they chose belonged to C. Lauer Ward, a millionaire businessman. It was just down the road from the garage that Starkweather had rented.

Ward had left for work by the time Starkweather drove round to the back door of the house. The Wards' maid, Lillian Fencl, answered. Starkweather threatened her with the rifle he was carrying, and walked in.

Lillian Fencl was deaf, and Starkweather had to write her notes to make himself understood. He told her to carry on making breakfast for Mr Ward's wife, Clara, who was the only other person in the house.

Headline danger

When Mrs Ward came down, she agreed to co-operate with Starkweather. One glance at the banner headlines about the Bartlett murders in the paper, which was lying on the kitchen table, told her who he was, and what he was capable of.

Starkweather waved Caril in. She brought the shotgun and some ammunition. Mrs Ward gave her a cup of coffee, and she went into the library.

For a while, Starkweather watched the other two women going about their domestic chores. He soon got bored, however, and began to wander around the mansion, trying out all the fancy furniture and indulging in wild fantasies of living the high life.

He got Mrs Ward to cook him breakfast and serve him in the library. 'They was real nice to us,' he said later, 'and I took it while I had it. I knowed it couldn't last long.'

Around 1 p.m., Mrs Ward asked to go upstairs to change. After she had been gone for a while, Starkweather went after her to check.

He claimed that as he walked along the hallway, Mrs Ward emerged from a bedroom and took a shot at him with a .22. She missed, rushed past him, and he threw his hunting knife into her back. Then he took out the knife, carried the wounded woman to her bed, and left her there.

He told Caril to hold a gun on the maid, then returned upstairs to find Mrs Ward trying to make a phone call. He bound and gagged her and covered her with a blanket.

Armed farmers

At around the same time, 25 armed police, and around the same number of armed farmers, were surrounding August Meyer's farmhouse. Starkweather's car had been found where he had abandoned it. The police believed he had taken shelter there.

They fired tear gas into the house. While they were waiting for the air to clear, a state trooper found Meyer's body in the wash-house. Shortly after, a farmer discovered the bodies of Carol King and Robert Jensen in the storm cellar. Within an hour, around 100 State Troopers were searching the frozen countryside.

Barricades

People in Bennet and Lincoln armed themselves and barricaded themselves inside their homes as news of the killings spread.

Back at the mansion, Starkweather was looking for loot. He took a clean shirt, and Caril packed some clothes.

At 5.30 p.m., the evening paper arrived. On the front page was a picture of Starkweather and Caril – both grinning – taken a few months before by Starkweather's landlady. There were also pictures of Caril's family. They clipped the pictures from the paper – they were found on Caril when she was arrested.

Starkweather told Caril to retrieve his knife from upstairs and to clean it. While she was up there, she splashed some perfume around to mask the smell of blood.

Starkweather found out that Mr Ward was due back around 6 p.m. He lay in wait by the kitchen door, while Caril watched from the front of the house to spot his Chevrolet coming up the drive.

According to Starkweather, he trained his gun on Ward as he came in the door, telling him that he would not be harmed if he co-operated. All Starkweather wanted was the car. Ward grabbed for the gun, and they fought for it.

The fight spilled into the basement. Starkweather finally got the gun back, and shot Ward as he ran back up the stairs. Ward kept going and Starkweather caught up with him at the front door, killing him with a shot to the head from close range.

Starkweather took Lillian Fencl upstairs and tied her up on the bed. He left Caril to watch her while he made a final search of the house, packing up some tinned food for their getaway. He rubbed some black shoe polish into his hair to hide its red colour, then loaded up Mrs Ward's Packard.

Starkweather and Caril left the house later that evening, driving past the Bartlett house on Belmont Avenue, then heading west out of town on Highway 34.

Next morning a relative of Lauer Ward went to his house to find out why he had not shown up at work. He found Ward shot and stabbed just inside the front door. The two women were upstairs, both dead from multiple stab wounds. The shape of the wounds suggested that the same slender, double-edged blade with which Carol King had been mutilated had been used to kill them. This knife was never found.

Starkweather insisted from the first that both women had been alive when he left. Caril's story was that her lover had told her he had killed Mrs Ward with a kitchen knife. She also said that she had actually been present when he stabbed Lillian Fencl repeatedly after tying her to the bed.

Panic

The news of the killings spread swiftly. The thought that Starkweather was still in the area spread panic through the streets of Lincoln. Gun stores ran out of stock as everyone armed themselves. The National Guard patrolled the near-empty streets in jeeps mounted with machine guns as the city was sealed off for a block-by-block search.

DEATH IN THE BADLANDS

After leaving the Wards' house, Starkweather kept driving through the night. As he and Caril went, they tossed their old clothing out of the window, along with a kitchen knife taken from Belmont Avenue and several written confessions, none of which were ever found.

In the early hours of the morning, Starkweather fell asleep at the wheel and only just managed to keep the car out of the ditch beside the road. He persuaded Caril that having sex would wake him up enough to continue driving, but ten minutes later he pulled off the road again and went to sleep.

They set off at first light, crossing the state border at around 9.00 a.m. They drove into the Badlands of Wyoming – so called because the countryside is scarred with ravines that provided shelter for lawbreakers in the old West. By noon they had reached the town of Douglas.

There, they heard on the radio that the bodies of the Wards had been found, and that the police had been told to keep a lookout for the Packard. Starkweather decided to find a new car as soon as possible.

About 12 miles beyond Douglas, Starkweather saw a Buick parked about 30 yards off the road down a narrow track.

Merle Collison, a shoe salesman, was asleep in the front seat. Starkweather rapped on the window. 'We're going to trade cars,' he said. Collison kept the door locked and ignored him.

Blasted

Starkweather walked back to the Packard, took his pump action .22 and shot at Collison through the window, twice, before the gun jammed. Collison agreed to hand over his car. Once he had opened the door, he was shot another seven times, blasting him back on to the floor.

Starkweather and Caril transferred their belongings to the Buick. Caril sat in the back with the weapons. Starkweather could not get the car started. The handbrake was jammed on. According to Caril, he turned to Collison's body for help and said, 'Man? Are you dead?'

Joe Sprinkle, a 29 year-old geologist, was driving east along the highway when he saw two cars parked on the other side of the road. Thinking there had been an accident, he turned round to see if he could help.

As he approached the Buick, Starkweather stepped out, levelled the pump-action rifle at him, and told him to help get the brake off. Sprinkle saw the body by the front seat and made a grab for the gun as he reached into the car.

They struggled into the road just as William Romer, a Wyoming Deputy Sheriff, drove by. He pulled up about 25 yards down the road. Caril got out of the Buick and ran towards him, saying, 'Take me to the police. He just killed a man!'

Quick getaway

When Starkweather saw the police car he spun around and let go of the gun. Off-balance, Sprinkle fell backwards into a shallow pit by the road-side. Abandoning his weapons in the Buick, Starkweather ran to the Packard and roared off the way he was facing, back towards Douglas.

Romer radioed in the news. A few miles down the road, Starkweather raced past another police car. In it were the Douglas Chief of Police, Robert Ainslie, and County Sheriff Earl Heflin. They gave chase. When Starkweather reached Douglas, he was travelling at around 100 m.p.h., and still had a good lead.

The mid-town traffic slowed him down, and Ainslie got close enough for Heflin to take a few pot-shots at the Packard's tyres with his handgun.

Starkweather sped past a truck on the inside, then drove through a red light. For a moment, Ainslie got close enough to lock bumpers with the Packard, but Charlie tore it loose and headed east out of town at 120 m.p.h.

Once they were beyond the city limits, Heflin started shooting at the Packard with his rifle. He shattered the rear windscreen.

A minute or so later the Packard slowed, then came to a stop in the centre of the road. Starkweather had been hit on the ear by flying glass. He thought he had been shot.

The police pulled up 100 yards behind. Starkweather got out and walked towards them.

They shouted for him to put his hands up. Starkweather ignored their orders. Ainslie shot at the ground in front of the advancing Starkweather. When they told him to lie down, he just reached behind him. Thinking he was going for a weapon, Ainslie fired at the ground again.

In fact, with a studied coolness, Starkweather was tucking in his shirt tail.

Once he was sure he looked his best, he lay down on the road and waited for the police to come and take him away.

WHEN LOVE DIES

Starkweather, convinced he was bleeding to death from the wound in his ear and whining that the handcuffs were too tight, was taken to jail in Douglas.

Deputy Sheriff Romer drove into Douglas with Caril. She told him she had been Starkweather's captive, and her family were being held hostage. Then, Romer claimed, she told him that she had witnessed all nine murders in Nebraska, contradicting her claim to have acted out of concern for her family's safety.

After this, Caril became incoherent. When she was put in a cell, she refused to wash or change and would not let anyone near her. She was sedated, and slept much of the next day.

The tiny jail was besieged by newsmen from across the country, clamouring to get to Starkweather. He would not speak to anyone, except to complain about his injuries.

He wrote a note to his parents, apologizing for the trouble he had caused the family, but ended, 'i'm not real sorry for what i did cause for the first time me and Caril have more fun, she help me a lot, but if she comes back don't hate her she had not a thing to do with the Killing all we wanted to do is get out of town.'

Lieutenant Henninger of the Lincoln police flew in to interview Starkweather. Pleased to see a familiar face, Starkweather confessed to all the killings save those of Clara Ward and Lillian Fencl. As far as he knew, he said, they were still alive when he left the Ward house.

The following morning, he was charged with killing Collison. However, the Governor of Wyoming, Millward Simpson, was happy for Starkweather to be extradited. Six lawmen from Nebraska flew to Douglas on the evening of Thursday, 30 January.

Starkweather and Caril came home in a convoy of four cars. Newspapers ridiculed the young killer as afraid to fly. But his escort, Sheriff Karnopp – who had known him since he was a boy – recognized that Starkweather simply thought he had a better chance of escaping from a car than a plane. Throughout the journey, he never gave up looking for ways to get away.

At an overnight stop in Gering, Nebraska, Starkweather wrote a pencil confession high on a cell wall, saying Caril had also killed but 'by the time anybody will read this I would be dead for all the killings then they cannot give Caril the chair to.' Next to it he drew a heart, with his and Caril's names inside it.

Caril travelled with Sheriff Karnopp's wife, and seemed to be in an extremely confused state. One of the first things she said was, 'Are my folks dead?'

She described the later murders, and said she was wearing Clara Ward's blouses and her suede jacket, which was bloodstained. She showed Mrs Karnopp pictures of her family that had been cut from a local paper at the Wards' house.

At 6.30 p.m., Charlie was delivered to the State penitentiary, where he was given a cell to himself. For the next few weeks he was intensively interrogated and tested. As there was no secure prison for a girl of Caril's age, she was kept in a mental hospital.

Both teenagers were charged with murder and pleaded not guilty, and it was decided that they would be tried separately, with Starkweather first.

The court appointed a Lincoln attorney, John McArthur, to look after Caril's interests, and Clem Gaughan and William Matschullat to represent Starkweather. They thought his best hope was an insanity plea, and prepared his defence accordingly.

Starkweather disagreed. He insisted that all the killings had been in self-defence. He refused to be dismissed as a madman, saying, 'Nobody remembers a crazy man.'

Starkweather's trial for murdering Robert Jensen began on 5 May 1958. Charlie made his court appearances wearing a suit provided by the prison. He travelled shackled and surrounded by armed men. There had been several threats on his life.

The prosecution's case was relatively simple. Starkweather had never changed his account of killing Jensen and had admitted that it was in the course of a robbery. The number of bullets Jensen had taken – all from behind – gave the lie to Starkweather's claims of self-defence. The prosecution rested its case on 13 May.

The defence began with a parade of 25 character witnesses. Starkweather rocked back in his chair, chewed gum and concentrated on acting cool as his life story unfolded. The only time he got really animated was when an ex-employer said he was the dumbest man who had ever worked for him. Starkweather turned red and had to be held back in his chair.

Gaughan read out some of Starkweather's confessions, hoping to illustrate his confused and abnormal state of mind.

On 16 May, it was Starkweather's turn to testify. The most dramatic moment of his testimony came when Gaughan asked him to clarify a point in one of his statements. 'Why were you mad at Caril Fugate at the cave?'

'For what she did.'

'What did she do?'

'Shot Carol King.' It was the first time that Starkweather had publicly called Caril a killer, although he had written to prosecutor Elmer Scheele the previous month to claim that Caril had shot King while he was trying to get the car out of the mud. He had also said that she finished off Collison after his gun had jammed. Gaughan read this letter into the record.

The psychiatric testimony began on 19 May. The three defence experts testified that Starkweather was suffering from a diseased mind, but admitted under cross-examination that his mental and emotional problems did not amount to a recognized illness such as schizophrenia.

None of them were prepared to assert that Starkweather was insane under the McNaughten rules – the legal standard of insanity in Nebraska.

Quick release

The prosecution psychiatrists agreed that Starkweather had an anti-social personality disorder, but was legally sane. Far from being 'only a point or two above an idiot', as Gaughan had characterized his client, Starkweather had an above-average IQ. Most damning of all for Starkweather was their assertion that, if he was pronounced insane, he would be committed to a mental hospital, where he would inevitably be found sane and released.

Gaughan and Matschullat made impassioned closing speeches aimed at saving their client from the electric chair. The prosecution concentrated on laying out the facts of the case and appealing to the jury to protect their community from this menace.

The jury were out for 24 hours. On 23 May they returned a guilty verdict and specified the death penalty.

Caril Fugate's trial began on 27 October. Under Nebraskan law, juveniles can be tried as adults for serious crimes, and Caril became the youngest woman ever to be tried for first degree murder in the USA.

Caril was tried for being an accomplice in Robert Jensen's murder. Although no one suggested that she had pulled the trigger, she had admitted taking his wallet. This made it easier to prove first-degree murder than in those cases where Starkweather had implicated her more deeply.

Much of the prosecution's case was the same as at Starkweather's trial. Starkweather was the prosecution's star witness. He no longer had any affection for Caril, and claimed not to care whether she lived or died.

Willing

His testimony, if the jury believed it, was enough to convict her. He said she had been in the room when he killed her mother and sister, and went with him willingly, expressing a desire to go down beside him on the highway. She had had plenty of chances to escape if she had wanted to.

Caril's attorney John McArthur, who passionately believed in Caril's innocence, was not able to shake Starkweather in cross-examination. Starkweather maintained that his earlier statements were 'a bunch of hog-wash', designed to protect her. He also said that she had known he was involved in Robert Colvert's murder.

Several witnesses to the couple's travels confirmed Starkweather's story of Caril's compliance. Deputy Romer and Mrs Karnopp repeated incriminating statements Caril had made to them.

The main defence witness, Caril herself, made a poor impression. She was dressed as if much older than her years, and delivered her answers in a clipped voice. Her attitude veered from confusion to outright hostility, and she resorted to claiming a poor memory whenever the questions became difficult to answer.

The jury took 24 hours to find her guilty, and she was sentenced to life imprisonment.

Charlie Starkweather made the most of his time in the State penitentiary. Although he missed the countryside, he enjoyed the attention he was getting, and the idea of his fame. Nothing pleased him more than reading his name in the newspaper. He put on weight, and he won the affection of the hard-bitten jailers who looked after him. He also said he had made his peace with God.

He spent a great deal of time laboriously writing his life story. He had always been pretty good at drawing, and in jail began to paint.

Delaying tactics

Legal manoeuvres delayed his execution. In April 1959 he fired his attorneys and represented himself at a clemency hearing. He spoke of his remorse, his new-found Christian faith and his belief that he had not been properly represented at his trial. The Parole Board was unmoved. An execution date was set for 22 May.

Starkweather's father contacted a federal judge and won a stay just an hour and a half before his son was due to die. The reprieve was short-lived. The execution was rescheduled for midnight on 25 June.

Starkweather wore a new shirt and jeans so he would look his best for the execution. When the prison officers came for him, he said, sardonically, 'What's your hurry?' and swaggered ahead of them, hands in pockets, to the electric chair.

Defiant end

When asked if he had any last words he pressed his lips together and shook his head. The executioner pulled the switch and 2,200 volts coursed through Starkweather's body. He had to pull it twice more before Starkweather was killed and pronounced dead at 12.04 a.m.

Before his body was brought out of the prison, police had to clear away gangs of teenagers who had been cruising the streets outside, their car radios blasting out rock 'n' roll.

CASE FILE: STARKWEATHER, CHARLES

BACKGROUND

Charlie Starkweather was born at home, in a shack in the poor quarter of Lincoln, on 24 November 1938. He was the third of the eight children – seven boys and a girl – of Guy and Helen Starkweather.

Guy Starkweather, a chatty, convivial man who liked a drink, was a carpenter and handyman, but a combination of a weak back and arthritis meant he could not always work. From 1946, Helen, slight and stoical, was the provider for the family, working at a succession of waitressing jobs.

As he grew up, Starkweather learned to respect and love his mother, but his relationship with his father sometimes degenerated into open hostility.

He had only happy memories of his first six years, which he spent playing with his elder brothers, Leonard and Rodney, fishing with his father, and helping his mother around the house. Though the family was poor, they never went hungry.

In 1944, Charlie began to attend Saratoga Elementary School. His first day there was a disaster, and he never forgot it. All the children were asked to come to the front to give a talk. When it came to Charlie's turn, his slight speech impediment caused his fellow pupils to laugh at him, and he broke down in confusion and humiliation.

As the day went on, he felt picked upon by the teacher, and thought the other children were ridiculing him on account of his short, bow legs and wild shock of red hair. Later he wrote, 'It seems as though I could see my heart before my eyes, turning dark black with hate of rages.' The next day at school he had his first fist-fight with another boy, and found that he enjoyed the experience.

Starkweather spent his whole school career in slow-learner groups, despite an above-average IQ. It was not until he was 15 that an eye-test revealed that he could barely see the blackboard from his usual position at the back of the class. At distances over 20 ft he was practically blind.

In his memoirs, he claimed to be getting into fights almost

every day in his later school years, though his teachers remember little of this.

Fighting friends

His reputation as a brawler brought him challenges from other boys in Lincoln, anxious to prove themselves. One of these was Bob von Busch. At the age of 15, Charlie and Bob fought one another to a standstill, then became friends. Charlie had very few friends, most of them boys he had fought with. In their company, he could be generous and amusing, but he faced the rest of the world with barely repressed hostility.

He dropped out of Irving Junior High School in 1954, and took a job at a newspaper warehouse. It was menial work, and Starkweather hated it. His boss thought he was retarded and treated him as such.

In 1955, Starkweather fought with his father and moved in with Bob von Busch and his father for a while. Both teenagers loved cars. They spent a lot of time at Capital Beach, the local auto track, where Starkweather raced hot rods and took part in demolition derbies. They also stole cars for joy-rides, and occasionally stripped them down for parts.

In 1956, von Busch started dating Barbara Fugate, and saw less of Starkweather, until he introduced him to Caril.

Starkweather quit his job at the warehouse. He had been working part-time with his brother Rodney, collecting garbage, since he was 13. Now he joined him full-time, for $42 a week.

Violence

Guy Starkweather co-owned his son's car, and forbade him from letting Caril – whom Charlie had taught to drive – use it. When, in the late summer of 1957, she was involved in a minor accident in the car, Guy hit his son so hard he knocked him through a window. Charlie left home for the last time.

At first, he went to live with the newly-wed Bob and Barbara in their cramped apartment, but later he moved into another room in the building.

PSYCHOLOGICAL PROFILE

Starkweather felt that everyone looked down on him, and he hated them for it. Childhood teasing, no worse than that suffered by thousands of others, cut him to the quick: 'In those younger years of my life I had built up a hate that was as hard as iron.'

He responded to taunts by withdrawing into black melancholy and fantasizing about getting even: 'I wanted in general revenge upon the world and its human race.'

Starkweather was not always honest about this. Some people believed he called attention to his physical characteristics in order to draw mockery against himself, and so legitimize his own burning resentment at the world.

He blamed the world for his poverty: 'They had me numbered for the bottom.' He was sure that people hated him 'because I was poor and had to live in a god-damned shack'.

Slow death

There was just one way out of this class trap: 'Dead people are all on the same level'. Perhaps it was to prove this point that he returned to the Country Club area of Lincoln after almost making good his escape. Ultimately, in Charlie Starkweather's eyes, everyone was guilty: 'The people I murdered had murdered me. They murdered me slow like. I was better to them. I killed them in a hurry.'

There were strong elements of paranoia in this, nowhere clearer than in his continued assertions that he only killed in self-defence, and that people kept coming at him. The four killings in which he implicated Caril were ones where the self-defence motive was obvious nonsense: the shooting and mutilation of Carol King, the multiple stabbing of two bound, middle-aged women in the Ward mansion, and the riddling with bullets of the unarmed Merle Collison in his car.

If the world was out to get him, he felt he would rather go out in a blaze of defiant glory than resign himself forever to a life of submission: 'Better to be left to rot on some high hill, and be remembered, than to be buried alive in some stinking place.'

The intense life of a criminal appealed as an escape from a life of drudgery. As he said when he was captured, he had always wanted to be an outlaw.

Starkweather had an unusual attitude to death. Although he kept quiet about it before his trial – he did not want his lawyers to use it as evidence of insanity – Starkweather had had a personal acquaintance with Death since he was 17.

Covenant

Death, in a shape that was half-human, half-bear, came to him in visions in the early hours of the morning, and convinced him that he had been singled out. He believed he had a 'covenant' with Death – what he called his 'death deal'.

He found thoughts of death comforting. After all, 'the world on the other side couldn't be as bad as this one'. Death came to him in a dream and took him to hell, but 'it wasn't hot like I'd always thought hell would be . . . it was more like beautiful flames of gold'.

Uncritical love

When he told others about his death deal, they had rapidly changed the subject, but Caril had said she would go with him all the way. Caril's uncritical love for him gave a sense of purpose to his thoughts of revenge: 'I started a new kind of thinking after I met her . . . Something worth killing for had come.'

His relationship with Caril was central to his vision of himself as a martyr: 'I wanted her to see me go down shooting it out and knowing it was for her . . .'

Killing Robert Colvert was a turning point. When he pulled the trigger, his rage disappeared, and the peace and serenity he remembered from his early childhood flooded through him. His murderous rampage exorcized much of his hate. Once his fate was settled, he allowed a gentler side of his character to be seen. Mike Shimerda, a prison guard who knew him, claimed: 'If somebody had just paid attention to Charlie, bragged on his drawing and writing, all of this might not have happened.'

Chapter 15

JOHN GEORGE HAIGH

THE ACID BATH
MURDERER

He was convinced he could commit the perfect murder, and he wanted to prove it. With his charming and courteous manner, he was able to entice his victims to their deaths and then destroy their bodies in acid. But the smiling, well-dressed man made one fatal error.

On Saturday, 26 February 1949, three men arrived at a small, backstreet storehouse in the Sussex village of Crawley. The storehouse, a brick-built shed on two floors, was surrounded by a six-foot wooden fence and secured by a mortice and padlock.

One of the men, a Mr Edward Jones, was managing director of a small engineering firm, Hurstlea Products, which owned the storehouse in Giles Yard, Leopold Road. The other two were Detective Sergeant Pat Heslin of the West Sussex Constabulary, and Police Sergeant Appleton, the village policeman.

Jones had already spoken to Heslin about the storehouse. His firm used it to store steel and other surplus materials and it was occasionally used by a business associate of his from London to do his own private work and experiments. This man was not an employee of the firm but came to Jones with various manufacturing jobs and orders, and from time to time suggested new engineering ideas.

Mr Jones' own impression, he told the detective, was that some kind of 'conversion work' was being done in the storehouse, but he could not say precisely what. His contact had borrowed the keys a few days before and had not yet returned them.

Inside the storehouse

So Heslin picked up a steel bar and prized the padlock open. At first glance. the whitewashed interior seemed quite ordinary. Paint pots, bits of wood and metal, old bottles and rags lay scattered on two rough benches along with various tools and implements.

Methodically, Heslin noted down other items inside the storehouse. All of them seemed in keeping with its purpose, although a peculiar mix – a rubber apron, heavily stained with chemicals, a large pair of rubber boots, a stirrup pump, a gas mask, some rubber gloves, a riding mackintosh and large carboys packed in straw and resting in metal frames. These were standard industrial containers for keeping dangerous acids in. In and around the yard, they found several 45-gallon oil drums – all of them in varying stages of corrosion.

But looking closer on a bench, Heslin began to understand why the police in London were so interested in Jones' colleague. There he found a small leather hatbox and a good quality leather briefcase. A dirty storeroom was a very curious place to leave important personal possessions.

The case contained various papers and documents, including three ration books and various clothing coupons. The contents of the hatbox were even more intriguing. It contained passports, driving licences, diaries, a cheque book and a marriage certificate, none of which bore the name of Jones' colleague. But most surprisingly of all, at the bottom of the box the detective found a .38 revolver and a supply of bullets.

Heslin was a sound, practical officer who did not look for exotic explanations when faced with the obvious. The gun pointed to murder. Nothing had been concealed and, clearly, whoever left it there had been very confident of avoiding suspicion. Heslin filed his report.

The officers waiting for the report were based in the fashionable, well-heeled district of London's Chelsea. They were investigating an unusual disappearance. Even in those days the police were accustomed to missing children and teenagers, and sometimes young women. But it was very rare for a dignified widow of 69 to disappear.

Gone missing

Mrs Henrietta Helen Olivia Robarts Durand-Deacon had been missing since 18 February. A wealthy woman, she had lived for years in the cosy atmosphere of the Onslow Court Hotel in Queen's Gate, one of Kensington's main thoroughfares. Her close friend, Mrs Constance Lane, noticed that Mrs Durand-Deacon was not at her dinner table that evening.

The next day, 19 February, after Mrs Durand-Deacon had failed to appear for breakfast, Mrs Lane was approached by a man who also lived in the hotel – a neat, short man with a trim moustache, of around 40, called

John Haigh. Mrs Lane had never liked him. There was something false about his glib smile and easy charm.

Haigh solicitously inquired after Mrs Durand-Deacon, saying she had failed to appear for an appointment with him the previous day. By now highly anxious, Mrs Lane spoke to a chambermaid, who said Mrs Durand-Deacon's bed had not been slept in. But Mrs Lane still waited. In 1949, respectable people, even close friends, did not lightly interfere in each other's lives.

On 20 February, Haigh again stopped at Mrs Lane's breakfast table, with the same oily concern. She told him bluntly she was going to the police. Observantly, she noticed how Haigh seemed to ponder this.

After breakfast, Haigh went up to Mrs Lane in the hotel lobby and suggested they go to the police station together. In his smart, grey overcoat and leather driving gloves, Haigh looked impressive at the wheel of his Alvis – a seemingly stylish, successful man with a cigarette placed racily between his lips.

Haigh's self-confident veneer helped him through the first shock. Mrs Lane had already known about Mrs Durand-Deacon's appointment with Haigh before he told her. Mrs Durand-Deacon had told Mrs Lane about it herself before setting off. Haigh smoothly explained to the police that 'dear' Mrs Durand-Deacon had, worryingly, not turned up. The interview over, Haigh promised to 'help all I can'.

It was a strange comment. Friends of missing people are assumed to be willing to help all they can.

Haigh had interested the police. His charm was superficial – they could see that. But there was something more substantial. Mrs Durand-Deacon had told Mrs Lane precisely why she had an appointment with Haigh. It was to discuss a business idea she had thought up. She wanted to manufacture imitation fingernails.

The idea was wholly Mrs Durand-Deacon's. What intrigued the police at Chelsea was why Haigh, supposedly a capable small businessman, should have endorsed such a bizarre idea. This was 1949. Rationing was still in force. Spending money was scarce, and credit not easy to come by. Who on earth did Haigh imagine he could sell false fingernails to?

Haigh's showy self-confidence left its mark on the detectives handling the case. They called on him the next day at the Onslow Court Hotel. Haigh told them again he would be happy to 'tell you all I know about it', and made a rambling statement. Its essence was that he had no idea where Mrs Durand-Deacon was.

Feminine intuition

Three days later, on Thursday, 24 February, Haigh was interviewed again at the hotel. He covered the same ground and repeated his catechism of goodwill, but this time Woman Police Sergeant Alexandra Lambourne, was present.

'Apart from the fact I do not like the man Haigh, with his mannerisms,' she wrote in her report. 'I have a sense that he is "wrong", and there may be a case behind the whole business.'

Sergeant Lambourne's intuition suddenly gave shape to her colleagues' uneasiness. Haigh was checked out. He had been jailed three times, twice for obtaining money by fraud and once for theft. Inquiries in London and Sussex showed that he owed money, and that he was struggling to pay his hotel bills.

When news arrived of the .38 revolver, and the obviously stolen documents being found in Haigh's storehouse, the detectives felt they were closing in on a callous 'smart-alec' who had gone too far. On 28 February, the day after the visit to the storehouse, Mrs Durand-Deacon's jewellery was located at a dealer's in Horsham, Sussex, and Haigh's description fitted that of the seller's. When a dry-cleaning ticket found in the hat-box led to the discovery of her Persian lamb coat, the case seemed to be over.

At 4.15 p.m. on the same day, Detective Inspector Albert Webb was waiting at the Onslow Court Hotel when Haigh's Alvis pulled up. When the Inspector asked him to come to the station for questioning, Haigh appeared completely unruffled.

'Certainly,' he replied affably, 'I'll do anything to help, as you know.'

Haigh took on a nonchalant air at the police station. He had arrived so promptly that no one was ready to interview him. He was placed in a Divisional Detective Inspector's office, where he sat, smoked and dozed off. At 6 p.m., he was given a cup of tea.

At 7.30 p.m., Divisional Detective Inspector Shelley Symes entered the office with Superintendent Barratt, and Inspector Webb.

Symes, an astute and experienced detective, began with some minor points. Haigh lied blandly about them, so Symes revealed that the revolver, the coat and the jewellery had all been recovered.

'Ah,' Haigh said, barely ruffled. He puffed on his cigarette. 'I can see you know what you're talking about. I admit the coat belonged to Mrs Durand-Deacon and that I sold her jewellery.'

'How did you come by the property?' Symes pressed him. 'And where *is* Mrs Durand-Deacon?'

The three detectives sat watching as Haigh smoked and thought. His collar and cuffs were immaculate, his tie in place, the shine on his shoes unsoiled. Haigh's composure was incredible. Even within moments of being found out his mind was at work trying to figure out some means of escape.

Finally, when ready, he spoke. 'It's a long story,' he drawled. 'It's one of blackmail and I shall have to implicate many others.'

Just then, the phone rang. Symes and Barratt were summoned from the room. Not knowing how much the police had on him or what they might come up with now, Haigh suddenly made up his mind. There was one chance for survival.

Left alone with the least senior officer, Haigh relaxed further. He spoke to Webb as to a friend, 'Tell me frankly, what are the chances of anyone being released from Broadmoor?' he asked.

Broadmoor was the institution for the criminally insane.

WITHOUT TRACE

Detective Inspector Albert Webb formally warned Haigh that he was not obliged to say anything. Haigh impatiently waved the warning aside and carried on regardless. 'If I told you the truth,' he said, 'you would not believe it. It is too fantastic for belief. I will tell you all about it,' he said. 'Mrs Durand-Deacon no longer exists. She has disappeared completely and no trace of her can ever be found again. I have destroyed her with acid. You will find sludge that remains at Leopold Road. Every trace has gone.

'How can you prove murder if there is no body?' Haigh asked.

Suddenly, Webb remembered the Sussex police report – the stirrup pump, the gas mask, the metal drums and the acid and sludge. Was this a fictitious yarn? What was Haigh talking about? Webb tried to imagine what else the acid might have been in the storehouse for, then hurried off to tell his senior officers.

Superintendent Barratt exploded. 'He's been having you on,' he told Webb. 'Fairy tales . . . nonsense.'

All three detectives recoiled from the idea. If Mrs Durand-Deacon was dead, as seemed all but certain, then they wanted a simple open-and-shut case of murder for greed. None of them had ever heard of anything as grotesque as dissolving people in acid. Moreover, Haigh had disclosed his line of defence: insanity. So self-assured had he been that he was more worried about getting out of Broadmoor, than finding his way into it.

In 1949, few detectives believed that a killer might be insane, unless he was visibly a ranting, incoherent lunatic beyond any form of self-control.

Haigh was hardly this type. To the Chelsea detectives, he was a glib, villain who held them in contempt. They probably feared that Haigh might manipulate the law, the psychiatrists and the courts and, finally, cheat the hangman.

The truth revealed

After Haigh had been formally cautioned, Inspector Symes impassively began writing down Haigh's statement. Apart from a brief interval for tea and cheese sandwiches, it took two and a half hours, with Haigh still happily smoking as he described how Mrs Durand-Deacon died.

'. . . Having taken her into the storeroom at Leopold Road, I shot her in the back of the head whilst she was examining some paper for use as finger nails,' he said.

286

'I then went out to the car and fetched in a drinking glass and made an incision, I think with a penknife, in the side of the throat, and collected a glass of blood, which I then drank.'

Haigh went on to describe how he removed Mrs Durand-Deacon's valuables – her Persian lamb coat, her rings, necklace, ear-rings and crucifix – and then put her body into a tank.

The detectives listened and watched without comment. Mad or sane, a true statement or pack of lies, they noticed how Haigh expressed himself with utterly unfeeling care. His grammar seemed to matter more to Haigh than his victim.

The statement had barely begun. 'I then filled the tank up with sulphuric acid by means of a stirrup pump from a carboy. I then left it to react.'

This was Haigh's way of saying he had set out to remove all trace of Mrs Durand-Deacon. But he suddenly seemed to remember something.

Break for tea

'I should have said that in between putting her in the tank and pumping in the acid, I went round to the Ancient Priors and had a cup of tea . . .'

The restaurant Haigh had referred to, fully named Ye Olde Ancient Priors, was nearby in Crawley Square. Inquiries showed that beside the cup of tea, after he had killed Mrs Durand-Deacon, he ate a poached egg on toast.

The evidence was bewildering. Detectives Symes, Barratt and Webb all understood what was being claimed: vampirism. At any rate, they were dealing with a man who could sit quite calmly, happily drinking tea in a public place immediately after shooting an elderly lady.

Haigh then described how he had taken the jewellery to the car, had dinner at the George restaurant, put the revolver in the hat-box and driven back to the Onslow Court Hotel where, the next morning, he paused at Mrs Lane's breakfast table to express his concern over Mrs Durand-Deacon.

The account of events inside the storehouse then resumed.

'On Monday, I returned to Crawley to find the reaction almost complete, but a piece of fat and bone was still floating on the sludge.'

Coldly clinical

'I emptied off the sludge with a bucket,' Haigh continued, 'and tipped it on the ground opposite the shed, and pumped a further quantity of acid into the tank to decompose the remaining fat and bone . . .

'On Tuesday, I returned to Crawley and found decomposition complete.'

Altogether, Haigh received £100 for Mrs Durand-Deacon's jewellery from Bull's Jewellers in Horsham, and £10 for her watch from a shop in

Putney High Street, south London. He repaid £36 of a loan of £50 made to him by Mr Jones of Hurstlea Products, owner of the storehouse, and reduced his overdraft of £83.

Haigh had been speaking for an hour or more, in painfully exact detail, concerned at all times to get everything in its right order. He had told stories of vampirism and genteel cups of tea, of greed and bankruptcy, of deceit and bad debts, and of forgery and fraud. But the story was not over.

The full horror

Haigh continued talking, smoking with cat-like pleasure as his revelations poured out. By the early hours of 1 March, he had confessed to five more murders.

The first had taken place on 9 September 1944. The victim was an old acquaintance, William McSwan, in a basement flat at 79 Gloucester Road, near the Onslow Court Hotel.

A year later, Haigh lured McSwan's trusting parents, Donald and Amy, to the same basement, and coshed both of them over the head. He forged Donald's signature to gain power-of-attorney over their estate. While selling one of their properties, Haigh met Dr Archibald Henderson and his wife Rosalie. For their killings he chose the Giles Yard storeroom.

Haigh said that in each case he had destroyed the bodies with acid after drinking a cup of their blood.

COMPLETING THE JIGSAW

The arrest of Haigh riveted the public's attention. Stories of acid baths, rumours of ritualistic blood-drinking, the remorseless killing of an elderly woman all generated disgust and fascination.

Haigh's immaculate appearance, slicked-back hair and all-weather smile increased the antagonism felt against him. His remand appearances before Horsham magistrates drew large, fiery crowds inside and outside the courtroom.

Young housewives jeered and shouted cat-calls while elderly men in caps, out for a morning stroll, peered forward for a glimpse of Haigh. Many others in the crowds looked worried and perplexed as they tried to read what they could on Haigh's unruffled features.

More confessions

To some, such as the women who stampeded towards Haigh on 1 April after he had been committed for trial. Haigh was purely evil. But others had begun to sense the bewildering contradictions in his character. His killings, they thought, might have been the act of a madman; the confidence tricks were not.

On 4 March, after being transferred from Chelsea to Lewes Prison in Sussex, Haigh asked to see Detective Inspector Webb, his former interrogator.

Haigh told Webb he thought it 'timely' to mention three more murders he had committed. Two of the victims, a woman and a youth, came from west London, the third was a girl from Eastbourne. This brought his total number of victims to nine.

By this stage, however, the authorities were concentrating on Mrs Durand-Deacon. Hers was the only murder Haigh was ever charged with. The police wanted a no-nonsense conviction, with public sympathy too outraged by the killing of an elderly lady for a reprieve to be granted.

Solid evidence

In the run-up to Haigh's trial, two complex scientific inquiries were launched. One, led by Scotland Yard, investigated the acidic remains at the Crawley storehouse. The other, for the defence, investigated Haigh's mind. The former proved simpler.

Dr Keith Simpson of London University, the pathologist attached to the Home Office, first carried out routine blood tests at the storehouse to ensure the bloodstains in the shed matched Mrs Durand-Deacon's blood group. He then turned to the weed-covered yard outside.

Following zig-zag scratches in the ground where Haigh had pushed the acid drum containing the body, Simpson found the spot where Haigh had claimed to empty the sludge. Soon, he noticed a stone 'the size of a cherry' and highly polished. It was a gallstone. Simpson handed it to DS Heslin, saying, 'There you are, Sergeant, that's the first trace of a human body.'

Haigh had never considered the possibility that some objects take longer to corrode than others. Gallstones, which are covered in fat, resist acid for some time. Chief Inspector Guy Mahon of the Murder Squad congratulated Simpson.

'I was looking for it,' Simpson snapped back. 'Women of Mrs Durand-Deacon's age and habits – 69 and fairly plump – are prone to gallstones.'

Mrs Durand-Deacon had, in fact, weighed 14 stone, but careless Haigh had left enough evidence to settle all questions of identification many times over. These included remains of the left foot, which Simpson painstakingly re-assembled with microscope and X-ray equipment. Scotland Yard's laboratory made a cast and found it perfectly fitted one of Mrs Durand-Deacon's shoes.

The sludge also included traces of pelvic bones, and two discs from the lower spinal column, a total of 18 fragments in all.

Killer: John George Haigh

Careless

Haigh's greatest error had been to miscalculate the time needed for acid to break down the acrylic resin from which false teeth are made. One set of dentures was found at the storehouse, and the dentist who made it confirmed that Mrs Durand-Deacon had been her patient.

Examination of a 24 square-foot area of topsoil, three inches deep, also revealed the handle of Mrs Durand-Deacon's handbag, a lipstick container cap, a notebook and other personal items. About 475 pounds of sludge and soil was removed, packed into boxes and painstakingly examined at the laboratory by the forensic team working on the case.

Simpson then moved into the workshop, where he found some of Haigh's clothing, and bloodstains on the wall. Sections of the plaster were removed and placed in storage. A hairpin was found in the grease at the bottom of one of Haigh's oil drums.

It was typical of Haigh to devise a wily, thorough plan only to see it ruined with elementary mistakes. But there is no sign that he was shocked, or even dismayed, by the collapse of his 'corpus delicti' beliefs.

Eternal optimist

Haigh was unquestionably optimistic. As one saviour or escape route vanished, so he would dream up a larger-than-life trust in the next.

First, no one would find the storehouse. Once found, no trace would be found of Mrs Durand-Deacon. With her identification complete, there was still Broadmoor, not the gallows, to look forward to. After confessing to nine murders, Haigh was still charming his fellow prisoners inside Lewes Prison.

Haigh generously handed cigarettes around in prison, when other inmates would have sold them. His shoes were always polished and, whether alone in his cell or the exercise yard, he carried his lemon kid gloves. One inmate joked that Haigh was 'the best-dressed prisoner of the year'.

Faking it

Several people who met Haigh in prison, before his trial, became convinced the stories of vampirism were a sham. Haigh was quite sure that he would be sent to Broadmoor and forecast that he would be released after five to ten years. Haigh found one inmate who had actually been inside Broadmoor, and plied him with questions about all the various symptoms of insanity.

His belief in his own charmed life remained. On being told he would be represented by Sir David Maxwell Fyfe, a Nuremberg prosecutor, Haigh wrote: 'I'm very glad to see we have got old Maxy. He's no fool.'

BROUGHT TO BOOK

Haigh's trial for the murder of Olivia Durand-Deacon opened at Lewes Assizes on 18 July 1949, and lasted two days. The case was heard by the foremost criminal judge of his day, Mr Justice Humphreys.

Haigh pleaded not guilty and set about doing crossword puzzles during the proceedings – a further indication of how unconcerned he was.

For all of the first day, the prosecution, led by the Attorney General, Sir Hartley Shawcross, produced evidence about the Crawley storehouse, the acid drums, Mrs Durand-Deacon's disappearance and Haigh's confessions. Each time, Haigh's counsel, Maxwell Fyfe, rose confidently in his black gown to say, 'No questions.' The case rested entirely on whether Haigh was mad or sane.

Convincing the jury

Pleas of insanity require expert evidence from psychiatrists. A jury's general impressions and intuitions have no formal standing: nor, in law, does the belief that anyone who repeatedly kills must be insane.

At the time of Haigh's trail, psychiatry was no longer in its infancy. But the art of giving plausible, coherent medical testimony about matters of the mind was still in its early days.

For his evidence to be plausible, a psychiatrist must himself be plausible while giving evidence in the witness box. He must speak in ways a practical-minded jury can understand, showing he shares their values. Above all, he must never be intimidated by the prosecuting counsel.

Dr Henry Yellowlees, the defence's only witness at Haigh's trial, lacked these qualities. A consultant and lecturer at St Thomas's Hospital in London, Dr Yellowlees was a withdrawn, scholarly-looking man in striped trousers and black waistcoat and jacket. At 61, he was experienced at giving evidence in big trials but was totally used to having his word taken as gospel.

Haigh's case rested on the M'Naghten Rules, the 19th-century guidelines concerning criminal sanity. They required a defendant to know what he was doing, and that it was wrong in law, before he can be held fully responsible.

Maxwell Fyfe rose to open his defence of Haigh, fully aware that not one single word had yet been said in his client's favour. Straight away, he addressed the central issue.

'The disorder of the mind which I submit has affected the reason of the accused is that rare, but quite well known, type of mental aberration which is called, in psychological medicine, pure paranoia,' he said.

Maxwell Fyfe went on to trace a link between the textbook ideas about this condition, and the perverted religious visions which Haigh claimed to be gripped by.

'In the case of pure paranoia,' he said, 'it really amounts, as it develops and gets a greater hold, to practically self-worship, and that is commonly expressed by a conviction in the mind of the patient that he is in some mystic way under the control of a guiding spirit which means infinitely more to him and is of infinitely greater authority than any human laws or rules of society.'

Yellowlees testified that Haigh was paranoid. Maxwell Fyfe asked him to expand on this.

'It is generally held to result from heredity and partly, or perhaps even so, from environment, by which I mean specially the early upbringing, the home surroundings and early experience,' Yellowlees replied.

Maxwell Fyfe asked his witness if he believed Haigh's claim to have drunk his victims' blood.

'I think it pretty certain that he tasted it,' Yellowlees said. 'I do not know whether he drank it or not. From a medical point of view I do not think it was important, for the reason that this question of blood runs through all his fantasies from childhood like a motif . . .'

He went on to describe how Haigh's paranoia could be detected in his love of hoodwinking people, and in his conceit and fantasy-world.

The psychiatrist, although rattled by questions from the judge, regained his composure and offered his interpretation of different facets of Haigh's life. Yellowlees said that there was 'a complete absence of sexual activity or interest and that in itself, of course, is an abnormal thing.' Maxwell Fyfe asked what this signified.

'It is an indication of a very great abnormality of some kind,' Yellowlees replied. 'It happens also to be stated in authoritative works that this is a thing you find in a paranoiac, who sublimates his sexual energies into this worship of himself and his mystic fantasy.'

Losing face

Several times during Yellowlees' evidence, the judge had interrupted to demand that the defence clarify some of its evidence. He objected, for example, to Yellowlees interpreting some of Haigh's claims and childhood experiences before these were established in evidence. Many of these objections were legal points directed at Maxwell Fyfe, who apologized.

The effect of the judge's interruptions, however, was to suggest that Yellowless was irresponsible, a child with naive ideas who needed scolding by men of the world. Despite the propriety of the judge's objections, their manner betrayed his absolute contempt for Yellowlees' evidence.

The defence struggled manfully to make up its lost dignity, and its portrait of a mocking criminal, driven and controlled by a nameless higher power, emerged eloquently and plausibly. For a short while, Haigh appeared worthy of pity as well as of loathing.

The defence examination ended. Whatever impression Dr Yellowlees had made was promptly ruined by the opening thrust of the Attorney-General's cross-examination.

'You said when you gave your evidence that you had seen the prisoner five times, you had examined him five times? That is not accurate, is it?'

Yellowlees, after some confusion and delving in his notes, apologized for his error. He then admitted he had no notes of the dates on which he had visited Haigh in prison, nor any idea of the total length of their meetings. The Attorney-General said this had been two hours and ten minutes.

'Is that right?' the Attorney-General asked.

'I do not know.'

'Is it about right?'

'I do not know.'

'Is it about right?' the Attorney General repeated.

'I have got no idea.'

Yellowlees was then asked, since Haigh was a notorious liar, what objective signs of insanity existed in him.

'There are no such things as objective signs of insanity,' Yellowlees replied, adding that his evidence was based on lifelong experience of 'cumulative' symptoms.

The Attorney-General asked him to name one.

'I am relying upon his verbosity, his egocentricity, the fact that he is unable to speak the truth, the fact that he has no shadow of remorse or shame,' replied Yellowlees.

Soon after, the Attorney-General put his case directly to the doctor. It was necessary to show that Haigh knew he was committing wrongs.

'I am asking you to look at the facts and tell the jury whether there is any doubt that he must have known that according to British law he was preparing to do and subsequently had done something which was wrong?'

'I will say "yes" to that if you say "punishable by law" instead of "wrong",' Yellowlees said.

'Punishable by law and, therefore, wrong by the law of his country?'

'Yes, I think he knew that,' Yellowlees replied.

Defence collapses

Quietly, in the way of English trials, a watershed had been reached and passed. Haigh's one witness, a man qualified to pronounce him insane and who actually appeared to believe he was, had testified that Haigh knew his crimes were acts of wrongdoing.

Maxwell Fyfe drew upon all his eloquence to plead the impairment of his client's mind. But as a lawyer, he knew his case was all but defeated. His speech lasted several hours, only to be followed by a cuttingly, contemptuously brief reply from the Attorney-General.

The judge, despite his earlier impatience with Dr Yellowlees, neglected nothing of value to the defence in his summing-up. He explored the theory of paranoia, examined Haigh's actions and personality. But he was obliged to prove insanity, and had not made out the semblance of a case.

The jury took a quarter of an hour to find Haigh guilty of murder. Sentenced to death, he was driven away from the court by grim-faced police officers, still smiling brightly and looking immaculate.

On the advice of his counsel, Haigh had not gone into the witness box since his word on oath would have meant nothing. Maxwell Fyfe also feared that Haigh's cocksure ways would have irritated the jury, as would his detailed, clinical description of the death of Mrs Durand-Deacon.

Strangely, it was the dryly academic Dr Yellowlees who managed to irritate the jury on Haigh's behalf.

Haigh's cheek let him down. If he had not mocked the police by saying they would never find Mrs Durand-Deacon's body, or insulted the court by doing crossword puzzles, or undermined his defence by inventing symptons of madness, he might have met a different fate.

END OF THE LINE

Haigh became prisoner No. 7663 at Wandsworth Prison, in south London. As a condemned man, he had finally to swap his smart green suit and shiny shoes for the prison suit worn in the death cell. By this stage, his hopes of being sent to Broadmoor had evaporated.

By law, the Home Secretary was bound to appoint psychiatrists to study Haigh, and all prisoners condemned to death. The three responsible for Haigh reported that he was sane.

Haigh never said anything more about the three further murders he had confessed to in Lewes Prison on remand. It has never yet been established whether or not Haigh ever committed them or whether he merely invented them to back up his plea of insanity.

Yet he still seemed to be in good spirits. Immediately after sentence, he had been taken down to the common room at Lewes Assizes. A court official asked if he would like to see the chaplain. Haigh had his feet up on the table, while sipping tea and puffing on a cigarette.

'I don't see much point in it, do you, old boy?' Haigh quipped.

Inside Wandsworth, Haigh wrote many letters. One was to Dr Yellowlees, thanking him for his help.

'All the outstanding personalities throughout history,' Haigh wrote, 'have been considered odd: Confucius, Jesus Christ, Julius Caesar, Mahomet, Napoleon and even Hitler . . . My headmistress at the High School and my headmaster at the Grammar School both reported that I was not a normal boy.'

On 24 July, five days after his trial ended, Haigh passed his 40th birthday in the condemned cell. His mother had sent him a card, but Haigh swept aside her suggestion of a visit, asking her to discuss it with his solicitor. The question was never raised again.

The final days

As the days wore on, Haigh finally lost the poise he had maintained since Mrs Durand-Deacon went missing. After spells of depression and petulance, he began compiling notes about his nightmares, particularly those concerning blood.

However, he never spoke openly about them, and neither to his guards nor in letters did he ever express remorse or shame for his crimes.

Though clearly depressed at losing his celebrity status once the trial was over. Haigh had lost none of his flair for showmanship.

He bequeathed his favourite suit, tie and socks to Madame Tussaud's so that the memory of his sartorial elegance would survive, even in the Chamber of Horrors. Haigh insisted that the model of him should have its shirt cuffs showing at least one inch below the sleeves of the jacket.

Accepting fate

Haigh did not appeal against his conviction, and the Home Office announced that there would be no reprieve. Soon afterwards, the Governor of Wandsworth Prison, Major A.C.N. Benke, received a request from Haigh to rehearse his own execution.

'My weight is deceptive,' Haigh said. 'I have a light springy step and I would not like there to be a hitch.'

Major Henke assured him there would be no difficulty and, despite Haigh's persistence, the request was turned down.

Haigh's letters to his parents from the death cell managed to preserve an air of peaceful acceptance. He wrote to them with affection – though some commentators believed that he was secretly gloating over the misery he had brought down on them. It has also been observed that Haigh seemed to feel as little pity for himself as he had for his victims.

The letters treated the approaching execution as a sad, tiresome event. Haigh neither reproached nor justified anyone, least of all himself.

His final letter, on the eve of execution, began:

'My Dearest Mum and Dad. Thank you for your very touching letter which I received this morning and which will, I suppose be your last . . .'

Haigh went on to say that though he found some parts of his Plymouth Brethren upbringing restrictive, 'there was much that was lovely'. He spoke of a 'sweet little note' he had received from someone, then raised himself into the kind of grandiloquent terms in which his father had always spoken.

Killer: John George Haigh

My mission

'We cannot change the inscrutable predictions of the Eternal . . . I, that is my spirit, shall remain earthbound for some time: my mission is not yet fulfilled . . .'

Haigh did not explain what this 'mission' was. The letter went on to describe how to switch the short-band channel of his radio to pick up American stations. This would be among the possessions sent to his family after his death.

There was no trace in the letter of any link in Haigh's mind between those 'lovely' days in childhood and the savagery of his criminal career. But Haigh himself had always aimed at leaving no trace – and boasted of this to the Chelsea police in February 1949.

In the end, the only mystery he kept was what he was truly thinking. The poise that had briefly deserted him returned.

Smiling brightly, Haigh was executed at 9 a.m. on 10 August 1949. Hundreds of people were crowded outside the gates of Wandsworth Prison when the official notice was put up. He was buried, as was customary in cases of execution inside the precincts of the prison walls.

On her death-bed, Haigh's mother, Emily, a broken woman, passed her son's letters to a friend for safekeeping, saying:

'We used to despise the people in the village because we thought we were God's elect.

'But we we're not.'

CASE FILE: HAIGH, JOHN GEORGE

BACKGROUND

John George Haigh was born in Stamford, Lincolnshire, on 24 July 1909. His parents were strict members of the fundamentalist Christian sect known as the Plymouth Brethren, and their religious views dominated Haigh's childhood.

Seeking to build a household 'that no wordly evil can penetrate', John and Emily Haigh banned newspapers, radio and even simple entertainments from the house. George, as they called their son, was forbidden to play sports away from school and was always dressed formally.

The family held prayer readings from the Bible at home every day, and George was brought up to believe in the complete, literal truth of the Bible – wars, slaughters, sacrifices and all. 'From my earliest years, my recollection is of my father saying "Do not" or "Thou Shalt not",' Haigh would later say.

Much of Haigh's boyhood was spent in Yorkshire, near Outwood Colliery, where his father was a foreman. As he grew older, George rarely mixed with other children, apart from at school. His parents looked down their noses at neighbours and would have nothing to do with those who were not involved with the Plymouth Brethren.

Grand visions

Outwardly, Haigh was cheerful and well-behaved – some parents would feel suspiciously so – but inwardly he wrestled with some of his father's grander visions. Haigh Senior had a blue scar on his forehead from having once been hit by a chip of flying coal. It was the 'Mark of Satan', he told young George. 'I have sinned and been punished,' he said. 'If you ever sin, Satan will do likewise.'

The boy was also repeatedly told that his mother, to whom he remained deeply attached, was literally an angel with wings. It was a story that was to remain printed indelibly on his mind.

At school Haigh was extremely lazy, almost ignoring those subjects he did not like, though he did show a flair for sciences. He soon became aware of the fact that he could lie easily, get away with it and not be punished – either by God or man. It was also at school that he developed his talent for forgery. It started off as a game but it was a gift that became crucial in his life of crime.

A more pleasant side of Haigh's character was his musical talent. Throughout his life his love of music and ability as a pianist won him many friends.

At 17, with no qualifications, Haigh left school. His first employer commented, 'He was lazy, he was always late. But he had a charm. I had to like him.'

In no time, the choir boy had become a con-man, first by stealing cars and then by obtaining money on hire-purchase agreements with fictitious addresses.

Spells in prison soon followed but, released from jail for a third time in September 1943. Haigh was even more determined to make his mark on the world. He got a job as a salesman for a small fancy goods manufacturer based in Crawley.

He soon began to gather a socially acceptable circle of friends. But in spite of the pleasant life in Sussex, Haigh was drawn back to the bright lights of London in the summer of 1944. He rented a bedsit and, with his savings, formed a company called Union Group Engineering at 79 Queen's Gate Terrace.

It was soon after this that he met William McSwann, for whom he had worked in 1936. As it turned out it was a fateful meeting for both of them.

PSYCHOLOGICAL PROFILE

Was John George Haigh insane?

Haigh's crimes baffled people by combining petty, calculating thefts, brutal violence and his bizarre methods of destroying the evidence. To this, he added his claim of vampirism.

In 1949, criminals were punished if they knew 'the nature and quality' of their crimes. But if they suffered from 'such defect of reason from disease of the mind' that they did not grasp fully what they were doing, they could still be convicted of offences, but spared the severest punishment.

These definitions were set out in the 'M'Naghten Rules' in 1843, following an attempt to kill the then Prime Minister, Sir Robert Peel, by a deranged assassin, Daniel M'Naghten.

Vampire?

Haigh never claimed that he was mad simply because he had killed six, possibly nine, people. The law has never recognised this approach to sanity.

Instead, he claimed he was a vampire.

It is easy to see the way his mind was working – what normal person kills up to nine people in cold blood, drinks their blood, drinks his own urine in prison – as he claimed to – remains cool, calm and smiling while the police net closes in on him, and compares himself to a German dictator, Hilter, and a Chinese philosopher, Confucius?

Haigh's solicitors recognized that much of this behaviour was merely odd, or perhaps perverse, but hardly enough to let their client escape the gallows.

The psychiatric evidence at his trial concentrated on Haigh's claims to have drunk his victims' blood, his fantasies and dreams, and on the scars of his fanatically religious upbringing.

Punishable acts

The only defence witness was Dr Henry Yellowlees, who spent only a very short period talking to Haigh in a prison cell. Yellowlees appears to have accepted that Haigh had dream-visions of forests turning into blood pouring down a crucifix, and told the court that Haigh was suffering from paranoia.

Yellowlees called this condition a 'disease' but was unable to convince the jury that Haigh had not known 'the meaning and quality' of his crimes. On the contrary, it was quite obvious that Haigh knew that killing, theft, forgery and destroying evidence were all against the law, and punishable.

Disconnected

The drift of opinion inside and outside court was that Haigh was inventing stories of vampirism, and of drinking his own urine, purely to save his neck. This impersonation of madness failed, and Haigh was convicted and hanged.

But psychiatrists and many other people have never been convinced that Haigh was just a callous killer trying to con the authorities.

One forensic psychiatrist has written that Haigh may have been so disturbed as to be disconnected from reality and all normal feelings, a condition that would explain his complete lack of concern for his victims.

Macbeth complex

This form of madness would not produce the symptoms of a raving lunatic.

Haigh's strange state of mind has led commentators to other murky theories about the mind. Some have spoken of a 'Macbeth complex' in which Haigh kept his hands spotlessly clean to free himself from guilt. Others have said that his parents' strict religious views encouraged him to feel sinful at such an early age that he spent the rest of his life searching for punishment.

One psychiatrist of the time believed Haigh could have saved himself by being less sly.

'Possibly Haigh did set out to feign insanity, not knowing he was already mad,' he wrote. 'If so, many people were taken in by it. They thought they saw through the sham, but missed the real madness beneath.'

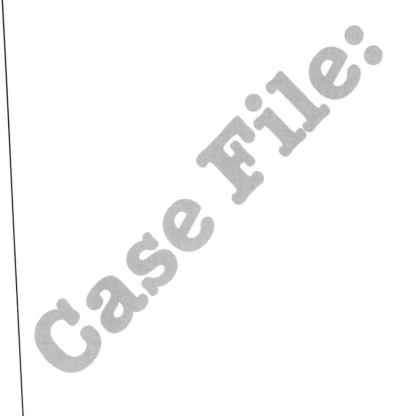

Chapter 16

DR HAWLEY HARVEY CRIPPEN

THE MILD-MANNERED MURDERER

The unassuming Dr Crippen fell in love with his secretary, but was tied to his wife whom he hated. The solution he chose was murder. In an escape bid that involved a catalogue of unbelievable mistakes, and a sea-chase spanning two continents, he came within a hair's breadth of success.

On 31 March 1910, Mrs Louise Smythson went to New Scotland Yard to report the disappearance of an old friend of hers called Cora Crippen. Cora – or to use her stage name as a music hall artiste, Belle Elmore – had last been seen exactly two months before by her friends and then, in an utterly uncharacteristic move, she had suddenly gone to America. She had given no advance warning to any of her friends, sent no form of communication to them on arrival and given no forwarding address for them if they needed to get in touch with her.

The first time that any of them were told of her departure had been on 2 February 1910, when a letter was delivered to the committee of the Music Hall Ladies' Guild of which she was the Honorary Treasurer. It announced that, because of the illness of a relative in America, she had to leave at very short notice and was hence resigning her position. She was in such haste that the letter had been written for her by her husband.

Just over a month later, her husband had announced that Cora was dangerously ill and a week later that her condition was critical, with double pleuro-pneumonia. On 24 March, he sent a telegram to one of Cora's closest friends announcing that she had died. Two days later he published an obituary notice in *Era*, the theatrical weekly newspaper.

Killer: Dr Hawley Harvey Crippen

Suspicious story

Cora's husband's behaviour was causing the greatest suspicion. All the information about Cora Crippen's whereabouts came through him and him alone, and yet he seemed unsure of where she was at any given time before she died.

He was even unsure of the details of her death. Although it was common knowledge to all Cora's friends that her relations were based around New York, her husband said she would be going to California instead. Only the husband himself had relations in California. His story seemed to be tripping itself up at every step.

He showed no intention of going out to America to deal with the funeral arrangements, saying that his wife would be cremated and her remains sent home. Friends who knew that Cora Crippen was a Catholic thought it strange that she should be cremated. Most condemning of all, Cora's husband now had a girlfriend, his secretary from work, living with him at his home. She appeared with him in public and had even taken to wearing his wife's jewellery. There was even a rumour that Cora's jewellery was being pawned. For her theatrical friends other circumstances were far too unusual to be left unreported. For Chief Detective Inspector Walter Dew, however, the facts were not yet convincing enough to justify an inquiry.

Dew explained that the number of missing persons in London was enormous and that he would need more evidence before feeling it necessary to take the matter up. He also pointed out that Cora Crippen had quite possibly eloped because of the difficulty she would have had trying to get a divorce. With regard to the apparent confusion of her husband's story, Dew suggested that it was because he was in a state of shock.

Same suspicions

Three months later, an American couple, Mr and Mrs John Nash, arrived at New Scotland Yard with the same story. They had just returned from a tour of American music halls only to find that Cora Crippen had rushed off to America in their absence and had since died there. When they went to see her husband about it, they found his manner suspicious and his explanation of events unsatisfactory. On this occasion, it was decided that Chief Inspector Dew should take matters further and go to see Dr Hawley Harvey Crippen of 39 Hilldrop Crescent, Holloway, North London.

Police visit

When Dew called at Hilldrop Crescent, Dr Crippen was at work in Central London and the Inspector instead spoke to his girlfriend, Miss Ethel Le Neve. He later described her as being quite attractive and neatly dressed. He also noticed that she was wearing a distinctive diamond brooch, which matched the description of one that had once belonged to Cora Crippen.

Inspector Dew and his sergeant then travelled into London to see the doctor at his office in New Oxford Street. Crippen was almost welcoming and appeared happy to tell the policemen all that he knew.

The majority of Crippen's statement was taken down in between his medical consultations and his tooth extractions. Crippen would dictate to the policemen for a while, return to his surgery and then come back to dictate some more. He admitted that Ethel Le Neve was his mistress and that their relationship had begun long before his wife had disappeared. He also conceded that his marriage to Cora Crippen had been far from happy.

More than this, Crippen admitted that the story of his wife's death had been a lie – it was to cover up for the fact of their failed relationship. The truth was that Cora had indeed gone to America, but she had gone to live with an old lover from the music hall stage, named Bruce Miller. It was because of the embarrassment of the break-up of their marriage, and because he wanted to protect his wife's reputation in front of her friends, that he had made up his original story.

The two policemen returned with Crippen to Hilldrop Crescent, where they made a cursory search. Finding nothing suspicious, Dew insisted that Crippen attempt to get in touch with his wife in America. Crippen appeared to do this, and even drafted an advertisement to be placed in the American newspapers, calling for Kunigunde Mackamotzki (Cora Crippen's maiden name) to contact Hawley Harvey Crippen. Inspector Dew left Crippen's house at 8.00 p.m. that night after getting Crippen to sign the statement he had just given.

Dew's interview with Crippen had taken place on Friday, 8 July and had lasted for nearly eight hours. Over the weekend, Inspector Dew examined Crippen's statement in detail.

Mis-match

Although there were a number of points he wished to clear up, his suspicions were not great. Crippen's marriage to Cora was well-known as a mismatch. It was also known that she had flirted outrageously with a number of young men over the last ten years. It was by no means impossible that she had become bored with her meek and subservient husband.

In fact, Inspector Dew had actively enjoyed Crippen's company, going with him to an Italian restaurant for lunch. 'Crippen made a hearty meal,' said Dew afterwards, 'and ate it with the relish of a man who hadn't a care in the world.'

On the following Monday, Dew returned to Hilldrop Crescent to talk to Dr Crippen, but was surprised to find the house empty. He checked at Crippen's office and was told that the doctor had not been in that day.

Killer: Dr Hawley Harvey Crippen

Two-day search

Inspector Dew ordered a complete search of the three-storey, nine-room house. Nothing of significance was found, so Dew turned his attention to the garden. It was the height of summer and the garden was in full bloom, but Dew and his colleagues dug up every rose bush, pulled up every flower and turned over every inch of soil, but all to no avail. After two full days of searching, the only room that had been left untouched was the tiny coal cellar, situated at the end of a short, gloomy corridor leading from the kitchen to the back door.

The cellar was dark and dusty. A small pile of coal lay in one corner; in another was a collection of branches. Dew got down on his hands and knees, and pried between the crevices of the brick floor. The mortar was old and loose and several bricks came up easily, revealing a bed of clay beneath the floor.

After digging about six inches, a nauseating smell filled the cellar, forcing Dew and his sergeant out into the garden for fresh air. Digging down a little further, they came across a shallow pit filled with a mass of human flesh, which had been covered in lime. Dew dug no further. Whether the remains were all that was left of Cora Crippen was not certain. Regardless of this, Dr Crippen and Ethel Le Neve were now under suspicion of murder.

KILLING FOR LOVE

Ethel Le Neve met Crippen when she was in her late teens. She lived at home in Camden Town where her family name was Neave – like Cora with her stage name of Belle Elmore, Ethel had made the French alterations as an affectation. Her elder sister, Nina, worked at the Drouet Institute for the Deaf in Kingsway, where Crippen was employed as consultant physician. When Nina left to get married, Ethel followed her as Crippen's private secretary.

Despite later claims that Crippen seduced Ethel and that she was clay in his hands, the relationship in fact developed gradually and on a foundation of mutual respect and then love. It was not until five years after they had first met each other that they slept together.

For Crippen, the relationship supplied a refuge from his own marriage, which was crumbling rapidly. Cora's extravagance and selfishness had increased since her lover, Bruce Miller, had returned to the United States. Despite the fact that Crippen had supplied her with virtually anything she wanted – including a collection of jewellery that was the envy of her friends – she had absolutely no respect for him. When he explained to her that he was in financial difficulties, her reaction was to go out at once and buy a new wardrobe of clothes.

Although she had failed in her dreams to become a music hall star, Cora compensated for this with her considerable social energy. Her forceful personality as well as her work on the committee of the Music Hall Ladies' Guild brought her in touch with the great names of the day, including her own heroine, Marie Lloyd. There were many visitors to Hilldrop Crescent, all of whom noticed how quiet and unassuming Dr Crippen was in comparison to his wife. There was no question in any of their friends' mind about who the dominant partner in the relationship was.

In 1906, Cora advertised for paying guests at Hilldrop Crescent so that she would have something to do to occupy herself. Four German students came to stay, one of whom, William Ehrlich, became a particular favourite of Cora's. Ehrlich noticed the degree of degradation that Crippen suffered at the hands of his wife. 'The doctor never lost his temper though his wife's reproaches were frequently unjustified,' he said afterwards. 'The husband must have possessed an extraordinary amount of self-control to endure his wife's stinging sarcasms for so long.' The degradation became all the worse when, in November 1906, Crippen returned to Hilldrop Crescent early one day to find Ehrlich in bed with his wife.

Silent hostility

Crippen hoped that Cora would at some stage leave Hilldrop Crescent and go and live with Bruce Miller. But she did not, and as the years went by, an atmosphere of silent hostility took over the house. Whereas Crippen and Cora had once kept up a pretence of fondness for each other in the company of other people, by 1908 they scarcely talked to each other.

Most of Crippen's time was taken up working for 'The Yale Tooth Specialists', where he had formed a partnership with an American named Dr Gilbert Rylance, who had a degree in dentistry. Rylance claimed that Crippen's role was merely to deal with the business side of the partnership, and that he played no active part in the dentistry itself. Rylance later described him as 'a smart man and wonderful organizer, very exact, with fine business methods'.

Jealous

But, according to Ethel Le Neve's father, Crippen had a far more direct involvement in the surgery. Assisted by Ethel, he carried out the extraction of teeth himself.

For Cora Crippen, the thought of her husband and Ethel Le Neve working so close together on a daily basis made her angry and jealous. She also disapproved of Crippen moving away from the practice of homoeopathy, which she felt was his best chance of earning the sort of money to which she had become accustomed. She was convinced that her husband's decision to set up the 'Yale Tooth Specialists' – a second-rate company that was destined to fail, in her opinion – had been influenced by Ethel Le Neve.

Cora Crippen had maintained a scornful indifference to her husband's affair with his secretary up until now. But with Ethel Le Neve starting to make Crippen's decisions for him, indifference was strengthening into an active dislike.

Ethel, in the meantime, was growing more and more unhappy about the situation. Although at first she had been prepared to play the part of the mistress, she had been trying to persuade Crippen to leave his wife as early as 1906. Ethel also found it painful to think that while she might spend much of the day with Crippen, he would return to Hilldrop Crescent every night.

She left home, first moving to her sister's house and then to a house in Highgate. In 1909, an unexpected development took place that Ethel believed would force the issue. She became pregnant. Even if Cora did not take off after Bruce Miller, she felt sure that Crippen would have no option but to leave his wife and marry her.

Miscarriage

In March of 1909, Ethel had a miscarriage. Cora Crippen who had known of her husband's relationship with his secretary for some time, found it a good opportunity to rub salt into the wound. Referring to Ethel as 'the little typewriter', she spread the rumour among her friends at the Music Hall Ladies' Guild that Ethel had had an abortion to spite Crippen. She even suggested that it was difficult to be sure who the father was. Crippen had learnt to be on the end of his wife's biting remarks, but it was another matter when they were aimed at the girl he loved.

On 19 January 1910, Dr Crippen went to William and Burroughs, his local chemist in New Oxford Street, and bought five grains of hyoscine (poison crystals). A fortnight later, on 31 January, he invited some friends, Paul and Clara Martinetti, to dinner at Hilldrop Crescent. When they left the house at 1.30 a.m. they were the last people, apart from Crippen himself, to see Cora Crippen alive.

Later that day, Ethel Le Neve arrived at work to find a message from Crippen left on her typewriter: '*B.E. has gone America . . . Shall be in later, when we can arrange for a pleasant little evening.*'

Complete folly

After that began a period, lasting over five months, of what with hindsight was complete folly. A day after Cora's disappearance, Ethel spent the first night at Hilldrop Crescent. She did not doubt what Crippen had told her about his wife's sudden departure to America and on 12 March, moved into Hilldrop Crescent on a permanent basis.

On 20 February, Ethel went with Crippen to the Criterion Ball, rubbing shoulders with Cora's theatrical friends and wearing her Rising Sun brooch. They walked together on the Holloway Road and went on holidays to Dieppe and Boulogne. Crippen announced the death of his wife by sending a telegram from Victoria Station, where he and Ethel were on their way to a holiday in Dieppe.

When the friends of Cora Crippen were confronted with the fact of her death, they were less than convinced. Despite informing the police of their misgivings, it was some time before Inspector Walter Dew appeared on the doorstep of 39 Hilldrop Crescent.

The police visit convinced Crippen that he and Ethel had to leave Hilldrop Crescent. The reason he gave Ethel was that the neighbours, particularly the Music Hall Ladies' Guild, would start gossip. He doubted he could face the office staff again now that they knew the police had been to see him. Their lives would be a misery. They must go away and start a new life.

Inspector Dew had spoken to Ethel on her own and had told her of Crippen's admission that Cora's death in America had been a lie. She was angry that Crippen had told her a direct lie for the first time, but she seemed to accept that he did not know where Cora was.

Strange disguise

It was while they were still at Hilldrop Crescent that the two of them decided that Ethel should travel disguised as a boy. Crippen has been described as a cold-blooded and ruthless murderer, but his plotting did not work well in this case and was comic rather than calculating. He roughly cut off Ethel's hair, and sent out one of his employees to buy a boy's suit. It was too small, and Ethel split the trousers the moment she put them on.

They never returned to Hilldrop Crescent. Arranging to leave the office separately, they met at Chancery Lane tube station and then went on to Liverpool Street to catch the train to Harwich.

They caught the night boat to Holland. In Rotterdam, Crippen took Ethel to have her hair cut properly. By this time, he had shaved off his moustache. Ethel had left her bowler hat on the boat and so a new straw one had to be bought for her. They went on to Brussels, where they stayed for ten days at the Hotel des Ardennes.

At first, Crippen planned to return to England and get a boat from Hull to America. He then saw an advertisement for boats sailing from Antwerp to Quebec and booked two second class berths, sailing on 31 July 1910. But on 15 July, he saw in the Belgian newspapers that the remains of Cora Crippen had been discovered and that the search was on for them. He returned straight to the booking office and changed the tickets to the earlier sailing of 20 July. They travelled under the assumed names of John Philo Robinson and Master John Robinson.

They tried to be as unobtrusive as possible, but inevitably had to mix with the other passengers and crew, including sharing dinner with the master of the *Montrose*, Captain Henry Kendall. It did not occur to Crippen that, by dressing Ethel up as a boy, they had made the fatal blunder in their attempt to escape.

TRANSATLANTIC MANHUNT

Captain Henry Kendall did not get a chance to introduce himself to the two passengers, John Philo Robinson and his son John, until the *Montrose* was out at sea. It immediately struck him that there was something odd about the couple. The boy's figure was strange – broad hips, small feet and delicate white hands. Kendall also noticed that although the father was not wearing spectacles he had the red marks on either side of the bridge of his nose that were the giveaway sign of someone who normally wore them.

He invited the pair to share lunch at his table and, during the meal, found an excuse to go to their cabin and make a search. He noticed that they had only a single suitcase between them and that the boy did not even possess an overcoat for the journey.

Later on that same day, Kendall went to look at a back copy of the *Daily Mail*, dated 14 July, which carried photographs of Dr Hawley Harvey Crippen and Ethel Le Neve. By closely examining the faces in each picture, Kendall became convinced that the two passengers he had just met were wanted in connection with the murder of Cora Crippen in London.

The following morning, Kendall took the Chief Officer into his confidence. When they were 130 miles west of the Lizard, Captain Kendall handed the radio operator the message that was to lead to one of the most publicized sea chases of all time.

Vital break

The telegram was passed from the Liverpool ship owners directly to New Scotland Yard, where it came into the hands of Inspector Walter Dew. For Dew it was the break he had desperately needed. It had been ten days since the discovery of Cora Crippen's body, and as every day passed it had seemed increasingly likely that Crippen and Le Neve would manage to get away.

By taking the White Star liner *Laurentic*, which left from Liverpool the following day, there was a good chance that Dew would arrive in Quebec ahead of Crippen. Although the *Montrose* had a three-day start, the *Laurentic's* running time was four days shorter. Dew persuaded his superior, the Assistant Commissioner, Sir Melville Macnaghten, that Captain Kendall's telegram was worth acting on and, after receiving his written authorization, he left London for Liverpool. He boarded the *Laurentic* travelling under the assumed name of Dewhurst.

Initially, there was doubt about the reliability of Captain Kendall's judgement. Inspector Dew was taking a risk of major public embarrassment if he arrived in Canada to find that he had been chasing the wrong couple. The police code name given to his journey was 'Operation Handcuffs' and it began in utmost secrecy. Even Dew's wife was not told of the purpose of her husband's journey before he left.

Positive identification

The police became confident that they had made the right decision after photographs of Ethel Le Neve and Crippen were positively identified by the travel agent who had booked their passage aboard the *Montrose* in Antwerp.

Captain Kendall, in the meantime, had made good use of the Marconi wireless system on board the ship to pass back a stream of reports about the couple to the *Daily Mail* and other newspapers. The public learned from Kendall that Crippen was growing a beard and 'looking more like a farmer every day', and that everything Ethel did made it more and more obvious that she was a girl.

Kendall was also kept busy making sure that neither Crippen nor Ethel became suspicious that they had been recognized. 'They have been under strict observation all the voyage, as, if they smelt a rat, he might do something rash,' Captain Kendall relayed to the press. He went around the ship removing all the English papers that mentioned anything about the murder.

Detective work

At the same time, Kendall tried to obtain further small items of proof as to the couple's real identity. He would call them as they walked on deck, using their assumed names, to see how slow they were to recognize them. On several occasions, it was only Ethel who turned to the Captain, and then apologized, saying the cold weather had made Dr Crippen go slightly deaf. Kendall had also read in the newspapers that Crippen had lived in San Francisco, Detroit and Toronto. By bringing them up in conversation, he confirmed that John Philo Robinson was familiar with these places.

Crippen and Ethel Le Neve were unaware of the fact that the attention of the world's press was being focused on their transatlantic journey to Canada. Ethel was confident that her identity remained hidden. 'It never entered my head,' she wrote afterwards, 'that the ship's officers had discovered my disguise.' To keep up pretences, she made friends with one of the boys on board the *Montrose*.

For most of the journey, Crippen was relaxed and seemingly confident about the future. Only once were his suspicions raised, as he overheard the wireless operator sending a dispatch. When he asked who the message was for, the wireless operator quickly said that he was asking the skipper of another ship whether any ice had been spotted near where they were heading.

Depression

Two days before *Montrose* was due to reach Father Point, Crippen's optimism left him. He gave Ethel all their money, telling her that he might have to leave her when they reached Canada. He suggested that she should go to Toronto and get a job as a secretary. She interpreted this as meaning Crippen would go ahead to find them somewhere to live. But his intentions seemed to be different. After his arrest, a note was found on the back of a visiting card that he had printed in Brussels in the name of John Robinson:

> 'I can't stand the horror I go through every night any longer, and as I see nothing bright ahead and money has come to an end, I have made up my mind to jump overboard tonight. I know I have spoiled your life, but I hope some day you can learn to forgive me. With last words of love, Your H.'

End of the chase

At his trial, Crippen denied he intended to commit suicide, which itself was a criminal offence. He said that a friendly quarter-master had agreed to stow him away when the ship reached Montreal, and that the note would throw Dew off the trail.

By the time the *Montrose* reached Father Point, the chase was over. Inspector Dew had already arrived and, disguised as a pilot in a brass-buttoned jacket and visored cap, was waiting to go aboard. While journalists stood by on a nearby pilot boat, Dew and a number of Canadian policemen approached Crippen.

'Good morning, Dr Crippen,' was all that Dew needed to say. Crippen's face showed doubt and uncertainty, as he recognized the officer who had interviewed him only three weeks before at his home in London. He asked what he was being arrested for, and then grabbed the warrant from the hands of one of the Canadian policemen. 'Murder and mutilation, oh God!' he said, before being manacled.

After spending 19 days in prison in Montreal, Crippen and Ethel Le Neve were brought back to England by Dew on the *Megantic*. They were kept separate during the voyage expect on one brief occasion, when Dew allowed them to meet. On 28 August 1910, they arrived in Liverpool.

COURTROOM THEATRE

Throughout the voyage back to England, Dr Crippen seemed only concerned with Ethel Le Neve's welfare, and in establishing her innocence. When they arrived at Liverpool docks on 28 August 1910, a large crowd was waiting for them.

Inspector Dew brought Crippen down the gangplank first, where a young man launched himself at Crippen waving a cane and had to be pulled away by the police. Ethel Le Neve followed, wearing a blue veil. They caught the 2.20 p.m. train to London. At Euston Station, they were met by jeering, threatening crowds, before being driven to Bow Street police station.

Corrupt defence

The next day, Travers Humphreys, appearing for the Director of Public Prosecutions, asked that the pair be remanded in custody for one week. Crippen already had a solicitor, Arthur Newton, who had volunteered to defend Crippen while he was still awaiting extradition in Montreal. Crippen had agreed willingly, not knowing the real intentions behind Newton's offer. Newton regarded Crippen's crime as a 'professional speculation', which would enable him to pay off his racing debts. He saw Crippen's trial as an opportunity to enhance his own reputation and also make money.

Newton was already renowned as a dishonest solicitor. Five years before, he had been jailed for six weeks for attempting to persuade certain key trial witnesses to leave the country. It was an enormous piece of ill-fortune for Crippen. Properly defended, he might just have escaped the gallows. As it was, by a combination of Newton and his own pigheadedness, he had no chance.

It was also bad luck for Crippen that Edward Marshall Hall, the outstanding defending barrister of his generation, was away on holiday. Newton had approached his clerk, but they disagreed over how Marshall Hall was to be paid. Given the celebrity of the case, it is likely that Marshall Hall would have reached some sort of compromise if he had been there. Instead, Newton walked straight out of his clerk's office and ten minutes later was briefing another solicitor, Alfred Tobin. Unfortunately for Crippen, Tobin lacked any of the flair and experience that might have been provided by Marshall Hall.

Killer: Dr Hawley Harvey Crippen

Death wish

Tobin had another problem. Dr Crippen seemed to have a death wish. He was receiving a very bad press – everyone was convinced that he was guilty and he was doing nothing to help himself. But he did have the beginnings of a defence. All he really had to do was admit to everything except the murder, making the most of Cora Crippen's infidelity, bad temper and drinking habits. With a strong defence barrister, there was the possibility of a manslaughter verdict, or even a defence on the grounds of accident. But he still insisted that the body found in the coal cellar at Hilldrop Crescent was not that of his wife.

The prosecution, meanwhile, had problems of its own. Inspector Dew, after his return from Canada, had slid into something approaching torpor, and was having to be chased to produce the evidence. The prosecution wanted proof that the pyjama top in which the body had been wrapped, could not have been bought before the Crippens moved into Hilldrop Crescent in 1905. Dew eventually provided evidence that it could not have been bought earlier than 1906. Crippen could not explain this away.

Over 4,000 applications were received for seats for the trial and 700 were granted. The trial opened at the Old Bailey on Tuesday, 18 October 1910. It had already been decided that Ethel should have separate counsel for her trial, which was to follow immediately after Crippen's.

The medical evidence was secure. Bernard Spilsbury, who was to become the greatest pathologist of his era, was at the start of his career. He was able to show that there was a scar on the flesh found in the coal cellar, which matched that of an operation Cora Crippen had undergone to remove one of her ovaries.

Crippen did as well as could be expected in the witness box. He stood up well to the relentless cross-examination. But he could not explain where his wife had gone, nor how the body, whose death occurred after the Crippens had moved in, found its way into his cellar. The newspapers were enthusiastic about his performance. 'Marvellous exhibition of nerve power,' said the *Daily Mail*, but it was of no help. On the fourth day, the jury retired, and returned after only 27 minutes of consideration to find Crippen guilty of wilful murder.

Lord Chief Justice Alverstone decided not to dwell on the 'ghastly and wicked nature of the crime.' After the judge's marshal had placed the black cap on his head. Lord Alverstone ordered that Hawley Harvey Crippen be 'taken from hence to a lawful prison, and from thence to a place of execution, and that you there be hanged by the neck until you are dead.'

Crippen showed no emotion. When asked if he had anything to say, he replied. 'I still protest my innocence.'

The trial of Ethel Le Neve was very different. She was represented by the outstanding F.E. Smith, later Lord Birkenhead.

Cross examination

In contrast to the plodding Tobin, Smith's was a brilliant performance. He made no attempt to conceal that she had been Crippen's mistress. The prosecution had emphasized that Ethel had gone into a decline at the time of Cora Crippen's death, implying that she was wracked by guilt and must have known about the murder. When Smith cross-examined Mrs Jackson, Ethel's former landlady, it became clear that Ethel was depressed *before* Cora's death and had then recovered. Was it not natural she should do so hearing that her lover's wife had left him?

Ethel Le Neve was acquitted and Lord Chief Justice Alverstone, who had also presided over Crippen's trial, congratulated Smith. But he never heard a word of thanks from Ethel.

COLD JUSTICE

After his conviction, Dr Crippen was sent to Pentonville Prison to await the hangman. He had only one real chance of the decision being reversed, and that was at the appeal hearing on Friday, 4 November. Crippen at first allowed himself some optimism, but when the Criminal Court of Appeal upheld his conviction, he gave up all hope.

Most of Crippen's time at Pentonville was spent thinking about Ethel Le Neve. He wrote a dozen letters to her in the month between his conviction and execution. Most of these were concerned with practical matters, such as how she would cope financially after his death and whether she would take his name in memory of him. She wrote him letters in return, but in accordance with Crippen's instructions, they were not kept. Along with his photograph of Ethel, they were buried with him after his execution on 23 November.

On the same day as Crippen's appeal, Ethel earned herself some money by posing for a magazine called *Lloyd's Weekly News*. She agreed to dress up in the same boy's outfit that she had worn during her escape aboard the *Montrose*. To some, this was evidence of her insensitivity and proved that she did not care about Crippen's fate. But she had already sold her life story to the same publication with Crippen's approval. 'You have, my wifie, most ably set forth important facts that must tell with great weight in the minds of the unprejudiced,' he wrote to her.

Mood of sympathy

After the initial hostility to Crippen, the public mood began to swing more and more towards sympathy as the date for his execution approached. A number of petitions calling for Crippen's reprieve, with over 15,000 signatures, were delivered to the Home Office. Arthur Newton said that hundreds of other signatures were arriving daily.

On 18 November, Crippen's 88 year-old father, Myron, died in Los Angeles. He had been living in poverty for some months, since Crippen's flight had cut off his remittance. The rooming-house keeper had allowed Myron to remain there rent-free and a local restaurant had sent him free meals. The *Coldwater Chronicle* reported that his death had been hastened by grief over his son's crime.

Reprieve failure

On 19 November, Winston Churchill, the Home Secretary who had been a spectator during the Crippen/Le Neve trials, turned down Crippen's petition for a reprieve. The news was delivered personally to Crippen in his cell by the governor of Pentonville prison, Major H. E. Mytton-Davies.

Like Inspector Dew before him, Mytton-Davies had developed a sympathy for Crippen that bordered on friendship. He also delivered personally Ethel Le Neve's final telegram at midnight on Tuesday, 22 November. When Crippen saw the Major for the last time the next morning, he asked him to accept his set of rosary beads and a ring, as a sign of appreciation for the consideration shown to him.

During the last few days the strain began to tell on Crippen. Having shown a healthy appetite in the days leading up to the reprieve application, he now began to look noticeably unwell. Two days before his execution, Crippen worked out a plan to commit suicide. But one of the warders noticed that part of his spectacles frame was missing and made a search of Crippen's clothes.

While he was in the lavatory, Crippen had broken off the steel arm of his spectacles and had hidden it in the inside seam at the bottom of his trouser leg. Crippen had intended to puncture an artery and bleed slowly to death while he slept on the eve of his execution.

Final farewell

Crippen saw Ethel Le Neve for the last time on 22 November. On the morning of Wednesday, 23 November 1910, he was hanged by the Chief Executioner, James Ellis, assisted by William Willis. No bell was rung because three other prisoners were awaiting execution after Crippen. A notice was posted outside the prison shortly after 9 a.m. where a large crowd was waiting.

While Crippen was being hanged, Ethel Le Neve, travelling as Miss Allen, was boarding the liner *Majestic*, bound for New York.

CASE FILE: CRIPPEN, HAWLEY HARVEY

BACKGROUND

Hawley Harvey Crippen was the son of a respectable family from Coldwater, Michigan. His grandfather, Philo, ran the local dry goods store, building up the business to be inherited by his father, Myron. Coldwater grew and the Crippen family grew with it. By the time of Hawley's birth in 1862, the store and house were the biggest in the town.

Hawley was an only child, and, coming from the richest family in town, he grew up spoilt and conceited. From his childhood, he was set on emulating his Uncle Bradley, Coldwater's family physician. Hawley attended the local school during the week, and read the Bible on Sunday.

His family – and especially his grandfather – were strict Christians, following a grim, strict and unforgiving Protestantism. After chapel every Sunday, Philo Crippen took his grandson on his knee, and sternly read him long passages from the Old Testament, drumming the Book of Proverbs or Isaiah, with their emphasis on the sins of the flesh, into the young child.

Crippen took his degree at the University of Michigan, and qualified as a doctor at the Homoeopathic Hospital in Cleveland, Ohio. It was not, however, a qualification that would have allowed him to practise in England without taking further examinations. It was whilst he was doing his internship at a Manhattan hospital that he married Charlotte Bell, then a student nurse.

Marital breakdown

The marriage seems to have been a failure. Charlotte, originally from Ireland, was born and brought up in a convent, and remained strongly Catholic all her life. Crippen's excitement at finally discovering the sins of the flesh quickly palled, with his wife visiting the confessional every time they slept together.

They travelled west to San Diego, where in 1888, Charlotte gave birth to a boy, Otto Hawley Crippen. Then four years later, after a journey to Salt Lake City, Charlotte died of apoplexy in the bitter cold of a Utah January. She had been due to give birth a few days later. Otto was sent to live with his grandparents in San Jose, California, while Crippen returned to New York, and opened a new practice.

It was six months later in July 1892, at his Brooklyn surgery, that Crippen first met his second wife. Kunigunde Mackamotzki, by then known as Cora Turner, was a bright 19 year-old, of Middle European stock. To the prematurely balding, 30 year-old widower, she was a creature to be nurtured and protected. She was impetuous, and her ruggedness and good humour appealed to him. In sharp contrast, Cora loved him for his distinguished air, his dependability and the security he offered.

Brief courtship

After a brief, six week courtship, they married on 1 September 1892, in New Jersey. But from the first, things went awry. Almost immediately, Cora had to have an operation to remove her ovaries. Now, to the deep disappointment of them both, she could no longer have children.

The early 1890s was a period of economic unrest in America. Homoepathic and conventional medicine alike were under financial strain. Doctors' bills went unpaid. Cora was forced to abandon the operatic singing lessons she had been taking since childhood, and, for a time, Crippen had to move in with her family.

The sharp-witted Cora soon realized that the New York public simply did not have the money for homoeopathic remedies, and she persuaded her husband to sacrifice his principles to become a quack.

Crippen began to sell patent remedies, and soon joined up with another 'quack' doctor, 'Professor' Munyon, running the offices of his Homoeopathic Remedies on East 14th Street. Cora also worked there as cashier, and the couple were forced to sleep in a room above the office.

Within a year, Crippen – described by Munyon as 'one of the most intelligent men I ever knew' – was promoted to general manager at the head office in Philadelphia. He went on to open Munyon's new office in Toronto. When he returned to Philadelphia, Cora left almost at once for New York, surrounded by a bevy of handsome young men.

In 1897, Crippen was offered the London office at an enormous annual salary of $10,000. Cora joined him after four months, hinting that she had had shipboard romances on the journey.

Vaudeville

Cora had long since abandoned her pretensions to opera, and had switched to vaudeville. She called herself Belle Elmore, and, because American acts were all the rage, she managed to find middle-of-the-bill work, earning about £3 a week before expenses.

However, her London debut, under her new stage name of Cora Motzki, at the Old Marylebone Music Hall, ended in failure after a week and her contract was not renewed. She was also putting on a good deal of weight and was known unkindly as 'The Brooklyn Matzos Ball'. She began to blame Crippen for her lack of success.

In this, she was not entirely fair to her husband. He had been neglecting Munyon's business to promote his wife when, out of the blue, he was recalled to Philadelphia. Munyon had discovered that Crippen had been described as 'acting manager' on a handbill for 'Vio and Motzki's Bright Lights Company'. He was sacked.

Love affair

There was worse to come. The Crippen marriage was now in ruins. Cora had taken up with a former boxer, Bruce Miller, now on the music hall circuit. Perhaps even worse, she had developed a taste for drink and an ungovernable temper.

It could never be said that Crippen was not a worker. First he joined another patent pill company, which went bust within the year, then he tried to market his own remedy 'Amorette'.

He set Cora up as a 'miniature painter' at their newer and cheaper flat in Store Street, near the British Museum, and in 1901 he joined the Drouet Institute, which prescribed patent plasters to be stuck behind the ears as a sure cure for deafness.

The firm spent the then enormous sum of between £20,000 and £30,000 a year on advertising what was later described as 'one of the biggest and most ambitious frauds on the deaf ever engineered in this country'. It was here, in 1902, that Crippen first set eyes on Ethel Le Neve.

PSYCHOLOGICAL PROFILE

Dr Crippen's defence during his trial was a blanket denial that the body found in the coal cellar at 39 Hilldrop Crescent was that of his wife. The reason he took this course was almost certainly to protect Ethel Le Neve at all costs from the risk of being prosecuted successfully as his accomplice. As a result, the exact truth of why Crippen murdered his wife – and why he murdered her on that particular night – will never be known.

However, the reasons can be pieced together with some certainty. Most obvious of all is the state of deterioration that Crippen's marriage had reached by the beginning of 1910. Cora Crippen had become a drinking, nagging, domineering, bossy and unfaithful wife. She ridiculed her husband in public and admitted that she scorned him as a partner. In itself, this portrait of Cora supplied what Inspector Walter Dew favoured as the prime motive for Dr Crippen's action: sheer hatred.

Hen-pecked

Yet Crippen was quite used to being the weak partner in the relationship. Psychologically, he was the archetypal hen-pecked husband. He was weak-willed, long suffering and was prepared to go to extremes of generosity to ensure that his wife stayed with him. There was something masochistic about his behaviour.

Because he had allowed this repressed role in the marriage to continue for so long, there had to be another ingredient that would fire him up with a hatred strong enough to want to kill his wife. This ingredient came out of his love for Ethel and his protectiveness towards her. When Cora Crippen began to apply the same scorn on Crippen's mistress as had been dealt out to himself the emotional balance began to tip dramatically.

Fear of divorce

Crippen had been in love with Ethel Le Neve for sometime. They had frequently talked about the possibility of him divorcing Cora, but the social stigma attached to such an action was sufficiently strong to stop them from going ahead. Dr Crippen, after all, had something of a social position in Holloway and risked the possibility of losing his job. In this respect his final resort to murder was fashioned as much by social pressures as by his own feelings.

Without taking the step of divorce the situation became increasingly intolerable. When Cora Crippen began to make disparaging remarks about Ethel, it became clear that the situation would have to change.

Deadly dilemma

Dr Crippen found that he was contending with two overwhelming emotions simultaneously – his love for Ethel and his hatred of his wife. If divorce was likely to be too awkward and too financially messy, Crippen was driven to another option which, if successful would solve all his problems at once.

Another motive that was directed towards Crippen, particularly by the prosecution during the trial, was that he was interested in his wife's money. The grounds for his accusation were the speed with which Crippen had pawned Cora's jewellery after Ethel Le Neve had moved in with him, and the fact that his own job was running into difficulties. Given the fact that Cora's jewellery raised only £175 and that Crippen's salary was a very comfortable £2,500 a year, the argument seems weak.

Chapter 17

DONALD HUME
THE DEADLY FANTASIST

A resourceful liar, he got away with murder after killing his first victim in a fit of rage. Ten years later, he shot dead a taxi driver in Switzerland during the last of his daring bank robberies. He was charming, clever and adventurous, but money seemed to slip through his fingers.

It had turned dark on Tuesday, 4 October 1949 when a dark-haired, slightly chubby man called Donald Hume was returning home with his dog Tony, a shaggy Alsatian cross.

Home was a maisonette above a greengrocers at 620 Finchley Road in north London. Hume lived near Golders Green and had been drinking in a nearby public house. It was 7.30 p.m. The shops were shut, but there were plenty of people bustling around.

As he approached the terraced building, Hume noticed a yellow Citroën parked outside. He tensed. Few people owned Citroën saloons in the lean post-war years, but Hume knew someone who did – a car dealer named Stanley Setty.

Shady dealings

Hume and Setty were partners in some shady dealings on the black market. Through Setty, a 46 year-old Iraqi-born Jew who had useful contacts in several countries, Hume had made a lot of money. At 29, he was beginning, in his own eyes, to make something of himself.

But Hume intensely disliked Setty, who talked down to everyone and wore expensive coats and ties and flamboyant jewellery. The registration number on the Citroën was CJN 444. It was Setty's car. Hume was angry that Setty had come to his home. When they had business to discuss, they usually met at Setty's garage or in nightclubs in the West End. It was always Setty who set up the operations, Setty who knew the contacts, Setty who financed the schemes.

All this made it important that Hume keep his own base independent of Setty. It helped him feel that he was his own man with other interests of which Setty knew nothing. The seven-room maisonette, where Hume lived with his wife Cynthia and their 11 week-old daughter Allison, was the first proper home of his own and he guarded it jealously.

The mere sight of the Citroën angered Hume, and he was a man aroused to fury very easily. But there was another reason why Hume felt affronted by the Citroën. A few weeks before, he had called on Setty at his yard in Cambridge Terrace Mews, in one of the wealthiest parts of London on the east side of Regent's Park. Hume had taken his dog, Tony, with him and, while the two men chatted, the dog had put claw-marks on one of Setty's cars.

Setty had burst into obscene abuse against the dog and kicked it viciously. Tony had whined in pain. Muttering an apology, Hume had petted the animal. But he had been white with anger. Setty either did not know or did not care how much Tony meant to Hume. Even his wife Cynthia was not allowed to share Tony with him. Hume had bought her a dog of her own.

Despised

After this incident, it became clear to Hume that Setty had no real respect for him. To Setty, Hume was a small-time operator, an underling to be discarded when no longer useful. Now, this man was on his property, throwing his weight around. Hume hurried up the stairs to his maisonette, on the top two floors, and was almost out of breath when he reached his sitting room, which overlooked the main road.

Setty, wearing a pin-stripe suit, was sitting on the sofa. 'If you come here again, it will be your lot,' Hume warned him. Setty looked at him mockingly.

'Who's going to stop me – you and who else?' he replied, and began to jeer. 'If I want to come here, I will.'

Moving towards Setty, Hume threatened to throw him down the stairs. 'You'll be the one to get slung down,' Setty said.

At this, Hume left the room and took down from the wall in the hallway one of his most treasured possessions. It was a German dagger, issued to Hitler's dreaded security force, the SS, during World War II. He returned to the sitting room and shut the door. 'Next time you come here, you'll get this,' he told Setty.

Setty fatally underestimated the depth of Hume's anger and resentment. Ignoring the dagger, he replied contemptuously, 'Go away, you silly bastard. What do you think you're doing? Playing at soldiers?'

Killer: Donald Hume

Bastard ... playing at soldiers ... The words summed up much of what had gone wrong for Hume in his life so far. 'There's no play,' he said quietly.

Still Setty failed to read the warning signs. When he tried to sweep Hume away, Hume attacked and the two men fell to the floor.

Finally, the large, bulky figure of the car dealer lay slumped against the sofa. He had been killed by repeated knife wounds to the chest.

Hume looked up and realized that the curtains were open. Anyone across the road could have seen the fight through the lace nets. The sound of the struggle on the floor must have been heard downstairs. Hume waited and listened, but there was no sound of commotion or alarm.

Removing evidence

Hume dragged Setty's body out into the hallway and through the dining-room door on the other side. From there, frequently pausing to catch his breath, Hume pulled the body through the breakfast room and the kitchen and, finally, into the coal cupboard which lay under a slanting roof at the back of the house.

Returning to the sitting room, he replaced pieces of furniture that had been knocked over in the fight. Soon the room was back to normal, except for the bloodstains on the light green carpet and the sofa. Fetching water and a cloth, Hume tried to remove these, and other spots leading to the coal cupboard. But he only made the stains worse.

He then found Setty's ignition key and let himself into the yellow Citroën. The time was 9.30 p.m. Twenty minutes later, he arrived at Cambridge Terrace Mews, where Setty usually kept the car. After checking there was no one around, he parked the car and made sure there were no fingerprints left on it.

After a short walk, Hume caught a taxi and arrived back at 620 Finchley Road at about 10.45 p.m. His wife was already asleep.

Hume checked that the sitting room and coal cupboard were as he left them, then lay awake all night, smoking cigarettes and planning his next move.

The body was too bulky to move in one piece, so Hume conceived of the grisly idea of severing the head and legs from the torso. This he carried out the following day, wrapping the torso and legs in felt and packing the head into a cardboard carton.

BURIAL AT SEA

Shortly before 3 p.m. on Wednesday, 5 October, Donald Hume drove down Dagger Lane, an approach road to Elstree Airport in Hertfordshire.

The car was a black, hired Singer saloon. With Hume were Tony, his dog, and two bundles wrapped in blankets and tied with cord. These contained the dismembered remains of Stanley Setty. A third bundle was still in the coal cupboard at Finchley Road.

At the airport control tower, Hume explained that he wanted to fly to Southend and back. The officials at Elstree knew him well and an Auster, G-AGXT, was put at Hume's disposal. He patted Tony goodbye and carried the parcels over to the aircraft.

Flight to sea

Half an hour later, cruising at 70 miles an hour, Hume eased the Auster starboard at 2,000 feet and headed out over the English Channel. Later he recalled, 'Sheer desperation was urging me on. I couldn't afford to be seen dropping suspicious-looking objects near Southend Pier.'

On a full tank, the Auster could fly for three-and-a-half hours. Hume pushed his outward journey to the maximum limit of his fuel capacity while allowing himself fuel to return to England. After more than an hour's further flying, the French coast came hazily into view and, beneath him, the waters seemed clear of shipping. From his raincoat pocket, Hume reached for the SS dagger and other incriminating objects. He threw them into the sea.

Hume then jettisoned the two parcels containing the remains of Stanley Setty. After scanning the surface of the water to make sure they had sunk, Hume swung the plane back towards England. It was about 4.30 p.m. and visibility was poor when he reached Southend Airport. With the strain telling, Hume made a poor landing in the dark, breaching the drill and halting in the path of another aircraft.

After arranging with the control tower to collect the Auster the following day, Hume took a taxi all the way back to 620 Finchley Road. He paid for it with part of the £100 he had kept from a wad of £1,000 which Setty had been carrying. Hume had destroyed £900 in £5 notes, which carried blood stains. He used the money he kept to pay off an overdraft.

It was about 8.30 p.m. when Hume got back to the maisonette. His wife Cynthia was upstairs. Hume checked the lower floor. That morning, he had cleaned the living-room floor and wiped everything on which Setty could have left fingerprints. He had taken the green sitting room carpet down to the cleaner's next door, and washed the floors. He bought a tin of dark-brown varnish stain to cover the areas where the cleaning had left scratches and abrasions. Hume had also cut away parts of the stained carpet underfelt, stretching it to cover the gaps.

He rang Elstree Airport, where he had left his dog for the night, and arranged for Tony to sleep in the Singer car.

Killer: Donald Hume

Dumping the body

The following morning, Thursday, 6 October – two days after the killing – Hume brought in a decorator to cover the sitting room floor in varnish. He went to Elstree and returned with Tony in the Singer at about 11 a.m. Hume asked the decorator to help him lift the bundle from the coal cupboard into the car.

At 2.30 p.m., Hume reached Southend Airport. The Auster had already been refuelled. As he was loading the aircraft, an engineer asked what the bundle was. 'Fish,' replied Hume. After a difficult take-off, the Auster headed out towards the Channel at a height of 3,000 feet. Visibility was poor. When the French coast again came into view, Hume dropped the aircraft to 2,000 feet and, almost tilting out of control, released the bundle. As it hit the sea its contents floated out.

By now, he was running short of fuel, and reaching Elstree would be impossible. Hume headed for Gravesend, where he landed at 6.30 p.m. Again, he caught a taxi home, with Tony as a fellow passenger.

Missing person

Setty's disappearance had already made headlines in the newspapers. The press went to town on the story of the shady car dealer with the celebrated wad of notes. That morning, two days after Setty had visited Hume's flat, the *Daily Express* ran the headline 'Dealer with 200 Fivers Vanishes.'

The police had been alerted by Setty's sister Eva and her husband. Also the car left by Hume in Cambridge Terrace Mews had been examined. Hume had not known that Setty usually put the Citroën in the garage, and the neighbours were surprised to find it in the open air next morning. One neighbour had heard it being parked on the night of 4 October, according to the newspaper reports which Hume studied carefully.

Later, Hume commented that 'at first the police, and the newspaper reporters trailing them around, seemed to be way off the scent.' One obvious line of inquiry was that Setty had been murdered for his £1,000-wad of banknotes. The police searched uncleared bomb sites for him in the areas of his known haunts and acquaintances.

On Friday, 7 October, three days after the murder, Hume went to Southend to collect the Singer car, and arranged for another pilot to fly the Auster back from Gravesend. The next day, Saturday, he read with alarm that the police had issued the numbers of the £5 notes which Setty had cashed on the afternoon he went to see Hume.

Hume had destroyed most of them, but the rest had either been deposited at his own bank, or given to taxi drivers in Southend and Gravesend. 'I failed to notice that the serial numbers were consecutive, and likely to be traced easily,' Hume later admitted.

For Hume, the news got worse. On 14 October, the Setty family offered £1,000 reward for information. On Friday, 21 October, parts of Setty's body were washed ashore on the Essex mudflats. Hume read the story in the newspapers. 'My victim's body,' he was to comment, 'had followed me home.' Police began inquiries in the Southend and Gravesend areas.

At 7.30 a.m. on Thursday, 27 October, a large squad of detectives surrounded 620 Finchley Road. Hume was taken to Albany Street police station for questioning. Three detectives were in charge of the inquiry. They were Superintendent Colin MacDougall, Chief Inspector John Jamieson and Detective-Sergeant Sutherland. It was clear to Hume that his movements on the days of the airdrops were known to them.

'Alright,' he said suddenly. 'I'll tell you what happened.' Hume then made a statement about three men, whom he called Mac, Greeny and The Boy, who had offered him £100 in £5 notes to drop two parcels from an aircraft. He had accepted the offer, Hume said, and the following day they had returned with a third parcel and an offer of £50 to repeat the flight. One had had a gun.

'After they had gone I began to have suspicions about that parcel,' Hume said in his statement to the police. 'But it was too late to draw back because I thought the police would never believe me if I went to them. They would have no time for shady characters like me.'

The next day, Friday, 28 October, Hume was charged with murder at Bow Street police station. 'No,' Hume said, 'I am absolutely not guilty.'

SAVING HIS SKIN

The trial of Donald Hume for the murder of Stanley Setty began in the No. 1 Court at the Old Bailey on 18 January 1950, before Mr Justice Lewis. The prosecution team was led by Christmas Humphreys. Hume, represented by R.F. Levy, KC, pleaded not guilty.

The 30 year-old defendant had made no effort to appear smart. His defence partly rested on the case that he was a shady character who had been afraid to take the police into his trust. Looking tough and a little dangerous, Hume wore a check jacket and flannel trousers. There was no sign of the RAF tie he had worn at his first remand appearance before Bow Street magistrates on 30 October.

Clear evidence

Little of the evidence was in serious dispute. The prosecution had already shown how closely they had traced Hume's journeys to Elstree and Southend, and the trail of the £5 notes carried by Setty. On 16 November, 23 prosecution witnesses had been assembled to give evidence when Hume was committed for trial.

Killer: Donald Hume

Hume's own story of Mac, Greeny and The Boy showed him to be guilty of complicity in a serious crime. But if the jury judged Hume to be a liar, he would almost certainly be hanged.

'The evidence will be almost entirely circumstantial,' Humphreys said in his opening speech. The story unfolded in largely uncontroversial detail. Humphreys did not delve deeply into Setty's character, describing him as 'a pavement car dealer.' When Humphreys came to deal with Hume's story of Mac, Greeny and The Boy, he said, 'It is a complete fantasy about three men, who do not exist outside Hume's fertile and romantic imagination.'

On the following morning, 19 January, Mr Justice Lewis, who had been taken sick, was replaced by another High Court Judge, Mr Justice Sellers. A new jury was sworn in, but this time Humphreys said he would dispense with an opening speech and let the jury try the case on the evidence alone.

It was on the third day of the trial, 20 January, that Hume's entire statement to the police was read out to a hushed court by Superintendent MacDougall. Hume and both sides' counsel studied the jury's faces, but they remained inscrutable. Cross-examining MacDougall, Hume's counsel retrieved some useful ground. The officer acknowledged that a careful examination of the maisonette had failed to produce a single Setty fingerprint. This is consistent with the defence case – that the dismemembered body of Setty was brought to the flat in three packages. Nor were there any bloodstains on Hume's clothing.

On the fourth day of the trial, Monday, 23 January, Levy opened the defence case. 'Hume does not pretend to be an angel,' he told the jury. 'He is no angel . . . He may be an exhibitionist, but it is not every liar who is a murderer.'

Levy challenged the prosecution's case that Setty could have been attacked, killed and dismembered in the flat with Mrs Hume present over much of the relevant period. He also tried to cast doubt on the expert testimony of Dr Henry Holden, director of the Metropolitan Police Laboratories.

Dr Holden had testified that human bloodstains were found in a corner of the sitting room carpet, after it had been cleaned and dyed, and on linoleum in the hallway. There had also been traces of blood discovered between floorboards in the sitting room, beneath those in the dining room, and also on the plaster and timbers in the flat below. The stains were of blood group O, Setty's group, but also that of four in every ten people.

In his opening speech, Levy suggested that stains found on the carpet could not have been blood because, although large enough to survive cleaning, they had left no traces on the underfelt.

Hume was then called to the witness box. Looking pale, but otherwise composed, he retold the story of Mac, Greeny and The Boy. The jury heard that Mac was a thickset man in his 30s, with fair hair. Hume spoke with impressive detail. Of Greeny, he said, 'He had a flashy green suit with exceptionally wide trousers, and plain suede shoes. I should say his height was about five foot six or five foot seven. He wore a tight overcoat with a belt and no hat. I should say he was either a Greek or a Cypriot.'

Hume shrewdly added more detail to these descriptions than he had offered in his original statements. This helped make them plausible, and avoided the impression that Hume had simply memorized a limited set of details. He also painted a vivid picture of The Boy, who had a 'receding forehead, sometimes wore steel-rimmed glasses and a very bright-coloured pair of brown buckled shoes.'

By this stage, Hume's imagination was working audaciously. 'I think he had a mac with him,' he said. After two hours of giving evidence, Hume faced a long, probing set of questions by Christmas Humphreys for the prosecution about the parcel.

'What did you think it was?'

'I thought it might have been part of a human body,' Hume replied.

'It was obviously part of a human body, wasn't it?'

'No, sir, not obviously.'

'When Setty was missing?' Humphreys persisted.

'I did not connect the two of them,' Hume insisted doggedly.

Humphreys then rattled the defendant by reading from Hume's statement in which he had said that it had occurred to him at the time that the parcels contained Setty's remains.

'What else could they have been connected with that spurts human blood unless it is a human body?' Humphreys asked. Hume did not reply. Later, Humphreys said that the three men were placing themselves at Hume's mercy and that Hume could have had the place surrounded by police before their second visit.

'No, I was scared stiff,' Hume said.

'Why not, if you are an honest man?' Humphreys asked. The jury had already heard Hume admit to impersonating an RAF officer. Now he spoke angrily from the witness box.

'I am not saying I am one hundred per cent honest,' he answered. 'I am saying I am a semi-honest man, but I'm not a murderer.'

The cross-examination continued the following morning, the fifth day of the trial. Hume recounted how he had cleaned up the blood dripping from the parcels. His counsel angrily interrupted Humphreys at one stage to complain that evidence was being misrepresented by the prosecution. This seemed to give the defendant confidence. When Humphreys suggested that Setty was murdered and dismembered in the maisonette, Hume replied, 'Absolute baloney.'

Hume then began to answer questions before counsel had finished them, and was told by Mr Justice Sellers to listen to the questions first. Goaded, Hume flared up when Humphreys accused him of lying.

'I am the one who knows whether I killed Setty or not, other than the men who murdered him,' he said. 'I have a clear conscience regarding the killing of the unfortunate man.'

The judge aggravated Hume further by saying, 'You are adopting this as a personal matter.'

'My life is a personal matter,' Hume said.

At the end of his evidence, Hume was asked by the judge if he could find Mac, Greeny and The Boy again. 'No,' said Hume.

Cynthia Hume followed her husband into the witness box. Her well-bred appearance may have improved Hume's standing with the jury. Defence counsel asked whether she had seen anything unusual over 4 October and 5 October, or any blood or bloodstained knives. She replied that she had not, and that Hume could not have dismembered a body in the home without her knowing.

Hume's counsel asked her whether she believed it possible for her husband to have murdered anyone in the flat during the evening before about 9 p.m. without her hearing a commotion. 'Quite impossible,' she replied. She was asked whether she heard any sound that suggested that violence was taking place, and again answered firmly with the single word, 'No.' Mrs Hume also testified that she would have remembered if her husband had not gone to bed later that night.

Cross-examined by Humphreys, Mrs Hume agreed that she knew little of her husband's life, and that she had not known of the visits by Mac, Greeny and The Boy.

Silent murder

In his closing speech for the defence, Levy concentrated on the complete lack of evidence that the alleged murder had caused a commotion. The neighbours, Cynthia Hume, the cleaning woman and the decorator had seen and heard nothing suspicious. 'Can you for a moment accept the fact that all these three men never existed?' he asked the jury. 'I submit that that man was murdered not by one man but several, and there you have Mac, The Boy and Green.'

Humphreys, for the prosecution, dwelt on the bloodstains and Hume's admission that he had disposed of Setty's body. He described the three strangers as a 'complete fabrication' and said that, if Setty was alive when he arrived at the maisonette on 4 October, then Hume must have taken part in murdering him.

The judge's summing-up began on the afternoon of the sixth day. Mr Justice Sellars quietly presented the strengths and weaknesses of each side's case, then addressed the central question of Hume's reliability.

'You may say, where his evidence is in conflict with somebody else's, that you may prefer the other person's . . . you will have to deal with that,' the judge said. At 12.30 p.m. on the trial's seventh day, the jury were sent out. They returned at 3 p.m.

'My Lord, we are not agreed,' the foreman said. 'I feel that it is doubtful that we shall reach a unanimous decision.'

Hume turned white in the dock. He had expected to be convicted of murder. Humphreys announced that the prosecution would not ask for a retrial. As a formality, a new jury was sworn in and instructed by the judge to return a verdict of not guilty without hearing evidence.

Hume still faced the charge of being an accessory to murder. He pleaded guilty and was sentenced to 12 years in prison. He bowed to the judge and was led down to the cells.

THE STICK-UPS

On 25 May 1958, a man with glasses and a moustache, wearing a dark blue suit, presented his passport to the official near the departure lounge at Ringway Airport, Manchester. The passport was in the name of Stephen Bird, a chemical engineer from Mortlake, Surrey. The holder was in fact Donald Hume. He was flying to Zürich, Switzerland, on business.

On 1 February, just over eight years after being sentenced at the Old Bailey, Hume had been released from Dartmoor Prison in Devon. He had received the maximum remission of sentence, a third of the 12 years. On his release he had earned £2,000 from the British newspapers for telling his story. Hume was carrying this money, in breach of laws governing the movement of currency, when he arrived at Ringway. Hume had no ties. Cynthia, his wife, had divorced him and he learnt sorrowfully that his dog Tony had been put to sleep.

When he arrived at Kloten Airport, Zürich, he was as he put it, 'rearin' to go'. He had money and plans, and he was on the look-out for women. Within a few weeks, Hume was posing not as the dull Mr Stephen Bird, but as Johnny Bird, a Canadian test pilot based in Montreal. In this role, he had found a girlfriend, a Swiss hairdresser called Trudi Sommer.

But Hume realized his lifestyle as the hard-drinking Johnny Bird was eating into his funds. He saw a way of replenishing them. 'Switzerland was just the place for me,' he was to say. 'The banks seemed a pushover. The staff are so kind, so gentle, so unsuspecting.'

Change of plan

By the last week of July 1958, he had revised this plan. He would rob banks in other countries and use Switzerland as his base. Hume flew to London. 'If anybody made a hole in a bank here, nobody would put the finger on me,' he was to say.

Staying in a hotel in Baker Street, in central London, Hume reconnoitred several banks and selected the Midland Bank in Boston Manor Road,

Killer: Donald Hume

Brentford, west London. At 9 a.m. on 2 August, Hume left his cases at an air terminal and arrived at the location with a canvas bag. He whiled away two hours with a pocket chess game, then entered the bank and asked about opening an account. The cashier explained how to do this, and Hume said he would call later.

At one minute to noon, Hume returned to the bank. The doors were closed at midday to new customers, leaving Hume alone with the staff. He drew out an automatic revolver.

'This is a stick-up,' he shouted, 'and I'm not kidding.' One of the cashiers, Frank Lewis, shouted in protest. Hume shot him in the stomach. 'No one else gets hurt if you do as I say,' Hume called out to the terrified staff. 'All I want is money.' Hume tied up the other three staff, two men and a girl. A few minutes later, some £1,500 in cash was inside his canvas bag. He asked about the large safes to the rear, but was told they contained only ledgers.

At about 12.10 p.m., he ran out of the bank, telephoned for a doctor, and caught a train at Kew Bridge station. Just over 24 hours later, he arrived in Zürich, via Paris, as Stephen Bird.

Trudi Sommer was beginning to realize there was more to her flamboyant boyfriend than flying aircraft. Before the bank raid, Hume had told her that he was a spy for the US espionage service, the Central Intelligence Agency. To explain his more frequent arrivals and departures, he told Trudi that he now also tested aircraft for the US Air Force in Europe.

Hume was relieved to read in the British press that the Brentford robber had apparently not been linked to him. But the reports said the robber had missed a large sum of money in the vaults. Realizing he had been fooled by the staff, Hume was determined to take revenge.

After waiting three months for the publicity surrounding the case to die down, Hume travelled to London by train, arriving on 5 November. He checked in at a hotel in Kensington as Donald Brown. The following day, he discovered that the Midland Bank in Brentford had been left empty. The branch was now housed a quarter of a mile away.

At 2.58 p.m. on 12 November, just before closing time at the bank, Hume stormed in, drew two guns and repeated his gangster-film line, 'This is a stick-up.' But the security system had changed. This time the staff ducked and ran out through the back, locking a door behind them.

Hume grabbed the cash he could see on the cashiers' counters. He could hear the alarm being raised and decided to leave immediately. As he tried to do so, the manager, Eric Aires, attempted to stop him. Hume opened fire and the manager collapsed. Like the cashier in the first raid, he would make a slow recovery.

Hume hastened once more to Kew Bridge, trying to keep cool while two police officers strolled past him. He boarded a train, jumped out while it was moving and finally reached Heathrow Airport. Returning to his Stephen Bird alias, he found his way safely back to Zürich. The bank raid had netted just £300.

330

Mounting worries

For a while, Hume brooded in Zürich. He and Trudi were engaged, but he was deeply worried about money and her growing suspicions of him. When she found one of his guns, Hume told her he was a spy not for the Americans, but for the Soviet Union.

For much of December 1958, Hume was in Canada, under an unknown alias. When he returned to Zürich, he was carrying £1,700. This amount, however, did not solve his financial problems. He decided to revert to his original plan. He would rob a bank in Switzerland.

FINAL FLING

On the morning of Friday, 30 January 1959, Hume, alias Johnny Bird, walked into the Gewerbebank in the Ramistrasse in central Zürich. He had had little sleep the night before and was nervous and drained. He wore brown casual trousers, a grey jacket and a blue pullover. Under his arm, he carried a cardboard box. Inside was a revolver.

Without saying a word, Hume put the box on a counter and fired the pistol through it. A cashier, Walter Schenkel, fell injured. Hume jumped over the partitioning and hit another cashier, Edwin Hug, with his gun. But Schenkel had managed to press an alarm button.

Hume grabbed some loose cash and ran out of the bank. A crowd led by Hug was already giving chase. Hume turned to fire, but the revolver jammed.

Almost out of breath, he reached a taxi rank in a square. A 50 year-old driver, Arthur Maag, saw the chase and tried to head Hume off. Hume fired the revolver again. This time the mechanism worked. Maag fell to the ground, dying. Hume was swiftly overpowered by an angry crowd, from which he had to be protected by police when they arrived in the square.

During questioning in custody, Hume tried various tricks to hide his identity. 'I ranted and raved . . .' he said, '. . . I did everything I could to conceal the fact that I was Donald Brown, formerly Hume.' The Swiss police, however, quickly discovered who he was and contacted Scotland Yard. Piece by piece, the two forces were able to complete the jigsaw of Hume's activities since he disappeared from view in May 1958.

While at the District Prison, Hume was examined by a psychiatrist, Dr Guggenbuhl-Craig. The psychiatrist concluded that Hume was sane in law when he shot Arthur Maag, the taxi driver. Hume never tried to test his play-acting skills on the doctor. The fight had gone out of him. 'This is the end of the line for me,' he told Dr Hans Stotz, the head of the Zürich detective force.

Hume's trial for the murder of Arthur Maag opened in the town of Winterthur on 24 September 1959, nearly eight months after Hume's arrest, and lasted five days. Besides murder, he was charged with attempted murder, armed robbery, threatening life and breaching the regulations governing foreign residents.

The defendant said at the outset that he accepted the prosecution case. But the trial was disturbed by continual shouts and interruptions from Hume, who wore earphones to hear an interpreter and was closely guarded by two police officers. On the first day, Hume became angry with the Court President Dr Hans Gut, and said to the interpreter, 'You tell him that if it comes to a slanging match, I will rip him to bits physically.' The threat was not translated.

Under the Swiss system, Hume was questioned by the Court President, or judge, rather than a prosecuting counsel.

'Why did you need the pistol?' Dr Gut asked.

'I felt lonely,' Hume replied.

Dr Gut took Humen through his London bank robberies as well as his life in Switzerland and his activities under the alias of Johnny Bird.

Dr Gut drew attention to a remark made by Hume to the Zürich police, which acknowledged that the Swiss robbery was doomed to failure.

'Why did you do it anyway?' he was asked.

'It's difficult to say,' Hume said thoughtfully, 'I didn't want my conscience to brand me as a coward.'

At other times, Hume returned to being coarse and abusive. There was a flash of his old impudence when he singled out the 16 year-old bank clerk who led the chase into the square after him. 'That young fellow, Fitze, deserves any reward to come from the Midland Bank. The others only joined in afterwards.'

Since Hume had not pleaded insanity, or diminished responsibility, there was little that his Swiss counsel could say. On 30 September, the jury was sent out. Three hours later, they declared Hume guilty of every charge. Switzerland had no capital punishment. Hume was sentenced to life imprisonment with hard labour.

He made no reply to the sentence. As he was led down the courthouse steps in chains, he tried to kick a newspaper photographer. It took several guards to bundle him into the police van which took him back to prison.

CASE FILE: HUME, BRIAN DONALD

BACKGROUND

Brian Donald Hume was born in Swanage, Dorset in December 1919. The exact date is not known. Hume was an illegitimate child, when the word 'bastard' was a stigma that few people were willing to admit to. Hume was keenly sensitive to this.

He had no clear idea of how his first two years were spent. Soon after his second birthday, he was sent to an orphanage at Burnham-on-Sea, in Somerset.

Few treats

According to Hume – whose recollections were uncorroborated – the orphanage was run by three ladies. He said that the children slept eight to a bed – four up, four down – and were given jam only on Christmas Day.

Discipline was severe. One common punishment, Hume said, was being kept alone for hours in the lampless cellar. Another was the product of a macabre imagination, though whether this belonged to Hume or one of the three ladies is impossible to know. The children would be threatened with a visit from an 'old green gypsy woman,' who would suddenly appear, issuing oaths and threatening to take the children away if they misbehaved.

Hume said that one night, locked in the cellar with another orphan, the green gypsy had appeared but that this time, he had recognized her as one of the three ladies and chased her out of the cellar. In his 'Confession', Hume tarnished a highly plausible story by saying that he chased her with a chopper left lying in the cellar.

He was about eight years old when the ladies told him he had been adopted. 'You're leaving here to go to your grandmother in London,' one of them explained. Before he left, they added that this was his mother's mother. The house was in Golders Green, north London, close to 620 Finchley Road, where Hume killed Stanley Setty over 20 years later.

The next six months were probably the happiest of Hume's childhood. He and 'Gran', as he called her, took to each other and Hume received the love that had hitherto been denied him. One of his favourite pastimes was going to the pictures. He liked violent gangster films best.

Hume was not happy when 'Gran' told him he was going to live with his aunt as an adopted child. This aunt lived in a village near Basingstoke, Hampshire, where she was headmistress of the local school. Hume was told to address her as 'Aunt Doodie' and her husband, a motor engineer, as Uncle Don. There were two sisters for Hume to play with, one by an earlier marriage of Aunt Doodie.

Real mother

Eighteen months later, news came that 'Gran' had died. Hume claimed that, after this, Aunt Doodie's attitude towards him changed, and he was made to feel a nuisance. There were rumours in the village about Aunt Doodie and the boy she had adopted. One day the maid, Doris, told Hume that he was really Aunt Doodie's son. From that moment, Hume hated his mother.

At the age of 14, Hume left Queen Mary's Grammar School. His mother got him a job as a live-in kitchen boy in Farnborough. After three months, he had had enough and returned home. Realizing he was unwelcome, Hume packed his bags one night and quietly left the house, saying goodbye to no one. That night, he slept in a haystack and in the morning he hitch-hiked to London.

One of the first things he did there was to visit Somerset House, the huge grey building that houses all records of births and deaths in Britain.

Hume discovered that what Doris had told him was true. Aunt Doodie was indeed his mother. The space for his father's name had been left blank.

PSYCHOLOGICAL FILE

In both England and Switzerland, the settings of his notorious crimes, Hume was considered to be a sane, intelligent man who should be held accountable for his ferocious bursts of violence.

In England, before the murder of Stanley Setty in 1949, he had only once received even a cursory psychological examination. This came in 1941, while he was recovering in hospital from a long bout of meningitis. A specialist reported that the illness had weakened Hume's ability to adapt to changing surroundings and ideas and that, at the age of 21, he was stuck in a set of adolescent attitudes – in other words, that he was immature.

In Switzerland, before his trial in 1959, Hume was examined at greater length by a reputable Swiss doctor, Dr Guggenbuhl-Craig. He reported that Hume was not mentally retarded or damaged in any way that would affect his moral sense, and that he did not suffer hallucinations or 'mad ideas'. At both his English and Swiss murder trials, it was accepted that Hume had not planned the killings of Stanley Setty and Arthur Maag.

Yet Hume's capacity for violence created an air which the Swiss doctor found 'so evil I often had shivers down my spine.' In England, some observers were disturbed less by the killing of the unsavoury Setty, than by Hume's dismembering of him on the floor of the family home.

Shame and rage

During Hume's early lifetime, illegitimate children were made to suffer harshly. But the distaste with which Hume was treated by his mother must also have been a factor in his subsequent rage against the world. As a respectable headmistress in a genteel village near Basingstoke, Hampshire, she sent her son away to an institution rather than accept the shame of his birth. Accepting him back, she pretended to be his aunt.

Hume was enraged by this deception. But it did not affect his belief that 'respectable' society was somehow better than he was. He was furious that, during the first raid on the Midland, the bank staff lied to him successfully about the money in the vaults. As he put it, 'I thought that people outside prison walls generally told the truth!' He swore revenge on the bank staff because 'nobody lies to Hume and gets away with it.'

But they did. The three ladies who masqueraded as the frightening 'green gypsy' fooled him and all the other orphanage children on many occasions, as did his mother, 'Aunt Doodie', until the village started gossiping. So, in effect, did the makers of the American gangster films who convinced Hume that a single cry of 'This is a stick-up!' would terrify every bank employee out of their wits. Hume hated to be seen as foolish or naive.

Inflamed

Rather than accept that 'respectable' society was no better than him, the bastard misfit, Hume seems to have been inflamed by it. It is interesting that the killings of Setty and Maag took place in what, outwardly, were genteel surroundings – his comfortably appointed maisonette in a respectable part of north London, and a quiet square in Switzerland. In the more violent setting of Los Angeles, which he visited in 1958 from Canada, Hume lacked the motivation to commit crime.

It is not known whether Hume's love of impersonation began because of the deceptions by his mother and the three ladies at the orphanage, or had already taken root inside him.

But there were many people in England who had more than a sneaking admiration for his story at the Setty trial in 1950 of the three shadowy, comic gangsters, Mac, Greeny and The Boy. It was exactly because they were so obviously modelled on the three investigating detectives that the story had such audacity.

Challenging

The impudent Hume seemed to be daring the court to prove he was lying, to prove that the system of justice was sound, and to challenge the educated, well-spoken barristers to outwit him. It was as if he wanted decent society to justify his admiration of it.

Chapter 18

EDWARD GEIN
THE HANDYMAN

I n 1958, the murderer of two young women and mutilator of 15 corpses, a harmless working odd job man, was committed to Wisconsin State insane asylum. His horrifying deeds had shocked America and provided the factual basis for Hitchcock's classic spine-chiller, *Psycho*.

The central region of Wisconsin, in the American midwest, is so flat and featureless that even the official state guide-book calls it 'nondescript'. In a more evocative Wisconsin phrase, it is the State's 'great dead heart' – bleak grassy plains scattered with lonely farmsteads and small towns. Raising a little livestock or growing patches of rye in the sandy, stony soil, farmers there in the 1950s could make only the barest of livings. For relief from this daily struggle, they would go hunting or meet in the town to drink beer.

In 1954, the aptly named town of Plainfield – no more than a group of clapboard stores and houses – had its own drinking den called Hogan's Tavern. The owner of the bar, Mary Hogan, a large buxom woman who had twice been divorced and was well into middle age, was by all accounts a colourful character with a questionable past.

Illicit atmosphere

Some said she had connections with the Mob, others claimed that she had been a celebrated Chicago madam and had bought the business with her ill-gotten gains. Whatever the truth of the matter, Mary Hogan had made a big impression on the conservative, God-fearing farming families of the area. While the men liked the warm but faintly illicit atmosphere of the tavern, it earned the outright disapproval of their wives and girlfriends.

On the afternoon of 8 December 1954, a freezing winter's day, a local farmer named Seymour Lester stopped by at the tavern for a drink. He found it open but deserted, with all the lights left on. When his calls for service remained unanswered, he began to grow suspicious. Then he noticed a newspaper-sized bloodstain by the door leading through to the back room. Sensing that something was seriously wrong, he hurried to telephone for help. Soon County Sheriff Harold S. Thompson arrived, accompanied by a number of hastily assembled Deputies.

Trail of blood

Their quick search of the bar revealed that it was empty. Mary Hogan's car was found parked at the back of the building in its usual place. The patch of blood, which by now had soaked into the bare pine floorboards and begun to dry, was streaked as if something had been dragged through it. Nearby lay a spent .32 calibre rifle cartridge.

Beyond the patch, a bloodstained trail led through the back door and out across to the customer's parking area, where it ended abruptly beside deep, freshly-made tyre tracks, recognizable to the Sheriff as those of a pick-up truck. The conclusion was inescapable: someone, almost certainly Mary Hogan, had been shot where she stood, and the body dragged outside into a waiting vehicle.

Yet there was no other sign of a struggle, and no evidence of a motive for the crime – the cash register was full and nothing else appeared to be missing. Thompson requested help from the State crime laboratory at Madison, some 60 miles away. But their forensic tests merely confirmed the Sheriff's conclusions as to the manner in which the crime had been committed, and could shed no further light on the case. Investigations in Chicago, Mary Hogan's former home, and an extensive farm-to-farm search of Pine Grove and the surrounding area came up with nothing. Mary Hogan had completely disappeared.

News of the mystery travelled fast, and as the weeks went by without the authorities turning up a single shred of new evidence, the question of 'Whatever happened to Mary Hogan?' began to crop up in talk all over the area. A month or so after her disappearance, one such conversation took place between a respected Plainfield sawmill owner, Elmo Ueeck, and the shy little handyman he had called in to mend a couple of fences. The fence-mender's name was Edward Gein.

Gein had lived on a farm six miles west of Plainfield since he was seven. Surrounded by nothing but woodland, fields and marsh, the farmhouse itself was a bare two-storey, L-plan white frame building where Gein lived alone. He was a shy, rather awkward figure who kept pretty much to himself. Following the death of his mother in 1945, he had received a subsidy from the US government for letting the land lie fallow. And as the farm began to fall into disrepair, Gein supplemented his income by doing odd jobs for his Plainfield neighbours.

It was in the capacity of handyman that the small, slightly built bachelor, in his early 50s with thinning fair hair and watery blue eyes, became well known to local residents. Though he was obliging, hard-working and trustworthy, most people regarded him as a little eccentric.

Strange comments

Ueeck did not bother with Gein much, even though he had known him for years. Along with the other residents of Plainfield, he found Gein extremely difficult to talk to – more often than not, Gein would look away nervously and lapse into an empty-headed lopsided grin, or else come out with some comment so strange and inappropriate that it would leave the other person lost for words.

On this occasion, however, Ueeck could not resist the temptation to tease Gein on the subject of Mary Hogan. Eddie was always particularly ill at ease when the talk turned to women, but Ueeck had seen Gein at Hogan's Tavern on several occasions sitting alone at the back of the bar, clutching a glass of beer. He and his friends had noticed the way Gein just sat and stared at the bar owner, lost in a world of his own. They supposed, with barely concealed amusement, that Eddie was in love.

Ueeck began by suggesting to Gein that if he had made his intentions to Mary Hogan a little plainer, she might at this very moment be cooking supper for him back at his farmhouse, instead of being missing, presumed murdered. Later he would recall that 'Eddie rolled his eyes and wiggled his nose like a dog sniffing a skunk,' before shifting from one leg to the other and lapsing into one of his familiar grins.

'She isn't missing,' Gein replied after a few seconds' deliberation. 'She's at the farm right now.'

Ueeck shrugged off what seemed like yet another of Gein's infrequent and rather pathetic attempts at humour. And although Gein was to repeat the claim to several other Plainfield residents in the weeks that followed, not one of them took it the least bit seriously. It was, after all, just the kind of crazy thing he would say.

SHOOTING SEASON

Like Mary Hogan, Bernice Worden was a plump, solidly built woman in her late 50s and a more than capable businesswoman. Unlike the bar owner, she was a devout Methodist who enjoyed an almost spotless reputation among her fellow Plainfield citizens.

Bernice had taken over as sole proprietor of Worden's Hardware and Implement Store in 1931 following the death of her husband. In the intervening years, assisted by her son Frank, she had built it into a thriving business to which every farmer in the area would turn at some time or another, for everything from agricultural machinery to rifle cartridges. In 1956 she was nominated Plainfield's first 'Citizen of the Week' by the local newspaper, and on the rare occasions when she was not working she could generally be found with her grandchildren, whom she adored.

On the morning of Saturday, 16 November 1957, she opened the store as usual, expecting a slow start to the day's trade. It was the first day of Wisconsin's nine-day deer hunting season, and most of Plainfield's male inhabitants – including her son Frank – were already out in the surrounding woodlands. The rest of the town was deserted and most of the shops closed, but Bernice Worden decided to keep her shop open, thinking that there would be a steady stream of visitors eager to replenish their supplies.

She soon had a customer. A little after 8.30 a.m. the small figure of Ed Gein shuffled up to the hardware store clutching an empty glass jug. Like everyone in Plainfield, Bernice found it hard to regard Gein as anything more than a simpleton, but lately he had taken to troubling her over the most trifling of details without actually buying anything. Only the night before, Gein had stopped off at the store to check on the price of antifreeze. On being given the answer he had stood there for several seconds with an idiot grin on his face before shuffling off into the dark.

Bernice had also been taken aback a few weeks before when Gein, out of the blue, turned up at the store and invited her to go ice-skating with him. The offer had been blurted out in a nervous, half-joking way and she had simply shrugged it off. Yet she was sufficiently unnerved to relate the incident to her son, and to point out that since then, she had seen Gein staring at her from inside his pick-up or from the other side of the street.

Alone with Eddie

The whole scene at Worden's on 16 November can only be pieced together from Gein's later confused recollections. Besides Bernice and Gein there had not been a soul in sight. Mrs Worden apparently filled the jug, returned to the front of the store and wrote out a sales slip. Gein then paid and left. A few moments later, he returned.

Picking a hunting rifle off the rack in the corner, he explained to Mrs Worden that he was thinking of changing his old .22 rifle for a more up-to-date gun which would fire a choice of calibre lengths. She agreed that the weapon he held in his hands was a good buy, and carried on with her work. Suddenly, while her back was turned, Gein reached into his pocket and slipped a cartridge into the rifle while pretending to inspect the action. A moment later he took aim – and fired.

First witness

Between 8.45 and 9.30 that same morning, Bernard Muschinski, the pump attendant at the filling station a little way down and across the street from the store, noticed Mrs Worden's delivery van pull out of the garage behind the building and head off down the road. He thought little of it. But a few hours later he walked past the store and was surprised to see the lights on. The front door was locked and Muschinski assumed that Mrs Worden had forgotten to switch them off.

The next person to see Gein was the sawmill owner, Elmo Ueeck. He had just shot a deer on Gein farmland and was making a hasty exit from the property with the kill tied to the front of his car. Ueeck was dismayed to see Gein's Ford sedan pounding down the road towards him – since he was sure that even Eddie would object to unauthorized hunting on his land. But as the two cars passed, Gein simply gave a friendly wave. Ueeck also remarked that Gein was driving at well above his usual speed.

Later, around noon, Ueeck's conscience began to trouble him and he drove back to the Gein farm to explain and apologize about the deer. He found Gein with his car jacked up, changing the snow tyres back to summer treads – a sight which struck him as odd, since there were already a couple of inches of snow on the ground. Gein was friendly and did not seem unduly bothered about the deer.

In the afternoon, Gein had a visit from another of his neighbours, his teenage friend Bob Hill and his sister Darlene, who asked whether he would mind driving them into town to buy a new car battery. Gein stepped briskly out of the house to meet them, his hands covered in blood. He explained that he had been dressing a deer. This puzzled Bob Hill, since Gein had always professed a distaste for butchery and claimed the sight of blood made him feel faint. But Gein said he would be glad to help, and after returning to the house to wash, he ushered them to his car and they set off for town.

Last supper

When Gein and the Hills finally returned to the Hills' nearby grocery store it was getting dark, and Bob Hills' mother, Irene, invited Gein to stay for supper. He accepted readily, little knowing it would be the last meal he would eat as a free man.

Some time earlier, shortly before dusk, Bernice Worden's son Frank had pulled into the Plainfield petrol station near the family store after an unsuccessful day's hunting. He was mystified to hear from the attendant, Muschinski, that the delivery van had been seen leaving the store early that morning. Frank had expected to find his mother still behind the counter, about to shut up shop. The two men had then confirmed Muschinski's earlier discovery that the door was locked but that the lights were still on, and Frank, who did not have a spare key with him, returned home to fetch one.

Among his other duties, Frank Worden was a Plainfield Deputy Sheriff, and like his mother, he was a steady, reliable person. But as he unlocked the door of Worden's Store and stepped inside, he could barely keep control of himself. The cash register was gone, torn from its place on the counter, and towards the back of the shop was a large patch of blood.

Frank telephoned Country Sheriff Art Schley in Wautoma, 15 miles away, then carried on searching the store for his mother. When the Sheriff and another Deputy arrived a quarter of an hour later, he had already made up his mind what had happened.

'He's done something to her,' Worden told them confidently.

'Who?' they asked.

'Ed Gein,' said Worden.

Frank Worden had not been idle during the time Schley and his Deputy took to drive from Wautoma to Plainfield. In his mind he replayed the conversations with his mother about Gein – how Eddie had been staring at her of late, how he had pestered her to go out with him, and how as recently as the previous night he had stopped off at the store to inquire about the price of antifreeze. Worden also recalled that Gein had asked him if he intended to go hunting next day. Could it be that Gein had been checking to see if the coast would be clear?

What had clinched it for Worden was the discovery near the blood patch of a handwritten sales slip for two quarts of antifreeze. It was dated 17 November and made out to Ed Gein. Sheriff Schley put out a general alert on the radio to bring Gein in for questioning.

Gein himself, meanwhile, had just finished eating with the Hills when a neighbour burst in to report news of Bernice Worden's disappearance. Eddie's only comment was, 'it must have been someone pretty cold-blooded.'

Irene Hill would later recall that she joked with Gein saying, 'How come every time someone gets banged on the head and hauled away, you're always around.' Gein, she remembered, had simply shrugged his shoulders and grinned.

Bob Hill suggested that Gein should drive the two of them into town to see what was going on. Gein happily complied, and the two men stepped out into the freezing snow-covered yard to start Gein's car. At that point, Traffic Officer Dan Chase and Deputy Poke Spees arrived looking for Gein.

Gein questioned

Chase and Spees had found the handyman's farm locked and empty when they had driven there a few minutes previously. Since it was well known that Bob Hill was one of Ed Gein's few friends, the Hills' store was the next logical port of call. Officer Chase stepped smartly across the yard and rapped on the window of Gein's car just as it was about to pull away.

Gein was ordered to get out and was escorted back to the squad car for questioning. Chase asked him to recount what he had been doing all day and where. Gein told him, and then Chase asked him to run through his story a second time. Immediately it became apparent that there were glaring inconsistencies between the two versions, and Chase told him so.

'Somebody framed me,' Gein retorted.

'Framed you for what?' Chase asked.

'Well, about Mrs Worden,' said Gein.

'What about Mrs Worden?'

'Well, she's dead, ain't she,' Gein replied.

'Dead!' exclaimed Chase. 'How d'you know she's dead?'

'I heard it,' said Gein. 'They told me in there.'

As soon as Sheriff Schley heard over the radio that his chief suspect had been apprehended, he went to Gein's farmhouse with Captain Lloyd Schoephoerster of the neighbouring Green Lake County Sheriff's office.

The door of the ground floor kitchen extension at the back of the house gave easily. Switching on their flashlights, the two men stepped inside. A moment later Art Schley felt something brush his right shoulder and wheeled round instinctively to see what it was. As his flashlight beam played across the object he gasped in horror.

There before him, hanging from the ceiling, was the headless corpse of a woman with a large, gaping hole where her stomach should have been. Schley's immediate thought was that the body had been trussed, dressed and skinned like an animal.

HOUSE OF HORROR

It took some time for the two policemen to get a grip on themselves, and for the full horror of what they had just witnessed to sink in. Eventually, Schoephoerster made it to the car and managed to radio for help. Then both men braced themselves and prepared to set foot back in the house.

A second look at the body revealed that it was hanging from a branch which had been sharpened and driven through the tendons of one ankle, the other foot having been slit below the heel and secured to the pole with wire. The body itself had been slit from the breastbone to the base of the abdomen, and the innardless insides glistened as if they had been scraped and cleaned. There was no head.

Only once had Schley seen anything like it before, and that was in an abattoir. Whoever it was – and Schley had little doubt it was Bernice Worden – had been slaughtered and expertly dressed for butchery as if they were a side of beef.

The body aside, it was hard to believe that a human being could live in such conditions. Everywhere were piles of stinking, rotting rubbish, with furniture, kitchen utensils and dirty, ragged clothes strewn anyhow. Cardboard boxes, empty cans and rusting farm implements littered the floor, giving the impression that the room had been overrun by some beast which had left a trail of filth and excrement in its wake.

Shining their flashlights around, hardly daring to let their eyes follow the beams, Schley and Schoephoerster then became aware of stranger sights – detective magazines and horror comics piled into boxes or dropped on the floor, a sink filled with sand, spatout chewing gum in an old coffee tin, rows of dentures displayed on the mantelpiece. Whoever had assembled this collection was evidently driven by some sickening force far beyond either man's comprehension.

Sickening search

It was not long before Gein's farm was choked with squad cars, as the help which Schoephoerster had requested began to arrive. To start with, the search through the house continued by flashlight and paraffin lamp. But then a generator was brought in, and as the house was bathed in the glare of police arc lights, the full horror of what was inside became apparent.

Scattered about the kitchen were a number of skulls, some intact, others sawn in half and used as crude bowls. Two of them had even been used to adorn the posts at the foot of Gein's festering, ragstrewn bed in the adjoining sleeping area. One of the chairs by the kitchen table turned out on close inspection to have a seat consisting of strips of human skin. There were other hideous artefacts – lampshades, wastepaper baskets, a drum, a bracelet, the sheath of a hunting knife – all fashioned from human remains.

Even worse was to come. As the investigators poked around, they uncovered boxes containing various bodily parts, each one of which had been cut away from an unidentified corpse with the skill and precision of a surgeon. There was a kind of vest fashioned from the skin from the top portion of a woman's body with a cord running through the back, and several pairs of human skin 'leggings'.

Most horrifying of all for the police searching the house was the discovery of a collection of death masks – genuine 'shrunken heads' of the kind more usually associated with only the most lurid tales of tribal cannibalism. Each of the nine masks consisted of the face and scalp of the victim, hair intact, which had been peeled from the skull and stuffed with rags or newspaper.

Silent witnesses

Four of these masks were found hanging on the walls around Gein's bed, silent witnesses to whatever bizarre nocturnal fantasies he had indulged in.

The others were found in bags, old cartons and sacks scattered there and in the kitchen. Some had been treated with oil to keep the skin smooth, and one still showed traces of lipstick. Another – shrunken but still recognizable to one of the officers present – belonged to Mary Hogan, the bar owner who had vanished three years before.

By this time, the assembled company of policemen, forensic experts and detectives on the scene were stunned into silence, their faces white with horror. Many of them were long-serving officers who had seen all kinds of gruesome crimes in their time, yet nothing could have prepared them for the house of corpses, bones and other human remains now before them. Even in the harsh frost of a Wisconsin November night, the stench was unspeakable. Searchers found the heart of Bernice Worden left in a plastic bag in front of the kitchen stove, and her still-warm entrails wrapped in an old suit nearby. But still the police searched on, grimly determined to find the one piece of evidence which had so far eluded them – the head of the corpse hanging from the rafters.

Beyond the kitchen and the sleeping area which led off it was the ground floor of the house proper. The door was securely boarded up, but within minutes the investigators had prised away enough of the planks to gain entry into the main living room.

Their torch beams shone down on an orderly and perfectly normal family room, in which the only thing out of place was the thick layer of dust that encased everything from the furniture to the ornaments above the fireplace. It was a mausoleum – a tomb which had been closed up and left by Gein exactly the way it was the day his mother died 12 years before.

Back in the kitchen, a pathologist who had been attempting to catalogue the ghastly remains suddenly spotted steam rising from an old feed sack lying in a heap of rubbish in the corner of the room. Pulling the sack out into the middle of the floor, he opened it up and found what everyone had been looking for.

Ghoulish trophy

The head of Bernice Worden was covered in dirt, and blood was congealed around the nostrils, but otherwise it was perfectly intact. The expression on the face seemed reassuringly peaceful, but the two investigators were taken aback by the sight of hooks driven through the ears with a cord stretched between them. Gein had obviously intended to hang Worden's head on his wall, along with the other ghoulish bedroom trophies.

As the night wore on, the search of Gein's farmhouse finally drew to a close. Bernice Worden's corpse was taken down from the rafters and labelled along with the other remains, which were then packed into plastic sacks and dispatched to Goult's Funeral Home in Plainfield so that a proper post-mortem examination could be carried out. No one present had been able to guess how many bodies had contributed heads, skins, or other parts to the grisly cache, but it was clear that far more than just those of Mary Hogan and Bernice Worden were involved.

The big question still left in the minds of the stunned, sickened police officers as they left Gein's farm that night, was – who did the other corpses belong to?

DIGGING FOR THE DEAD

While the gruesome discoveries were being made at his farmhouse, Edward Gein sat quietly in the Wautoma County jail guarded by the arresting officers, Chase and Spees. At 2.30 a.m. on Sunday, 17 November, Sheriff Schley returned from the nightmare scene in Plainfield.

Over the next 12 hours, Gein was questioned almost continuously, without an attorney present, but continued to stay silent. In the meantime, the initial autopsy report on Bernice Worden confirmed that she had died from a .22 calibre gunshot wound to the head.

The following morning, Monday, 18 November, Gein broke his silence. He said he had shot Mrs Worden, loaded her corpse into her truck and driven it out to a nearby pine forest. Leaving the truck there, he had walked back to town to fetch his car, then driven back to the forest. The corpse was transferred from the truck to the car and then taken to Gein's farmhouse, where it was trussed up and butchered.

Cannibalism

All these details were included in a statement District Attorney Earl Kileen issued to the press that morning. He then added one or two more speculative details of his own, specifically that some of the victims' body parts found at the farmhouse appeared to belong to 'young people', and the way Mrs Worden's corpse had been mutilated, it had 'looked like cannibalism'.

Soon the reporters were filing the most lurid details of the case back to newspapers as far away as Chicago. In the meantime, Kileen himself went to interview Gein, who said he could remember none of the details of Bernice Worden's killing because he had been 'in a daze at the time'.

Under further questioning, Gein said he thought it had all been an accident. Why then, asked Kileen, had he stolen the cash register? Gein said that he 'hoped to strip it down and examine the mechanism' to see how the machine worked.

Kileen pressed him on what he had done with the body. Gein began describing how he had trussed it up and bled it into a bucket, then buried the fresh blood in a hole in the ground.

Asked if he thought he had been dressing out a deer, Gein replied 'That is the only explanation I can think was in my mind.'

Gein was asked to account for the numerous skulls, pieces of skin and other human remains found at the farm. Adamant that, to his knowledge, he had murdered no one else besides Bernice Worden, Gein told astonished detectives that he had obtained the bodies from graveyards.

He explained that over the last few years he had on occasion been gripped by a sudden compulsion to rob graves. In many cases he had known the victims while they were still alive and had read about their deaths in the local paper. He would drive to the cemetery on the night of the burial, remove the body from the freshly dug grave, and fill the grave in again to leave it in what he cheerfully described as 'apple pie order'.

Gein admitted that on many of these nocturnal expeditions he panicked on reaching the grave and drove straight home again. He could not remember how many bodies he had actually obtained, and once more offered the excuse that he was 'in a daze'. When asked if he had ever enjoyed any kind of sexual relations with the stolen corpses – a question already foremost in the minds of his interrogators – he shook his head and cried, 'No! No!', before adding that they 'smelt too bad'. Gein also strenuously denied charges of cannibalism.

Robbery charge

On Monday afternoon, Ed Gein appeared in court charged only with armed robbery of the cash register from Worden's store. The DA's office wished to postpone any murder charges until the forensic evidence was completed and the prisoner had been subjected to a lie detector test. Afterwards he was driven out to the farm, where he showed the police and a posse of accompanying reporters the spot where he had buried Bernice Worden's blood.

That afternoon Gein was also interviewed by detectives from La Crosse – his home town – about the disappearance four years previously of a 15 year-old girl named Evelyn Hartley. The results proved inconclusive. Gein was also questioned by sheriffs from neighbouring Portage County on the subject of Mary Hogan, whose head they already knew had been discovered at the farm. Lapsing into confusion and frequent bouts of silence, the prisoner denied knowing her at all, though he did concede he had visited her bar for a drink once or twice.

The following day, the press contingent, which had by now taken up more or less permanent residence in town, were finally allowed inside Gein's farm to see for themselves the squalor in which the 'Butcher of Plainfield' had been living.

Though now confronted by hard fact, imaginations ran riot and a fresh flood of horror stories appeared on front pages all over the country. Some reports suggested there were as many as 50 bodies buried around the farm. Others claimed that Gein had handed out packages of human flesh to unsuspecting neighbours, and most linked his name with every disappearance in Wisconsin over the last ten years.

Meanwhile Gein himself was taken to the State Central Crime Laboratory in the state capital, Madison, to be interviewed while connected to a lie detector. In the nine or so hours of questioning which followed, he confessed to having worn the 'clothes' he had made out of human skin. He also caved in on the subject of Mary Hogan, admitting that he thought he had murdered her, while remaining 'very hazy' about the precise details. As far as the death of Bernice Worden was concerned, he continued to maintain that it had been an accident, and would do so for the rest of his life.

Later in the interview, the questions turned to Gein's grave-robbing exploits. If the soil was soft enough, he would remove it by hand and prise open the lid of the burial casket with a crowbar to expose the body. Sometimes Gein only removed the head – by sawing across the neck and then snapping the spinal cord. On other occasions, he would remove other parts as well. A few times he had removed the entire body, then replaced the casket lid and refilled the grave.

Throughout the interrogation, Gein remained his usual quiet, co-operative self. He described his deeds without any apparent remorse, and only became flustered and reticent when the questioning returned to Mary Hogan's or Bernice Worden's murder. Joe Wilimovsky, who operated the lie detector, was sure that what he was hearing was the truth. He was also struck by the calm way Gein described how he had sawed through skulls or disembowelled bodies.

Afterwards, DA Kileen made a statement in which he said that Gein would be charged with the first degree murder of Hogan and Worden 'in a day or two', but that his office was satisfied he had had nothing to do with other disappearances. He then informed reporters, much to their fury, that the State Attorney General had ordered a news blackout of the entire case.

Committed

Thereafter, events began to move more swiftly. On Thursday, 21 November, Gein was formally charged, and the news embargo temporarily lifted to allow three reporters into his cell for an interview. On the following day, at the preliminary trial hearing, Gein's attorney entered a plea of insanity, and the judge committed Gein to the Central State Hospital for the Criminally Insane in Waupun pending psychological tests. The focus of the case now shifted to his grave-robbing exploits.

Kileen announced at the hearing that Gein had given police a list of the victims whose resting places he had violated. Subject to the permission of relatives, the authorities hoped to exhume a number of graves the following week. One of the people on the list was a Mrs Eleanor Adams, who had died six years before, in 1951.

Rumours

Pat Danna, the sexton of Plainfield Town Cemetery, insisted, however, that it was simply not possible for a single man to do what Gein had alleged. And in any case he was sure none of the graves in his charge had been disturbed. As the mystery deepened a rumour spread that someone had assisted Gein in his grave-robbing activities.

On Saturday, a rumour spread that Gein was taken back to the farm a second time, where he showed the police a trench which he said contained the cremated remains of Mary Hogan's body. The trench was duly excavated, and the remains of considerably more than one corpse removed for examination. By the following Monday, under mounting pressure from all sides to find out where the bodies had come from, Kileen ordered Eleanor Adams' grave to be opened.

The ground in the cemetery was frozen that day, and it took Danna and his assistant more than an hour to dig down as far as the burial casket. As the earth was scraped away from the casket, the cover was seen to be split in two. Having removed the pieces, Danna and his assistant reached in and lifted off the lid of Mrs Adams' coffin. It was empty, save for the rotting burial shroud, and something else – a 12 inch steel crowbar.

The assembled group then moved to another grave named on Gein's list, some 30 yards away from the first, and began a second excavation. Before they had even dug a few feet, the workmen began to uncover what were unmistakably human remains. When the coffin was finally reached and opened, it came as no surprise to find it empty. Gein's story was confirmed. In the case of Mrs Adams he had removed the body in its entirety. At the second grave, he had apparently removed what he wanted, then hurriedly covered up the evidence.

What no one could even begin to guess at this stage was how many more graves had been violated.

ASYLUM FOR PSYCHO

On Wednesday, 27 November, police were directed by Gein's neighbours to a rubbish pit on his property, some way from the farmhouse. Gein, they said, was often to be seen digging there, though they had always assumed that he was simply burying rubbish.

Excavation of the site uncovered another near-complete skeleton, the skull of which seemed rather large for a woman and contained a gold tooth. This in turn gave rise to speculation that the body was that of local farmer Ray Burgess, who had disappeared with a friend while on a hunting expedition back in 1952.

After the discoveries of the past two weeks, the people of Plainfield were convinced that the monster who had been living undetected in their midst for so long was capable of anything. However, forensic tests proved that the body was that of a woman.

Gein, meanwhile, was subjected to exhaustive psychological tests by doctors at the Central State Hospital. A second lie detector test appeared to confirm that apart from Bernice Worden and Mary Hogan, Gein had confined his butchery and mutilation activities to the bodies of women who were already dead. He finally admitted to stealing nine corpses, all of middle-aged women.

Once again he calmly described what he had done with the dismembered heads, limbs and other body parts. It appeared that on occasions he had donned the human skin vest and leggings and proceeded to pace around his farm. The thought of this butcher-transvestite, trampling by nightfall through the stinking debris and rotting remains that littered his living quarters, disgusted his interrogators. Yet Gein himself appeared to see little wrong with mutilating bodies that were already dead, and seemed proud of the anatomical knowledge his handiwork displayed.

The psychological tests, which included the standard Wechsler adult intelligence test, showed that Eddie Gein was in many ways 'quite bright' – even above-average – but that he had great difficulty expressing himself or communicating with people in anything other than the simplest terms. The psychologists at the hospital put this down to some previous 'severe emotional disturbance', stating that it prompted Gein into fits of irrational behaviour followed by extended periods of calm and remorse.

They also discovered that his sexual-emotional development was severely retarded, causing him to retreat into a bizarre fantasy world in which his feelings towards women became confused with grief over the death of his mother, and fear of transgressing his own peculiarly straight-laced moral code. Bernice Worden and Mary Hogan, Gein claimed, were 'not good women'. He did not go so far as to suggest they deserved to die, but rather that they were fated to meet violent ends, and that he was merely acting as the instrument of their deaths.

On the subject of the mutilated corpses, Gein conceded that he had once entertained the idea of bringing his mother back to life through the body of another woman. He had been disappointed when the plan he tried had failed.

He said that in the years since his mother's death he had seen 'faces in the leaves' and 'smelt strange odours'. In fact, the odours continued to trouble him even as he sat in the Central State Hospital, facing interrogation. When asked what the odours smelt like, he replied chillingly, 'They smell like flesh.'

Insane conclusion

On 18 December, the doctors who had questioned Gein held a final meeting to review the evidence, under the chairmanship of Dr Edward F. Schubert,

Director of the hospital. Their conclusion was that he was insane, and therefore not mentally competent to stand trial. The decision was taken to remand Gein in hospital until after Christmas, and psychologists' recommendations were forwarded to the State Attorney General.

Gein was brought before presiding Judge Bunde on the morning of 6 January 1958, and sat impassively in the dock chewing gum while three psychologists – including Schubert – gave expert evidence. After listening to their opinions, Bunde had no hesitation in endorsing the hospital recommendations, and Gein was committed indefinitely to the State mental hospital.

The decision raised a storm of protest among the residents of Plainfield, many of whom were infuriated that the man who had made their town a byword for murder and grave-robbing would not be standing trial. In an effort to placate them, Attorney General Walter Honeck wrote a letter stating that Gein's incarceration did not automatically rule out a trial at some time in the future, and that he would be examined at regular intervals to see if his mental condition showed any signs of improvement.

In March, just as the dust was beginning to settle, a fresh row erupted over the announcement that Gein's farm and its contents were to be sold by auction, and that potential purchasers could inspect the property for a fee of 50 cents – a charge necessary, it was claimed, to discourage 'casual sightseers'. Quite apart from the thought that others stood to gain where Plainfield had so evidently lost, the date of the auction – 30 March, Palm Sunday – was seen by the more religious people of the town as a direct affront.

As it turned out, the auction never took place. On the evening of 20 March, the sky was illuminated by the sight of Gein's farm in flames, while the residents of Plainfield stood by and witnessed what many believed was devine retribution. Among their number was the town's fire officer, Bernice Worden's son, Frank. The cause of the fire was never discovered, and Gein's own comment on hearing the news was, 'Just as well.'

More remains

But the Gein story was not over. In May 1960, dogs scrabbling in a trench on what had once been Gein farmland discovered a fresh pile of human bones, including arms, leg bones and a pelvis. The mad little handyman's eventual tally, once all the remains had been analysed, catalogued and accounted for, came to 15 bodies, including the two murder victims Bernice Worden and Mary Hogan.

Gein flourished in his new 'home' and was a model prisoner. He got along well with the warders, and, in marked contrast to the other inmates, never showed signs of requiring sedation. He also demonstrated considerable skill at handicrafts in the prison workshops, and with the small salary he was paid he bought a short-wave radio, becoming something of a 'radio ham'.

Fit for trial

In January 1968, however, District Judge Robert Gollmar received a letter from the hospital authorities stating that in their opinion Gein was now mentally fit to stand trial. Though Gollmar, on reviewing the case, thought that such a trial would be a waste of time and money, he felt that the assurances given by Attorney General Honeck to the people of Plainfield had to be honoured. Gollmar, therefore, authorized the proceedings to go ahead.

The trial, which took place the following November and lasted just a week, was, on a point of American law, bifurcated – in other words, it would simultaneously establish whether or not Gein had committed murder, and if he had, whether or not he was sane enough to know what he was doing.

For the first time, a jury and public gallery were to bear witness to the gruesome findings at the Gein farmhouse.

Split decision

The jury heard numerous psychologists recall for the second time their interviews with Gein, and how – on the subject of grave-robbing at least – the little man seemed hardly aware that he had done anything wrong.

When the verdict came, it was a surprise to no one – though Gein had the strange distinction of being found guilty and not guilty on the same day: guilty of murder, not guilty because of his obvious insanity.

Gein himself remained, as always, quiet and docile throughout. After Judge Gollmar had ordered him to be returned to hospital and declared the case finally closed, he rose from the dock and shuffled through the assembled ranks of reporters and photographers. The Plainfield Butcher was on his way home to the Central State Hospital in Waupun.

CASE FILE: GEIN, EDWARD THEODORE

BACKGROUND

Augusta Gein gave birth to her second son on 27 August 1906. She had prayed it would be a girl – her stern Lutheran upbringing and her marriage to drunken George Gein had developed in her a loathing of men. Their loveless union had already produced a son, Henry, in 1902.

Augusta vowed that this son, Edward Theodore, would never be like the lustful, godless men she saw around her. From the first, Eddie's life was to be totally dominated by his mother.

Augusta ran the family grocery store in La Crosse, Wisconsin, virtually single-handedly. Her husband spent most of his time and money in local bars. She was a harsh disciplinarian, quick to punish, slow to give comfort, and unable to provide her sons with a mother's love.

In 1913, the Geins started a new life as farmers. After spending a year on a dairy farm some 40 miles east of La Crosse, the family finally settled at an isolated farmstead just outside the small town of Plainfield.

Mother's shadow

For the first 16 years of his life, school was Gein's only real contact with the outside world. But as fast as Eddie found a friend, Augusta would object to the boy's family. In her eyes, everyone was a threat to the moral purity of her son. She would quote endlessly from the scriptures, reminding Gein that boys were sinners in the image of their fathers.

Gein withdrew from contact with other children. Contemporaries later recalled him as being shy and feeble.

He also professed an aversion to blood or killing – common sights in a rural community where hunting and livestock farming were a way of life. Yet he devoured horror comics and books about violence. It was the one subject that would get him talking, though often the conversation would end abruptly when Gein came out with one of his macabre comments.

Gein's father died in 1940. By the mid-1940s, the family farm business was struggling, and Eddie and Henry took on extra work to supplement the family income. Gein admired his brother, but tension grew between them after Henry suggested that Gein's closeness to their mother might not be healthy.

Fire fighters

In the spring of 1944, Henry died in mysterious circumstances. He and Eddie had been fighting a fire near their farm when they became separated. Eddie led a search party straight to the spot where Henry lay dead. Though there was bruising on Henry's forehead, his death was attributed to asphyxiation by smoke.

Shortly after her elder son's death, Augusta Gein collapsed with a stroke. Over the next 12 months Eddie nursed her lovingly back to health, only to see her die a few weeks later in December 1945.

At the age of 39, Gein was alone in a world he barely understood. Within five years, he would retreat into another – a world in which the coldness, violence and repression of his childhood would become hideously twisted in his mind.

PSYCHOLOGICAL PROFILE

The case of Edward Gein is, from a medical point of view, one of the most complex in criminological history. Voyeurism, fetishism, transvesticism and necrophilia all reared their ugly heads.

Yet as the true story emerged, it became clear that these perversions were merely manifestations of a deeper psychosis – a disorder of the mind which had its roots in Gein's extraordinary relationship with his mother.

Mother love

When psychiatrists first began to speculate about what dark inner force had driven Gein, the phrase 'Oedipus complex' was frequently mentioned. Gein, they supposed, was in love with his mother, and that following her death he became obsessed with finding a substitute for the only person to whom he had ever been able to show affection.

At first he experimented with dead bodies, mutilating them hideously in his efforts to gain sexual and emotional satisfaction. Later, claimed the theorists, the striking similarities between his mother and the two murder victims (both were heavily built, middle-aged businesswomen with strong personalities) moved Gein to murder as his desire to possess both women totally took control.

However, the official psychiatric reports on Gein demonstrate that the 'mother love' theory is in fact an over-simplification of what really took place in his mind, especially when read in the light of recent medical findings.

Shattered mind

Edward Gein, the reports state, was a schizophrenic, a man whose mind was shattered by the inner turmoil of conflicting personalities. Research suggests that schizophrenia begins in childhood, when the young mind is confronted by something so terrible, so unbearable, that it buries it away in the subconscious and replaces it with a personality, or personalities, better able to deal with the situation. So it was in the case of the shy little boy whose every waking moment was dominated by the rigid discipline and religious fanaticism of his cold, unloving mother.

As a child, Gein craved his mother's love, yet time and again it was refused. Worse, his mother despised men, holding up Gein's father as an example of male inadequacy. If Augusta Gein loathed men, the inference drawn by her son's impressionable mind was that she hated him too. Try as he might, he could never please her, never gain her love.

Thus Gein's mind developed a new personality to explain this sorry state of affairs. 'Edward number two' could not be loved by his mother, or by any woman, because he was unworthy. He could only worship the person who tolerated this unworthiness – his mother.

Mother hate

But what about 'Edward number one', the normal, healthy personality whose only crime was to seek a love that was not there? It began to fester in Gein's subconscious, nurturing the anger it felt towards the person who had repressed it. 'Edward number one' hated his mother.

As the years went by and Gein became steadily more isolated from the outside world, the blind worship and feelings of inadequacy engendered by personality number two were reinforced with every scolding that Augusta Gein gave her son. But at the same time, the frustration felt by personality number one continued to seethe inside Gein's mind. He wanted to love women, yet it was they, in the shape of his mother, who prevented him from doing so.

Inner conflict

After Augusta Gein's death, it seems likely that her son's mind was thrown into fresh turmoil. With his mother gone, reasoned personality number two, who was there left to love him? Simultaneously, personality number one began to stir from its resting place deep in Gein's subconscious, sensing that the time for freedom had now arrived.

With all the normal channels for expressing love still blocked, Gein began by finding solace in the graveyard. Personality number two was still very much in control at this stage, so it was 'natural' that he should seek out the bodies of women who resembled his mother, the only woman he could ever love. Sex in any normal sense was out of the question, so Gein resorted to other fetishistic and necrophile practices as alternative outlets for the physical urges he felt inside him.

Unfortunately the sight of living women, specifically Mary Hogan and Bernice Worden, then began to arouse him, and as it did so the anger felt by personality number one became inflamed. The closer he got to Hogan and Worden, the angrier he began to feel. These women were evil, he told himself, because a part of him sought to love them while another never could.

The exact truth can, of course, never be established. But in all probability, when Edward Gein murdered Mary Hogan and Bernice Worden, he was really murdering his mother.

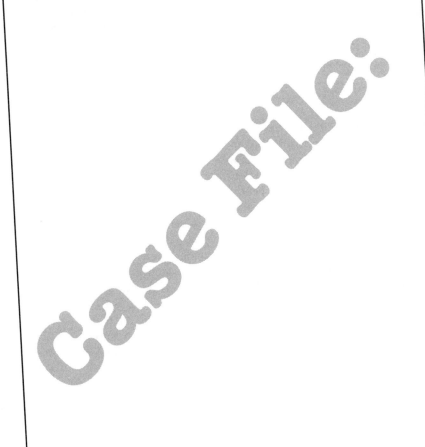

Chapter 19

DAVID LASHLEY

THE BEAST

In April 1977, some 10 weeks after her disappearance, the body of a young Australian woman was found on a common near St Albans. She had been savagely raped and murdered. Police became convinced that her killer was a known criminal, but it was to take 13 years to bring him to justice.

On the evening of Friday, 4 February 1977, Janie Shepherd, a 24 year-old Australian living and working in London, left the luxury flat in St John's Wood where she lived with her cousin Camilla and Camilla's husband Alistair Sampson. At about 8.40 p.m. she gave them a brief hug and a happy smile and ran down the steps saying 'I must dash, I'm frightfully late'. She climbed into her dark blue Mini and vanished.

Janie had planned to spend the weekend with her boyfriend, Roddy Kinkead-Weekes, who lived in Lennox Gardens, Knightsbridge. He expected her around 9 p.m. Janie Shepherd lived only three miles away and had promised to drop in at a supermarket to pick up some groceries for supper. When she had not arrived by 9.30 p.m., Kinkead-Weekes rang the Sampsons' flat. Camilla and Alistair had gone to the cinema but their maid told him that Janie had left 50 minutes earlier. He rang the flat again at 10 p.m. and then, increasingly worried, at half-hourly intervals.

The Sampsons returned home around midnight. There was still no word from Janie Shepherd and they quickly shared her boyfriend's alarm. They rang all the main London hospitals to check if there had been any accidents but the replies were negative.

Finally, at 3.15 a.m. on Saturday, 5 February, Alistair Sampson reported Janie Shepherd missing to St John's Wood police station, and Roddy Kinkead-Weekes did the same at Chelsea police station. Janie Shepherd was not the sort of girl to drop into a pub or club on her own, and if her car had broken down or she had run into friends unexpectedly, she would certainly have rung Kinkead-Weekes.

A happy, stable girl, Janie had no known reason for wishing to disappear on her own. She and Kinkead-Weekes were deeply in love. But Shepherd was the heiress to a fortune (her stepfather was Chairman of British Petroleum in Sydney) and the possibility that she could have been kidnapped occurred immediately to police and family alike. Her description and details of her car were circulated within the hour. The car was checked on the police computer to see if it had been stopped or seen anywhere. Throughout a long, anxious weekend, her friends and family sat and waited for a ransom demand, but none came.

The police, piecing together Janie's last known movements, discovered that on the day of her disappearance, she had left the Caelt Art Gallery in Westbourne Grove, west London, where she worked, and driven straight home. Finding that she had left her keys at the gallery, she had to ring the bell. Camilla let her in and an apologetic, but excited, Janie had rushed up the stairs, refused a cup of tea and packed for her weekend with her boyfriend. At 7 p.m. Kinkead-Weekes had telephoned to suggest they spend a quiet evening at home. Janie had agreed and they had planned a meal of smoked trout, celery and cheese. Janie said she would buy the food on her way over.

When she left the Sampsons' flat in Clifton Hill at 8.40 p.m., she was wearing jeans tucked into Cossack boots, a man's check shirt over a thin polo-necked sweater, and a thick white cardigan with a reindeer motif. In her big red satchel bag she had £40 in cash, a change of underwear, and a black sweater with a vivid red polo-neck and bright green cuffs. She also took a tapestry she was making and some balls of coloured wool.

The contents of her bag strongly indicated that she was expecting to spend a homely weekend with a friend.

Mini for sale

When Janie left home that Friday night her car was clean and shiny. A week earlier, she had decided to sell it and had cleaned and polished it for potential buyers. She had placed an advertisement in the London *Evening Standard* for four consecutive days and had put a large 'For Sale' notice in the rear window.

On Tuesday, 8 February, four days after her disappearance, Janie's car was found in Elgin Crescent, Notting Hill Gate. It was parked on a yellow line and streaked with mud. Detective Roger Lewis of St John's Wood CID had been put in charge of the investigation and, with no ransom demand being yet made, was already in serious doubt that Janie Shepherd would ever be seen alive again. The discovery of the car strengthened his fears. There were two parking tickets on the windscreen. One was dated Monday, 7 February, and timed at 11.45 a.m., the other was dated Tuesday, 8 February, at 12 noon. The outside condition of the car was so noticeable that witnesses were later found who remembered seeing it as early as 1.10 a.m. on the previous Saturday.

Outlandish evidence

Inside, the condition of the Mini was even worse. Chief Superintendent Henry Mooney of Scotland Yard's Murder Squad was called in to oversee the investigation. He said that one look at the interior showed him that 'something outlandish' had taken place. There were two parallel slash marks in the sun-roof. It was obvious that a struggle had taken place.

In the car police found Shepherd's Cossack boots and red shoulder bag but the £40 in cash and her National Westminster cheque card were missing. So were her change of clothing, the tapestry and the balls of wool. The 'For Sale' notice was still in the back. The police also found two receipts in the red handbag. One was from the Europa Foods supermarket in Queensway, the other was from a self-service garage in Bayswater, showing that Janie had topped up the 7 gallon petrol tank of her Mini with three gallons of four star petrol on the night she went missing.

This enabled the police to make a rough assessment of how far the car could have been driven into the countryside. Given the amount of petrol left in the tank it looked as though the Mini could have travelled 75 miles, but there was no clue as to any direction. An early analysis of the soil embedded in the tyres showed traces of chalk and flint, of oak and beech leaves, and of coloured fibres which suggested that the car had been stuck in mud and that Janie's tapestry had been used to give the wheels leverage in an attempt to drive away.

That left a huge area to be explored – Oxfordshire, Surrey, Hertfordshire and even Wiltshire. The detectives believed that somewhere in one of these counties was the clue to Janie Shepherd's disappearance.

TRAIL OF HEARTBREAK

Scotland Yard's involvement in the Janie Shepherd case began when forensic evidence revealed that the soil on the bodywork and tyres of Janie Shepherd's car came from as many as four different counties. Police forces in the four counties were alerted but the search began in the Notting Hill area of west London.

The supermarket receipt indicated that Janie had bought smoked trout, as she had promised her boyfriend, as well as yoghurt, tomatoes and chicory. At the Europa store in Queensway, the counter girl, a schoolgirl earning pocket money for the weekend, remembered Janie because 'she looked like an actress or a model'. When the police searched the scruffy back streets in the area, they found the food Janie had bought thrown into various backyards.

On 11 February, detectives used helicopters to search the gardens of derelict houses lying between St John's Wood and Notting Hill, the embankment of the Grand Canal, waste land and old bomb sites in north London. They also used infrared cameras to scour a 70-mile radius from Notting Hill over any district with soil similar to that found on the abandoned car. Body-sniffing dogs, trained by the same methods as drug-sniffing dogs, were used for the first time in a murder investigation in Great Britain.

Detective Chief Superintendent Henry Mooney of Scotland Yard, the man responsible for the arrest and conviction of the Kray twins, made a direct appeal to the public for information.

The police also distributed posters showing Janie smiling and a picture of her dark Mini. Newspapers carried full descriptions of the clothes and jewellery Janie was wearing when last seen by friends. The jewellery included a gold 'Woodstock' charm, a present from Roddy Kinkead-Weekes, that she wore on a chain given to her by her mother. She had also worn a Gucci digital watch on a grey leather wristband, a heavy gold bangle and an unusual gold Russian wedding ring of interesting design.

Samples of the soil were examined by mineralogists from the huge chemicals company ICI, scientists from London University and many other experts in an attempt to pinpoint where Janie Shepherd might be found. On Wednesday, 9 February, her distraught mother and stepfather, Angela and John Darling, arrived in London from Teheran where John had been working. DCS Mooney could offer them little hope. The state of the car, which was still being examined, suggested that the worst had happened to their daughter.

Mr and Mrs Darling stayed in a flat in St James's, prepared to keep a vigil in the hope of receiving a ransom demand. They were willing to pay one without hesitation but, as the days passed, they felt the need to do something practical.

DCS Mooney showed both shrewdness and sympathy by providing them with the results of the forensic evidence as it took shape day by day and, armed with Ordnance Survey maps, Mr and Mrs Darling drove out to those parts of the country where the soil was similar to that found in Shepherd's car.

For 65 days they explored copses, common lands, beauty spots, hedgerows and little-used lanes, bravely looking for the very discovery they dreaded. Detective Chief Inspector Roger Lewis and a team of 50 officers and cadets were making similar searches in the Chilterns, an area which the scientists thought might yield results, and squads of police hunted through other counties.

The pressure on the police was increased by the knowledge that the longer the search, the less chance there was of finding sufficient evidence to identify the culprit.

Meanwhile, routine inquiries were made. Known sex offenders were questioned and this resulted in what DI Lewis described as 'spin-off' arrests as other crimes were uncovered. Altogether, 18 people were detained in connection with other offences as a result of the Janie Shepherd investigation.

False trails

Inevitably, there were many misleading reports. The caretaker of a block of flats in west London reported having seen a dark-coloured Mini, with a blond girl and a man of Arabic appearance inside, parked in his area. The caretaker said he had noticed them because their car radio was very loud and because he had gone out to explain to them that they were parked on private property. On 11 March, the police were called to a dry cleaners to examine a navy blue cashmere coat which had been taken in, covered in mud, but which had not been collected. When the police arrived, it had already been cleaned.

DCS Mooney examined all the records of Scotland Yard and at Notting Hill looking for similar sexual attacks on women. His diligence almost paid off. The files showed that in June 1976 a young woman had been sexually assaulted in her car less than half a mile away from the street where Janie's car had been found. The victim on that occasion had spent the evening with her boyfriend and around midnight had driven back to her flat in Chesterton Street, Kensington. As she was parking, a man approached and asked the time. While she glanced at her watch he wrenched the door open, pushed her into the passenger seat and drove her to a railway arch in a back street, where he held her captive for two hours at knife-point, raping her and attempting to strangle her. As a woman walked past pushing a sleeping child in a pram her assailant told the girl, 'If you call out, I'll kill you first, then the woman and child'. He also told her how much he hated white women, slashed one of her wrists, then jumped out of the car and ran away. Somehow she managed to drive herself home with one hand, keeping the other in the air to try and stem the flow of blood. When she arrived she collapsed into the arms of a neighbour who called the police. During her four day stay in hospital she gave police a vivid description of her attacker, helping to construct an Identikit of a black man with a scar on his face. The picture was shown on the British television show Police Five. It later came to light that a woman friend of the man had warned him to change his image, which he did.

Prime suspect

The police closely examined their files in search of similar crimes. A suspect who might have been high on their list was overlooked because his file did not record him having a scar on his face. The suspect's name was David

Lashley. In 1970 he had been sentenced to twelve years imprisonment for rape, indecent assault and robbery. In four of the five cases with which he was charged he had assaulted and robbed women in their own cars. Lashley was paroled in 1976, partly because he had come to the rescue of a warder during a riot in the prison.

DCS Mooney sent his men to Lashley's home in Beaconsfield Road, Southall. They returned with the information that Lashley did indeed have a scar on his cheek. Lashley was taken in on 17 February for questioning about the Chesterton Street case and on suspicion of abducting Janie Shepherd. On an identification parade, Miss A., the woman from Chesterton Street, picked him out unhesitatingly. Lashley was remanded in custody in Brixton prison and charged with rape and attempted murder.

According to Mooney, Lashley confessed to the Chesterton Road case though Lashley himself was to deny this. He insisted that he knew nothing about Janie Shepherd and had an alibi for the night she disappeared.

On 4 February, Lashley said in a statement he had gone to the north of England with a girlfriend and returned to London in the early evening. At 5.30 p.m. he had been at work as a car-sprayer, and from 7 p.m. was at home watching television. He had gone to bed at 9.30 p.m. His friends corroborated the statement.

But what had been an intuitive move on Henry Mooney's part impeded the search for Janie Shepherd's body. In custody, Lashley was protected by the law. He was under no obligation to see anybody unless it was in connection with the charges that had been made. Nobody could force Lashley to talk. While he was languishing in Brixton Jail, Angela and John Darling continued their daily searches through the English countryside. But they were now resigned to never seeing their daughter again, and hoped only that her body could be found to be given a decent burial.

On three consecutive Friday nights, the police staged a reconstruction of Janie's visit to the Queensway supermarket, working on the premise that people are creatures of habit and might have noticed somebody hanging around the area.

Some 6000 people were questioned during the investigation, but finally the police had to cut the number of men involved in the search for Janie Shepherd's body. On 12 April, 1977, ten weeks after she disappeared, Angela and John Darling abandoned their efforts, returning to Australia heartbroken but convinced Henry Mooney was right in thinking that Lashley had murdered their daughter.

DEVIL'S DYKE

It was the Easter school holidays and two young boys, school friends and neighbours, decided to go for a bike ride on Nomansland Common, a popular stretch of open land near Wheathampstead in Hertfordshire. The day was clear and bright, and the boys cycled up the rough footpaths, among gorse bushes and hawthorn trees.

Suddenly they spotted what they thought was a pile of rags and went to look. But curiosity quickly gave way to fright and they dropped their bikes and ran. So it was that on Monday, 18 April, six days after Angela and John Darling had returned to Australia, eleven year-old Dean James and Neil Gardiner, who was a year younger, had found what the police of four counties were looking for. They had discovered the body of Janie Shepherd.

A glimpse of hair

At first, the boys tried to convince themselves that they must have seen a dummy. They crept back to retrieve their bikes, barely daring to look at the bundle of rags but Dean thought he saw what looked like blonde hair. They pedalled quickly home, too frightened to stop and tell anyone what had happened. It was dusk before Dean finally blurted out to his father, Peter James, that he was sure he had seen a real body on the common. Mr James immediately contacted the local police. The boys were questioned and their fright convinced the police that this was no prank.

Accompanied by their fathers, the boys led the police to the spot in the bushes. The body lay in a light dip, only 25 yards from the B651 road from St Albans to Wheathampstead, in an area used extensively by model aircraft enthusiasts and motorcyclists, known locally as Devil's Dyke.

Detective Chief Superintendent Ronald Harvey, the head of the Hertfordshire CID was summoned and the area was cordoned off. An urgent call was placed to Professor James Cameron, a leading pathologist from the London Hospital, Whitechapel, and his colleague Bernard Sims, a forensic dentist.

After preliminary tests, the body was removed to St Albans mortuary. By the time DCS Mooney arrived, who had led the investigation for nearly 11 weeks, the case had become the property of Ronald Harvey. The body was found fully clothed in jeans, striped socks and a black sweater with a vivid scarlet polo-neck and bright green cuffs. There were gold rings on two fingers of the right hand and on one finger of the left hand. Around the neck was a gold chain with a Woodstock charm attached to it. There was no doubt that it was Janie Shepherd.

At 11.15 p.m. Professor Cameron and Bernard Sims began a post-mortem examination that lasted four hours. Cameron noted ligatures on the outside left ankle above the socks, indicating that the feet had been bound before death with the right leg placed in front. There were also ligatures on the upper arms, extensive bruising on the upper arms and chest and what may have been finger-nail marks on both the breasts. There was additional bruising on the back of the left foot, the right shin, the right thigh and the left temple. Janie Shepherd had fought for her life.

Despite the bruising to the left temple there was no indication of a fracture of the skull, but the lungs and heart revealed elements of asphyxia. Cameron concluded that the victim had died from compression of the neck. By 3.15 a.m. Bernard Sims had completed his identification, using Janie Shepherd's dental charts.

On 19 April, Angela and John Darling were woken at 8 a.m. at their home in Sydney, Australia, to be told of the discovery. Only a few weeks before, the distraught couple had been in England searching for Janie, and had been within three miles of the spot where she was found.

The finding of a body usually sheds some light on the circumstances of death, but, in Shepherd's case, it confused the situation. When Shepherd left her cousin's flat in Clifton Hill on the evening of 4 February, she had been wearing a check shirt over a fawn sweater and a thick white cardigan over jeans and boots. When found, she was clothed in the jeans, unzipped although still buttoned at the waist and she was wearing the black, red and green sweater she had packed in her big red satchel. Her underwear had also been changed.

Lost evidence

The area was minutely explored but neither the missing garments, nor Shepherd's tapestry and wool, were found. The post-mortem had revealed that she had been sitting upright before her death but the degree of decomposition made it impossible to tell whether she had been raped or indecently assaulted. Semen had been found inside her Mini, but at that time, there was not the technology to identify semen groups. After four days, the time it took to locate the Mini after Janie disappeared, nothing conclusive could be learnt from it.

The inquest on Janie Shepherd opened on 22 April 1977, in St Albans. The coroner, Dr Arnold Mendoza, adjourned the hearing for further forensic tests to be made both on the body and the car. On 24 October, the inquest was reopened before a jury. Professor Cameron testified that Shepherd had died of compression of the neck but that he was unable to say whether the compression was manual or caused by some hard object. He added that she had been bound hand and foot and that the extensive bruising on her body suggested that she had either struggled desperately or had been beaten up. The court also heard evidence from Alistair Sampson, who spoke of Shepherd's good health and high spirits on the night of her disappearance, and from Roddy Kinkead-Weekes, who gave evidence about Janie's schedule for the evening.

The court also heard that, despite statements from 825 people, her killer had not been identified. The jury returned a verdict of murder by person or persons unknown. That afternoon, Janie Shepherd was laid to rest. Her remains were cremated at Garston Crematorium near Watford in a service

Killer: David Lashley

attended by Angela and John Darling, Roddy Kinkead-Weekes, and a few close friends.

THE BEAST

When Angela and John Darling returned to Australia on April 12, 1977, their one consolation was a firm assurance from Henry Mooney that one day he would bring their daughter's murderer to justice. He promised to keep in touch, even though he was to retire in June of that year, and he exchanged letters and Christmas cards with Mr and Mrs Darling throughout the long wait.

Angela Darling never gave up hope. In June 1988 she once more wrote to the Home Office requesting any fresh information. Whether she was aware that David Lashley, Mooney's prime suspect, was due for release in February 1989, has never been disclosed, but the Home Office contacted the Hertfordshire police with a suggestion that the case be reviewed.

The brief went to Detective-Superintendent Ian Whinnett who called in Detective-Constable Mick Farenden, an officer who had been on duty on 18 April 1977, when Dean James' father had reported the finding of the body.

Farenden had been celebrating the promotion of some colleagues but, within hours, he had set up an incident room at St Albans police station. Eleven years had elapsed but Farenden was familiar with the contents of all the boxes in which the evidence had been stored. The Hertfordshire police had been made aware of Henry Mooney's opinions early in the investigation, while Lashley was in Brixton Prison on remand for the double rape and the attempted murder of Miss A.

At the time of Mrs Darling's letter, Lashley was in Frankland Prison, Durham, a high security jail where, even after 11 years, he was still a Category A – or dangerous – prisoner. Whinnett and Farenden travelled north to talk to the prison personnel and there they discovered some extraordinary information.

Careless talk

Although there was no record of Lashley ever having received any formal psychiatric treatment, prison officers had written down the reports on Lashley from fellow inmates. The gist of these remarks, which could have been dismissed as gossip or attempts by informers to curry favour, were consistent over the years. Lashley was eaten up with hatred for the police – and women. He had once said quite simply, 'When I get out, there are two things I am going to do. First, I am going to get even with the police. Then, I am going to go on a rape and murder campaign against females. If you think Hungerford was bad just wait and see when I'm free.'

At the top of his hit list in the police was Henry Mooney and his family. It was said that he planned to use a machete. As a result, a meeting was organized between officers of the Hertfordshire and Metropolitan police forces at which Henry Mooney was present, even though retired.

The re-investigation started with a team of seven officers systematically reading through every statement taken in 1977 and tracing the people who had made them. It took Mick Farenden three months to find the checkout girl from the Europa supermarket.

One by one, the witnesses were tracked down, but the man whom nobody – prisoners, police officers and prison warders alike – wanted to see back on the streets of London was finally delivered up to justice by a criminal with a conscience.

The police were no nearer to finding conclusive evidence against Lashley, when a prisoner from Frankland recounted a conversation he had had with Lashley in the sawmill where they worked.

Confidante

Lashley was a loner, but he confided in Daniel Reece, who was serving a long sentence for rape and other offences. It was not, however, the similarity of their crimes that cemented their friendship, so much as their shared passion for fitness and body-building. The two men spent hours in the prison gym, practising weightlifting. Lashley regularly lifted 700 pounds, a weight only the strongest men in Britain can achieve.

It was after reading a piece in a newspaper about a black man receiving a long sentence for rape that an enraged Lashley turned to Reece, a white man, and said, 'He should have killed her. If I had killed that one (Miss A.) like I did the other, I wouldn't be here now.'

Lashley went on to describe in extraordinary detail how he had abducted 'a nice-looking blonde' after seeing her get out of her Mini and go into a shop in Queensway. He had noticed the 'For Sale' in the rear window and waylaid her on her return. He had grabbed her in the car and flourished a butcher's knife, cutting the roof of the car to demonstrate how sharp it was, driven to some dark place in the Ladbroke Grove area where he ripped her clothes to shreds with the knife and raped her.

Lashley told Reece that she had put up a terrific struggle but he had insisted on making her tell him how much she was enjoying it. He then demonstrated to Reece how he had killed her. Having re-dressed the body, he had strapped her into the passenger seat, driven out into the country and thrown the body into some bushes.

This alleged confession, coupled with Lashley's previous statements about his plans for his release, disturbed Reece. Finally, he confided in a prison officer after stating categorically that he would not, under any circumstances, discuss the matter directly with the police. Reece said that his reason for offering the information was his concern for the safety of white women on the street. He believed that a criminal such as David Lashley should never be released.

It remains unclear exactly when the prison authorities released this report to the Hertfordshire police. But after it was received, one particularly chilling detail emerged in the files. According to Reece, Lashley had laughed as he described how the body had swayed in the front seat on the long drive to Hertfordshire. Amongst the few sightings of a dark-coloured Mini on the night of 4 February 1977, was an account by a young couple who had seen a blonde girl, apparently drunk, in a car being driven by a man with dark hair.

Damning evidence

The pathologists' report tallied with Lashley's description of the killing. The details had not been released at the inquest and Reece, unaware of the report, could not have made them up. The files on the cases which in 1969 sent Lashley to prison with a sentence of 12 years were re-opened and the victims questioned all over again. The similarity and patterns of the attack were like those made against Janie Shepherd and Miss A.

All but one of the victims had been attacked in small cars outside their own homes while parking. The only exception was a woman who, returning home, had believed Lashley's story that he was visiting a friend who lived in the same mansion block. She had let him in through the front door but, as she opened her own door, he had tried to push her inside. Her screams had sent him running.

One hour later he raped a woman in her Morris Minor outside her home in south-west London. All the women were blondes. All had been robbed of cash as well as raped and told that if they screamed, they would have their necks broken. He had been tracked down by his own car number plates and picked out separately by each woman at police identification parades.

No escape

By November 1988, a combined team of Hertfordshire and Scotland Yard detectives was convinced it had enough evidence to prosecute Lashley. But there were still some unresolved questions about procedure. It had to be decided whether to interview Lashley about the murder of Janie Shepherd in prison, or wait for his release in February 1989. The detectives decided to wait, but in January 1989, the news of the re-opening of the Janie Shepherd case and of the imminent release of the unnamed prime suspect – a vicious rapist – was released to the press.

It became front page news and could have easily cost Daniel Reece his life. When Lashley read the papers, he turned on Reece saying, 'You've grassed on me. You are only one I've confessed to.' Lashley was transferred instantly to Durham Prison, another high security jail, but Reece was beaten up a few days later by other prisoners. On Sunday 16 February, Lashley was transferred back to Frankland. It is customary for a prisoner to be released from the prison where he was serving his sentence.

At 7 a.m. on Monday 17 February, Lashley walked towards the gates, escorted by prison warders. As they went he turned to a prison officer and said, 'The police are waiting for me, aren't they?' He was right. DS Ian Whinnett and DC Mick Farenden were outside. Lashley was free for barely 30 seconds before they charged him with the murder of Janie Shepherd and bundled him into a high security van, standing by to take him to St Albans police station.

His arrest received wide news coverage and, by the time he appeared in St Albans Magistrates Court for remand on Thursday, 10 February 1989, the police had been given further vital evidence against him by prison officers at Parkhurst, the high security prison on the Isle of Wight. There a prisoner named Robert Hodgson alleged that Lashley had as good as confessed to the Shepherd killing in Wakefield Prison, where, in 1981, they were both doing time. Lashley had asked Hodgson what he was in for. Hodgson replied that he had been convicted of killing a woman in a car. 'What did you do with the body?' Lashley is said to have asked. When Hodgson said he had left it in the car, his fellow criminal Lashley replied, 'You should have done like me and shoved it in some woods'.

Lashley was remanded in Brixton prison and committal proceedings began at St Albans Magistrates Court at the end of May 1989. Both Reece and Hodgson gave evidence and a small account of the proceedings appeared in the *Times* and *Guardian*, as Lashley requested that reporting restrictions should be lifted. As a result, a third prisoner stated that Lashley had confessed to the crime. On 2 June 1989 Lashley was committed for trial for the murder of Janie Shepherd.

JUST DESSERTS

On Tuesday, 7 February 1990, 13 years to the month after Janie Shepherd disappeared, David Lashley walked into the dock of St Albans Crown Court under a heavy guard of policemen. He had not withdrawn his threat to 'get' several prison warders and police officers. Lashley pleaded 'Not Guilty' to the murder of Janie Shepherd, which had occurred sometime between 4 February and 18 April 1977.

Michael Kalisher, QC, prosecuting, told the court that although within a fortnight of Janie's disappearance, Lashley had been arrested under suspicion of committing the crime, it had been thought that the evidence was insufficient for a prosecution. Kalisher then read out the sworn statement from Daniel Reece. 'The Crown will contend that the confession was so detailed, so accurate, and so consistent with the known facts about the murder that it could only have come from the murderer himself. It is overwhelming and, in a sense, too horrifying to be anything other than the truth.'

A ghastly demonstration

During the three-week trial, Daniel Reece, the chief witness, described how Lashley had demonstrated how he had murdered Janie Shepherd.

Reece claimed that Lashley had held his own neck in one hand, and pressed the fist of his other hand hard against his own windpipe. As he went through these actions, Lashley explained that this was how he had killed Janie Shepherd.

The pathologist's report, made by Professor Cameron in April 1977, had concluded that death had been caused by compression of the neck but its detailed findings had never been made public. Reece could not have known them. Reece said that Lashley had claimed to have eaten some of the food Janie had bought, mentioning salmon rather than the smoked trout she had purchased. But even that slight mistake made Reece's statement all the more authentic. Also, Lashley was supposed to have said that he had thrown the rest of the contents of her shopping into the gardens around Queensway on his return from Hertfordshire and that he had almost panicked when the car stuck in the mud after he had abandoned the body. He had to get out and push it to start. The forensic examination of the mud-covered car after it was found on 8 February, 1977 in Elgin Crescent, bore the signs of wheel spin on the tyre. This detail had not been made public.

Thorough research

Police research into Lashley's background had shown that he was quite familiar with the area where the body was found. He had been a van driver for a Hertfordshire school outfitters in the Hatfield and St Albans area, and he visited his stepson who had lived in the National Children's Home in Harpenden during the 1960s.

Lashley and his wife, Jean, used to take the boy and his friends out to play on Nomansland Common. There were other minor points of evidence against Lashley, such as the chewing gum packets, of a type he used, which had been found in the Mini. Janie did not chew gum. Cigarette butts of a kind that Janie did not smoke were also found.

Technology could now identify semen groups and the semen found in the Mini gave a reaction for an A-secretor. David Lashley was an A-secretor.

The smallest evidence

The police diligence had been extraordinary. They had kept, in a small plastic bag, the peanut shells found in Janie's Mini and also in Lashley's Vauxhall Victor, which he used as a delivery van. Also detectives had traced all the women involved in Lashley's previous crimes, and these women were all willing to repeat their testimony against Lashley during his trial for Shepherd's murder.

Lashley had an alibi. When first interviewed on 12 February 1977, he had denied all knowledge of Janie's fate, stating that he had travelled to Leicester with a girlfriend. Then, he checked in at his place of work for the following day's orders and arrived at his aunt's home in Beaconsfield Road, Southall, west London, where he had a room, at around 7 p.m.

Quiet evening

According to Lashley, he had watched television and gone to bed at 9.30 p.m. Thirteen years later his aunt, Mrs Eurthra Smith, corroborated this story under oath. She had supported Lashley's alibi in 1977 and she repeated it in 1990. He had gone to bed early, his aunt explained, and had complained of feeling unwell. She had stayed up to watch the rest of the evening's programmes and, after the closedown, had checked the front and back doors and all the rooms in the house. Lashley was then fast asleep, she told the court.

Throughout the case, Mrs Angela Darling sat in court wearing the Woodstock charm on a chain and one of the rings that had been found on Janie's body. When she took the witness box, the judge, Mr Justice Alliott, expressed his concern for her well-being, but Angela Darling told him she was there at her own request. She told the court that DCS Henry Mooney had told her many years before that he suspected a man of the murder, but Mrs Darling said she could not remember when she had first learned the name of this suspect. In the witness box she was trembling and nervous but she had sat unflinchingly through all the horrific details of Janie's abduction, rape and murder listening to tales of mutilation and humilitation her daughter had suffered at her killer's hand.

On Monday, 19 March 1990, the jury retired for two and a quarter hours, and returned with a unanimous verdict: Guilty. There were cheers from the public gallery and tears from Angela Darling before Mr Justice Alliott could quieten the court to pass sentence. Life imprisonment, the automatic sentence for murder, can, in practice, mean parole, after a term of seven to nine years. But in Lashley's case, the judge chose his words extremely carefully.

'The decision is such that whoever is responsible must have the utmost, careful regard before you are ever allowed your liberty again,' he told

Killer: David Lashley

Lashley. 'In my view you are such an appalling, dangerous man that the real issue is whether the authorities can ever allow you your liberty in your natural lifetime.'

The family of Janie Shepherd were triumphant. 'Justice has been done,' said Angela Darling. 'We have always prayed this would happen.'

CASE FILE: LASHLEY, DAVID

BACKGROUND

David Lashley was born on 30 September, 1939, in St Lawrence, Barbados. His record shows no signs of any juvenile delinquency. Leaving school at the age of 13 in 1953, he went into apprenticeship as a car-sprayer for the local Rootes factory. He developed an ambition to come to London and Rootes offered him a place at their factory in west London. Lashley lived in a room at his aunt's house in Southall, west London. In the early 1960s, he met a young, blonde, white woman who was pregnant by a former boyfriend. Lashley would walk her to her home in west London at night, worried about her being out alone on the dark streets. Vulnerable and very scared, the 19 year-old girl became dependent on Lashley's kindness and soon after the birth of her son they set up home together.

Lashley loved his new family life and was tender and considerate towards the boy but when, in 1962, Jean gave birth to their own daughter, Sandra, he began to change. In a violent row over a cracked tea-cup in the sink, Jean suffered three broken ribs. Horrified by his own behaviour, Lashley begged Jean both to forgive him and marry him, which she did.

Soon after, a son was born and from that time Lashley became obsessively jealous about his blonde wife and her past. He wanted her to place her first son in a children's home, demanding to know why he should work for another man's child. The arguments became more and more violent and, on one occasion, Lashley grabbed a chair and beat Jean with it until she lost consciousness.

Jean, who had herself been brought up in orphanages, gave in after a time. She was frightened for her two children and placed her illegitimate son in the National Children's Home at Harpenden. But this made no difference to the atmosphere at home or to Lashley's jealousy. His sexual demands became more brutal, and were utterly unaccompanied by love or affection. By now he had become a van driver for a school outfitters in Hertfordshire and was convinced that every time he left home his wife was indulging in an affair.

Full of hate

In 1965 Jean became pregnant again but Lashley told her he could not afford more children: she must have an abortion. He literally dragged her to a back street abortionist, who bungled the operation. The baby died nine days after birth. By that time Lashley was so full of hate that he ignored the funeral. That was the turning point. When Lashley stayed out late at night, Jean was indifferent.

But during that time, when the tabloids printed headlines about 'The Beast of Shepherd's Bush', an unknown prowler who raped young women in their cars, it never occurred to her that it could be Lashley. Then, one evening, Jean went out to make a telephone call while a friend minded the children. While she was out, Lashley returned home and raped the friend on the kitchen floor. The girl – also a blonde – was in a state of shock when Jean returned. When confronted, Lashley would say only 'she asked for it'. A few days later, Lashley was charged with the rape and the indecent assault of five women.

PSYCHOLOGICAL PROFILE

There is a huge chasm between the people who kill because of some unbearable conflict between love and hatred, and those to whom others have become mere symbols. The first are usually desperate people driven beyond endurance, unable to look openly at themselves and their problems. So they resort to violence in their own homes, get caught and end up shamed and repentant.

It is when the failure to deal with the inner self focuses on others, on strangers, that the real trouble begins.

The spreading of that pain and rage makes such people very dangerous to society, all the more so as even close relatives, friends or workmates are usually unaware of the pent-up emotions which are simmering deep inside.

Killer: David Lashley

It is sometimes claimed that multiple killers want to kill that part of themselves they subconsciously recognise. In the case of David Lashley it seems that jealousy and the fear of losing his wife's love became the spur that led to Janie Shepherd's murder.

As a young man, Lashley had fallen in love with a blonde girl. He was then new to London, a boy from Barbados living in a big city for the first time. He was not a drifter, but had a ready-made job and ambitions to be a successful boxer when he met Jean, a young white girl who was pregnant by a man who had deserted her. He was happy to look after her and her son. They were friends first, lovers later and, following the birth of their daughter, husband and wife.

White trash

It was soon after this event that Lashley started to become obsessional about Jean's past. The phrase 'white trash' was being bandied about by black militants in the mid-1960s but, whatever the background influences, political or emotional, the nice boy was turning into an angry man.

There is no record of Lashley taking drugs but smoking marijuana was part of the subculture of the time, and there was a hardening of black attitudes towards the police (there were almost no black officers). Whatever caused the hatred between Lashley and his wife, it was probably aggravated by guilt at having separated Jean from her first-born son, who, because of Lashley's unreasonable jealousy of him, had been put in a national children's home.

In time, the hatred Lashley felt grew into an extreme hatred of all whites, particularly blonde women, as Lashley fought a losing battle to remain in control of his domestic life. According to his wife, his sexual needs at this time were inexhaustable. It is possible that the revulsion she came to feel, and could not conceal, added to his need for revenge.

His choice of women driving small cars is difficult to understand, but Lashley was a big, strong man and perhaps the confined space would have increased his power over his victims. They were trapped, helpless. A rapist is by nature a bully, and bullies are almost inevitably cowards, so they are invariably armed, either with a gun or a knife. Most of them rob as well as rape, the women being anxious to hand over money in the hope of escaping the threatened ordeal.

Unfortunately, their acquiesence often encourages the violent side of their attackers.

For Lashley, rape gave him the illusion of mastery and control. Serving a prison sentence for it between 1977 and 1989, he may have brooded about letting his victims go. His hatred would probably have deepened when his wife divorced him. Perhaps he resolved that, next time he raped, he would leave no witness behind. That doomed potential witness was Janie Shepherd.

Chapter 20

JOHN REGINALD CHRISTIE
THE RILLINGTON PLACE KILLER

In 1949 a mother and child were viciously strangled at 10 Rillington Place. For this crime, Timothy Evans was hanged. But when three years later another six bodies were carried out from the house, it became shockingly clear that British justice had miscarried.

The shabby, ground-floor kitchen was finally going to be cleaned up. Beresford Brown, the Jamaican tenant who lived in a room on the top floor, was delighted. The whole house had looked a mess ever since the war. Number 10 Rillington Place was situated in what is now London's wealthier district of north Kensington. In March 1953, the terraced cul-de-sac, with crumbling stone doorways, had turned into one of the most neglected streets around Ladbroke Grove.

Brown had seen all types of tenants moving in and out of the house. Many of them had been drifters, hardly caring how they lived. Everyone in the district had known about the dreadful business in 1949, when the young Welshman, Timothy Evans killed his wife and baby. They had hanged him.

The last link with those days had gone. John Christie, the quiet, balding little man who had lived on the ground floor had left. He seemed just to come and go, often bringing down-at-heel women back for a few hours, or a few days. But now he had gone for good. First his wife had left, then he followed.

Beresford Brown was cheery. The previous day, the landlord had called to find that Christie had illegally rented his flat to two sub-tenants, a couple called Reilly. They had paid Christie £7.13s – three months' rent in advance.

The landlord promptly told the couple to be out by the morning, and had given Brown permission to use the ground-floor kitchen. Here was a chance to use it as a home, not the depressing, rubbish-filled slum Christie had left behind.

No one knew or cared where Christie had gone. He had left the same morning that Mr and Mrs Reilly arrived, borrowing one of their suitcases to pack some lady's things in, as well as some photographs and frames. Christie had told them he was being transferred to Birmingham, and that his wife had gone ahead of him.

Brown warmed to his task. Over the next few days, he carried piles of clothes, rubbish and filth into the tiny backyard, alongside the wash-house. The kitchen had peeling walls, ageing paint and no amenities. Eventually, he cleared the rubbish and was ready to make a start.

He found a place where he could put up some brackets to hold a radio set, then tapped what he thought was a rear wall. It sounded hollow. Brown tapped again, and pulled away a strip of the peeling wallpaper. There was no wall there at all, but a papered-over wooden door to an alcove.

Disbelief

Brown shone his torch into the opening. At first he could not believe what he saw. Throwing down the torch, he ran to the second floor to fetch another tenant, Ivan Williams. Cautiously they went downstairs and shone the torch into the alcove.

Sitting on a pile of rubbish was a partially clothed woman's body. She was wearing a white, cotton pique jacket, held by a safety pin, a blue bra, stockings and a pink suspender belt. Brown raced off for the police.

Detectives immediately discovered that 10 Rillington Place concealed not one, but several bodies. The first woman found in the alcove was attached by the bra straps to a blanket wrapped around a second body. Behind them was a third, covered in an old woollen blanket, tied at the ankles with a plastic flex. All three women had been strangled.

By the early hours of the next day, 25 March, a fourth dead woman had been found beneath some rubble in the front room. She was Ethel Christie. The police called a halt for the night. Officers were posted outside the house, and a guard remained there for several weeks.

In the press, detectives announced 'the most brutal mass killing known in London'. There was one 'vital witness' they believed could help them in their inquiries. His name was John Reginald Halliday Christie. A description of the slight, middle-aged former tenant was circulated. Football crowds were asked to report any sighting at once. Christie's face appeared in every national newspaper.

Excavation work in the tiny garden at Rillington Place revealed the skeletons of two more women. Medical tests showed that they had been buried for approximately ten years. A leading pathologist, Dr Francis Camps, stated that both had been sexually assaulted and strangled. The skull of one woman was missing.

The search went on. Long rods were put up the chimney. An old-fashioned copper boiler was removed. Detectives and doctors came and went as crowds gathered at the entrance of the small cul-de-sac.

Of Christie, there was no sign. The police had not yet tracked him down, but the press knew where to find his former colleagues. During the war, Christie had been a Special Constable with the Emergency Reserve at the Harrow Road police station in west London. One of his former workmates remembered Christie well.

'I worked with him on all kinds of crime investigations,' the officer told reporters. 'He was always secluded and reticent and never mixed with the boys. But he knew his job. In his time, he had brought to justice thieves, blackmailers, fraudsmen and men who were found guilty of sexual assaults on women.'

The day he left Rillington Place, Christie had booked into Rowton House in King's Cross Road for seven nights. But he soon moved on, wandering uneasily, often lost, across distant parts of London. Sometimes he found himself in East Ham and Barking, miles from home. Then he would make his way back to the north Kensington area.

Christie passed much of these days in cafes. In one in Pentonville Road, north London, he met a woman called Margaret Wilson, and offered to procure an abortion when she confided that she was pregnant. It was quite common for troubled women, even complete strangers, to tell Christie their problems.

Though neither handsome nor scintillating, Christie was aware of his mysterious charisma. 'I could hardly go anywhere but women would want to talk to me,' he would say later, 'dozens of them.' On another occasion, he insisted, 'It wasn't me who did the chasing. Girls were attracted to me.'

Unconfirmed sightings

There were many 'sightings' of Christie. He was seen sleeping in a van, he had boarded a north-bound coach, he had gone abroad. Dozens of reports were received.

A woman who lived in Rillington Place, Florence Newman, reported that she had seen Christie hanging around the cul-de-sac. One newspaper, the *Daily Sketch*, carried a photofit of what he was believed to be wearing – a light brown trilby, a double-breasted overcoat with padded 'spiv' shoulders, a belt with a black leather buckle, blue tie, pink striped shirt and brown shoes. When Christie was finally apprehended, he was wearing none of these things.

It was on 29 March 1953, at 11.20 in the evening, that Norman Rae, chief crime reporter on the *News of the World*, received a phone-call. 'You recognize my voice?' the caller asked the reporter.

Rae did. He would have known that gravelly grate anywhere. Like policemen, crime reporters have long memories. Rae had met Christie before, in 1950, during the trial of Timothy Evans.

Close to collapse

'I can't stand any more,' the voice went on. 'They're hunting me like a dog and I'm tired out. I'm cold and wet and I've nothing to change into.'

Christie told Rae that in return for a meal, a smoke and a warm place to sit, he would give the *News of the World* a story about himself. Rae warned him that, afterwards, the police would have to be called in. Christie said that he understood this, and a meeting was arranged for 1.30 a.m. that night, outside Wood Green Town Hall in north London.

Rae and his driver parked outside the Town Hall, away from the street lamp, opened the car door and waited. There was a rustle in the bushes. Then, by chance, two policemen approached on their beat, unaware of the meeting. Thinking he had been betrayed, Christie fled.

Putney arrest

Two days later, 31 March, PC Thomas Ledger saw a man leaning over the embankment by Putney Bridge. 'What are you doing?' he asked. 'Looking for work?' The short, middle-aged man said he was waiting for his unemployment cards.

'Can you tell me who you are?' PC Ledger continued.

'John Waddington, 35 Westbourne Grove,' came the reply.

The alert young officer studied the man's face, then asked him to remove his hat. The balding features confirmed Ledger's suspicion. The hunt for Christie was over.

Inside the police van, Christie was asked to empty his pockets. Various bits and pieces were pulled out, including a newspaper cutting of Timothy Evans' trial in 1950.

FALSE CONFESSIONS

Timothy and Beryl Evans moved into the top-floor flat at 10 Rillington Place during Easter, 1948. Evans, then 24, had spotted a 'To Let' sign outside the building while the couple were living with his mother and stepfather. Beryl was pregnant, and the couple needed to find a place quickly.

In October, their baby girl, Geraldine, was born. For the first time in their married life, the Evans' seemed able to settle.

One floor below them lived Charles Kitchener, a lifelong railwayman who had lived at No 10 since the 1920s. He kept himself to himself, but his failing eyesight meant he spent more and more time in hospital. The ground floor was occupied by the Christies. Timothy and Beryl got on quite well with them. Ethel Christie seemed fond of the baby, although Evans was troubled that John Christie clearly found Beryl attractive.

Later, the Evans were given the opportunity to move to a flat elsewhere. But Beryl was happy at Rillington Place and wanted to stay. Ethel Christie had promised to keep her eye on Geraldine whenever Beryl was at her part-time job.

Unwanted pregnancy

In the summer of 1949, Beryl became pregnant again. She was dismayed. The couple had little money coming in, and there were still hire-purchase payments to make. Beryl decided to have an abortion. Her husband, with his Roman Catholic upbringing, was against this, but Beryl was adamant. She was still a very young woman, only 19, with no interest in being tied to her home.

Making inquiries, she found that there was a back-street abortionist just a few miles away in the Edgware Road who would do the job for £1. She told several people of her intentions. One of them was Christie.

Medical qualifications

Using his celebrated charm, Christie persuaded Beryl that he could perform an abortion for her in the house. Evans was furious and went downstairs to challenge Christie. Had he any medical knowledge, Evans demanded to know. Certainly, Christie told him, and slyly showed Evans what he called 'one of my medical books'.

It was nothing more than a first-aid manual of the St John's Ambulance Brigade, but Christie knew that Evans was barely literate. Moreover, the drawings would impress him.

Evans did his best for his family, and worked long hours, often leaving the house at 6.30 in the morning and not returning before early evening. Mr Kitchener from the middle floor was in hospital having an operation to save his sight. For most of the day, Beryl and the Christies were alone at 10 Rillington Place.

It is impossible to determine exactly when the operation took place. Workmen were at No 10 around this time, making repairs to the damp plaster in the water closet and washroom.

On either 6 November 1949, or the day after, Evans came home to find Christie waiting for him. The operation had not been a success, Christie told Evans. Beryl had died.

If Evans went to the police, it was possible that Christie would be charged with murder, certainly with manslaughter, as abortion was illegal. Cunningly, he persuaded Evans to help him move Beryl's body into the absent Mr Kitchener's flat. In doing this, Evans became an accessory to murder.

Evans wanted to take the baby, Geraldine, round to his mother, Mrs Probert. Christie dissuaded him, promising that he and his wife would find someone to look after her. When Evans returned from work on 10 November, Christie was again waiting, this time to say the child had been taken to a couple in East Acton who would look after her.

Christie also offered to help Evans another way. He said he would help to dispose of Beryl's body by putting it down a drain.

Return to Wales

In the days that followed, still helped by Christie, Evans sold the household furniture for the large sum of £40, even though some of it was still on hire-purchase. Evans bought himself a camel coat for £19 out of the proceeds. He told Christie's wife that he was going to Bristol, but after destroying the bloodstained bedding on which Beryl had died, he went to South Wales to stay with his aunt and uncle.

There was no peace for Evans in Wales. His mind was tortured. After a brief return to London, he told his family that Beryl had walked out on him. There were also letters from his mother, complaining about having to pay his debts. Evans finally decided there was only one thing to do. He walked into Merthyr Vale police station and told the detective-constable that he had disposed of his wife.

Web of lies

Evans' attempts at cunning merely exposed his naivety. He thought he could clear himself without implicating Christie. Evans told the police that he had obtained a bottle containing something for his wife to procure a miscarriage. The bottle, he said, had been given to him by a man he met casually in a transport cafe, between Colchester and Ipswich. His wife had found the bottle just before he went to work. He had returned home to find her dead, although he had not told her to drink the contents. He had opened a drain outside the front door, put his wife's body down it, and arranged for someone to look after the baby girl.

The Merthyr Vale police contacted Notting Hill, who sent officers to search the manhole outside 10 Rillington Place. It took three of them to lift the cover. The drain was empty. Back in Merthyr, Evans was told the news but insisted he had lifted the manhole cover by himself and pushed Beryl inside.

When challenged directly by a detective, his statement collapsed. He made a second, this time implicating Christie as the abortionist.

Arrested for theft

Another search took place at Rillington Place. It was not very meticulous. The thigh bone of one of Christie's victims, Muriel Eady, was propped against the garden fence, and left unnoticed. The search failed to unearth any bodies, but what police did find was a stolen brief-case. This was enough to get Evans arrested.

Christie was asked to attend the police station, and gave a masterful performance, drawing on the sense of brotherhood that existed even between former colleagues in the force. He gave details of the Evans' quarrels, and of complaints by Beryl of her throat being grabbed.

Another, more determined search was made at Rillington Place. This time police found what they were looking for. The body of Beryl Evans was found wrapped in a green tablecloth behind a stack of wood. The body of Geraldine was found behind the door, with a tie around her neck.

A pathologist, Dr Donald Teare, reported that both victims had been strangled. Beryl's right eye and upper lip were badly swollen, and there were signs of bruising in her vagina. Dr Teare thought of taking a swab but 'others thought it unnecessary'.

To the police, it was now a 'simple domestic' matter. Evans was brought back to London on Friday, 2 December 1949. The group arrived at Paddington Station at 9.30 p.m.

Less than half-an-hour later, Evans made a first brief statement at Notting Hill police station, saying he had strangled Beryl with a rope and put her in the outside wash-house after the Christies had gone to bed. Two days later, he had strangled the baby and put her there, too.

Evans immediately made yet another, much longer statement – his fourth in all. It took 75 minutes to write it down and read back to him. This repeated the earlier confessions Evans had made, but went into far more detail, saying that Beryl had been getting him into deeper and deeper debt.

Evans was charged with murdering his wife and daughter. The Crown decided to proceed only on the killing of the baby. There would be no possible sympathy for such a crime.

Timothy Evans' trial for murder began at No 1 Court at the Old Bailey on 11 January 1950, before Mr Justice Lewis.

The Crown was represented by Mr Christmas Humphreys KC (King's Counsel). Evans' defence was led by Malcolm Morris, a handsome man, well over 6ft tall, with a beautiful speaking voice, which he had previously used to great effect with juries.

Humphreys opened the case to the jury, laying stress on the confessions.

There was also the evidence of the Christies. In the witness box, John Christie won sympathy by telling the judge that he had difficulty in speaking because he had been gassed during World War I. His service as a special constable confirmed the impression of a sound, dutiful citizen.

Morris would have liked to base the defence on the second Merthyr confession. But it was now established that Beryl had died not from the abortion, but from strangulation. He suggested that Christie knew something more about the deaths of Mrs Evans and her daughter. Christie said, 'It's a lie.'

Gaining sympathy

Christie denied taking part in the abortion, or having medical books, and said that he had been in bed with enteritis and fibrositis on the day of Beryl's death. His disabilities again won the judge's sympathy.

Evans gave evidence poorly. True or false, his own version of events showed him appallingly lacking in decent feeling or regard for the law.

The judge summed up against Evans, and the jury was out for only 40 minutes. The verdict was guilty and the sentence, death by hanging.

To the end, Evans maintained that Christie had killed both Beryl and Geraldine. To his solicitors, counsel, family, priests and prison officers, he repeated the same story. After his appeal was lost on 20 February, Evans waited patiently for a reprieve from the Home Secretary.

Some public disquiet about the verdict already existed. A petition with 1,800 signatures was presented to the Home Office. But a reprieve was not granted.

Evans was received back into the Roman Catholic Church and, at 8 o'clock in the morning on 9 March 1950, he was hanged.

HOME FOR TEA

It was three years after Evans was hanged that Christie was arrested and found guilty of murder. The news caused a sensation – two murderers had lived in the same house.

Christie was sent to Brixton Prison, and, once inside, made no secret of his violence against women. Solicitors, fellow inmates and eventually the press were treated to self-righteous, detailed accounts of his killings.

Christie compared his first victim, Austrian Ruth Fuerst, to an artist's first painting. 'It is the same with me when I try to remember my first murder,' he told the *Sunday Pictorial* newspaper. 'It was thrilling because I had embarked on the career I had chosen for myself, the career of murder. But it was only the beginning.'

Killer: John Reginald Christie

The charmer

If Christie's appearance had been shabby and anonymous, he still saw himself as a charmer of ladies. He dismissed comparison with Boris Karloff, an actor noted for horror films. 'More like Charles Boyer, me,' Christie would say, referring to one of the most romantic film actors of the day.

But through his boastfulness, Christie's basic fear of women was plain. Coquettish women, in particular, seem to have troubled him the most. 'Women who give you the come-on wouldn't look nearly so saucy if they were helpless and dead,' he said. Christie also took pride in concealing his violent intentions from the women he took back to Rillington Place, until, as he put it, 'it was too late'.

In prison, Christie astutely realized that the main issue at his trial would be his own personality. He had always been a mass of contradictions. In the evenings, he would go out for a walk with his wife on his arm, tipping his hat to acquaintances. Yet one day he would kill her.

When he and Ethel visited her family in Leeds. Christie spoke of his 'big house in London' with servants. But he never earned more than £8 a week, the going rate for a junior clerk.

In 1939, just before the war broke out. Christie had been accepted as a Special Constable. To all intents and purposes, he seemed a reformed character. But his petty-mindedness soon showed. He and another Special were known as 'the rat and the weasel'. Locals began to fear his footsteps, and it was on the beat that he met the tall, dark-haired Ruth Fuerst.

The Austrian girl's pay in a munitions factory was poor and she began to supplement her income by prostitution. Soon, she had a baby by an American soldier.

She met Christie while he was trying to trace a man wanted for theft. Ruth asked him to lend her ten shillings and Christie, seeing his chance, invited her to 10 Rillington Place for the first time.

One hot August afternoon in 1943, while Mrs Christie was away in Sheffield, Ruth called again.

'I was rather backward and shy about the act of love-making on this occasion, but she was encouraging,' Christie was later to say. 'After the affair was ended. I strangled her.'

Christie went on to describe what he called the beauty of her appearance in death, and the peace he felt. Equally grotesque was his stealthy, nocturnal burial of Ruth Fuerst after his wife unexpectedly returned home.

Christie left the police at the end of 1943, and found work at the Ultra Radio Works in west London. There he befriended Muriel Eady.

He knew that Muriel suffered from catarrh and said he knew a remedy. Muriel visited Rillington Place one afternoon in October 1944 and, after the cup of tea enjoyed by all of Christie's victims, was shown a patent inhaler. This was a square jar with a metal lid containing perfumed water.

There were two holes in the lid and, unknown to Muriel, a tube in one was connected to a gas pipe.

So clever

Confident that the perfume would disguise the smell of gas, Christie persuaded her to inhale. Then, as Muriel became drowsy, he 'made love' to her and strangled her.

'My second murder was a really clever murder,' he would write, 'much, much cleverer than the first one. I planned it very carefully.'

Suddenly, as far as is known, the murders ceased. Apparently, it was another ten years before Christie killed again.

Act of mercy

On 14 December 1952, Christie was awakened, in his own account, by convulsions suddenly being suffered by Ethel. His wife was by now elderly and arthritic. Christie said he could do nothing to restore her breathing and decided to end her misery in the kindest way. Ethel Christie died from strangulation. 'For two days I left my wife's body in bed. And then I pulled up the floorboards of the front room and buried her,' he later said. This act of mercy caused him much pain, he claimed. 'From the first day I missed her. The quiet love she and I bore each other happens only once in a lifetime.'

Any semblance of normality Christie might have maintained vanished with the death of his wife. He sold most of the furniture and lived in the flat with his cat and dog to which he was devoted.

Between December 1952 and March 1953 Christie stalked, lured and murdered three more women. Kathleen Maloney was killed after she had posed nude while Christie took photographs. Her body was then bundled into an alcove in the kitchen. Rita Nelson had just found out that she was pregnant, when she disappeared on 12 January. Hectorina MacLennan was his final victim. She met Christie in a cafe and was offered accommodation. It was something of a surprise when she turned up with her boyfriend, Alexander Baker, in tow. They stayed at Rillington Place for three nights. On 6 March, Christie followed them to the Labour Exchange. While Baker went in to sign on. Christie persuaded Hectorina to come back to the flat. She told Baker and later he went to find her.

Christie had given her a drink and started to get his gas appliance to work. She saw it, became unhappy and there was a struggle. He strangled her, had sex with her and then placed her body in a sitting position with her bra hooked to Maloney's legs to keep her body in an upright position.

His pride in his artistry was undimmed. Christie was keen to show that a decent, respectable grace was present in his actions. 'I gave them a merciful exit,' he said.

Christie's confessional outpourings, however, did not mean that he intended to plead guilty to murder. He was still a ruthlessly, calculating man who hoped to cheat the gallows by proving that his homicidal mania was, in some way, excusable. Clearly, no jury would accept this if it believed Christie had killed a baby.

The prosecution was equally concerned not to implicate Christie in Geraldine's death. It would mean they had hanged an innocent man.

MERCY KILLINGS

Christie's trial began in the No. 1 Court at the Old Bailey on 22 June 1953. In the same courtroom, three years before, he had stood in the witness box and denied killing Beryl Evans. Now, he would retrace his footsteps and admit that he had.

Like Timothy Evans, Christie was tried on only one sample charge. Yet by now, the entire country knew that a mass-killer of women would be on public view, being tried for his life. Christie had by this stage confessed to seven killings: two women in 1943, Beryl Evans in 1949, his wife Ethel in 1952 and the other three women in early 1953.

His counsel, Derek Curtis-Bennett KC, was eager for the courts to hear of all these cases and 'any others of which the prosecution may know'.

It had been a painstaking task by the police to unearth the full extent of events at Rillington Place. At 6 a.m. on 18 May, Beryl Evans' body had been exhumed from its grave at Kensington Borough Cemetery in Gunnersbury for examination by the three leading pathologists of the day – Keith Simpson, Francis Camps and Donald Teare. The body of Geraldine, which lay with her mother, had not been exhumed.

There had been lengthy efforts to identify the victim's bones. In the case of Ruth Fuerst, Christie's first known victim, her skull had been reconstructed out of 110 separate pieces.

Christie wrote to an old acquaintance from prison that he was 'fuddled' and dazed by his predicament. He longed for sweets, cigarettes and the 'taste of an apple' but also spoke of the prison warders' consideration.

At the end of his formal confessions, he had written, 'I wish to state that I am most grateful to the police in charge for the kindly way in which I have been treated at Putney police station.'

Christie took care in his written confessions to provide explanations for each killing. The prostitutes had forced themselves upon him and things had got out of hand. His wife had to be put out of her pain.

Eady and Beryl Evans had also been given forms of mercy killings, according to Christie.

The Old Bailey courtroom was packed. Distinguished people from many walks of life were present. Christie, dressed in a blue, pin-stripe suit, was charged with murdering his wife and pleaded not guilty.

Insanity plea

Christie's counsel, Curtis-Bennett, told the jury that he would establish a defence of insanity under the M'Naghten Rules. These date back to 1843, when defendants were not allowed to give evidence on their own behalf. The rules state that a man is not guilty in law if, at the time of his actions, he did not know he was doing wrong.

'You can have no doubt, doctors or no doctors, that at the time he did each of these killings, including that of his wife, he was mad in the eyes of the law,' said Curtis-Bennett.

Christie walked to the witness box, apparently almost in tears, and took half a minute to mumble the oath. He constantly clasped his hands, pulled an ear, tugged his collar and smoothed his bald head as he answered questions. He could recall some murders, and not others.

Asked by his counsel if he had committed any murders between 1943 and 1949. Christie replied 'I don't know.'

'Do you mean you may have done?'

'I might have done. I don't know whether I did or not.' Christie said, but he was more definite when questioned about 1949 itself.

'Did you kill the baby, Geraldine Evans?'

'No,' came Christie's reply.

The judge, Mr Justice Finnemore, pressed Christie on his evidence at the Evans' trial, Christie became evasive.

'You were not lying about the baby, but why did you lie about Mrs Evans?'

'Well, I was accused of killing both of them,' Christie said.

The medical evidence was divided. Dr Jack Hobson, senior psychiatrist at Middlesex Hospital, met Christie ten or more times in prison, and gave evidence of his supposed horror of masturbation, and of public houses. In fact, Christie frequented run-down pubs, and semen stains were found on his clothing.

Hobson said that, under the M'Naghten Rules, Christie was not responsible. 'The tricks of memory are avoidances of getting down to disturbing topics to preserve his own self-respect rather than to avoid incriminating himself.'

The Crown's medical witnesses rejected this. In particular, Dr Desmond Curran of St George's Hospital, expressed the view that Christie was 'abnormal and conceited' but not suffering from any form of hysteria.

On the fourth day of the trial, the judge began his summing up. The jury was sent out at 4.05 p.m. and returned 82 minutes later.

'Do you find the prisoner guilty or not guilty?' the jury was asked.

'We find him guilty.'

Through tears of pity, Mr Justice Finnemore passed the death sentence. Christie said nothing.

TO THE GALLOWS

Christie's execution was only three weeks away. With his trial over, there were clamours for a more wide-ranging inquiry. Could two stranglers have operated independently, unknown to each other, in such a tiny house?

Christie was sentenced on 25 June 1953. Next day, the Labour opposition in Parliament pressed a reluctant government to review the entire Rillington Place affair. On 6 July, the Home Secretary, Sir David Maxwell Fyfe, appointed the Recorder of Portsmouth, John Scott Henderson, to study 'whether there is any ground for thinking there may have been a miscarriage of justice'.

Scott Henderson had to move quickly. His report had to be compiled before Christie went to the gallows. The task was immense. Before his appointment, he had been asked to study all the relevant documents in the Evans case. To these were now added the Christie documents. Scott Henderson had also to hold discussions with counsel for both Evans and Christie, and with numerous other officials in the case.

Scott Henderson also held a 75-minute meeting with Christie himself. Christie's permission for this had been obtained by a senior police officer assisting the inquiry. The officer had warned Christie that he would be questioned about Geraldine Evans, but gratuitously added that there was no evidence that he had killed her.

The report, presented on 13 July, bewildered people on both sides of the debate. It concluded that the case against Evans for murdering his daughter had been overwhelming. Moreover, the report said, Evans had also murdered his wife. In other words, Christie had told the truth at Evans' trial, but lied at his own, and that there were two stranglers at 10 Rillington Place.

Christie in his death cell, enjoyed a status that had during his life never before been conferred on him. But two days before his execution an old acquaintance found him a broken man. 'I don't care what happens to me now. I have nothing to live for,' said Christie. His solicitor announced there would be no formal appeal against the conviction or the sentence.

Christie wrote to another friend that he was in reasonable sorts and enjoying the food. 'I could really compliment our cook,' he wrote. 'It is really well cooked and plentiful. I am even putting on weight.' He was possibly suffering from the condemned cell syndrome of 'weight grief'. Many prisoners relieved of the ordeal of the trial actually put on weight while awaiting execution.

Christie sold his story to the *Sunday Pictorial*. But his lurid descriptions of the crimes did nothing to lift the veil of their mystery. Few people, apart from abolitionists, mourned that Christie would soon be executed, but the events of 1949, and the murders of Beryl and Geraldine Evans, needed further explanation.

Dr Hobson, the psychiatrist who testified for the defence at Christie's trial, was refused permission to see Christie again.

Hobson was outraged by this, believing that Christie's decaying memory could still be revived, and the exact fate of Geraldine Evans discovered if handled delicately.

The Evans family and their supporters were not satisfied. There had been medical evidence of an attempt to penetrate Beryl Evans sexually after her death. This had not been produced at Evans' trial, but if true then it becomes inconceivable that Evans killed his wife. The lawyers considered it too awful to present evidence of necrophilia to a jury. In 1949, science was not yet able to carry out conclusive tests on semen.

There was also evidence from the workmen who renovated Christie's flat. Evans' supporters claimed this could have shown that Evans' dates for the killings were wrong, and that the bodies could not have been in the wash-room when he said they were. But the workmen were never called to give their evidence.

Suspicion also fell on Christie's claim, made at Evans' trial, that his bad back prevented him from lifting weights. He had not complained about this until after Beryl Evans' death. Was it not possible that the pain was caused by lifting her body?

There was a crowd of about 200 people outside Pentonville Prison at 9 a.m. on the morning of 15 July 1953. People had come from Scotland, Wales, Ireland, and even from as far as Australia and the United States.

One lorry driver announced he had managed to get himself an overnight run and reached the prison 'just in nice time'. Despite this, the authorities had expected a larger and more troublesome crowd. There were none of the incidents seen at Wandsworth Prison earlier in the year when a teenager of limited mental powers, Derek Bentley, was hanged for killing a police officer.

A dozen constables stood with arms linked, as reinforcements stood by, outside the gates. Inside, the public executioner, Albert Pierrepoint, stood ready with Christie.

At 9.10, a warder appeared at the gates with a black-edged notice which he pinned up on the board. It was announced that John Reginald Halliday Christie had been executed.

CASE FILE: CHRISTIE, JOHN REGINALD

BACKGROUND

John Reginald Christie was born on 8 April 1898 in Black Boy House, Halifax.

His father, Ernest, was a designer for Crossley Carpets at Dean Clough Mills. Christie senior was a founder member of the Halifax Conservative Party, and a leading light in the Primrose League – an organization promoting purity among the working-classes. He was also the first Superintendant of the St John Ambulance Brigade, Halifax branch.

Christie's mother, Mary Hannah, was known as 'Beauty Halliday' before her marriage, and was keen on amateur dramatics.

Christie, one of seven children, had a large share of his mother's affection, but dreaded his disciplinarian father. 'We almost had to ask if we could speak to him,' he would one day write while in Pentonville Prison.

But the boy had a share of his father's ill-temper and meanness, and found few children to play with.

Schooldays

Christie sang in the school choir, and became a scout and then assistant scoutmaster. At school, he was top of the class in arithmetic and algebra. He was good with his hands, able to repair watches and make toys. Once at work, he emulated his father by helping in the first-aid room and reading medical books.

'I always made certain. I mastered any subject I took up,' he would say later. 'But once I mastered it, my interest ended.'

Three events in his early youth had a formative influence on Christie. When he was eight, his maternal grandfather died and he saw the body. Christie later described the trembling sensation he felt as both fascination and pleasure.

A second event was really a continuation of the dominance his sisters had over him. They were always bossing him about. Then one day his elder married sister invited him to her home in Halifax and, while she was fastening her shoes, the young

John saw her leg up to her knee. Although told it was nothing to be embarrassed about, he blushed furiously.

Sexual disaster

The third came in his teens after leaving school. Christie was working in the Gem Cinema, Halifax. One day, he and some friends went down a lane known as the Monkey Run. They paired off, and he found himself with a girl more sexually experienced than himself. He could not perform the sexual act. Word got around and Christie became known as 'Reggie-No-Dick' or 'Can't-do-it Reggie'. He never forgot the humiliation he experienced.

There were more disasters to follow. At 17, Christie was caught stealing while working as a clerk with the local police. He was sacked and his father banned him from the house.

Job followed job, and Christie became a drifter; clerk, shoemaker, clerk again, out of work, destitution. Sometimes he would sleep on his father's allotment and his mother would take him food.

Marriage at last

At 18, he was called up for service in World War I and sent to France. Two years later in June 1918, he was gassed. Christie dwelt on this disability at Evans' trial, but how serious it was has never been exactly known. For a short while, however, he received a disability pension.

On 20 May 1920, he married the placid, passive and ill-fated Ethel Waddington. A year later, working as a postman, he was caught stealing money out of letters. Christie was jailed for nine months.

Two years later, he was in trouble again but treated leniently. Magistrates bound him over for posing as an ex-military officer, and put him on probation for violence.

In 1924, Christie was jailed for another nine months, this time at Uxbridge Petty Sessions for larceny.

Hard labour

Accounts of his next few years vary. Christie had been deserted by his wife, and continued to drift. In 1929, he was again before the courts, for attacking a prostitute with whom he was living. The magistrates called it 'a murderous attack' and gave Christie six months' hard labour.

In 1933, after yet another spell in prison for stealing a car from a Roman Catholic priest who befriended him, Christie wrote to Ethel, asking her to go back to him. She did, and remained with him until her death.

PSYCHOLOGICAL PROFILE

At his trial, Christie's sole defence was a plea of insanity. His counsel even went as far as to declare that when he killed his victims he was 'as mad as a March hare'.

There was no way, however, of hiding the fact that he was fully aware of his intentions to have sex with unconscious women - witness the apparatus he constructed to gas Ruth Fuerst and Muriel Eady.

Even the argument that Christie suffered from hysteria could not be expected to help him. In psychiatry, hysteria is used to refer to a mental condition of selectively and unconsciously erasing unpleasant memories.

This may have been true in Christie's case, but it says nothing of what went through his mind while he was planning and conducting his murders. And while Christie's sexual preferences were undoubtedly peculiar, sexual deviance is not in itself evidence of insanity.

But why would an outwardly respectable and mild man go to such extreme lengths to satisfy his sexual cravings?

Virile male

The way in which Christie laid great stress on how women found him attractive, illustrates how desperately he wanted to be regarded as a virile male. Even in court when he was arguing for his life, he took great pains to point out that several of his victims seduced him before he murdered them.

But many men suffer such blows to their self-esteem in their early years without becoming killers. To find the additional information for a full portrait of his psyche we have to look at his disturbed relationship with his father who was authoritarian to an extreme degree, ruling over his household in a tyrannical fashion. In such an atmosphere Christie's growth to maturity was severely stunted. It should come as no surprise that many times he joined organizations with distinctive uniforms - scout, scoutmaster, soldier, postman and policeman – where his clothes would define him in the eyes of the world.

Respectability

From this emerged a craving to be recognized as a full and respectable member of society. Christie dressed smartly, took pride in being seen with his wife on his arm, and constantly sought to give the impression he was knowledgeable on a wide range of subjects.

His past, with a series of convictions for crimes of varying severity, did not match his public image. In addition, he also possessed a violent streak. The underdeveloped personality mixed with his aggressive behaviour combined to form a devious killer with dubious sexual desires.

But his undisputable skill in manipulating gullible people let little stand in his way. Yet, there remains one lingering mystery of Rillington Place: how Timothy Evans yielded to Christie's will once Beryl Evans had died.

State of shock

Although Evans was foolish and unable to read or write, he was not mentally deficient as has often been claimed. So why was it that when he returned home on 8 November 1949 to find his wife lying dead upon a bed did he not call the police?

He was almost certainly in a state of shock, and with no one else to turn to. Christie was the only person who could 'help' him. Maybe Christie gambled on Evans being at his most suggestible, arguing, with the force of an ex-policeman, that to involve the law would only bring suspicion down upon Timothy's head.

There was also the issue of moral responsibility. Being a Catholic, Evans would have believed that his wife died while committing the major sin of attempting an abortion. Therefore, although not directly involved, he may well have believed that he was partially responsible. Christie probably convinced himself of Evans' guilt and therefore found it easy to give evidence that sent him to his death.

THE FALKLANDS WAR
A DAY-BY-DAY ACCOUNT FROM
INVASION TO VICTORY

*"This book presents the reality of the
conflict and dispels any inaccuracies
and over exaggerations published at
the time ... I encourage you to read it
and relive the personal experiences and
fascinating stories of the Falklands
war 25 years on."*

From the foreword by
Simon Weston OBE

ISBN 978-0462-09909-5 / £9.99

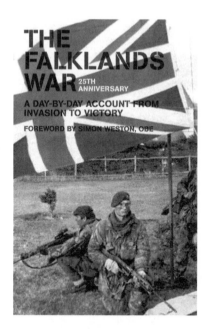

VOICES FROM WORLD WAR II
TRUE ACCOUNTS OF THE
SECOND WORLD WAR BY THOSE
WHO EXPERIENCED IT

This book provides a history of the
Second World War from the point of
view and experiences of the ordinary
fighting men and women and the
civilians on the home fronts of both
Allied and Axis powers. Eyewitness
accounts uniquely convey the heroism
and horror of war. Each major
campaign of World War II is covered
through the tales and experiences of
those who were there. As a result, the
book represents a fascinating, first-
hand account of what the Second
World War was really like.

ISBN 978-0-462-09911-8 / £12.99

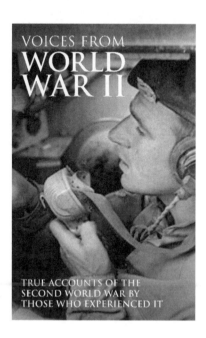